No Blank Check

Concerns about unaccountable executive power have featured recurrently in political debates from the American founding to today. For many, presidents' use of unilateral power threatens American democracy. *No Blank Check* advances a new perspective: Instead of finding Americans apathetic towards how presidents exercise power, it shows the public is deeply concerned with core democratic values. Drawing on data from original surveys, innovative experiments, historical polls, and contexts outside the United States, the book highlights Americans' skepticism towards presidential power. This skepticism results in a public that punishes unilaterally minded presidents and the policies they pursue. By departing from existing theories of presidential power which acknowledge only institutional constraints, this timely and revealing book demonstrates the public's capacity to tame the unilateral impulses of even the most ambitious presidents. Ultimately, when it comes to exercising power, the public does not hand the president a blank check.

Andrew Reeves is Professor of Political Science and Director of the Weidenbaum Center on the Economy, Government, and Public Policy at Washington University in St. Louis. He is coauthor (with Douglas Kriner) of *The Particularistic President: Executive Branch Politics and Political Inequality*, which received the 2016 Richard E. Neustadt Award for the best book published in the field of the American presidency.

Jon C. Rogowski is Professor in the Department of Political Science at the University of Chicago. He is coauthor (with William Howell and Saul Jackman) of *The Wartime President: Executive Influence and the Nationalizing Politics of Threat*, which won the 2014 William H. Riker Prize for the best book published in political economy.

No Blank Check

The Origins and Consequences of Public Antipathy towards Presidential Power

ANDREW REEVES

Washington University in St. Louis

JON C. ROGOWSKI

University of Chicago

CAMBRIDGE
UNIVERSITY PRESS

University Printing House, Cambridge CB2 8BS, United Kingdom

One Liberty Plaza, 20th Floor, New York, NY 10006, USA

477 Williamstown Road, Port Melbourne, VIC 3207, Australia

314–321, 3rd Floor, Plot 3, Splendor Forum, Jasola District Centre,
New Delhi – 110025, India

103 Penang Road, #05–06/07, Visioncrest Commercial, Singapore 238467

Cambridge University Press is part of the University of Cambridge.

It furthers the University's mission by disseminating knowledge in the pursuit of
education, learning, and research at the highest international levels of excellence.

www.cambridge.org
Information on this title: www.cambridge.org/9781107174306
DOI: 10.1017/9781316795811

© Andrew Reeves and Jon C. Rogowski 2022

First published 2022

A catalogue record for this publication is available from the British Library.

ISBN 978-1-107-17430-6 Hardback
ISBN 978-1-316-62647-4 Paperback

Contents

Figures

Tables

Acknowledgments

As the semester began in the fall of 2013, it seemed that the United States was moving towards a war footing in Syria. Near the end of August, more than a thousand people had been killed outside Damascus in a chemical weapons attack. Intelligence reports indicated that the attack had been carried out by the Syrian government under its president, Bashar al-Assad. A year earlier, American President Barack Obama indicated that the use of chemical weapons by the Assad regime would constitute a "red line" and prompt a US military response. As haunting images of those killed and injured by the attacks circulated around the world, military personnel, defense analysts, and even Obama himself appeared to believe that military intervention was inevitable.

But that isn't what happened. Rather than initiate military strikes by invoking the president's war powers, as Obama and his predecessors had done in similar situations, at the end of the month President Obama instead announced that he would seek congressional authorization before conducting military strikes in Syria.

Like many other projects, this book has its origins in hallway conversations. *Why had Obama forgone the opportunity to exercise a power he conceivably could have claimed? Why didn't he follow through on a threat he himself had made?* That we were asking these questions suggested to us that political science scholarship on the presidency had missed something important about presidential decision-making. Through these discussions in Seigle Hall at Washington University in St. Louis, we began our collaboration to discover why presidents sometimes choose *not* to exercise authority they might claim to advance preferences they appear to hold.

We conducted a survey later in the fall of 2013 in a first attempt to make headway on this question. Fortuitously, our colleague John Patty invited us to co-organize a conference at Washington University in St. Louis that was held the following summer. There, we presented our initial findings on the nature of public attitudes about presidential power. We are grateful to John for the opportunity to invite an impressive group of scholars to St. Louis. We are also grateful to conference participants, particularly Chuck Cameron, for incisive and formative feedback on the project at this early stage.

Our initial findings were compelling enough (to us, at least) to suggest the benefits of conducting additional surveys. We were fortunate to successfully make this case to Steve Smith and Betsy Sinclair, who directed The American Panel Survey (TAPS) at Washington University in St. Louis. TAPS became a centerpiece of this project and it is difficult to imagine how we would have written the book without it. We thank Steve and Betsy for generously allowing us to field our survey questions on TAPS, and the Weidenbaum Center for the Economy, Government, and Public Policy at Washington University in St. Louis for supporting TAPS. We also thank Michelle Torres and Patrick Tucker, then-graduate student fellows with the Weidenbaum Center, for answering our many questions about TAPS and providing us with additional data from the survey. We also thank Delia Bailey and Joe Williams for providing survey data collected by YouGov, and Kyle Dropp for generously fielding one of our survey experiments through Survey Sampling International.

As the project grew, so did our collaborations. We were privileged for the opportunity to work with excellent graduate student collaborators, Min Hee Seo and Andrew Stone. Portions of our work together appear in Chapters 3 and 5.

Gwen Calais-Haase and Matthew Thomas provided excellent assistance with gathering and analyzing data from the historical polls used in Chapter 7. Jon also acknowledges financial support from the Dean's Competitive Fund for Promising Scholarship and the Faculty of Arts and Sciences Tenure-Track Publication Fund at Harvard.

Once drafted, many individuals and audiences challenged us to refine our argument and encouraged us to continue moving forward with the project. We are grateful to Zoe Ang, Steve Ansolabehere, Eric Beerbohm, Adam Berinsky, Lucas Boschelli, Sarah Brierley, Charles Cameron, Brandice Canes-Wrone, Jamie Carson, Fang-Yi Chiou, Dino

Christenson, Jeff Cohen, Brian Crisp, David Doherty, Dan Ford, Justin Fox, Jim Gibson, Will Howell, Gbemende Johnson, Peter Kastor, George Krause, Doug Kriner, Kenny Lowande, Michael Lynch, Ken Mayer, David Miller, Terry Moe, Ben Noble, Guillermo Rosas, Larry Rothenberg, Brandon Rottinghaus, Ben Schneider, Joel Sievert, Betsy Sinclair, Steve Smith, Andrew Stone, Margit Tavits, Sharece Thrower, Jennifer Wolak, and audiences at American University, Purdue University, the University of Georgia, the University of Houston, the University of Rochester, Texas A&M, the University of Virginia, Vanderbilt University, Washington University in St. Louis, and the American, Midwest, Southern, and Western Midwest Political Science Associations.

At Cambridge University Press, we thank our excellent editors, Robert Dreesen, Sara Doskow, and Rachel Blaifeder. For assistance with copy editing, we thank Amanda Pearson and Sofia Jarrin. We also thank Peter Christenson for designing our cover.

Some of our earlier research from this project is published in articles that appear in *Presidential Studies Quarterly*, *American Journal of Political Science*, *Journal of Politics*, and *Legislative Studies Quarterly*. We are grateful to the editors and reviewers of each and appreciate the journals' willingness to grant permissions for us to use portions of those articles in this book.

For their constant love and support, we thank our families. Finally, words cannot express how much we owe to Katie Ford Reeves and Aaron Welo. We dedicate this work to them.

Introduction

Joe Biden sought the presidency for most of his professional life. After winning election to the US Senate in 1972, Biden entered the race for the 1988 Democratic Party nomination but withdrew before the first contest. He didn't last much longer when he sought the 2008 nomination. But 2020 was his year, and what a year it was.

Even for a man who had eyed the presidency for more than thirty years, Biden entered the White House with no shortage of challenges to address. He was inaugurated on January 20, 2021, in the midst of the deadliest four weeks of the COVID-19 pandemic in the United States (Gamio and Leatherby 2021). The nation's economy contracted at the highest rate in recorded history in spring 2020 (Siegel and Van Dam 2020), and annual growth in 2020 was the lowest it had been since World War II (Siegel, Van Dam, and Werner 2021). After the killings of George Floyd, Breonna Taylor, and other Black Americans by police, race relations were at their lowest point in decades (*Economist* 2020). The country's reputation among foreign allies had declined precipitously (Pew Research Center 2020). And the riot at the US Capitol two weeks before Biden's inauguration had shocked the nation and the world.

While running for president, Biden had issued a slew of policy pledges (Moore 2020). Yet upon becoming president-elect, Biden expressed reluctance to advance those promises with the stroke of a pen through unilateral action. On a call with civil rights leaders in December 2020, for example, Biden explained his views about the limits to executive power:

So there's some things that I'm going to be able to do by executive order. I'm not going to hesitate to do it, but ... I am not going to violate the Constitution. Executive authority that my progressive friends talk about is way beyond the bounds. And as one of you said ... there is a Constitution. It's our only hope. Our only hope and the way to deal with it is, where I have executive authority, I will use it to undo every single damn thing this guy has done by executive authority, but I'm not going to exercise executive authority where it's a question, where I can come along and say, "I can do away with assault weapons." There's no executive authority to do away that. ... you can't do it by executive order. We do that, next guy comes along and says, Well, guess what? By executive order, I guess everybody can have machine guns again. So we gotta be careful. (Grim 2020)

Despite his reluctance, Biden made quick use of his presidential pen during his first days in office. Most of his efforts rolled back directives that had been issued by the Trump administration and implemented emergency measures for addressing the raging pandemic. Yet for some observers, this was a case of too much, too soon. A week into his administration, the *New York Times* Editorial Board (2021) implored the president to "ease up" on unilateral action. This plea came despite the Board's full-throated endorsement of Biden during the 2020 campaign in which it cited approvingly his "bold agenda aimed at tackling some of America's most pressing problems."

Biden's cautious approach to executive power helps illustrate a central claim of this book. Americans have deep-seated skepticism about presidential power. This skepticism is not always made explicit in the public's day-to-day political expressions, but it is a latent force in American political culture forged at the founding of the nation and ingrained in grade-school civics lessons. It is not a legalistic or intellectual understanding of the text of the US Constitution or Declaration of Independence. Rather, this skepticism reflects a belief that the separation of powers, especially in their protection from tyranny, is sacrosanct. Just as Americans celebrate the Declaration of Independence – an indictment against monarchical executive power – or cheer against King George III in the musical *Hamilton*, the public has inherited a wariness towards executive power. This latent force influences how Americans evaluate presidents and their policies and provides the political incentives for the familiar push-and-pull found in interbranch political conflict.

1.1 THE POLITICS OF PRESIDENTIAL POWER

Nowhere is political power more contested in the American political system than it is with the presidency. The approaches of recent presidential administrations underscore the point. President George W. Bush embraced the unitary presidency theory as a justification for conducting twin wars abroad and domestic surveillance at home. President Obama used the administrative presidency to overcome congressional recalcitrance to change policies ranging from immigration to drug enforcement. And President Trump aggressively utilized unilateral directives and emergency power to fulfill campaign promises and policy objectives. Critics challenge recent administrations on the bounds of presidential authority just as they contest the merits of the presidents' policy objectives.

The terms of these interbranch disputes are clear: when political institutions share power, clashes over who holds authority and to what ends are inevitable. The public's extraordinary expectations for its presidents provide incentives for presidents to claim additional authority in hopes of meeting public demand. Yet presidents' congressional opponents waste little time in pushing back. They accuse presidents of subverting the US Constitution by claiming power that belongs to the legislative branch. For instance, when President Obama directed the Department of Homeland Security in 2014 to modify its enforcement of deportation laws, Republican leaders criticized the president's "brazen power grab" (Shear 2014c).

This conflict over power is a fact of life for virtually every presidential administration. This conflict unfolds on a public stage as presidents and their allies justify the exercise of presidential authority while opponents criticize its use. These exchanges are inherently political and invite the public to evaluate the competing arguments. The public's response to these debates is an important determinant of their political resolution.

Over the last century, concerns about weak and ineffectual presidents have been supplanted by worries of an imperial presidency (Schlesinger 1973). These worries focus on whether and how presidents are held accountable for the use of power. The framers of the Constitution intended their system of checks and balances to keep any one branch of government from accumulating too much power, but, as Madison observed in *Federalist*, no. 48, "a mere demarcation on parchment of the constitutional limits" was not self-enforcing. Instead, the political process also enforces limits on presidential power. Because the president and members of Congress require popular support for their continued service in office, public opinion provides a means to resolve conflict over presidential power vis-á-vis Congress.

How do Americans evaluate presidential power? Have they inherited the skepticism of executive power, as expressed by the founding generation? Or, owing to their embrace of the presidency as the best institutional vehicle for advancing the public interest, do they endorse a more expansive view of presidential authority? Or, as yet another alternative, on questions of presidential power, do Americans' partisan and ideological affiliations carry the day without regard for the principles that shaped the design of the US Constitution? These are the questions we address in this book.

1.2 THE RISE OF PRESIDENTIAL POWER

Textbook accounts of American government identify the emergence of the modern presidency in the early twentieth century. Scholars differ about why and when exactly this transformation occurred, but it is indisputable that contemporary presidents confront challenges largely unimaginable by their predecessors. With these new trials come elevated expectations. In response, modern presidents have claimed authority and exercised power in ways that broke with the practices of their predecessors.

The presidencies of Theodore Roosevelt and William Howard Taft are an instructive contrast in theories of presidential power. Roosevelt championed a stewardship theory of the presidency, and he viewed the powers of his office as expansive especially when they were in the service of the desires of the American people. Reflecting in his autobiography on how this theory guided his approach to the presidency, President Roosevelt recalled, "I did and caused to be done many things not previously done by the president and the heads of departments. I did not usurp power, but I did greatly broaden the use of executive power" (1913, 357).

Roosevelt's successor, William Taft, did not follow Roosevelt's philosophical lead, hewing instead to a more traditional philosophy regarding presidential governance. Taft's more conservative view was that "the President can exercise no power which cannot be fairly and reasonably traced to some specific grant of power" from the Constitution or an act of Congress (Taft 1916, 140).

Roosevelt's and Taft's divergent philosophies of the presidency were pitted head-to-head as they ran against each other for president in 1912. Taft, the incumbent, viewed the contest as "a crusade to defend the Constitution and the rule of law against the pure democracy threatened by Roosevelt, who was increasingly sounding like a demagogue" (Rosen 2018, 94). In the end, Taft was crushed in the contest, receiving the fewest electoral votes of any incumbent president in history. In the three-way contest, Woodrow Wilson, with his expansive view of presidential powers closely akin to that of Roosevelt, was the victor.

With few exceptions, since the Taft administration, presidents have seen it in their political interests to claim powers that may extend beyond even a Hamiltonian view of the presidency. Summing up the trajectory of presidential power, one account notes that,

> Although Presidents Calvin Coolidge and Herbert Hoover adhered to Taft's strict constructionist vision of the presidency, all presidents since Franklin D. Roosevelt have embraced what the historian Arthur M. Schlesinger, Jr. called the imperial presidency, drawing on Theodore Roosevelt's and Woodrow Wilson's idea of the president as a steward of the people. (Rosen 2018, 123)

The transformation of the presidency following Roosevelt's vision represented a victory for Progressives. Around the turn of the twentieth century, Progressive reformers sought to modernize and democratize government administration and its procedures. Recasting the role of the presidency in the American system of government lay at the center of many of these efforts. The key argument for Progressives – which is often articulated by contemporary proponents of presidential supremacy – relates to the president's unique relationship with the mass public. No other political actor, they argue, is elected by the entire country. Therefore, the president is best positioned to understand and advance the national interest and to represent the political views of a national constituency.

Yet Progressive-era reformers recognized that achieving their vision required that the presidency acquire more institutional authority. As Henry Jones Ford (1898, 215) proclaimed, "While the presidential office has been transformed into a representative institution, it lacks proper organs for the exercise of that function ... [N]o constitutional means are provided whereby he may carry out his pledges." Presidents and political observers thus used Progressives' arguments to advocate for shifting institutional power towards the presidency and away from Congress. For instance, Congress endorsed the theory of presidential representation to endow the president with greater agenda-setting powers and administrative capacity in the decades following the Progressive Era (Dearborn 2019a, 2019b). As presidential expectations steadily grew during the second half of the twentieth century, presidents lay claim to an increasingly wide range of powers. Today, presidents routinely act on their own to effect policy outcomes through a wide range of means – all without involving Congress.[1] The ascendance of the presidency in the American

---

[1] It bears mentioning that this phenomenon is by no means new. Presidents since Washington have drawn upon their powers to create the nation's policies on their own. Yet

political system has been accompanied by debates over how far, exactly, presidents can and should wield power to meet their herculean expectations. While Theodore Roosevelt's theory of the presidency has won out over the past century, we argue that the public's deference for the rule of law and related skepticism of executive power is more reflective of Taft's philosophy.

1.3 CAMPAIGNING ON UNILATERAL POWER

Presidents could hardly be blamed for seeking new ways to achieve their goals when their formal authority is so limited. The assumption that presidents seek to employ whatever means allow them to achieve their goals is found in virtually every standard account of the presidency. Just as pursuing the reelection imperative is a prerequisite for legislators who hope to achieve their political and programmatic goals, maintaining and expanding the presidential toolkit is essential for success-oriented presidents. According to this view, pursuing a robust approach to power is inherent in the contemporary presidency.

While modern-day presidents may embrace Roosevelt's governing philosophy, their rhetoric suggests a reluctance to stray from Taftian principles. As candidates pursue the presidency, their ambivalence or downright antipathy towards unilateral powers is apparent. As questions of executive power have become increasingly salient in recent presidential campaigns, candidates have repeatedly gone out of their way to run *against* the presidency and have promised to restore it to its more humble roots. During the 2008 campaign, for example, Barack Obama argued, "[t]he biggest problems that we're facing right now have to do with George Bush trying to bring more and more power into the executive branch and not go through Congress at all. And that's what I intend to reverse when I'm president of the United States of America" (quoted in Karl 2014).

Then-candidate Obama also criticized the Bush administration for its aggressive use of signing statements, arguing that "it is a clear abuse of power to use such statements as a license to evade laws that the president does not like or as an end-run around provisions designed to foster accountability" (Savage 2007). Obama further argued that the American people ought to evaluate presidents on the basis of how they intended

---

the extent to which presidents rely on these tools as part of their governing strategy is unique to the modern era.

to exercise power while governing. "Any President takes an oath to, 'preserve, protect and defend the Constitution of the United States,'" he said. "The American people need to know where we stand on these issues before they entrust us with this responsibility – particularly at a time when our laws, our traditions, and our Constitution have been repeatedly challenged by [the Bush] Administration" (Savage 2007).

Obama's chief opponent for the 2008 Democratic presidential nomination, then-Senator Hillary Clinton, expressed similar views in similarly direct terms. "I think you have to restore the checks and balances and the separation of powers, which means reining in the presidency," she argued (Bombadieri 2007). Clinton further expressed opposition to the unitary executive theory most prominently attributed to Vice President Dick Cheney, which Clinton said, "[had] been a concerted effort by the vice president, with the full acquiescence of the president, to create a much more powerful executive at the expense of both branches of government and of the American people" (Bombadieri 2007). Obama's running mate, then-Senator Joe Biden, further addressed Cheney's contribution to presidential power during the 2008 vice presidential debate. According to Biden, "Vice President Cheney has been the most dangerous vice president we've had probably in American history. The idea he doesn't realize that Article I of the Constitution defines the role of the vice president of the United States, that's the Executive Branch. He works in the Executive Branch" (*New York Times* 2008).

During the 2008 presidential campaign, Obama, Clinton, and Biden each made clear their opposition to not only the Bush administration's policies but also its embrace of a stronger and more unilateral presidency. Though each of these Democrats sought the presidential office for themselves in the 2008 campaign, they promised to pursue their policy objectives through a more constrained vision of executive power.

Four years later, President Obama found himself on the receiving end of criticism from Republican presidential candidates for his use of executive power. According to Representative Ron Paul, for instance, Obama did not "respect constitutional limits on executive power" and proved to be even "worse than his predecessor" (*New York Times* 2011). Senator Rick Santorum went further, accusing the Obama administration of an "arrogance" that "surpasses the Nixonian period … This is a president who uniformly disregards the Constitution, disregards the rules that are put in place" (Lee 2012).

The 2016 presidential campaign saw even more pointed criticism of Obama's use of power from candidates vying to replace him. Ben

Carson said that Obama's "executive self-aggrandizement has elevated political interests over the executive duty of faithfully enforcing the law"; if elected, Carson committed to refraining from "the unconstitutional practices of making law through executive orders" (Savage 2016). Senator Rand Paul sounded a similar note, arguing that "unconstitutional claims of authority by the President" had dramatically increased presidential power over the previous decade. In contrast, Paul pledged "to restore our constitutional system of separation of powers, which allows the American people to decide how they are to be governed" (Savage 2016). Senator Ted Cruz went a step further, arguing that the first thing he would do after taking the oath of office would be to "rescind every illegal and unconstitutional executive action taken by Barack Obama" (Chen 2015).

Candidate Donald Trump sounded the harshest and most persistent criticisms of President Obama's use of executive power. In January 2016, Trump objected to what he referred to as the "executive order concept" in response to Obama's use of administrative action to regulate gun access. According to Trump,

You know, it's supposed to be negotiated. You're supposed to cajole, get people in a room, you have Republicans, Democrats, you're supposed to get together and pass a law. [Obama] doesn't want to do that because it's too much work. So he doesn't want to work too hard. He wants to go back and play golf. (Krieg 2016)

In another interview that month, Trump elaborated upon his objections to Obama's use of unilateral powers, telling a morning news show that "the problem with Washington [is] they don't make deals. It's all gridlock. And then you have a president that signs executive orders because he can't get anything done. I'll get everybody together" (*Fox and Friends* 2016). At a town hall the following month, Trump told his audience that "the country wasn't based on executive orders ... you can't do it" (Lemire and Colvin 2017). He went even further in March 2016, promising that he would scale back his use of unilateral powers were he to be elected. Candidate Trump said that, while Obama "sign[s] them like they are butter," President Trump would "do away with executive orders for the most part" (Trump 2016a). His criticism of President Obama's unilateral actions continued through the general election. In September 2016, for instance, Trump noted that, as if to draw a contrast between Obama and himself: "Right now, we have an executive order president" (Benen 2017).

Unilateral power once again figured prominently in the candidates' rhetoric during the 2020 election cycle – and this time among candidates from both parties. A feature in the *New York Times* profiled 2020 candidates' proposals for "reforming executive power after Trump" (Bewetherick et al. 2019). In announcing a long-shot primary challenge to President Trump, former Representative Joe Walsh accused the Trump administration of being a "walking billboard for the need to curb abuses of presidential power" and echoed the familiar refrain of presidential candidates to work with Congress to reign in the powers of the imperial presidency. Democratic candidates were just as adamant and expressed nearly unanimous calls for scaling back unilateral powers. Senator Cory Booker observed, as so many other candidates had, that the US system of separation of powers was imperiled because of the "unhealthy" flow of authority to the executive branch. Senator Kamala Harris expressed support for the "goal of restoring our constitutional separation of powers and reducing opportunities for abuse." Similarly, Senator Amy Klobuchar argued that the Trump administration had "ignored ... checks and balances" and that the president had instead "pursued his divisive agenda by undermining our democracy and exploiting executive power."

As this evidence suggests, candidates in recent presidential elections have avoided advocating for a more muscular set of powers. This observation raises several questions. First, why would presidential candidates back away from unilateral power if voters were generally unconcerned with it? If, as conventional wisdom suggests, the public is unaware of or disinterested in questions of political procedure, presidents (and presidential candidates) should not bother dedicating precious time to discussing this issue. Second, why would would-be presidents dissociate themselves from unilateral power if this position could limit their ability to achieve their political objectives? Contemporary presidents and presidential candidates promise to do something about virtually everything. Voters expect nothing less. Increased levels of congressional gridlock reduce the opportunities for presidents to achieve their promises via legislation. Such conditions would seem to increase the appeal of unilateral approaches for presidents who hope to satisfy their constituencies. Yet their rhetoric suggests that as candidates, the men and women who want to become president (some of whom do) perceive limits to the acceptability of unilateralism as a means to an end.[2]

---

[2] Scholarship on presidential rhetoric provides a fuller treatment of how presidents convey their understanding of the office and its powers (Campbell and Jamieson 1990, 2008;

1.4 ACCOUNTABILITY AND UNILATERAL POWER

Concerns over executive power featured prominently in the founding of the United States and have, at various times in American history, been represented in robust political debates. Along with presidential claims to new powers come cries that presidents are exceeding or abusing their authority. Each new presidential administration begets alarming books, law review articles, and op-eds that warn of the increasing power of the presidency.

Accountability – and its absence – is usually front and center in debates over presidential power. In *The Imperial Presidency*, one of the most prominent indictments of presidential power, Schlesinger viewed presidential accountability and presidential power as inextricably linked. According to Schlesinger (2004, ix), "The American Constitution ... envisages a strong Presidency within an equally strong system of accountability. When the constitutional balance is upset in favor of Presidential power and at the expense of Presidential accountability, the office can be said to become imperial."

Political scientists and other observers have leveled similar criticisms of presidents' uses of unilateral authority. Some view executive orders as incidents of "unaccountable power and a way of evading both public opinion and constitutional constraints" (Mayer 2002, 9). In comments on the nomination of Brett Kavanaugh to the Supreme Court, one constitutional scholar complained of Judge Kavanaugh's "indulgent interpretation" of "constitutional questions of executive power," which would "effectively undermine a President's accountability to law" (Shane 2018, 1). Following the Senate's acquittal of President Trump after his first impeachment by the House, one commentator lamented the "degrading of presidential accountability" (Sorkin 2020).

Debates over presidential power are arguments over the appropriate scope of political power. In the extreme, unbound executive power is a dictatorship whereby an executive exercises absolute authority without regard for the rule of law. In the US system of separation of powers, members of Congress often complain about executive power in these very terms. Near the end of President George W. Bush's administration, Senator Arlen Specter argued that historians would regard the post–9/11 Bush presidency as an era of "unbridled executive power"

Tulis 1988). In contrast with this research, we are interested primarily in how the public understands the office and its powers.

(Mahler 2008). Eight years later, Senator Mike Lee (R-UT) sounded similar notes and argued forcefully against the "arbitrary, unaccountable government-without-consent that Congress now for its own selfish reasons enables the executive branch to practice" (Lee 2016). In his opening statement supporting Congress's 2019 impeachment inquiry into President Trump, Representative Adam Schiff (D-CA) argued that "the balance of power between our two branches of government will be irrevocably altered" if the president is exempt from Congress's efforts to hold the president accountable through oversight (Paz 2019). Speaker Pelosi (D-CA) likewise criticized the Senate's "betrayal of the Constitution" for acquitting President Trump, arguing that Senate Republicans had "embraced this darkest vision of power" offered by the president's legal team in which "Congress and the American people have no right" to hold the president accountable for abuses of power (Pelosi 2020).

Unaccountable unilateral power is tyranny, the fear of which loomed large in debates about institutional design at the American founding. Delegates to the Constitutional Convention considered the presidency with their rebellion against the "absolute Tyranny" of King George III over the North American colonies still fresh in their minds. The absence of an executive under the Articles of Confederation contributed substantially to governmental failures in the early republic. This experience underscored the need to enshrine robust executive power in the young nation's new constitution. After debate, convention delegates settled on an executive branch headed by a single individual – the president. Keenly aware of the anti-Federalists' skepticism towards executive power, authors of the Constitution proposed that an elected executive, along with interbranch competition, would limit the president's accumulation of power. As Mansfield (1989, 295) argues, "the task of political science in *The Federalist* was to show that an energetic executive could be republicanized."

For the Founders, presidential accountability was the antidote for tyranny. *The Federalist Papers* emphasized that the need for popular support constrained American presidents. The task of creating an accountable chief executive was "the objection that most concerned the Founding Fathers" (Schlesinger 1973, 386). In *Federalist*, no. 68, therefore, Alexander Hamilton emphasized that "the sense of the people should operate in the choice" of the president "to whom so important a trust" is invested. Hamilton went on to argue that the president "should be independent for his continuance in office on all but the people themselves." Concerns about accountability motivated the design of the office itself, as Hamilton justifies the unitary executive in *Federalist*, no. 70, on the basis of accountability considerations. If executive authority were to be divided across members of a plural office, Hamilton argued, it would be difficult to attribute specific decisions to individual executives and would therefore be more difficult for the public to hold those individuals accountable for their behavior. In his words, "the plurality of the Executive tends to deprive the people of ... the restraints of public opinion." Arguments at ratification further turned on the accountability relationship enshrined in the office's design. The Founders accomplished the twin goals of creating an energetic yet accountable president because "the Constitution would facilitate presidential energy and enable the people, Congress, and the courts to detect and prevent abuses of the same" (Kitrosser 2015, 49).

The nature of this accountability was a distinguishing characteristic of the newly created presidency. A political commentator in Virginia noted that "[t]he United States are the scrutinizing spectators of [the president's] conduct" (quoted in Kitrosser 2015, 48). The Supreme Court further affirmed the political constraints on presidential action in *Marbury v. Madison*, a case that involved the reach of presidential authority. Chief Justice John Marshall wrote that "the President is invested with certain important political powers, in the exercise of which he is to use his own discretion, and is accountable only to his country in his political character, and to his own conscience." In addition to establishing the principle of judicial review, *Marbury v. Madison* speaks to the accountability of presidents in exercising their power to appoint judges. Even while establishing the judiciary's most important power, Marshall noted the nebulous nature of presidential power and the influential role of the public in holding it to account.

Questions about presidents' accountability for the exercise of power have been raised in some of the most extraordinary moments in the history of the republic. Even as President Abraham Lincoln contemplated unprecedented measures in his attempt to preserve the Union, scholars linked public opinion with the president's ability to act with Hamiltonian "decision, activity, secrecy, and dispatch." Rossiter (1956, 47) noted that

Lincoln is supposed to have said that he could do anything with "public sentiment" but nothing without it or against it ... The President draws immense authority from the support of the American people, but only if he uses it in ways they understand and approve, which generally means ways that are fair, dignified, traditional, and familiar.

The public reaction to some of Lincoln's orders tempered his subsequent exercise of authority. In 1863, former congressman and Ohio gubernatorial candidate Clement Vallandigham was arrested for violating an order issued by one of Lincoln's generals that prohibited speaking out against the Union or expressing favor for the Confederacy. The act caused consternation among his cabinet and "roused" a "furor of anger … in the country," and one newspaper declared the act "the tyranny of military despotism" (Donald 2011, 420). In response, Lincoln commuted Vallandigham's sentence. Shortly thereafter, the same general attempted to suspend an anti-war newspaper. Lincoln, who had been chastened by the response to the previous arrest, overruled him (Donald 2011, 21). Public opinion also factored heavily into Lincoln's decision to ultimately issue the Emancipation Proclamation. He "began preparing public opinion for a proclamation of freedom" by consulting with African American leaders and by publishing a letter where he argued that his primary goal was to save the Union (Donald 2011, 366–369). During the Civil War, Lincoln expanded the powers of the presidency in unprecedented ways, yet even in this context, public opinion shaped his political options.

During the administration of Franklin Roosevelt, the Brownlow Committee convened to discuss how to better organize the White House to allow the president to meet contemporary governing challenges. The committee proposed "giv[ing] the President authority commensurate with his responsibility … [and] hold[ing] him to strict accountability for the exercise of that authority" (Brownlow 1955, 114). Acknowledging the expansion of presidential authority during the Roosevelt administration, Rossiter (1956, 54–55) argued that the public would hold these powers to account. He observed that,

If [the President] flouts either the considered judgments or ill-considered prejudices of any vocal segment of the people, if he chooses to roam too far outside the accepted limits of presidential behavior, he will find himself exposed to all those enemies who multiply like mosquitoes in a Jersey August whenever a President plays the game too hard. No President, certainly no peacetime President, ever wielded more power with less need to worry about the political consequences than Franklin Roosevelt in 1933, yet even then the assumption was abroad that there were some steps he could not take, some measures he could not recommend to Congress, in his effort to rescue "a stricken Nation in the midst of a stricken world."

Presidents must anticipate how their behavior influences future public opinion. Popularity can be fleeting, and thus presidents cannot rely solely on their public standing today to determine what political boundaries may exist tomorrow. Even popular presidents eschew actions that they might prefer to take because of their calculation about the potential political reaction. Observers of politics must consider not only how public opinion affects what presidents do but also what dissuades them from undertaking that which they would otherwise choose to do. If the president forges ahead, "he invites the one disaster from which Presidents rarely recover: the loss of genuine popular support" (Rossiter 1956, 56).

Consistent with the arguments advanced by the authors of the Constitution, a president's need for continued political support provides a source of accountability for his behavior. Theories of democratic accountability posit that voters supply incentives for elected officials to represent their interests. Election-seeking presidents, for instance, are understood to pursue policies and generate outcomes that voters support. Should presidents stray too far from public opinion, this perspective posits, they risk declining approval ratings and damaging their (or their partisan successor's) electoral fortunes.

The rhetoric of the authors of the Constitution and others invokes a public that carefully monitors how presidents exercise their power and dutifully sounds the alarm when the commander-in-chief exhibits tyrannical impulses. But does this accountability exist? If so, how does it operate? Elections facilitate popular control of political officials through the principal-agent relationship. Voters (the principals) select officials (the agents) to act on their behalf. If officials fail to behave in ways desired by the principals, voters can replace them at the next election. Therefore, elections provide incentives for officials to reflect public preferences by virtue of voters' abilities to sanction or reward them based on their performances.

For public accountability to exist in the context of presidents' exercise of power, two conditions must be satisfied. First, the American public must have preferences over how presidents wield power. Second, they should apply those preferences when evaluating presidential performance. Evidence that the public satisfies these two conditions means that presidents and their use of authority are subject to "the discipline of consent" that reflects "the genius of democracy" (Schlesinger 2004, 388).

1.5 PUBLIC EVALUATIONS OF PRESIDENTIAL POWER

Elite rhetoric aside, do Americans care about the use of presidential power? Do they have opinions over how presidents get things done?

Do they hold presidents accountable for the *means* with which they pursue their policy *ends*? In other words, do citizens hold presidents accountable for exercising unilateral political power? We briefly survey three competing perspectives on how Americans view presidential power and its use.

1.5.1 The Partisan Electorate

One dominant view of mass political behavior emphasizes the partisan nature of the electorate. This view offers a pessimistic perspective on the potential for presidential accountability. According to this view, presidential power is not a salient or accessible topic for most Americans, and thus they do not view it through a principled lens. Instead, Americans apply short-term heuristics – particularly partisanship – when evaluating presidential power. In particular, Americans who share the president's partisanship may support expanding the president's power while those who are aligned with the opposing political party may not. Pundits and political scientists consistently assert the dominance of partisanship in contemporary public opinion (Klein 2016; Mellman 2017), as the public reflexively applies its partisan identities when evaluating political events, receiving political information, and even while participating in the labor market and making decisions about whom to date (Gerber and Huber 2010; Huber and Malhotra 2017; McConnell et al. 2018). Americans may also engage in partisan "cheerleading" (Sears and Lau 1983) by expressing greater support for presidential power with a copartisan president in office as a means of expressing their affinity for the president. In this view, Americans vacillate between expressing support for and opposition to presidential power depending on their alignment with the president's political orientation. This perspective therefore expresses a rather dim view of the potential for Americans to hold presidents accountable on the basis of their use of power.

A related view emphasizes Americans' attitudes towards the president currently in office. Americans who think highly of the president – because, for example, they support his policies, approve of his job performance, or admire his leadership – may express greater support for expanded presidential power. For example, critics of President Trump note that "the higher President Trump's approval rating, the more dangerous he is" (Levitsky and Ziblatt 2018, 192). This view holds that presidential approval is the currency of presidential power; as presidents accrue more of the former they can expect to marshal more of the latter. Applied to public opinion, Americans' beliefs about presidential power may pivot with their support for the person holding the office as opposed to their attitudes towards the office itself.

1.5.2 Deciders-in-Chief

A second perspective suggests that Americans entrust the presidency with great power and support its exercise. Political commentators, campaign consultants, the public, and presidents themselves routinely extol the virtues of presidential leadership. According to survey research, supermajorities of the public endorse the view that "[a]n ideal president provides strong leadership" (Kinder et al. 1980, 319), prompting political strategist David Moore (1995, 205) to argue that "the single most important value of the American public is respect for strong presidential leadership." Likewise, presidents perceived as strong leaders are viewed more favorably by the electorate (Cohen 2015). Americans' support for strong leadership may be expected to manifest in their support for a muscular and robust set of powers belonging to the presidency.

This view is consistent with scholarship that links the development of the modern presidency to Americans' increased appetites for presidential power. According to this scholarship, presidents now occupy a more central role in American government than in earlier periods of the nation's history. As Lowi (1986, 20) explains, "[H]aving given presidents maximum power to govern and all the help they have ever asked for, the public has rationally focused its expectations on them, counting on them to deliver on all the promises they explicitly made." Accordingly, the public may accept and even demand vigorous presidential activity, even if it comes through the exercise of illegal or constitutionally dubious powers. This view asserts that "opting not to act – indeed, merely being perceived as not acting – comes at a great political cost" to American presidents (Howell 2013, 125). Rather than recoiling at the ambitions of power-seeking executives, this perspective posits that Americans endorse bold action from their presidents and evaluate them based on whether they wield power in a sufficiently assertive manner.

1.5.3 Constitutional Veneration

We advance an alternative perspective that argues that Americans have attitudes over how presidents exercise power. These attitudes reflect values over the inviolability of the system of government expressed in the Constitution. Americans embrace a "literary theory" of separation of powers and express hostility towards presidential power (Pious and Pyle 1984, 153). This view emphasizes Americans' high levels of reverence for and approval of the Constitution (Brown and Pope 2019; Levinson 2006; Stephanopoulos and Versteeg 2016; Zink and Dawes 2016). Americans' constitutional affinities are ingrained from an early age and in the classroom as they learn civics and American history (Pious and Pyle 1984). Accordingly, Americans may be hostile to the concentration of power within the presidency and exhibit what Posner and Vermeule (2010) characterize as "tyrannophobia." This view suggests that Americans harbor negative evaluations of presidential power and hold presidents accountable by withholding their support following its use.

Despite the importance of accountability in democratic systems, we know little about how these mechanisms operate with respect to the exercise of power. Our analyses here provide the first empirical record and systematic evaluation of how the public views presidential power and its use. As Hibbing and Theiss-Morse (1996, 29) wrote a quarter-century ago, "In the case of the executive branch, almost nothing exists on public support for the institution itself. Much attention has been devoted to support for the person occupying the position of president, but not so for the institution of the presidency." That remains largely the case today.

On the theoretical side, no existing account explains how the public evaluates the power of the presidency against their own partisan interests, ideological loyalties, and approval ratings of individual presidents. What Americans think about presidential power and the conditions under which those attitudes are deployed when evaluating presidents, then, is the stuff of speculation. Understanding how the mass public views presidential power and holds leaders accountable for its use is important not only because "[p]ower restrained by accountability and consent is more likely than arbitrary and unrestrained power to produce wise policy" (Schlesinger 2004, 491) but also because the nature of accountability shapes the potential "scope of executive abuses" (Posner and Vermeule 2010, 113).

1.5.4 Presidential Responsiveness to Public Opinion

Theories of political accountability emphasize how elections induce officials to respond to public opinion. There is considerable evidence of issue-based accountability, particularly in the context of legislative

(Adams et al. 2017; Ansolabehere and Jones 2010; Canes-Wrone, Brandice, and Cogan 2002; Shor and Rogowski 2018) and judicial (Ansolabehere and White 2020; Bartels and Johnston 2013; Christenson and Glick 2015) politics. These findings generally show that the public bases their evaluations of legislators and judges on whether they behave in ways that reflect the public's political leanings. A smaller body of literature documents issue-based accountability in the context of the presidency. In studies on presidential elections, voters select presidential candidates on the basis of issue congruence (Jessee 2009, 2010, 2012). These findings are consistent with the role of elections as a screening mechanism that allows the public to choose candidates who will advance policies they support. Analyses of voters' responses to presidential unilateral actions show that presidential approval ratings are responsive to the public's level of agreement with the policies presidents have created (Ansolabehere and Rogowski 2020).

Research on presidential behavior, moreover, provides evidence that electoral incentives encourage presidents to behave in ways consistent with the public's policy views. For instance, presidents propose budgets that are conditionally responsive to the public's spending preferences (Canes-Wrone and Shotts 2004). Presidents' support for congressional legislation is also strongly responsive to the public's policy preferences (Erikson, MacKuen, and Stimson 2002; Stimson, MacKuen, and Erikson 1995). American foreign policy decisions, including those made by the president, are also constrained by the level of public support for them (Baum and Potter 2015). And Rogowski (2019) provides evidence of an association between public opinion and presidents' uses of unilateral directives, showing that presidents issue more directives for topics that the public believes are salient and for which they support more governmental involvement. This scholarship provides evidence consistent with the conclusion that "popularity-seeking presidents take a stand in response to public opinion or in anticipation of it" (Page and Shapiro 1992, 349). In an important exception, however, Druckman and Jacobs (2015) argue that presidents strategically manipulate public opinion to simulate responsiveness while they advance policy ideals that are often at odds with most Americans' interests.

Though theories about strategic interactions among political institutions often have not explicitly incorporated public opinion (but see Groseclose and McCarty 2001 for a prominent exception), some accounts of presidential behavior entertain the possibility of such a function. In discussing how presidents use vetoes, Cameron (2000, 17–18) considers whether public opinion might "stop a president from pursuing his supporters' objectives even in the teeth of congressional opposition." Likewise, Moe and Howell (1999a, 866) argue that courts' decisions to uphold or strike down unilateral actions may be influenced by the popularity of the presidents' actions.

Understanding the nature of public accountability of executive power strikes at the heart of democratic viability. As in most presidential systems, the chief executive occupies a unique position within the American political system. Unlike Congress and the courts, the president and the presidency are one and the same. As a consequence of the unitary presidency:

The President is in a position to do serious damage, if not irreparable injury, to the ideals and methods of American democracy. Power that can be used decisively can also be abused grossly. No man can hold such a concentration of authority without feeling the urge, even though the urge be honest and patriotic, to push it beyond its usual bounds. We must therefore consider carefully the various safeguards that are counted upon to keep the President's feet in paths of constitutional righteousness. (Rossiter 1956, 33)

Levitsky and Ziblatt (2018, 191–192) underscore the importance of public opinion for the safety of democracy. They argue that "would-be authoritarians" endanger democracy to the extent they have widespread public support. Yet this account conflates support for individual politicians and public attitudes about how those officeholders should rule. If the mass public responds to how officeholders go about achieving their objectives, even politicians with high levels of popularity may risk public blowback.

The assumption that the public evaluates presidents on the basis of outcomes alone dominates the study of the presidency – and to great consequence. Presidents enter office with a variety of objectives and goals, and perhaps chief among them is to secure subsequent electoral support from voters (Kriner and Reeves 2015; Moe 1985). To do so, presidents have incentives to respond to public opinion (Cohen 1999; Edwards 1983; Jacobs and Shapiro 2000) and thus pursue policies that the public supports. As a consequence of this singular focus on the purposes of presidential action, scholars attribute a wide range of presidential behavior – including vetoes (McCarty 2009), executive orders (Howell 2003; Rogowski 2019), and public appeals (Canes-Wrone 2006; Kernell 2006) – to the president's focus on the public's policy preferences. Indeed, the public's demand for increased policy responsiveness from presidents is widely posited to explain the ascendance of the modern presidency (Lowi 1986; Neustadt 1990) and presidents' increased reliance on unilateral tools (Howell 2003; Moe and Howell 1999a, 1999b). If the public also scrutinizes the ways these policy outcomes are achieved, these attitudes may affect the incentive structures for presidents to take action. As Canes-Wrone (2006, 192) observes, "The relationship between a chief executive and his or her public can significantly affect the ways in which formal institutions operate in practice." To make progress on this question, however, we require a theory of public opinion that considers the means through which political outcomes are realized.

1.6 AN OVERVIEW

In this book, we present a new theoretical perspective and assemble comprehensive original data to study accountability over the use of power. We argue that public support is no blank check on unilateral presidential powers. Rather, legacies of colonial rule and the American founding are reflected in contemporary public opinion about the presidency. We advance three primary claims. First, Americans view executive power with skepticism and prefer national policymaking to be the domain of Congress rather than the presidency. While Americans may desire that presidents channel public opinion by articulating ambitious policy agendas, they prefer that Congress legislate rather than the president to enact those agendas via fiat. Second, Americans' attitudes towards executive power are not mere reflections of party loyalties to a particular president; rather, they reflect their beliefs about the separation of powers and their commitments to the rule of law. The American public meaningfully distinguishes their attitudes towards the presidency from their evaluations of its occupant. Third, the public brings these attitudes to bear when evaluating presidents and their records in office. Americans hold presidents accountable not only for *what* they accomplish but also for *how* they wield power. Our argument implies that responsiveness is driven not just by demand for particular policies but also by the public's fundamental normative expectations about the separation of powers and how policies ought to be achieved. More generally, our argument suggests that public opinion towards presidential power structures the terms of interbranch conflict in contemporary American politics.

Our focus on public opinion and the use of power provides new theoretical and empirical insight into the presidency, the politics of policymaking, and political representation and accountability. First, our argument suggests that while scholarship on the presidency has been concerned chiefly with characterizing its influence in a system of separated powers, it has overlooked the political dynamics that accompany its acquisition and use. According to one dominant perspective, presidential power is "the power to persuade" (Neustadt 1990, 11). Presidents wield influence to the extent they are successful in convincing other political actors that what the president wishes them to do is in their own best interests (Neustadt 1990). More recent research shows that persuasion may not be the only means through which presidents can effectively wield the power of the office. Howell (2003) argues that presidents can leverage ambiguities in Article II to advance policy initiatives via direct action that Congress otherwise could not. Yet both of these perspectives take the president's authority as exogenous; neither of these accounts, or any others, studies how presidents attempt to accumulate and legitimate their power or their success in doing so.

We put front-and-center the politics that animates interbranch conflict and produces accusations of presidential overreach. We focus on how the American public views presidential power and how those views structure the incentives for competing claims to power. We begin in Chapter 2 by presenting a behavioral perspective on the relationship between the mass public and the American presidency. In contrast with a large literature that argues that Americans evaluate presidents and policies solely on the basis of their partisan and ideological views, our account emphasizes Americans' evaluations of governing procedures. We focus particularly on the skepticism with which Americans have viewed executive power since the nation's humble beginnings. This skepticism initially manifested in the exclusion of an executive branch from the nation's original governing document, the Articles of Confederation, and the limited powers granted to governors in early state constitutions. Once the need for an independent executive became clear by the mid-1780s, Alexander Hamilton, among others, devoted substantial ink in *The Federalist* to justifying the need for a presidency and emphasizing the strict limits on its powers. We argue that this skepticism is found in American public opinion today, borne of political socialization that emphasizes veneration for the US Constitution and prescribes a limited policymaking role for the executive. While constitutional questions may not occupy most Americans' thoughts on a regular basis, we argue that these core values towards executive power structure how Americans view policies achieved through unilateral action and the presidents who exercise that power. They also affect how political elites respond in turn.

The next section of the book presents original survey data to evaluate our argument about public opinion towards executive power. In Chapter 3, we introduce our approach to measuring Americans' attitudes towards institutional powers of the presidency and describe the surveys we conducted to implement it. We then provide new evidence from surveys conducted between 2013 and 2018 that characterizes Americans' aggregate orientations towards executive power. In documenting these attitudes, we note the relative stability of attitudes even as the Obama presidency ended and the Trump presidency began. We also contrast attitudes towards unilateral power with presidential approval and find that the latter is both more variable and more polarized than the former. We also contrast attitudes towards unilateral power with presidential approval and find that presidential approval is both more variable and more polarized than attitudes towards unilateral actions.

Chapter 4 presents evidence about the origins of attitudes towards executive power. We demonstrate that these attitudes reflect evaluations of the current president as well as more fundamental conceptions about the nature of the office, which are rooted in constitutional commitments. We show that support for the rule of law durably predicts support for unilateral presidential powers across a wide array of contexts. Together with the findings in Chapter 3, the results in this chapter suggest that Americans distinguish their views of the current president from more fundamental attitudes about the institution of the presidency.

In Chapter 5, we interrogate individual-level change and continuity in support for unilateral action. Taking advantage of the panel nature of our survey data, we examine within-respondent changes in support for unilateral powers. While we find strong cross-sectional support that presidential approval is related to support for unilateral powers, we find no evidence that within-respondent shifts in presidential approval result in changing views of the institutional power of the office. We also leverage the election and inauguration of Donald Trump to examine how the person holding office affects attitudes towards the institutional authority of the presidency. Even across presidencies, most respondents maintain their views of the bounds of presidential powers. The last section of the chapter connects our work to scholarship on presidential mandates and explores how aggregate public support for the president's policy goals affects individual-level attitudes about the exercise of power.

In Chapter 6, we examine how the attitudes we document affect evaluations of policies pursued via unilateral action. We present results from a series of survey experiments we conducted with nationally representative samples of Americans. The experiments varied the policy goals presidents wished to accomplish and the means by which presidents sought to attain them. We find that Americans provide systematically more negative evaluations of both presidents and their policies when they use unilateral actions. In an era of persistent congressional gridlock, we also show that Americans prefer that presidents take *no* action rather than advance their goals via unilateral power, even if this results in no change in policy outcomes. In both cases, moreover, we find that these patterns apply to individuals who both support and oppose the policy in question; that is, the negative effects of unilateral action among individuals who oppose the president's policy position are not offset by positive effects among those who share the president's policy views.

The preceding chapters evaluate perceptions of presidential power in contemporary American politics. In Chapter 7, we present a wider and more historical view of Americans' attitudes towards presidential power. The effects we document in Chapter 6 are not simply artifacts of today's hyperpolarized environment or the contemporary status and salience of American presidents. Instead, we present evidence from dozens of national polls conducted between the presidencies of Franklin Roosevelt and Donald Trump to show that Americans almost always reflexively reject expansions of presidential power, and that these attitudes influence their evaluations of how presidents have historically wielded prerogative powers. We then revisit four historical cases in which presidential power was contested to show how the public's attitudes about executive authority reflected the contemporary debates on the topic.

Concerns about power and accountability in presidential systems are by no means limited to the United States (see, e.g., Crisp, Olivella, and Rosas 2020; Linz 1990). Chapter 8 ventures beyond the United States and evaluates attitudes towards executive power in comparative perspective. We present evidence from surveys conducted in more than fifty countries in Africa and the Americas that the relationships we document in the United States are widely generalizable. Americans are not unique in expressing skepticism towards executive authority, and at the individual level these attitudes are consistently structured by commitments to core governing principles. At the country level, we further show that aggregate attitudes towards executive power are associated with institutional and political contexts. Our findings suggest attitudes towards executive power are structured by a common set of factors around much of the globe. They also suggest the capacity for domestic audiences to hold their political leaders accountable for how they exercise power.

The concluding chapter returns to the ideas that motivated our study and discusses the implications of our argument and findings for the presidency, representation and accountability, the separation of powers, and democratic theory.

2

Watchmen in the Night?

Holding Presidents Accountable for Power

In the debate during impeachment proceedings against President Richard Nixon, Congressman James Mann (D-SC) ruminated on whether Nixon's fate was enough to deter future presidents from abusing power. Representative Mann said, "We should strive to strengthen and protect the Presidency. But if there be no accountability, another President will feel free to do as he chooses. The next time there may be no watchman in the night" (US Congress, House of Representatives 1974). Theodore Sorenson, who had served as an advisor to President John F. Kennedy, sounded an optimistic tone after considering Mann's foreboding warning. He concluded that,

In this country we are all, as citizens and voters, entrusted with governmental and political power. If Watergate spurs us all to understand better those fundamental principles and strive more diligently for that intellectual and moral integrity, then it can truly be a watershed for this country.

The next time there will be watchmen in the night – all of us. (Sorenson 1975, 160)

To what extent does the American public live up to Sorenson's notion that it guards against presidential abuses of power? In this chapter, we present a behavioral perspective about how voters view presidential power and its exercise. We consider how – when given compelling evidence of mass polarization and disinterest in questions of political process – Americans could muster any serious attitude towards the exercise of unilateral power by presidents. The answer, we argue, is rooted in deep-seated values towards the rule of law, originating in childhood as Americans learn about civics and celebrate the American founding. Our perspective posits that Americans draw upon these attitudes when evaluating presidents and

25

their behavior, ultimately shaping the politics of presidential power in ways that have gone largely unnoticed and unappreciated.

2.1 EXPECTATIONS AND PRESIDENTIAL INCENTIVES

Voters hold presidents accountable for a wide range of phenomena and expect presidents to do something about virtually everything (Neustadt 1990, 7). Likewise, presidents enter office with a variety of objectives and goals. Perhaps chief among them is to secure subsequent electoral support from voters (Kriner and Reeves 2015; Moe 1985). To do so, presidents have incentives to promote outcomes the public values and advance policies that the public supports. Presidents' approval ratings and electoral performances, for instance, are responsive to unemployment rates (Mueller 1970; Park and Reeves 2020), personal income (de Benedictis-Kessner and Warshaw 2020), mortgage delinquencies (Healy and Lenz 2017), trade-related job losses (Margalit 2011), the allocation of federal spending (Kriner and Reeves 2015), foreign policy crises (Oneal and Bryan 1995), and war casualties (Karol and Miguel 2007). Presidential evaluations also reflect phenomena that are outside the control of any president such as natural disasters (Gasper and Reeves 2011), local property tax increases (Sances 2017), and the outcomes of sporting events (Healy, Malhotra, and Mo 2010). Still other research shows that the public bases their choices for president on which presidential candidates support their policy beliefs (Jessee 2012) and penalizes presidents who implement policies they oppose (Ansolabehere and Rogowski 2020). These incentives send presidents searching for avenues to showcase their accomplishments, advertise their policy views, and demonstrate their leadership skills.

It is no surprise, then, that presidents rely on unilateral powers to try to satiate the country's enormous appetite for presidential action. These powers are exercised through a variety of forms. For instance, presidents issue executive orders and memoranda to change how executive agencies administer policies (Howell 2003; Lowande 2014; Mayer 2002; Moe and Howell 1999a). In terms of distributive benefits, presidents can direct federal resources such as disaster relief, grants, and federal contracts towards preferred constituencies (Gordon 2011; Kriner and Reeves 2015; Reeves 2011; Rogowski 2016) and adjust tariff schedules to advantage favored industries and/or industries in electorally valuable jurisdictions (Lowande, Jenkins, and Clarke 2018). Presidents can also strategically exempt states and localities from abiding by the requirements of federal statutes, sometimes in exchange for adopting the president's preferred policies instead (Howell 2015). These tools allow presidents to affect political outcomes without congressional involvement.

In many instances, the president can achieve similar objectives through either legislative or unilateral means. In August 2013, President Obama considered launching a missile strike against Syria in retaliation for President Bashar al-Assad's use of chemical weapons. While Obama and many members of Congress argued that the strikes did not require congressional approval, other legislators argued that the president risked setting a precedent for future presidents to violate the separation of powers if he did not involve Congress. Obama ultimately sought congressional approval for an outcome he could have achieved unilaterally.[1]

In other instances, presidents may be able to implement policies through unilateral means that are identical to those that could be achieved via legislation, yet the practical implications are often similar and the measures offer symbolic importance. In 2014, President Obama issued Executive Order 13658 to raise the minimum wage for federal contractors to $10.10 per hour (Goldfarb 2014). While this policy did not apply universally across US employers, it affected wages for some of the two million federal contract workers and signaled a commitment to an increased minimum wage. Obama's use of executive power to benefit federal employees was credited with spurring action by private employers and state and local governments to increase wages for workers (Shear 2014a). Similarly, in 2014, Obama issued Executive Order 13672, which forbade the federal government from discriminating on the basis of gender identity and prohibited federal contractors from discriminating on the basis of sexual orientation and gender identity. The order appeared to reflect a recognition that similar protections – through more sweeping in their scope – could not be implemented via legislation such as the Employment Nondiscrimination Act, which had stalled in Congress (Goldfarb and Eilperin 2014). Obama used executive action to make progress on an issue for which legislative action seemed unlikely.

Most scholarship argues that the public cares mostly – if not exclusively – about whether political officials deliver outcomes and produce policies that they prefer. This is the dominant perspective in studies

---

[1] Congress ultimately failed to provide authorization for the use of military force, and Republicans later criticized Obama's inaction on Syria. Polls showed that the public was opposed to military intervention in Syria (Landler and Thee-Brenan 2013) but also believed that President Obama should receive congressional approval before taking any action (Murray 2013).

of American political representation, whether focused on presidents or members of Congress. According to this view, the public is unlikely to evaluate a president's successes or failures on the basis of how those outcomes were achieved. This view is also consistent with research on public opinion, which posits that the public is more likely to have clearly defined preferences over "easy" issues, which Carmines and Stimson (1980, 80) characterize as those that are symbolic rather than technical, address policy ends rather than means and have been on the public agenda for some time. Satisfying none of these three conditions, the public may simply hold "non-attitudes" on the topic of presidential power (Converse 1970). These non-attitudes would reveal randomness and instability (Campbell et al. 1960; Converse 1964, 1970; Zaller 1992) when the public is asked to consider the procedures through which presidential outcomes are achieved. This perspective further suggests that the public's non-attitudes limit the opportunities for them to hold presidents accountable for how outcomes are achieved.

As a consequence of this singular focus on the purposes of presidential actions, scholars attribute a wide range of presidential behavior to presidents' electoral motivations. The strengthened connection between the public's expectations and presidential behavior is often cited as an explanation for the ascendance of the modern presidency (Lowi 1986; Neustadt 1990) and presidents' increased reliance on unilateral tools (Howell 2003; Moe and Howell 1999a). If, however, the public also scrutinizes the ways these policy outcomes are achieved, the prospects for presidential accountability may extend beyond the public's approval of those outcomes. The public may hold meaningful attitudes about the tools wielded by presidents that may affect the incentives for presidents to take action.

Existing scholarship has paid less attention to public responsiveness to a presidential decision to employ legislative or unilateral means. Most studies ignore or rule out the potential for the public to evaluate presidents on the basis of how political outcomes were achieved.[2] What were the implications for presidential accountability, for example, when President Obama mandated a minimum wage for federal employees through executive action rather than by signing legislation? Understanding how attitudes towards political *processes* affect attitudes about *outcomes* is thus important for characterizing the degree to which the American public

---

[2] Studies that consider how presidential approval affects the number of executive orders presidents issue reach mixed conclusions (Deering and Maltzman 1999; Krause and Cohen 1997; Mayer 1999), but they do not examine whether public opinion influences a president's choice between unilateral and legislative means.

can effectively serve as Representative Mann's "watchmen" and hold presidents accountable for their exercise of power.

2.1.1 Presidential Accountability in a Partisan Era

Most studies of voter accountability posit or assume that voters focus on readily accessible and easily obtained information. This follows from an understanding that voters are relatively uninformed and operate in low information environments (Downs 1957; Popkin 1994). Voters are mostly unable to identify their elected officials (Delli Carpini and Keeter 1996), much less pay attention to the processes through which policies are made. In 2010, only 26 percent of Americans knew the number of votes to break a filibuster (Pew 2010). Similarly, a survey conducted in 2018 showed only about a third of Americans could name the three branches of government (Annenberg 2018). Even Speaker Pelosi declared that, "The American people don't care about process" (Harwood 2010).

Instead, major theories of voter behavior emphasize sociological and psychological attachments as key factors in shaping political evaluations. Mechanisms such as partisanship (Campbell et al. 1960), ideology (Downs 1957), one's social contacts (Berelson, Lazarsfeld, and McPhee 1954), and political endorsements (Lupia 1994) operate as heuristics through which voters' information costs are significantly reduced. These theories suggest that presidential evaluations may depend less on performance and more on readily available cues voters use to form political judgments.

In an age of polarization, partisan predispositions may be a powerful substitute for attitudes towards political processes. Partisanship acts as a "perceptual screen" (Campbell et al. 1960) for how Americans perceive and experience the political world. According to Key (1949, 285), "Although the great issues of national politics are potent instruments for the formation of divisions among the voters, they meet their match in the inertia of traditional partisan attachments formed generations ago." Accordingly, partisan attachments influence a variety of political views, ranging from economic assessments (Gerber, Huber, and Washington 2010) to attitudes on domestic spying (Pew 2013) and views of US relations with Russia (Reinhart 2018). Partisanship may often substitute for considered reflection on political issues, particularly in a context of elite polarization (Berinsky 2009; Druckman, Peterson, and Slothuus 2013). While models of democratic representation often rest on the notion that voters express their views through elections on the major political issues of the day, some research suggests that voters simply "adopt the policies that their favorite politicians prefer" (Lenz 2012, 3). Drawing from what Huddy, Mason, and Aarøe (2015) term the "expressive model" of party identification, partisanship is often described as "a helluva drug" (Klein 2016) due to its omnipresent association with political attitudes and behaviors.

In a world where voters do not hold policy positions independent of their leaders, how are they to muster any feelings towards the means their elected leaders employ? Less salient process issues may be especially susceptible to being driven entirely by partisanship. Research on attitudes towards congressional procedures finds that the public's attitudes towards the Senate filibuster are strongly associated with the partisan alignment between voters and the Senate majority party (Smith and Park 2013) and the policy for which the filibuster is used (Doherty 2015). Given these findings, a citizen's shared partisanship with the president may entirely drive support for the president's exercise of power.

In behavioral studies of the presidency, partisanship and presidential approval loom large as drivers of public opinion. In contemporary American politics, copartisanship with and support for the president are practically one and the same. Recent presidents' approval ratings have been increasingly polarized across party lines, with the presidents' copartisans nearly unanimous in their support and members of the other party nearly unanimous in their opposition (Jones 2019). Not only do voters express presidential approval as a function of their partisanship, but they also reconsider their partisanship so that it is aligned with their evaluation of the president (Montagnes, Peskowitz, and McCrain 2019; Tucker, Montgomery, and Smith 2018).

A variety of studies suggest that partisanship and presidential approval are the sole drivers of attitudes towards presidential power. Sievert and Williamson (2018) show that respondents' partisanship and presidential approval were the most important predictors of evaluations of the veto power. Individuals who shared the president's partisanship and approved of the current president were significantly more supportive of the president's right to veto legislation passed by Congress. Another analysis used survey experiments to manipulate whether respondents were told that a president pursued outcomes via unilateral action and found that "partisan cues and policy preferences, alone, shaped assessments of" the presidential actions they examined (Christenson and Kriner 2017a, 346). They conclude that partisan attachments "all but overwhelm [Americans'] underlying constitutional concerns" when considering presidents' unilateral power (Christenson and Kriner 2017a, 347).[3]

The outsized roles that partisanship and presidential approval are believed to play in the public's evaluations of its presidents may leave little room for Americans to consider how presidents govern in office. According to one account, "The prevailing consensus is that Americans will support the power grabs of the presidents they already support and disapprove power grabs when they already disapprove of the president" (Stein 2016). Another notes that, "Executive orders are about process. It's a means of making public policy. And the public is largely unmoved by insider-y process stories despite the attention they get in DC" (Sullivan and Craighill 2014).

For Americans to hold presidents accountable for how they wield power, two conditions must be met. First, Americans must have preferences over the tools presidents use to govern. That is, the public's attitudes about the power of the presidency must be distinct from their evaluations of the president currently in office. While partisanship and presidential approval may be associated with how Americans view presidential power, for the accountability mechanism to operate these quantities cannot be mere reflections of each other. Second, Americans must draw upon these attitudes when evaluating presidential uses of power. That is, when presidents bring about some policy outcome, evaluations of those outcomes should reflect, at least in part, Americans' preferences towards the governing tools presidents use to accomplish it.

Our central thesis is that citizens have beliefs and values over the exercise of political power and that they bring these values to bear in their political judgments. Our primary focus is on the president's use of unilateral action to accomplish something contentious and over the objection of another branch. In this chapter, we consider why citizens – most of whom approach politics with low levels of knowledge, strong partisan attachments, or both – respond to how presidents govern. In making our case, we argue that citizens draw upon core values that shape how they think about the American presidency. These beliefs are shaped through political socialization and relate to Americans' understanding of the structural features of US governance. In turn, these beliefs shape how Americans evaluate presidential behavior. In contrast with the

---

[3] For an alternative view about the relationship between voters' constitutional concerns and evaluations of unilateral power, see Christenson and Kriner (2017b).

perspectives discussed, our theoretical argument suggests that Americans indeed meet the requirements to function as "watchmen in the night."

2.2 HOW PEOPLE VIEW POWER

Presidential power may not at first glance appear to be a subject about which Americans express enlightened public opinion. Most citizens are not experts on the president's constitutional powers. Presidential power rarely makes the front pages of newspapers or is the topic of headline stories on evening newscasts. It typically does not rank among the political issues that weigh on the minds of most Americans and thus is unlikely to be the subject of conversations at dinner tables, in barbershops, at workplaces, or in churches. Given these conditions, one could be forgiven for suspecting that Americans' beliefs on this subject exemplify the definition of a non-attitude (Converse 1970).

In contrast with this conventional wisdom, we contend that the public possesses clear preferences about presidential authority and its exercise. Three initial observations support our claim. First, Americans are closely attuned to their presidents. The president is the most visible and politically salient figure in American society. Since 1946, for instance, Gallup has surveyed Americans on their most admired men and women.[4] In only eight of those seventy-three years – none of them since 1980 – was a president not described as the "most admired" man (Gallup 2019). Reflecting this vast public interest, media outlets perceive incentives to provide extensive coverage of presidents. According to Eshbaugh-Soha (2013, 549), "That the president dominates the daily news cycle is an often-repeated truism of political science." Presidents can generate further upticks in both public attention and media coverage by speaking directly to the nation, as they often do in times of crisis or to rally support for a new policy proposal (Kernell 2006). Americans are thus likely to have at least some passing knowledge of what their presidents do given the volume of attention they pay to them.

Second, citizens express interest in how and for what purposes presidents wield power. In 1999, for example, the House of Representatives Rules Committee convened a hearing on executive branch lawmaking. Several members of Congress commented specifically on the volume of constituent-initiated communications they had received on issues of executive power. As Representative Deborah Pryce (R-OH) testified,

---

[4] This poll was not conducted in 1976.

"Judging by my constituent mail, I think it is fair to say that the public awareness of the power of executive order has increased, and Congress should be able to explain to the public why the President is establishing policy without congressional approval" (US Congress House Committee on Rules Subcommittee on Legislative and Budget Process 1999, 7). Similarly, Representative Doc Hastings (R-WA) noted that "I at home hear a great deal from my constituents on particular executive orders. In fact, I daresay there is not a town hall meeting that I have that somebody brings up an executive order, which means that they are probably in tune with what's going on" (US Congress House Committee on Rules Subcommittee on Legislative and Budget Process 1999, 39). More recent survey evidence also suggests that the public is aware of presidents' exercise of power. An *Economist/YouGov* (2014a) poll showed that half of Americans watched President Obama's November 2014 speech that announced his actions to defer deportation proceedings for certain undocumented immigrants, and a study conducted by the Pew Research Center showed that 78 percent of respondents had heard "a lot" about President Trump's executive actions in 2017 that restricted individuals from certain countries from entering the United States. The available evidence, then, suggests that while executive orders may indeed be an "insider-y" way of making public policy, Americans are familiar with and attuned to presidents' uses of power, particularly on higher-profile matters.

Third, the public's lack of knowledge about the details of executive orders and other tools of presidential power does not mean that they have no opinions about their use. Americans know little about the specifics of the tax code, for instance, yet they express clear and consistent preferences about proposals to increase taxes. And despite many Americans' ignorance of the details of foreign policy, public opinion on this issue is rather coherent (Holsti 1992). Even on complicated issues about which Americans have relatively low levels of knowledge, accountability mechanisms induce officeholders to respond to public opinion (Carmines and Stimson 1980; Baum and Potter 2015; Lupia and McCubbins 1998). Americans do not have to be experts in constitutional or administrative law to have attitudes about executive power and to bring them to bear when evaluating presidents who wield it.

What might be the source of these attitudes? While voters may not have encyclopedic knowledge about the institution of the presidency, they do possess core values about American governance (Feldman 1988; Goren 2001; McClosky 1964). According to Kinder and Kalmoe (2017, 102), these values manifest as "beliefs that certain modes of conduct or certain end states are desirable. Values transcend particular objects and specific situations; they are relatively abstract and durable claims about virtue and the good society." Individuals can make political evaluations of policies and actions based on the extent to which they "are consistent or inconsistent with certain important beliefs and values" (Feldman 1988, 418).

Core values influence citizens' basic ideas about the structure of government. Even in the absence of specific knowledge about the details and mechanics of the tools of unilateral action, core values shape citizens' assessments about the acceptability of unilateral authority. Core democratic values such as egalitarianism, tolerance, and support for minority rights are strong predictors of attitudes towards specific policies (Feldman 1988), political procedures (Smith and Park 2013), and political institutions (Caldeira and Gibson 1992; Gibson and Caldeira 2009). While offering a skeptical view about the public's ideological coherence, Converse (1964, 211) recognizes that "a few crowning postures" can "serve as a sort of glue to bind together many more specific attitudes and beliefs, and these postures are of prime centrality in the belief system as a whole." Our argument is not that voters have well-formed and ideologically constrained views about the presidency and the separation of powers, but that they possess values relating to the proper exercise of political power and bring them to bear when evaluating presidential behavior.

In this respect, our argument is that the presidency is not especially unique among political institutions in how it is evaluated by the public. The public's evaluations of political institutions beyond the presidency reflect, at least in part, the procedures employed in those institutions' uses of authority. In the context of the courts, for instance, the perception that judicial procedures are fair is an important source of the courts' legitimacy (Gibson 1989); likewise, the means by which judges are selected influences how the public views their impartiality (Gibson 2012). In the legislative branch, perceptions of the lawmaking process influence public attitudes towards Congress (Hibbing and Theiss-Morse 1996, 2002) and individual legislators (Doherty 2015). More generally, public opinion towards political institutions reflects perceptions of institutional fairness (Doherty and Wolak 2012; Lind and Tyler 1988), and support for political leaders is responsive to the procedures those leaders employ (Tyler, Rasinski, and McGraw 1985). As the world's most powerful elected official, we expect that a president's evaluations also reflect how they wield authority.

Presidents routinely invoke political processes when appealing to the public. For instance, in debates over the Affordable Care and Patient

Protection Act, both President Obama and members of Congress took each other to task for the procedures they employed. During his 2010 State of the Union address, President Obama argued that decreased public support for health care reform was due to a lack of transparency in how the proposed legislation was debated in Congress. President Obama noted that "the process left most Americans wondering, 'What's in it for me?'" (Obama 2010). Obama's decision to highlight "unsavory legislative maneuvering" was described by observers as a "new element of tension" in the president's relationship with congressional leaders (Harwood 2010). Just as politicians may attempt to shape public opinion on specific policies (Jacobs and Shapiro 2000), presidents' public appeals suggest that they believe public opinion can also be moved by criticizing unpopular political tactics. Presidents have no monopoly on criticizing the procedural machinations of adjoining branches, leaving presidents vulnerable to criticism when exercising power in ways the public disapproves.

2.3 THE RULE OF LAW AND PRESIDENTIAL POWER

Arguments over the bounds of executive power usually contest where the rule of law ends and tyranny begins. These debates extend beyond contemporary American politics across time as far back as 1215 and the signing of the Magna Carta. They provoke questions that animate conflict in any country with an executive who desires power. In the United States, arguments over the scope of executive power preceded the inception of the nation and motivated the initial calls for independence. The growth of executive power is at the heart of contemporary fears over democratic backsliding both in the United States and around the world.

Political officials often emphasize the sanctity of rules and procedures of politics. In a discussion of the first impeachment trial of Donald Trump, John Dean, White House Counsel to President Nixon, noted that "process determines results. And if you ignore process, you are really ignoring the way the machinery is going to produce and what it will produce" ("New Day [Transcript]" 2020). To this, Joseph Lieberman, former vice-presidential candidate and Connecticut Senator, added, "We're a rule of law country. That's one of the ways we distinguish ourselves. And rules of law are all about process. Of course, it's about the result in the end, but how you get to the result is really critically important and distinguishes us as Americans" ("New Day [Transcript]" 2020). As Dean and Lieberman highlight, when elites follow the rules, citizens view outcomes as legitimate.

Not all debates invoking procedural issues are equally salient. In the context of legislative politics, for example, citizens may react to broad process questions like the willingness to compromise (Harbridge and Malhotra 2011), but not to more technical issues over parliamentary procedure (Smith and Park 2013). The public may not react strongly to, for example, an executive proclamation versus an executive memorandum. But debates over presidential power are different.

Arguments over presidential power are typically about faithfulness to the US Constitution. At their most feverish, these arguments engender treasonous allegations that may scar legacies. Proponents of presidential power and those presidents who use those powers are often cast as courtiers and kings. In considering claims that his father "harbored monarchical sympathies," John C. Hamilton, son of Alexander Hamilton, lamented that the charge meant that "men like his father 'are to be handed down to posterity as traitors to the feelings of the people and to the Constitution they had formed and sworn to maintain'" (Meacham 2008, 288). These impulses were not limited to the founding. Rather, American skepticism of kingly power was present at the "birth of the Republic and decades on" and created "political problems" for future presidents (Meacham 2008, 288).

We argue that attitudes towards presidential power are rooted in core values about deference and obedience to the rule of law. This does not imply a legalistic understanding of the Constitution but rather a set of values over the inviolability of the law. The rule of law "ensures political rights, civil liberties, and mechanisms of accountability which in turn affirm the political equality of all citizens and constrain potential abuses of state power" (O'Donnell 2006, 3). In democratic systems, its importance owes to its "primary function … to impede tyranny" (Gibson 2007, 593). In a system in which authority is both shared and separated across the branches of government, increases in the authority of the presidency reduces the authority of other adjoining branches.

The rule of law is especially relevant for characterizing views towards unilateral powers. Scholarship on American political thought characterizes executive prerogative "as a disturbing anomaly in a normally rule-bound system of government" (Fatovic 2004). Support for the rule of law comes into conflict with support for executive power, as individuals with strong commitments to the rule of law are likely to perceive a president's use of unilateral authority as inconsistent with the president's role in a democratic system. Strong beliefs in the rule of law are associated with a view that "neither citizens nor leaders are free to act in any way they please" (Gibson 2007, 594) and so these individuals may balk, despite their political predispositions, towards unilateral presidential powers. Strong believers in the rule of law are more likely to view laws as inviolable and see the exercise of unilateral executive powers as a violation of the political order.

These are the very terms by which many popular critics of presidential power cast their arguments. In an editorial published in 2015, Representative Randy Forbes (R-VA) accused President Obama of sending a message that "the rule of law doesn't matter." Throughout his presidency, headlines proclaimed that President Obama "must respect the rule of law" (Paxton 2015), was "undermining the rule of law" (Thomas 2015), engaged in "rule of lawlessness" (Roff 2015), put "politics above the rule of law" (Napolitano 2013), and generally behaved in a "lawless" manner (Will 2014). This pattern continued under President Trump, with a nearly constant barrage of news stories and opinion pieces that accused the president of "[undermining] the rule of law" (Denning 2019), showing "unbroken disdain" (Biskupic 2020) and "contempt" (Toobin 2018) for the rule of law, and conducting "war" (McManus 2019) on the rule of law.

We argue that Americans apply these attitudes about unilateral power when evaluating presidential outcomes. They do so by providing more negative assessments of policies and outcomes that are achieved via the president's use of unilateral power. This assessment reflects the public's beliefs about whether unilateral power is a legitimate means of policy-making. Research on process-based evaluation characterizes legitimacy as "the belief that authorities, institutions, and social arrangements are appropriate, proper, and just" (Tyler 2006, 376). Citizens view policy outputs as legitimate when they believe there is "something rightful about the way the laws came about" (Friedman 1998, 256). Legitimacy thus has some parallels with the concept of "diffuse support," which consists of a "reservoir of favorable attitudes or goodwill that helps members to accept or tolerate outputs to which they are opposed or the effects of which they see as damaging to their wants" (Easton 1965, 273).

Our argument implies that Americans view the institution of the presidency through different lenses relative to how they evaluate the occupants of that office. The public's support for an institution – as apart from the individuals inhabiting those institutions – is an important measure of that institution's legitimacy. In the context of presidential power, public attitudes towards those powers serve as an indicator of the public's acceptance of those powers, even when they are wielded to achieve policy goals individuals do not personally support. Discussions of legitimacy have occurred most commonly in scholarship on institutions outside of the executive branch.[5] Citizens do not evaluate the Supreme Court solely on the basis of their impressions of the chief justice, nor do their attitudes about their congressional representative directly map on to their assessment of Congress as a whole. Scholarship on attitudes towards Congress and the courts advances various arguments to explain why attitudes towards individual officeholders differ from attitudes towards the office itself, but this research agrees that the public employs different considerations when evaluating political institutions and the individuals who comprise them.

2.4 THE ORIGINS OF VIEWS OF THE EXECUTIVE

We argue that public attitudes towards unilateral power are part of an American ethos. This ethos has persisted since the nation's beginning, and it reflects a reverence for the principles that are enshrined in the Constitution and are reinforced through political and civic socialization. These values are not uniquely American – we show later in the book that these sentiments exist to varying degrees around the world – but Americans show deep veneration for the rule of law and profound disdain for unilateral power.

2.4.1 The Role of Political Culture

A distinct political culture has characterized American public life almost from the nation's beginning. Tocqueville (1963 [1840]) argued that American identity is rooted in widespread public agreement on a common set of core values (or mores). Louis Hartz reached a similar conclusion more than a century later. Hartz (1955, 9) attributed "many of the most peculiar American cultural phenomena" to a "fixed, dogmatic liberalism" and "the national acceptance of the Lockian creed."

One distinctive feature of American political culture is its opposition to the concentration of power in a single executive. This is reflected by the observation that "Americans are basically individualistic and skeptical of authority" (Edwards 1989, 14). Posner and Vermeule (2010, 113–114) sound a similar theme, observing that "American political culture ...

---

5 Rogowski (2020) and Yackee and Lowery (2005), however, study public support for the federal bureaucracy.

features deeply entrenched suspicion of the executive." Mansfield (1989, 1) presents a more nuanced perspective and describes American thought towards executive power as ambivalent:

Even though the assumption regarding the necessity of executive power is universal, there are always some and sometimes many living under free governments who grumble about strong executive actions they find distasteful. They deplore and oppose them as the practices of tyranny, calling them by one of the many contemporary equivalents for that term which our prudery requires and our experience makes very familiar. Yet the protestations subside soon enough as if in recognition of necessity, unless indeed the tune is changed and clamor begins for strong executive actions which the formerly disapproving now find beneficial.

Mansfield's account emphasizes that while Americans recognize executive power as something of a necessary evil, their resistance towards it is nearly automatic.

Mansfield's (1989) description of the ambivalence towards executive power is not peculiar to modern political life. These debates are reflected in the tension between the county's founding documents. The Declaration of Independence presented an indictment of kingly power, while the US Constitution revived an energetic executive after the failed efforts of the Articles of Confederation. To persuade skeptical Americans about the necessity of a chief executive, many of the arguments presented in *The Federalist* defended against the idea that the office of the presidency was too strong. This tension persisted beyond the founding, as contestation over presidential power has been a consistent theme in political debates since then. On January 3, 1848, for example, the US House of Representatives voted to censure President Polk for "unnecessarily and unconstitutionally" starting the Mexican War by provoking hostilities on American soil (Fisher 2010). Over a century later, the *Washington Post* predicted that President Truman's seizure of the steel industry in April 1952 would "go down in history as one of the most high-handed acts committed by an American president" (*Washington Post* 1952). In 2014, the House of Representatives voted to authorize Speaker John Boehner to sue President Obama for overstepping his constitutional authority in delaying the employer mandate in the Patient Protection and Affordable Care Act of 2010. The contentious nature of unilateral executive power is unsurprising, given the origins of the office. The debates of the Founders revealed a stark divide between "a definition of executive power more consistent with the royal prerogative of Britain than with the republican principles of the Constitution" (Rakove 2009, 172).

These founding-era debates were enshrined in the Constitution through the design of our political institutions. As Howell (2013, 129) notes, "An important strain of American political culture ... finds its earliest expressions in America's revolt against the reach of monarchical power across the Atlantic, and the subsequent efforts of a newly independent people to design a system of government that would protect against executive tyranny." The new government reflected the tension discussed above between the need for a strong executive and skepticism about the extent of its powers. Howell (2013, 130) continues:

> That the Framers were willing to confer new authority on the presidency, however, did not signify an abandonment of their concerns about despotism. ... In the same instance that the Founders endowed an office with new authority to act, they constructed a set of institutional safeguards meant to frustrate those who would fill the office. ... Presidents were to act, but the basis for such action would always be contested.

The constitutional system designed in Philadelphia in 1787 put Congress at the center of American government. Article I of the Constitution concerns the legislative power. As Madison wrote in *Federalist*, no. 48, "In republican government, the legislative authority necessarily predominates." The titles of contemporary textbooks explicitly reference Congress as the "first branch" (e.g., Ginsberg and Wagner Hill 2019; Theriault and Edwards 2019). Today, this understanding is manifested in what Pious and Pyle (1984, 153) term the "'literary' (or ninth-grade civics) theory of separation of powers" in which "Congress legislates and the executive executes." This characterization of the Constitution is encoded in how contemporary Americans think about the presidency.

Americans' reverence for the Constitution helps to ensure that this understanding is perpetuated. In *Federalist*, no. 49, Madison expresses his wish that the Constitution will be viewed with a "veneration which time bestows on everything, and without which perhaps the wisest and freest governments would not possess the requisite stability." By all accounts, Madison's wish has been fulfilled. In his classic text, Hofstadter (1948, 13) argues that "Americans venerate [the Constitution] so deeply." More recent scholarship concurs. According to Zink and Dawes (2016, 538), the public's "widespread reverence for the Constitution serves ... as a focal point for agreement among the citizenry." Similarly, Hibbing and

Theiss-Morse (1996, 125) conclude that "Americans love the constitutional structure and the abstract principles underlying the political system in the United States." Americans' "constitutional attachment" (Zink and Dawes 2016, 538) leads them to "find the notion of seriously criticizing it almost sacrilegious" (Levinson 2006, 17). Importantly, public esteem for the Constitution need not – and does not appear to – reflect specific knowledge about the Constitution. For example, Brown and Pope (2019, 1136) conclude that Americans' "reverence seems to be based on something other than a deep knowledge of the document." Instead, the public views the Constitution through a somewhat mythical lens, in turn shaping how they perceive the American political system in general and the presidency in particular.

2.4.2 Civic and Political Socialization

In 1875, President Grant addressed Congress and pleaded with them to join his crusade for public education. In doing so, he explicitly linked education with the preservation of democracy. As Chernow (2017, 812) describes,

Grant embroidered this theme of the need for mass public education to resist "tyranny and oppression … whether directed by the demagogue or by priestcraft." Educating the citizenry, he asserted, was the optimal way to protect democratic institutions.

Given the historical and institutional legacies of the colonial experience, political socialization may cultivate skepticism about a more expansive presidency than what the Founders proscribed. After all, Americans are not born with an innate hesitancy towards presidential power. Civic instruction through informal and incidental activities, however, is the most important source of children's ideas about politics (Greenstein 1965, 45). As young children, Americans have an idealized – almost heroic view – of the president as the central authority of government (Carter and Schap 1987; Dennis and Webster 1975; Easton and Dennis 1969; Greenstein 1969, 1975; Hess and Easton 1960). Yet this initial orientation rapidly changes as children mature. In an examination of who children identify as "the chief lawmaker," Easton and Dennis (1969, 176) found that as they "grow older they realize that representative bodies exist and that these bodies help to make the laws. … [C]hildren … begin to understand the correspondingly more limited legal powers of the president." It appears that, "[k]nowledge tempers the image of the kind of power the President should have" (Easton and Dennis 1969, 176). By eighth grade, less than one-fifth of students believe that president should have an absolute final veto of all laws (Easton and Dennis 1969, 173).

This trend is not only a rejection of presidential power but also an embrace of the legislative supremacy of Congress. Easton and Dennis (1969, 120) find that "by the middle grades the child is increasingly prone to identify Congress as both the chief source of lawmaking and a more representative symbol of our government than the President." While still in childhood, Americans come to "see government with Congress as its center" and "law as its most visible product" (Easton and Dennis 1969, 120). In an extension of Greenstein (1969), a study from the 2000s confirms that the "presidency still reigns with unparalleled importance and maintains the paramount status within the country" (Carter and Teten 2002, 460) but also finds that children have become more cynical with respect to the specific officeholder. The authors speculate that, compared to the 1950s, children more "actively separate the *office* from the *individual*" (Carter and Teten 2002, 460). Similarly, Oxley et al. (2020, 141) find that, though children do not have favorable views of the president, "the institution of the presidency continues to be held in high esteem." Children quickly move from understanding government through their idealized views of the president to an institutionalized view focused on the constitutional principles of legislative supremacy and separation of powers, among other principles. Analogous arguments and findings exist with respect to development of attitudes towards the US legal system (Tyler and Trinkner 2018).

The deference for separating the presidency from its occupants persists beyond childhood. In surveys from 2008 to 2012, overwhelming majorities of Americans saw the Constitution as an "enduring document that remains relevant today" as opposed to "an outdated document that needs to be modernized" (GfK Roper 2012). Between 69 and 75 percent of Americans favored the former over the latter position. These findings support the conclusion that citizens approach the US Constitution with "veneration and reverence" and are resistant to change it (Brown and Pope 2019).

The US Constitution and its tenets of separation of powers and checks and balances is a major source of frustration to presidents, especially in the backdrop of increasing expectations heaped upon the president. In analyzing the modern presidency, many have lamented the constitutional weakness of the office (Howell and Moe 2016; Sorenson 1975; Suri 2017), even while Americans hold the president "responsible for the fall of every sparrow" (Sorenson 1975, 159). In an indictment of the Constitution as a "relic," Howell and Moe (2016) argue that granting the president more power in the form of general fast-track authority is the solution for the US's gridlocked system. The Constitution, by this account, is an impediment to a more effective presidential government. Yet Americans' dedication to their cultural understanding of the Constitution stands as a barrier to more radical changes that would shift greater institutional power towards the presidency.

Through formal education, most Americans have been exposed to the principles of separation of powers, checks and balances, and the like. Many Americans espouse views consistent with those Shane (2009, 27) terms "pluralists," who "interpret the checks and balances system to emphasize the roles that the Constitution assigns to the multiple institutions of our national government in holding each other to account." These commitments color the ways Americans evaluate presidential power and, we argue, shape how they evaluate presidential actions.

2.5 STEPPING BACK

The account we have outlined in this chapter generates several testable hypotheses. First, as a descriptive matter, our argument implies that Americans hold low opinions of executive power. We study these attitudes in depth.

Second, we examine the relationship between public attitudes about presidential power and individuals' commitments to the rule of law. As we outlined, Americans with stronger commitments to the rule of law should be more resistant to executive power. We do not expect that this is the *only* factor that is associated with these attitudes. Still, we expect that opinions about unilateral power are not merely reflections of Americans' partisan loyalties and evaluations of the current president. Instead, Americans' commitments to core democratic principles are associated with how they view the presidency.

Third, we argue that Americans hold presidents accountable for how they wield power. Our account of presidential accountability posits that Americans penalize presidents for exercising power in ways they do not approve of. In particular, we expect that the public grants less favorable evaluations to presidents who achieve their goals through unilateral rather than legislative means. If the evidence is consistent with this hypothesis, our findings would indicate that presidents may incur popular costs on the basis of how they wield power. Understanding how the public responds to unilateral actions clarifies how presidents' concerns for their public standings shape their unilateral decision calculus.

We further consider that the effects of unilateralism will vary in systematic ways. Presidents do not exercise their powers within a vacuum, and the context in which presidents act may shape evaluations of presidential power. Just as presidential approval ratings are sensitive to context (Krosnick 1990; Tesler 2012), context may also shape both the public's demand for presidential action and evaluations of its use. For instance, the public may be more supportive of unilateral action for issues of national security, an area where American presidents have particular sway.[6]

Our argument further implies that differences in public support for unilateral powers across various contexts result from a slackening of the constraints that shape opinion towards unilateral powers. For instance, the public could be more supportive of unilateral action in national security matters because the rule of law is less binding on such issues. This is an articulation offered by Locke and Hamilton in favor of vesting executives with emergency powers. Locke's theory of executive prerogative argued that "it is fit that the laws themselves should in some cases give way to the executive power" (Locke 2003 [1690], 375). Thus, overall support for unilateral powers and the importance of the factors that shape these attitudes may vary across contexts in ways that reflect the realities in which presidents govern.

2.5.1 Power, Accountability, and Counterfactuals

Evaluating our argument has important implications for characterizing the nature of presidential accountability. If our argument is correct, we expect to observe that American presidents face penalties for exercises of power that the public views as improper. Strategic presidents would avoid such uses of power to a far greater extent if Americans were inattentive and unresponsive to its use. Our argument thus suggests that accountability mechanisms enable the American public to "tame the Prince" (to borrow from Mansfield 1989), rendering the presidency less dangerous to American democracy than its critics often allege. Our argument stands in contrast to leading perspectives on presidential accountability.

The views outlined in the introduction tend to take a dim view of the capacity of the American public to hold their presidents accountable for

---

[6] National security is not the only context in which public support for unilateral action may vary. We discuss additional contexts in Chapters 3 and 6.

the exercise of power. Political philosophers such as John Locke have expressed concern about executive prerogative in similar terms. Locke (2003 [1690], Second Treatise, chap. 229) asked,

Which is best for mankind, that the people should be always exposed to the boundless will of tyranny, or that the rulers should be sometimes liable to be opposed, when they grow exorbitant in the use of their power, and employ it for the destruction, and not the preservation of the properties of their people?

However, he also expressed skepticism that the public could be roused in a manner effective for constraining tyrannical rule.

It is true, such men may stir, whenever they please; but it will be only to their own just ruin and perdition: for till the mischief be grown general, and the ill designs of the rulers become visible, or their attempts sensible to the greater part, the people, who are more disposed to suffer than right themselves by resistance, are not apt to. (Locke 2003 [1690], Second Treatise, chap. 230)

Locke expressed the view that the public was too passive and viewed politics as too distant to actively monitor and enforce the bounds of prerogative; accordingly, Kleinerman (2007, 218–220) proposes that Locke's concerns make the case for establishing clear demarcations of the limits on executive power so that there can be "manifest evidence" when "the constitution has been breached" by the executive.

This pessimistic conclusion about political accountability and presidential power shares much in common with liberal legalists as described by Posner and Vermeule (2010). Liberal legalism, in their telling, "is intensely anxious about executive power, and sometimes goes so far as to define tightly constrained executive power as an essential element of the rule of law" (Posner and Vermeule 2010, 3). This accounting suggests that while Americans may express low levels of approval of executive power in the abstract, they are ill-equipped to act upon those beliefs. Popular will provides no means for constraining the ambitions of power-seeking executives, absent constitutional provisions that place limits on how they can exercise power.

A second alternative perspective allows for a more limited and conditional role of public opinion in presidential accountability. According to Christenson and Kriner (2017a, 347), "Most Americans evaluate unilateral action through the same partisan cues and policy preferences that they use to make other political judgments." This perspective suggests that Americans view presidential power through the same lenses as they see the president, and it suggests little prospects for accountability for the use of power apart from the normal give-and-take of partisan politics. To the extent the public *can* be rallied to oppose a president's power grabs, this perspective posits a decidedly top-down mechanism. Christenson and Kriner (2017b, 782) argue that popular resistance to presidential actions can only be mobilized by elite political actors – notably, members of Congress – whose public opposition to the president "can activate [voters'] underlying constitutional concerns." In this telling, accountability mechanisms enable voters to sanction presidents only when members of Congress mobilize the public to do so. Our argument, in contrast, posits that accountability mechanisms operate from the bottom up and do not depend on the mobilization of public opinion by the president's political opponents.

Still other perspectives suggest that there are limits on presidents' exercise of power, but they do not specify how those limits are enforced. According to Rossiter (1956, 56), for instance,

[The President], like the rest of us, has been raised in the American tradition; he, perhaps better than the rest of us, senses what the tradition permits and what it forbids in the conduct of high office. If he knows anything of history or politics or administration, he knows that he can do great things only within "the common range of expectation," that is to say, in ways that honor or at least do not outrage the accepted dictates of constitutionalism, democracy, personal liberty, and Christian morality.

This perspective acknowledges the role of political culture in setting the bounds for what is socially and politically acceptable from American presidents. It is unclear, however, what incentives exist to constrain presidents from venturing beyond "what the tradition permits." If presidents indeed have superior knowledge about what is allowable and what is forbidden, as Rossiter proposes, the American public may depend solely on the president's own self-discipline as a means for respecting their beliefs about the use of power.

Our argument instead offers an account that places the agency relationship between presidents and voters front and center. But while we argue that presidents make decisions in the shadows of potential political constraints, we offer a novel take on how voters hold officeholders to account by focusing on how the public constrains the use of power rather than the choice of policy. Our claims are perhaps most similar to that advanced by Posner and Vermeule (2010, 5), who argue that, in contrast with the concerns expressed by liberal legalists, "even an imperial president is constrained by politics and public opinion." Our argument has important implications for how we interpret empirical patterns of presidential behavior. Numerous studies document presidents' increasing reliance on unilateral power. These studies focus primarily on how the separation of powers affects presidents' use of power. We argue for a more expansive understanding of the relevant counterfactuals that accompany figures on, for instance, the number of unilateral directives presidents issue. If the public constrains presidents' exercise of power, we would expect that presidents draw upon those powers much less frequently than they would if political accountability played no role in disciplining presidential behavior. Earlier in this chapter, we outlined the vast expectations presidents inherit when they enter office. To what extent do presidents draw upon executive powers to live up to them? Our account offers a more sober view about the extent to which presidents are free to pursue their objectives independent of political and institutional constraints.

2.5.2 Our Approach

Our book sits somewhat unconventionally at the intersection of public opinion, political behavior, and the presidency. In what follows, we present evidence to test the theoretical account offered in this chapter. Throughout, we provide new empirical findings about the structure of public opinion, and the values citizens bring to bear in how they evaluate policies and presidents. A substantial portion of our evidence is from original surveys of Americans from the Obama and Trump presidencies. We also rely on survey experiments to make causal claims about the relationship between unilateral action and public opinion. Though we base our theory and evidence on behavior, our substantive implications are just as relevant for students of the presidency. Our findings about public opinion and political behavior provide new insight about political conflict over presidents' use of power and the incentives for its exercise.

Ours is not the first scholarly study of public attitudes about the president. But our focus extends beyond how Americans view any particular president. Instead, we are interested in examining how Americans understand the *presidency*. This focus represents a sharp disjuncture between our study and previous research dedicated to understanding the sources of presidential approval or the predictors of presidential election outcomes. These indicators are meaningful for our research to the extent that they inform us about the nature of political accountability, how it operates in the context of presidential power, and how it may shape the incentives for presidents to take action. For these reasons, we proceed differently from previous scholarship. In the first half of the book, we collect an extensive volume of original survey data that draws upon survey instruments we design to understand whether citizens possess the hypothesized values we outline in this chapter.

In the second half of the book, we use several original survey experiments to evaluate many of the core theoretical and empirical claims we make in this book. Survey experiments are used relatively infrequently in the context of the presidency, in part because behavioral studies of the presidency have tended to draw from observational data (Cohen 2017). We use survey experiments with a particular purpose in mind: namely, we seek to identify how the public would react *if* the president were to take a particular action. We can only identify the potential electoral costs of presidential behavior if we ask voters to evaluate an action a president could, but ultimately did not, take. In designing our studies, we sought to strike a balance between realistic scenarios and plausible counterfactuals in order to test our theoretical perspective. Though causal inference in research on political institutions can be challenging – particularly in the context of the presidency for which the number of presidents is small – we hope that our approach provides clear advantages and stimulates additional thinking about inference in presidency research. To bolster these analyses, we also rely on other approaches to test our account of the correlates and consequences of public opinion about executive power. We conduct new analyses of historical polls from as far back as the 1930s to understand the dynamics between public opinion and the use of power in other historical contexts. We also devote a chapter to study attitudes towards executive power outside the United States using survey data for citizens of twenty-six countries of the Americas and thirty-eight countries in Africa.

3

How Americans View Presidential Power

The theoretical perspective we develop in Chapter 2 addresses three central empirical questions about public opinion and the presidency. To what extent do Americans accept the exercise of presidential power? What structures these attitudes? And how do Americans evaluate presidents and their accomplishments? In this chapter, we focus on answering the first of these questions and laying the groundwork for the analyses in later chapters that will build upon its answers.

We establish basic empirical facts about the landscape of public opinion towards the American presidency. Previous scholars and pollsters have not dedicated much attention to understanding how Americans view the institutional power of the most powerful office on earth. Providing an answer to a fundamental question – *how does the public evaluate presidential power?* – requires us to develop and validate new measures of public opinion. In this chapter, we describe our measurement and methodological approach to data collection and begin to test our hypotheses about the nature of public attitudes towards the presidency.

3.1 MEASURING SUPPORT FOR UNILATERAL POWERS

A large body of scholarship characterizes Americans' attitudes towards government by studying public trust and confidence. To the extent this research has evaluated attitudes towards specific institutions, it has focused mostly on the judicial and legislative branches. For instance, studies evaluate perceptions of legitimacy of the Supreme Court and other lower courts (e.g., Ansolabehere and White 2020; Bartels and Johnston 2013; Caldeira and Gibson 1992; Christenson and Glick 2015; Gibson, Caldeira, and Spence 2003; Rogowski and Stone 2021) and attitudes towards Congress (e.g., Doherty 2015; Hibbing and Theiss-Morse 1996, 2001, 2002; Smith and Park 2013). While the correlates of presidential approval have received substantial attention (e.g., Edwards, Mitchell, and Welch 1995; Gronke and Newman 2003; Mueller 1970), few studies evaluate attitudes towards presidential power. With the prominent exception of Aberbach, Peterson, and Quirk (2007), data on public opinion towards executive power is mostly uncharted scholarly territory.

We developed several survey instruments to assess attitudes towards distinct yet related dimensions of presidential power. The statements asked about unilateral policymaking, unilateral judicial appointments, and unilateral agency implementation. We present the full question wording in Table 3.1. We designed the questions with three main principles in mind. First, we sought to abstract away from formal language and legal terminology that describes presidents' use of power. We hoped to avoid the framing effects found in related research that has studied attitudes towards political institutions and the power they exercise (Nicholson 2012). We were also concerned that formal language could artificially generate differences in response patterns on the basis of political information or sophistication. If some respondents were familiar with the definition of "executive order," for example, while others were not, these groups may exhibit different response patterns even if their underlying attitudes about presidential unilateralism were similar. Instead, we designed statements that described the practical consequences of a president's exercise of power.

Second, the questions were designed to measure respondents' conceptions of the presidency rather than their evaluations of any particular president. This is an important challenge for behavioral studies of the presidency. Americans distinguish their support for their individual member of Congress from their views of the collective institution, but a single individual serves as president and occupies the office of the presidency. To encourage respondents to evaluate how power should be distributed across political institutions rather than offer their view of the current president, we prompted respondents to consider "the office of the presidency and not any particular president."

Third, the questions reflect the nature of presidential power in a system in which power is shared across political institutions. Presidential authority expands at the expense of the other branches of government and threatens the balance of the separation of powers system. Each of our questions asks respondents to report whether they support the president's exercise of power relative to another branch. The survey instruments reference both the president and an adjoining political institution, such that respondents' endorsement of presidential power comes at the expense of some other branch of government.

Each of these survey instruments addresses a prominent aspect of unilateral executive power and bears on a president's interbranch relationships. Most scholarship and popular discussion around presidential power focuses on the issues raised by our unilateral policymaking question, which concerns a president's ability to make policy directly. Using tools such as the executive order, the courts have recognized the president's authority to create new policies that carry the force of law. Presidents influence judicial decision-making primarily through the judges they appoint, and recent scholarship focuses on how presidents use recess appointments to appoint nominees who may otherwise not have received Senate confirmation (Black et al. 2007; Hogue 2004). Finally, reflecting what Kagan (2001) terms "presidential administration," presidents have the opportunity as head of the executive branch to influence policy implementation by directing agency behavior and issuing directives and memoranda (Lowande 2014).

The three questions displayed in Table 3.1 were asked nine times over a four-year period that began in January 2014. These questions appeared on the January 2014, May 2014, January 2015, June 2015, October 2015, October 2016, November 2016, May 2017, and January 2018 waves of The American Panel Survey (TAPS). The panel nature of these data permit an unprecedented exploration of continuity and change in both aggregate and individual-level public opinion towards the presidency over the course of two presidential administrations.

Throughout the book, we draw on both our own original surveys as well as those conducted by others. In the aggregate analyses that follow (and elsewhere), we rely on nationally representative surveys of US adult citizens that we conducted as part of TAPS, a monthly panel survey administered to approximately 1,700 respondents. TAPS was conducted monthly between 2012 and 2018 by GfK/Knowledge Networks with a national probability sample. Respondents were recruited by drawing their addresses from the US Postal Service's computerized delivery sequence file. The sample was drawn from four strata: 18-to-24-year-old Hispanics; all other Hispanic adults ages 25 and older, or age unknown; 18-to-24-year-old non-Hispanic adults; and all other adults who are non-Hispanic or of unknown ethnicity and ages 25 and older or age unknown. Survey weights were calculated to account for selection probabilities by the stratified sampling procedure and the probability of selection within

TABLE 3.1 *Question wording for unilateral power survey instruments*

Unilateral action	Question wording
Policymaking	A president should have the right to enact policies without having those policies voted on by Congress.
Judicial appointment	The president should be able to appoint judges of his choosing regardless of whether the US Senate agrees with his selections.
Agency implementation	A president should have the authority to decide how executive agencies will implement bills passed by Congress.

households based on the random choice of a respondent from among all eligible adults residing in the household. These weights generalize response patterns from the survey to approximate a simple random sample of the English-speaking US adult population. The survey was administered online and internet access was provided for respondents who did not already have it. Full demographics of respondents across each wave are shown in Table A.4 in the Appendix to Chapter 3.

Our survey instruments measuring unilateral action were presented to respondents as statements. We asked whether they agreed or disagreed with each. Questions in the first four waves were accompanied by four-point scales that asked respondents to indicate whether they "strongly agreed," "somewhat agreed," "somewhat disagreed," or "strongly disagreed" with each of the items shown in Table 3.1. In most waves, these response options were also accompanied by a neutral option for which respondents "neither agreed nor disagreed." In some waves, however, this response option was replaced with either a "don't know" option, or in other months both the neutral and the "don't know" options were available. The complete unweighted distribution of responses across response options are shown in Tables A.1 through A.3 in the Appendix to Chapter 3. In our analyses that follow, we generally distinguish respondents who provided a positive response from those who did not, yet we take care to explore the robustness of our analyses and inferences to our chosen measurement strategy given the diversity in the sets of response options.

3.2 AMERICANS' ATTITUDES TOWARDS PRESIDENTIAL POWER

We study Americans' attitudes towards presidential power using our survey data described in Section 3.1. Figure 3.1 presents the overall

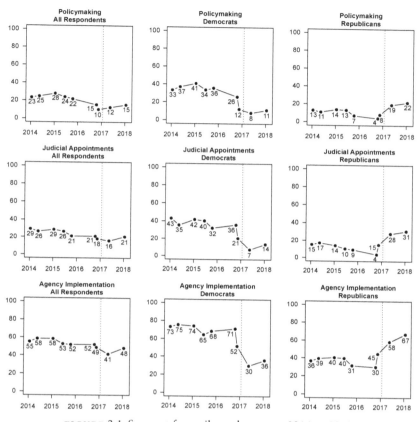

FIGURE 3.1 Support for unilateral powers, 2014 to 2018

Note: Plots show the percentages of respondents who approved of unilateral policymaking (top row), judicial appointments (middle row), and agency implementation (bottom row). Plots in the left column show results for all respondents while the middle and right columns show results for respondents who identified as Democrats and Republicans, respectively. Observations to the left of the vertical dotted line are from the Obama presidency and observations to its right are from the Trump presidency.

percentages of respondents in each survey wave who supported unilateral policymaking, unilateral judicial implementation, and unilateral agency implementation (i.e., expressed agreement with the three survey instruments). These data are weighted to national population parameters and each row corresponds to one of the three items about presidential power described in Table 3.1. The first row presents support for unilateral policymaking, the middle row shows judicial appointments, and the bottom row shows support for agency implementation. The columns show support for the full sample and then by partisanship. The left column shows response patterns for all respondents in the sample, while the center and right columns display results for respondents who identified as Democrats or Republicans, respectively. Respondents who identify with or lean towards one of the major parties are distinguished as partisans (Keith et al. 1992; Klar and Krupnikov 2016). Each of the plotted points corresponds to one of the nine survey waves.

Figure 3.1 provides evidence of three primary patterns. First, as the left column of plots shows, support for unilateral action in each of these surveys is low. Only about a fifth of respondents approved of unilateral policymaking, ranging from a low of 10 percent in November 2016 to a high of 28 percent in January 2015. Support for a president's ability to issue unilateral judicial appointments is only marginally higher and ranged from 16 percent in May 2017 to 29 percent in both January 2014 and January 2015. A larger share of respondents – about half – agreed with a president's ability to direct agency implementation of policy, ranging between 41 percent (May 2017) and 58 percent (May 2014 and January 2015). The greater support for this item relative to the other two questions suggests that the public may recognize the president as the head of the executive branch. This acknowledgment may lead respondents to have broader support for a president's ability to direct an agency within the executive branch compared to other unilateral tools that bear upon other branches of government.

Second, Figure 3.1 shows that aggregate support for unilateral powers is relatively consistent across time. Support for each power varied by an average of around 3 percentage points from one wave to the next. We benchmark these patterns against presidential ratings in the same waves, shown in Figure 3.2. The most notable contrast between Figures 3.1 and 3.2 involves the transition between Presidents Obama and Trump. Aggregate presidential approval drops by 14 percentage points between November 2016 and May 2017, with Democrats and Republicans moving dramatically in opposite directions. While we see some change in attitudes towards presidential power over the same period, which we explore in detail in Chapter 5, the change in presidential approval is considerably larger than any of the wave-to-wave movements in attitudes about presidential power. The contrasting patterns suggest that while presidential approval responds to changes in the political environment and the president's performance, our measures of attitudes toward presidential powers–at least at the aggregate level–are less responsive to short-term changes in the political context.

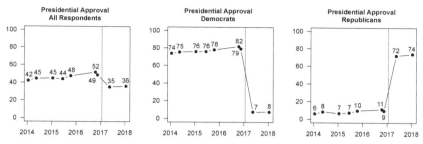

FIGURE 3.2 Presidential approval ratings, 2014 to 2018

Note: Plots show the percentages of respondents who approved of the current president's job performance. The left plot shows results for all respondents while the middle and right plots show results for respondents who identified as Democrats and Republicans, respectively. Observations to the left of the vertical dotted line are from the Obama presidency and observations to its right are from the Trump presidency.

Third, our measures capture attitudes towards presidential power that are distinct from views of the current president. As we discussed, respondents expressed varying levels of support for our questions about unilateral power. If response patterns were reflections of support for the sitting president, we would instead expect these responses to be consistent across the three items. We also find that attitudes towards presidential power sometimes move in opposite directions from presidential approval. Consider the left column in Figures 3.1 and 3.2. Approval of President Obama's job performance went up by four points between October 2015 and October 2016 (from 48 to 52 percent); in contrast, support for unilateral policymaking decreased by seven points (from 22 to 15 percent) over the same period while levels of support for judicial appointments and agency implementation remained the same. We would not observe these divergent patterns across measures if our new survey items were indicators of attitudes towards the president.

Finally, we find that there is more bipartisan agreement over presidential power than there is for the president himself. The center and right columns of Figures 3.1 and 3.2 show data for respondents who identify as Democrats and Republicans, respectively. Predictably, we find that Democrats and Republicans differ in their evaluations of presidential power. During the Obama administration, for instance, an average of 31 percent of Democrats approved of unilateral policymaking compared with an average of 10 percent of Republicans. We observe similar partisan differences for evaluations of judicial appointments, whereby an average of 36 percent of Democrats and 12 percent of Republicans approved of such appointments, and for agency implementation, whereby an average of 61 percent of Democrats and 37 percent of Republicans approved. Likewise, during each of the two waves conducted during the Trump administration, Republicans were more supportive of presidential power than Democrats.

Yet while these partisan differences are both substantively and statistically significant, they pale in comparison to the partisan gulf in evaluations of the sitting president. During the Obama administration, more than three-quarters of Democrats generally approved of the president's job performance compared to around 10 percent of Republicans. Likewise, an average of 73 percent of Republicans approved of President Trump's job performance compared to 8 percent of Democrats. Our data reveal that Americans express much more agreement across party lines in their attitudes towards presidential power than in their evaluations of the current president. Not only does a large share of the public express skepticism about – if not hostility towards – presidential power, but these views are held more widely across partisan lines compared with their evaluations of contemporary political figures.

The measures we introduce in this section provide new descriptive portraits of Americans' views towards the powers belonging to the office of the presidency. These data provide initial evidence consistent with our theoretical perspective that Americans express relatively limited support for presidential power. Moreover, Americans' judgments of the president appear to be distinct from their evaluations of the scope of presidential power, with considerably greater partisan consensus on questions of presidential power relative to many of the other issues that generate contemporary political debate.

3.3 POLITICAL CONTEXT AND SUPPORT FOR UNILATERAL POWER

Our new measures describe Americans' attitudes towards unilateral power in the abstract. Yet presidents do not exercise powers in a vacuum. The larger political environment, the relevant policy domain, or the president's relationship with other political actors may also shape the public's demand for presidential action and condition their evaluations of its desirability.

Existing research documents several contexts that shape public opinion towards the presidency. First, the public may be more willing to accept the use of presidential power to achieve the president's policy priorities. Presidents dating back to Andrew Jackson have used their election to claim popular mandates for their programmatic agendas (Azari 2014; Dahl 1990); to the extent these presidents' claims resonate with voters, the public may be more accepting of the presidents' use of power to achieve their priority items (e.g., Edwards 1989; Peterson et al. 2003).

Second, the public may be more supportive of unilateral action on issues of national security. In this arena, American presidents have particular sway because of Article II authority and the domestic politics associated with the "two presidencies" thesis (Wildavsky 1966). According to Bryce (1995 [1888], 48–49), for instance, the authority of the president "expands with portentous speed" during war, because "immense responsibility is then thrown on one who is both the commander in chief and the head of the civil executive." Because they have "the inevitable tendency to enhance the prestige and influence of the presidential office" (Sturm 1949, 139), wars and foreign crises often induce a "rally-around-the-flag" effect (Brody 1991; Mueller 1973) and exalt the president in the public's eye. George W. Bush's Homeland Security Presidential Directive 1, which establishes the organization and operation of the Homeland Security Council, justifies its action based on "the national security function" to "secur[e] Americans from terrorist threats or attacks" (Bush 2001). Presidents are less responsive to public opinion on foreign affairs than for most other issues, possibly because presidents can expect relatively wide latitude – and thus greater support – from the public in this policy domain (Canes-Wrone and Shotts 2004). Similarly, legislators are more deferential to the president during periods of war (Howell, Jackman, and Rogowski 2013).

Third, public support for presidential power could also depend on the policymaking capacities of other political actors. The public desires responsive government, and gridlock may frustrate agendas that the public supports. Gridlock in Congress tends to reduce public evaluations of that institution (Ramirez 2009), and the public may be more willing to support a president's use of power to overcome legislative inaction. The inability to spur congressional action is precisely the scenario that motivated President Obama's "We Can't Wait" campaign (Lowande and Milkis 2014). President Obama articulated this justification for unilateral action in his May 2014 radio address when he stated, "I want to work with Congress to create jobs and opportunity for more Americans. But where Congress won't act, I will" (Obama 2014c). Research in comparative politics similarly identifies legislative intransigence as a factor that leads to executive unilateralism and circumvents normal constitutional processes (Linz 1990).

We investigated how these conditions affect attitudes towards presidential power by embedding an experiment in a survey administered in September 2014 by Survey Sampling International (SSI). Unlike TAPS, which utilized a national probability sample, SSI recruited respondents from an opt-in internet panel to complete surveys conducted online. The use of data from a nonprobability sample raises an important methodological issue. Because the survey was not administered to a sample designed to represent the national population, the results may have decreased external validity. The demographic characteristics of the sample might differ from the characteristics of the target population, and nonprobability samples in online panels tend to be younger and more white than the national population. There also may be features of individuals that select into taking our survey that are correlated with how they respond to its questions.

We address these issues of external validity through two aspects of our analysis. First, in testing our hypothesis experimentally, randomization assures that estimates of our treatment effects are unbiased within the context of our sample. Characteristics of individuals in our sample – even those unobserved or unobservable – are unrelated to the treatment condition to which they are assigned. Though our sample is not nationally representative, our survey experiment will produce unbiased treatment effects. Other work has shown that survey experiments conducted with nonrepresentative samples closely approximate those with high-quality national sampling frames (Berinsky, Huber, and Lenz 2012; Coppock 2019). These findings indicate that even if our sample is not fully representative, the treatment effects we estimate are likely to generalize to the US population.

Second, in analyzing our survey experiments, we use survey weights so that the demographic composition of our sample is comparable to the demographic composition of the national population. Using survey weights allows us to estimate the population average treatment effect (PATE). Weights for the SSI data were constructed via ranking based on gender, race, Hispanic origin, age, education, Census region, income, homeownership, and marital status. Using survey weights allows us to estimate treatment effects as though the demographic characteristics of our sample are comparable to the demographic characteristics of the national population. As Miratrix et al. (2018) shows, however, differences between the PATE and the sample average treatment effect (SATE) estimated without the use of weights may indicate the presence of heterogeneous treatment effects. Therefore, while we focus on reporting the

PATE in our main analyses, we consider both quantities when estimating experimental treatment effects.

A total of 2,048 respondents completed the survey in September 2014. Each respondent was randomly assigned to either the control group or one of three treatment groups, and received one of the following prompts:

- **Control:** The president should have the right to enact policies without having those policies voted on by Congress.
- **Presidential priority:** When a president feels strongly about an issue, he should have the right to enact policies without having those policies voted on by Congress.
- **Gridlock:** When Congress will not act, a president should have the right to enact policies without having those policies voted on by Congress.
- **National security:** In matters of national security, a president should have the right to enact policies without having those policies voted on by Congress.

The number of respondents in each condition was, respectively, 506, 496, 533, and 513. These conditions certainly do not exhaust the set of contextual circumstances that might affect the public's support for unilateral action. Nonetheless, the context described by each condition is politically salient and relatively common, and they all connect to existing scholarship on the presidency and public opinion. After we presented respondents with one of the four statements shown, we asked them whether they agreed with the statement along a four-point scale; for simplicity, we collapsed responses to a binary indicator of support.

We evaluated the effects of the contextual conditions by comparing the mean level of support for unilateral power in each context condition to mean support among respondents in the control condition. Overall, 37 percent of respondents in the control condition supported the president's right to enact policies without involving Congress. This figure is somewhat higher than what we found in the TAPS data shown earlier in this chapter, perhaps attributable to the difference in sampling frames. For our purposes, however, we are more concerned with how support for unilateral power in the other conditions varies relative to this baseline.

Figure 3.3 displays these comparisons. We describe the three conditions on the y-axis. The plotted points show the differences in mean support between each condition and the control condition, where more positive numbers along the *x*-axis indicate greater support for unilateral power relative to the control group. The horizontal lines are the 95 percent confidence intervals associated with the mean differences. The dashed vertical line at zero indicates the null hypothesis of no difference in support between the control and the treatment conditions.

We find that respondents are no more likely to support unilateral power when a president feels strongly about the issue that the directive addresses. The magnitude of the difference is minimal (-0.004) and statistically indistinguishable from zero. The other two treatment conditions, however, significantly increased respondents' approval of unilateral action. Respondents in the *Gridlock* condition were 10 percentage points more approving of unilateral power relative to the control group. The effect was even larger among respondents in the *National security* condition, who were 13 percentage points more approving of unilateral power relative to the control group. The differences between these effects, however, are not statistically significant.

We find similar results when estimating the sample average treatment effects, which are calculated without survey weights.[1] Support for unilateral power is 3 percentage points lower in the *Presidential priority* condition relative to the control, but, as with the population average treatment effects, this difference is not statistically significant. However, the effects of the *Gridlock* and *National security* conditions are both positive and statistically significant, increasing support for unilateral power by 15 and 17 percentage points, respectively, compared to the control condition.

The findings in Figure 3.3 help to contextualize the patterns shown earlier in this chapter. The figure also provides some evidence that the public evaluates presidential power on the basis of the political and institutional context in which it is exercised. While the public is not willing to indulge a president's use of power on issues that the president has prioritized, during periods of legislative gridlock and on matters of national security the public expressed greater support for presidential power. Even in these contexts, however, support for unilateral power does not exceed 50 percent. Our data do not indicate, therefore, that the public endorses a president-centered view of government even when other institutions may be paralyzed or when national security is at stake. Instead, Figure 3.3 suggests that Americans' constitutional concerns related to executive power and checks and balances temper their support for the unilateral presidency.

---

[1] These results are shown in Figure A.1 in the Appendix to Chapter 3.

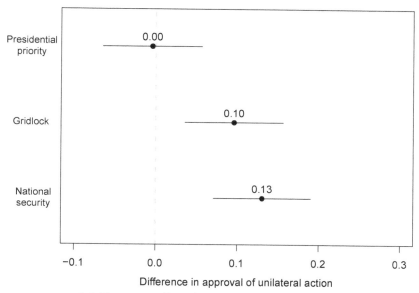

FIGURE 3.3 Treatment effects for context on approval of unilateral policymaking

Note: Data from an experiment conducted in September 2014 by Survey Sampling International (SSI). Points show the population average treatment effects of each condition relative to the control condition where no context was provided. Positive values along the *x*-axis indicate greater support for unilateral power for the context shown along the *y*-axis. Horizontal lines are the ninety-five percent confidence intervals associated with the mean differences in support.

3.4 VALIDATING THE SURVEY INSTRUMENT

Using the measures we developed and reported in Sections 3.1 and 3.2, we will test many of the hypotheses generated by our theoretical perspective in Chapter 2. Before doing so, we consider the extent to which question wording drives the attitudes we observed. In doing so, we address the extent to which the public holds meaningful attitudes towards presidential power.

When it comes to views of executive power, do Americans have "high quality opinions" that are "stable, consistent, informed, and connected to abstract principles and values" (Chong and Druckman 2007, 103)? The American public generally fall short of this criteria as individuals' policy preferences often change over short periods of time (e.g., Campbell et al. 1960; Zaller 1992), exhibit low levels of internal consistency (e.g., Converse 1964), and are sensitive to minor differences in survey question wording (e.g., Rasinski 1989; Sniderman and Theriault 2004).[2] Scholars generally explain variability in public attitudes as resulting from a lack of information or due to the presence of competing considerations (Alvarez and Brehm 2002; Hochschild 1981; Zaller 1992). Given the prominence of the American president and the salient views that many have towards the person holding the office, individual-level opinion about the powers of the office may simply mirror presidential approval. Our aggregate findings in Section 3.2 do not make clear whether the public holds stable and consistent attitudes towards more abstract questions about American governance that are more divorced from everyday political news and events.

In addition to lack of information, scholars also note the influence of framing effects. For example, one study found that citizens conditioned their tolerance for abhorrent speech on the basis of whether it was presented as a matter of freedom of speech or public disruption (Nelson, Clawson, and Oxley 1997). Other studies find, however, that public opinion responds to frames in a largely rational manner (Druckman 2001) or is mostly immune to framing effects on salient issues (Bechtel et al. 2015). These studies highlight a central challenge to drawing inferences from our survey questions. Are the attitudes we observe ephemeral? Do they dissolve away or radically change with the introduction of additional information?

To examine these questions, we conducted a series of survey experiments to examine the stability of individual attitudes towards unilateral power. These analyses investigate the degree to which respondents' assessments of unilateral power are sensitive to how their attitudes are elicited. If individual attitudes towards unilateralism reflect core values about American governance and are largely fixed, we expect to find limited changes in support for the use of unilateral powers under varying political and institutional scenarios. However, if individuals take account of the circumstances surrounding a president's issuance of a unilateral order, we expect attitudes towards unilateralism to vacillate as a function of short-term considerations. We consider a range of factors that may influence how Americans view presidential power, including the identity of the president, the nature of the unilateral tool, the role of historical and

---

[2] In the context of the presidency, presidential rhetoric may affect public opinion by priming factors the public uses to evaluate the president (Druckman and Holmes 2004), though these relationships may be conditioned by the availability of partisan cues (Harrison 2015).

legalistic justifications, political context, and the specific policies enacted through unilateral action.

Our examination is at once methodological and substantive. Methodologically, we probe the differences that question wording makes for levels of public opinion in the context of political procedures and the presidency. Substantively, identifying how the public reacts across different political and institutional contexts allows us to understand the circumstances under which presidents have the greatest support to act unilaterally. Understanding how public opinion changes in response to frames or semantic differences in question wording can provide guidance to survey-based and experimental research that seeks to understand the relationship between political institutions and public opinion.

We used a series of survey experiments to study the effect of question wording on attitudes towards presidential power. In each experiment, we capture a baseline level of support for the president's use of unilateral powers using one of the same instruments we reported in the first part of this chapter. This is measured using respondents' agreement with the statement: "Presidents should be able to make new policies without having those policies voted on by Congress." We construct several variations to the baseline statement to reflect varying contexts. We then randomize respondents into either the baseline condition or one of the contextual variations, and measure the treatment effects of the variations relative to the baseline.

We conducted our survey experiments in July and August 2016 with a total of 6,933 respondents who were recruited to participate in five surveys through Amazon's Mechanical Turk (MTurk).[3] Each of the five surveys had approximately 1,400 respondents. In contrast with the TAPS survey data presented earlier in this chapter, respondents recruited via MTurk are not representative of the national population. Consistent with other research, our MTurk respondents were disproportionately white (78 percent of respondents), male (52 percent of respondents), young (42 percent of respondents were between 18 and 29 years old), and well educated (56 percent of respondents had at least a bachelor's degree) (Paolacci and Chandler 2014).[4] Treatment effects estimated from

---

[3] We conducted our experiments during a presidential election year, which may represent a heightened level of public attention towards presidential powers. As this factor was present for respondents in all of our treatment groups, it does not risk confounding our results.

[4] See Table A.5 in the Appendix to Chapter 3 for our sample's demographic and political characteristics.

convenience samples of survey respondents, including those recruited from MTurk, are very similar to those obtained from experiments conducted using nationally representative samples (Berinsky, Huber, and Lenz 2012; Coppock 2019; Levay, Freese, and Druckman 2016). We test our hypotheses by comparing the treatment effects of variations in question wording with respect to the baseline question stem.

Our survey experiments evaluated how three sets of question wording variations affected respondents' attitudes towards unilateral power. The following outlines the theoretical motivation for each and describe the items we used to evaluate them.

Presidential identity: How do attitudes towards unilateral power depend on which president exercises it? If individuals evaluate the use of unilateral powers differently depending on who occupies the White House, this would suggest that attitudes towards unilateral action are a product of an individual's political beliefs rather than their principled beliefs about American governance. On the other hand, if attitudes towards unilateral action exhibit little movement depending on who the president is, this provides evidence of the consistency of individual views towards unilateral power. Reflecting the survey's timing during the 2016 presidential election campaign, we asked the following three variants in addition to the baseline question:

- *Future Trump president:* If Donald Trump becomes president, he should be able to make new policies without having those policies voted on by Congress.
- *Future Clinton president:* If Hillary Clinton becomes president, she should be able to make new policies without having those policies voted on by Congress.
- *Future president (generic):* Future presidents should be able to make new policies without having those policies voted on by Congress.

While respondents may have had varying assessments of who was likely to succeed Obama, these question wordings were intended to remove the focus from the current president. Respondents were randomly assigned to answer one of the three "future" questions or the baseline question. If attitudes towards the identity of the president supersede attitudes towards unilateral power, we would expect to see significant differences across conditions that reflect partisanship or support of the respective candidates.

Unilateral tools: Are public attitudes towards unilateral power sensitive to the means through which presidents exercise it? Presidents have many unilateral tools at their disposal, and political discussion occasionally references the specific means through which presidents exercise unilateral power. For example, a 2014 *USA Today* article highlights how many of President Obama's unilateral policies have been implemented through memoranda rather than the more historically common executive orders (Korte 2014). We study whether the public differentiates between these tools when evaluating their support for their use, or instead treats variants of unilateral actions as one and the same, drawing little distinction between the different tools the president can wield. To the degree the public does not fully distinguish between the tools presidents employ, evaluations of unilateral action may be responsive to the practical consequences of the president's action. For instance, respondents may react differently when presidents act unilaterally to either direct military affairs as commander in chief or instruct cabinet secretaries to take a particular action. If support for presidential power depends on the type and nature of the action the president takes, attitudes and preferences over unilateral action may be relatively malleable.

To evaluate these possibilities, respondents were randomly assigned to a condition that either included the baseline question or that described various forms of unilateral action, including executive agreements, executive orders, national security directives, proclamations, and memoranda, and which addressed the president's authority to use administrative power to control the operations of the executive branch. These seven variants include:

- *Direct cabinet:* Presidents should be able to direct cabinet secretaries to make new policies without having those policies voted on by Congress.
- *Direct military:* Presidents should be able to initiate military operations without having those operations voted on by Congress.
- *Executive order:* Presidents should be able to issue executive orders to make new policies without having those policies voted on by Congress.
- *Executive agreement:* Presidents should be able to issue executive agreements to make new policies without having those policies voted on by Congress.
- *Proclamation:* Presidents should be able to issue proclamations to make new policies without having those policies voted on by Congress.
- *Memorandum:* Presidents should be able to issue memoranda to make new policies without having those policies voted on by Congress.

- *National Security Directive:* Presidents should be able to issue national security directives to make new policies without having those policies voted on by Congress.

To the extent respondents' support for unilateral action reflects their underlying procedural values, we do not expect that their attitudes will vary substantially across each of these question wordings. Instead, we expect that respondents evaluate unilateral powers based on their views about the president's role in a system of separated powers.

Precedents and justifications: Are attitudes towards unilateral power responsive to the invocation of historical precedent and presidential justifications for its use? Presidents have often justified the expansion of power by pointing to historical precedent for their actions and the constitutional authority that permits them. For example, President Obama cited unilateral actions taken by his predecessors in justifying his immigration reform efforts (Obama 2014a). Moreover, modern presidents may be able to curry popular favor by linking their unilateral efforts to those taken by well-regarded presidents, such as George Washington and Franklin D. Roosevelt. We also draw upon ideas of presidential representation to investigate whether respondents approve or criticize a president's use of unilateral powers.

We examine how various justifications for presidential action affect the public's attitudes towards unilateral powers. The public's relatively low levels of knowledge about and attentiveness to issues of unilateral power may render their attitudes on this issue susceptible to persuasion through a president's efforts to contextualize his actions. On the other hand, if the public has entrenched attitudes about executive power, we would expect to find little evidence that appeals to historical precedent and other justifications meaningfully affect public support for unilateral action.

We test the effectiveness of presidential justifications by drawing upon descriptions of historical circumstances in which presidents exercised unilateral powers. We also examine whether individuals are sensitive to political and constitutional justifications for unilateral action. The full set of question wordings includes:

- *All presidents:* Presidents since George Washington have used unilateral powers like executive orders to make new policies on their own.

- *FDR presidency:* While he was president, Franklin D. Roosevelt issued over 3,000 executive orders to make new policies on his own.
- *Japanese internment:* During World War II, President Roosevelt used his unilateral powers to incarcerate over 100,000 Japanese Americans in internment camps.
- *Courts upheld:* The Supreme Court has ruled in favor of the president's constitutional authority to use his unilateral powers to make new policies on his own.
- *Vague Constitution:* The Constitution is vague when it comes to defining the president's unilateral powers.
- *Legal scholars concerned:* Some legal scholars argue that presidents have taken unilateral powers too far.
- *National constituency:* Presidents should be able to make new policies unilaterally since the president is elected by the entire country.
- *Particularism:* A president should be able to make new policies unilaterally even though he can disproportionately distribute benefits to certain constituents.

To the extent the public bases their view of presidential power on how it is justified or framed, we expect that approval of unilateral action will differ among respondents in each of these conditions compared to the baseline question wording.

3.4.1 Results

Figure 3.4 shows the results. Each label along the *y*-axis corresponds to one of the question wordings we have discussed. The plotted points show the effect of the question wording on the proportion of respondents who expressed support for unilateral powers. Positive numbers along the *x*-axis indicate that the question wording increased support over the baseline question, whereas negative numbers indicate lower support for unilateral power relative to the baseline. The horizontal lines are the 95 percent confidence intervals of the differences in proportions and the dashed vertical line represents the null hypothesis of no difference in approval relative to the baseline question.

Two key findings stand out from Figure 3.4. First, most of the question wordings had substantively modest effects on respondents' approval of unilateral power. All but one of the question wording variations affected approval of unilateral power by fewer than 10 percentage points, and many of them affected approval by only a few percentage points. Overall,

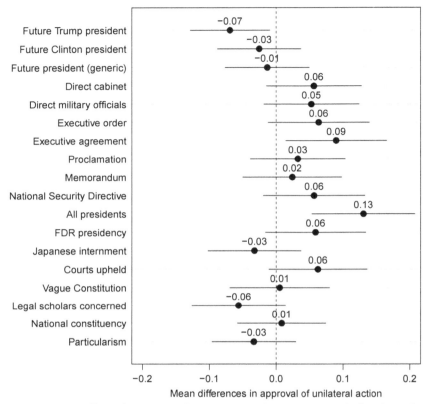

FIGURE 3.4 Effect of context and question wording on approval of unilateral
action

Note: The *y*-axis presents the difference in support for each experimental condition (presented on the *x*-axis) and the control condition, which is the approval for the baseline unilateral powers question. Horizontal bars represent 95 percent confidence intervals around the treatment effects.

the figure suggests that attitudes towards unilateral power are relatively stable across a vast set of contextual differences.

Second, only three of the eighteen question wording variants yielded statistically significant differences. Relative to the baseline question wording, approval of unilateral power was 7 percentage points lower among respondents who were asked to consider a future Trump presidency or who were asked to consider generic "future presidents." Respondents were also 9 percentage points more supportive of unilateral powers in the context of executive agreements than in the baseline question. We found the strongest results for the effect of the justification question wording that contextualized unilateral action by explaining that all presidents had exercised unilateral powers, which increased approval of unilateral action by 13 percentage points. However, we note that our statistical tests erred on the conservative side in that we did not account for the multiple comparisons we conducted; when doing so via the Bonferroni correction, in which we divide our threshold for statistical significance (0.05) by the number of comparisons (18), only one of the differences – corresponding to "All presidents" – is statistically significant.

On the whole, our additional analyses provide little evidence that attitudes towards presidential power are susceptible to framing, priming, or information effects. Instead, the vast majority of our question wording variations generated responses that were indistinguishable from our baseline question about presidential unilateral power. These findings provide evidence that Americans' self-reported evaluations of presidential power are "real attitudes" according to the criteria described by Chong and Druckman (2007) and other public-opinion scholars, and they provide confidence in using our survey instruments to study the nature and consequences of Americans' attitudes towards presidential power.

3.5 EVIDENCE FROM ALTERNATIVE QUESTION WORDING

Our survey instruments provide consistent evidence documenting Americans' skepticism towards presidential power. Our analyses in the previous sections suggest that these instruments capture genuine attitudes among the public about the institution of the presidency. Yet other research reports "little evidence of a public inherently skeptical of unilateral action" (Christenson and Kriner 2017a, 336). To what extent are our descriptive inferences a product of our chosen measurement strategy?

Fortunately, between 2016 and 2018, the Pew Research Center (2016, 2017b, 2018) conducted nationally representative surveys of Americans on their views of national political institutions. These surveys include an item that assesses opinions about the distribution of power across the branches of government, with a focus on whether the president's power should be expanded. The item asks respondents to choose which of the following statements best reflects their views:

- "Many of the country's problems could be dealt with more effectively if US presidents didn't have to worry so much about Congress or the courts," or
- "It would be too risky to give US presidents more power to deal directly with many of the country's problems."

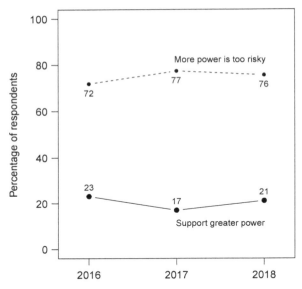

FIGURE 3.5 Attitudes towards presidential power
Note: Data are from surveys conducted by the Pew Research Center in 2016, 2017, and 2018. Points indicate the percentages of respondents who agreed that giving the president more power would be "too risky" (dashed line) or would enable the country's problems to be solved "more effectively" (solid line).

This instrument has the benefit of being distinct from our more specific questions on presidential power, yet it clearly taps generic assessments of the relationship between the presidency and other governing institutions. This item was fielded on surveys conducted in August 2016, February 2017, and March 2018.[5] These dates correspond well to the dates of the TAPS items described in Section 3.1.

The Pew data show patterns that are strongly consistent with what we found using our own survey instrument. Figure 3.5 shows the aggregate distribution of responses in each version of the survey. In each year of the survey, large majorities of respondents agreed that "it would be too risky to give US presidents more power." Only around 20 percent of respondents expressed the belief that empowering presidents relative to the other branches would be a more effective way of addressing the nation's problems. The distribution of responses for these items is quite similar to

[5] The 2016 survey was fielded between August 9 and 16, with a sample size of 2,010. The 2017 survey was fielded between February 7 and 12, with a sample size of 1,503. The 2018 survey was fielded between March 7 and 14, with a sample size of 1,466.

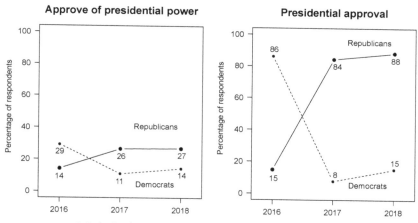

FIGURE 3.6 Attitudes towards presidential power (by political party)
Note: Data are from surveys conducted by the Pew Research Center in 2016, 2017, and 2018. The left plot shows the percentages of respondents who agreed that giving the president more power would enable the country's problems to be solved "more effectively." The right plot shows the percentages of respondents who approved of the current president's job performance. Republican respondents are plotted with the solid lines and Democratic respondents are plotted with the dashed lines.

response patterns for our unilateral policymaking question, in which only about a quarter of TAPS respondents believed that the president should be able to make new policies without involving Congress.

Figure 3.6 distinguishes the patterns by respondent partisanship. The left plot shows responses to the question described above and the right plot shows presidential approval ratings reported in the same survey. Both plots demonstrate that Americans' evaluations of both the presidency and the current president vary across partisan lines. In the left plot, for instance, Democrats endorsed a more powerful presidency in 2016 when Obama was president, while Republicans endorsed a more powerful presidency when Trump was president. And as the right plot shows, Democratic and Republican respondents expressed starkly different levels of approval of the current president based on whether they shared the president's partisanship. However, just as we showed in Figures 3.1 and 3.2, majorities of Americans from both political parties oppose a more expansive characterization of presidential power, and these attitudes are considerably less responsive than approval ratings to the changing partisanship of the president.

Figures 3.5 and 3.6 provide strong support for our characterization of attitudes towards presidential power. Supermajorities of the public oppose an expansive view of the president's role in the American political system. These patterns are consistent across a large number of variations in question wording and when using altogether different measurement strategies. These additional analyses provide confidence that our survey instrument both characterizes real attitudes towards presidential power and that the patterns reflected in the data are robust to the specific instrument used to measure these beliefs.

3.6 DISCUSSION

Our objective in this chapter is to sketch the contours of American public opinion on matters of presidential power. To do so, we introduce new measures that we fielded on nine waves of a nationally representative panel survey and validate our interpretation of them.

The evidence in this chapter depicts a public that is skeptical about, if not outright hostile towards, presidential power. Support for presidential power is persistently low across time. Strikingly, Americans exhibit high levels of agreement on this issue across partisan lines and especially compared with their approval of the current president. Again and again, across both panel and cross-sectional settings and when investigating several different survey instruments, we find that evaluations of presidential power do not simply reflect the public's aggregate partisan identification or approval of the sitting president. Evidence from survey experiments we conducted further shows that while public opinion on questions of presidential power meaningfully varies across political contexts, it is generally invulnerable to alternative phrasings and question wordings. Far from being ignorant or naive on matters of presidential power, we have presented systematic evidence to characterize the nature of Americans' "tyrannophobia" (Posner and Vermeule 2010).

The data presented in this chapter provide a foundation upon which we build much of our subsequent empirical analyses. We turn now to the task of characterizing individual-level attitudes towards presidential power before studying their consequences for citizens' evaluations of presidents and their policies.

4

Support for the Rule of Law and Attitudes towards Power

In Chapter 2, we present our theoretical argument that Americans have views of the presidency that are distinct from their approval of the individual president. We hypothesize that citizens express disapproval towards unilateral power by presidents because of deeply held core values towards the rule of law. In this chapter, we submit this argument to empirical testing. We study the structure of attitudes towards unilateral power, paying particular attention to the relationship between individuals' commitment to the rule of law and their support for unilateral action.

A series of analyses provides consistent support for our perspective. First, in an analysis of nearly twenty-seven thousand survey responses on attitudes towards presidential power from seventeen hundred individuals taken over nine waves from 2014 to 2018, we find that those with higher levels of support for the rule of law are more opposed to presidents acting alone – even after accounting for presidential approval. Second, we demonstrate the durability of this relationship over time and across various substantive contexts, including national security, congressional inaction, and presidential prioritization. Finally, we analyze how presidential approval, time, and political knowledge condition the relationship between support for both the rule of law and unilateral powers. In total, we find that core democratic values are the wellspring for antipathy towards executive power. Across numerous contexts, citizens draw from these considerations consistently to resist expansive presidential powers even when they approve of the individual officeholder.

4.1 LAWLESS PRESIDENTS

When presidents exercise unilateral power, they are frequently denounced by critics as tyrants or kings. The very term "imperial presidency" invokes the president as emperor. Because presidents issue unilateral directives without the explicit consent of the other branches, citizens may view them as actions that skirt the constitutional process.

Americans are acutely sensitive to accusations that their executive is acting as a monarch or tyrant. When a president is "charg[ed] with kingship," it "touch[es] core American anxieties" (Meacham 2008, 288). During debates over ratifying the Constitution, Patrick Henry warned in 1788 of "a great and mighty President, with very extensive powers – the powers of a King" that would follow from the Constitution, which Henry argued "squints towards monarchy" (quoted in Wirt 1817, 280).

Complaints relating to presidents' exercise of power are typically accompanied by claims that the president is violating the rule of law and disrespecting the separation of powers established by the US Constitution. Critics attacked President Andrew Jackson, who transformed the use of the presidential veto, for violating the constitutional authority of the legislative branch. When Jackson vetoed funding for the Maysville Road Project, his rival Henry Clay complained that "We shall be contending against a principle which wears a monarchical aspect" (quoted in Meacham 2008, 141). During the 1832 election, the anti-Jacksonians lambasted his Bank veto with one headline reading, "THE KING UPON THE THRONE: The People in the Dust!!!"(Meacham 2008, 219). According to his critics, by exercising the veto, Jackson had made "a mockery of the premier operating principal of the Jeffersonian regime – executive deference to the legislature" (Skowronek 1993, 172).

Jackson's use of the veto – a constitutionally granted power – is a hallmark of his historical legacy. Jackson's order in 1833 to remove deposits from the Bank of the United States further fueled charges of tyranny. These charges were enshrined in the political cartoon "King Andrew the First," which depicted Jackson as a monarch in full regalia holding a scepter in one hand and a presidential veto in the other as he stepped on a torn-up Constitution. Often, a list of charges would accompany the cartoon, including that Jackson "placed himself above laws."

During his presidency, critics accused Barack Obama of disrespecting and violating the US Constitution through his use of unilateral powers. One critic developed a "top ten list" of ways in which Obama had violated the Constitution and claimed that the Obama administration was "the most lawless in U.S. history" (Shapiro 2017). The Editorial Board of the *Wall Street Journal* noted a recess appointment to the National Labor Relations Board as evidence that Obama's was the "most lawless Administration since Richard Nixon's" (Editorial Board 2015). Another commentator compared Obama's Deferred Action for Childhood Arrivals (DACA) executive action to Watergate and accused Obama of "constitutional bankruptcy" for showing such "indifference to the rule of law" (Rubin 2012).

Jackson and Obama are not unique among presidents for being accused of the dictatorial use of unilateral powers. Even Abraham Lincoln and Franklin D. Roosevelt, who are routinely lauded as among the greatest in American history, were criticized for abusing their authority. Rossiter (2005 [1948], 224, 226) characterized Abraham Lincoln's presidency as a "dictatorship" whose "amazing disregard for the words of the Constitution was considered by nobody as legal." Lincoln's embrace of presidential power led to accusations of "executive tyranny" for acts from the Emancipation Proclamation to the suspension of *habeas corpus* (Donald 2011). Copperhead Democrats further denounced Abraham Lincoln as "the usurper, traitor, and tyrant" (quoted in Weber 2006, 167) and his assassin exclaimed "sic semper tyrannis!" upon shooting Lincoln in the back of the head. During Franklin Roosevelt's first reelection campaign, the American Liberty League characterized the 1936 election as a referendum on whether "we are to continue to enjoy a government of laws and not of men, or shall have foisted upon us an Americanized copy of Old World dictatorship" (quoted in Goldstein 2014, 296), with the latter intended as a warning for what lay ahead with a second Roosevelt term. Today, accusations that presidents act as though they are kings are commonplace (Litman 2018; The Editorial Board 2018).

Pundits, commentators, and historians are not the only groups to levy charges of tyranny against the president. In summer 2014, Speaker of the House of Representatives John Boehner announced he would seek action to bring a lawsuit against President Obama. Boehner charged that President Obama had overstepped his authority by delaying the implementation of a provision of the Affordable Care Act without a vote of Congress. Boehner justified the suit on account that,

The President has circumvented the American people and their elected representatives through executive action, changing and creating his own laws, and excusing himself from enforcing statutes he is sworn to uphold – at times even boasting about his willingness to do it, as if daring the American people to stop him. (Boehner 2014)

In other words, Boehner was suing the president over Obama's perceived violations of the rule of law. In explaining his actions, he references the American people and suggests that they may be activated to stop Obama's executive actions.

From administration to administration, critics of presidents invoke similar complaints about unilateral action. A president wielding unilateral power is a tyrant who mocks the democratic delineations of power outlined by the US Constitution. By disregarding these proper bounds of authority, critics argue, the emperor-president gleefully shreds the US Constitution as the Founders turn in their graves. The oft-invoked victims of and plaintiffs in these usurpations are the American people.

These attacks implicitly assume that citizens care about how presidents wield their power. If these critiques are to damage the president's reputation, citizens must have values relating to how presidents exercise executive power. These values, we argue in Chapter 2, reflect deference and respect for the constitutional political system borne from an indictment of kingly powers.

Values concerning how presidents exercise power do not reflect legalistic applications of constitutional clauses; instead, they reflect beliefs about the inviolability of constitutional principles that are ingrained through grade-school civics education and political socialization. Our argument draws on a conception that posits that "the most important manifestation of the rule of law is its representation in a nation's culture – the beliefs, expectations, values, and attitudes held by the populace of a country" (Gibson 2007, 598). In Chapter 3, we show that support for unilateral powers was low and substantially distinct from presidential approval or partisanship. In this chapter, we explore the relationship between core democratic values and support for unilateral powers while accounting for presidential approval and other individual-level characteristics.

4.2 MEASURING SUPPORT FOR RULE OF LAW

We evaluate our hypothesis regarding attitudes about the rule of law and support for presidential power using our data from TAPS described in Chapter 3. We measure support for the rule of law with a five-item battery that is commonly found in the literature and presented in Table 4.1. Respondents were asked whether they strongly agreed, agreed, were uncertain, disagreed, or strongly disagreed with each statement in Table 4.1. We draw on five waves in which the rule of law questions were asked: March 2013, May 2014, May 2015, October 2015, and May 2016.

Scaling these variables generates a measure of belief in the rule of law ranging from one to five with low values indicating weak support for

TABLE 4.1 *Question wording for support for rule of law survey instruments*

It is not necessary to obey a law you consider unjust.

Sometimes it might be better to ignore the law and solve problems immediately rather than wait for a legal solution.

The government should have some ability to bend the law in order to solve pressing social and political problems.

It is not necessary to obey the laws of a government that I did not vote for.

When it comes right down to it, law is not all that important; what's important is that our government solve society's problems and make us all better off.

Note: Each question is answered along a five-point scale ranging from agree strongly to disagree strongly.

this principle.[1] As previous studies have found, Americans have a high appreciation for the rule of law (Gibson 2007). Support is also highly stable over time. Studying attitudes towards the rule of law from 1995 to 2005, Gibson (2007, 604) reports that "Americans have remained relatively steadfast in their commitments to the rule of law" even as terrorism and American engagement in war reshaped many other political priorities.[2] According to our argument, we expect that individuals with stronger support for the rule of law will be less supportive of unilateral action.

Figure 4.1 presents the full distribution of our measure of support for the rule of law over the five waves we utilize in the analysis that follows. Support is consistent across waves. The mean ranges from 3.81 to 3.94, and the median ranges from 3.8 to 4.0. Across the five rule-of-law questions, respondents, on average, indicated they disagreed (i.e., scoring a four on the five-point scale) with the statements about the violability of law. As other studies have shown, there is relative stability in these views. If we consider within-respondent changes across waves, the median respondent-level standard deviation is 0.35. At the individual level, the

---

[1] The Cronbach's alpha for this scale was high in each wave, ranging between 0.75 and 0.77.
[2] For more on the measurement and use of this rule-of-law measure, see Gibson (2004), Gibson and Caldeira (2009), Gibson and Nelson (2015, 2018).

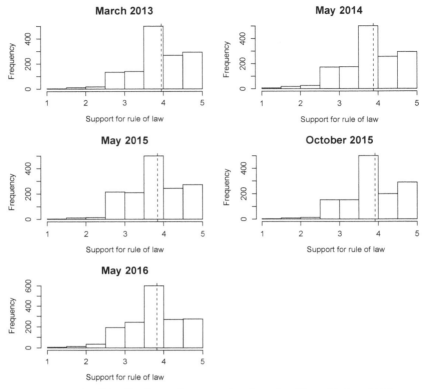

FIGURE 4.1 Distributions of support for the rule of law, 2013 to 2016

correlations in the rule-of-law measure are robust across time, ranging from 0.55 to 0.67 between each pair of waves.

Many studies show that this measure of the rule of law is associated with diffuse support for the Supreme Court (inter alia, Gibson and Nelson 2015). From other questions within TAPS, we see evidence that support for the rule of law is related to a deference for and faith in the US Constitution. For example, respondents who support rewriting the Constitution to give the president more power score significantly lower on the rule-of-law scale. Likewise, those who believe the Supreme Court is unlikely to make a mistake in deciding the constitutionality of a law show significantly higher support for the core value. Thus, building on the research of others, and as suggested by correlations within TAPS, we rely on support for the rule of law as an indicator of support for constitutional deference, which runs deep in American culture.

4.3 DETERMINANTS OF SUPPORT FOR UNILATERAL ACTION

We now turn to a multivariate analysis of attitudes towards unilateral power. Our focus is the extent to which support for the rule of law is associated with attitudes towards presidential power while accounting for an array of additional individual-level characteristics.

Our dependent variables are binary indicators of support for our three unilateral actions – policymaking, judicial appointments, and agency implementation – from nine waves of data from January 2014 to January 2018.[3] In the analysis that follows, we analyze nearly twenty-seven thousand responses from almost seventeen hundred respondents covering two presidential administrations and several congressional and presidential election years.

We also account for the respondent's approval of the individual president, which some argue is the primary and lone determinant of support for presidential powers. We measure presidential approval as a four-point scale that ranges from strongly disapprove to strongly approve. As presidential approval increases, we expect that individuals will be more likely to support unilateral action. We use this measure rather than partisanship for two reasons. First, recent scholarship shows that individuals' partisan identities can change across time and that these changes often reflect their evaluations of the current president (Montagnes, Peskowitz, and McCrain 2019; Tucker, Montgomery, and Smith 2018). In the short term, presidential approval is a more accurate assessment of respondents' attitudes towards the current occupant. Second, since we measure presidential approval as opposed to partisanship, the coefficient on this variable can be interpreted in a consistent way across the Obama and Trump administrations despite their different political parties. In Chapter 5, we further explore how the change in presidential administration clarifies our results. Also, in Table B.3, we conduct our analyses using copartisanship of the president and the respondent instead of presidential approval and find substantively similar results.

Since our dependent variables take on values of one and zero, we estimate linear probability models where the unit of analysis is a

---

[3] As we describe in Chapter 3, our first four waves provided respondents with a four-point response scale (strongly agree, agree, disagree, strongly disagree) while the last five waves added an option to also respond "neither agree nor disagree." For the first four waves, we collapse our measures of support into a binary indicator of support. For the final five waves, we code as missing those who answer neither agree nor disagree. In the Appendix to Chapter 4, we include alternative specifications with models and coding.

respondent in one of our nine waves of TAPS from January 2014 through January 2018. To account for individual-level drivers of attitudes, we include measures of age, income, and education and indicators for whether the respondent is male, Black, or Hispanic. We also include fixed effects for each wave of the survey and cluster standard errors for each respondent. In Appendix B, we report results from logistic models as a robustness check.

4.3.1 Results

Table 4.2 presents models of support for unilateral policymaking, unilateral judicial appointments, and unilateral agency implementation. We find consistent results across each measure of attitudes towards presidential power. The coefficients for presidential approval are positive and statistically significant in each model. This finding provides strong evidence that presidential approval is associated with attitudes towards unilateral powers. But, while presidential approval is an essential determinant of attitudes towards unilateral power, it is not the lone determinant.

Table 4.2 shows that core beliefs towards the rule of law also structure views of executive action. The coefficients for the rule of law are negative and statistically significant for each dependent variable, indicating that individuals with strong commitments to the rule of law were less supportive of unilateral powers. These findings provide robust support for our hypothesis.

Since the results are from a linear probability model, the coefficients are directly interpretable as the expected change in the probability of support for a unilateral action given a one-unit increase in the independent variable. For example, a one-unit increase in support for the rule of law, which ranges from one to five, yields a 0.07 decline in supporting unilateral policymaking. For judicial appointments, that relationship is 0.04 and for agency implementation it is 0.06. Across the three measures of support for unilateral power, support for the rule of law is associated with a decline in endorsing presidential fiats.

We can also consider the relationship between moving from the lowest to the highest levels of support for rule of law. Since the range of the measure is from one to five, moving from the lowest to the highest levels of support represents a four-point increase. In the context of support for unilateral policymaking, this maximum increase in support for the rule of law is associated with a decline in the probability of supporting unilateral powers of 0.29 ($-0.073 \times 4 = -0.292$). For unilateral

TABLE 4.2 *Model of support for unilateral powers*

	Policymaking	Judicial appointments	Agency implementation
Presidential approval	0.111*	0.111*	0.170*
	(0.005)	(0.005)	(0.005)
Support for rule of law	−0.073*	−0.039*	−0.061*
	(0.009)	(0.008)	(0.011)
Male	0.026*	−0.013	0.060*
	(0.012)	(0.012)	(0.016)
Income	−0.000	−0.005*	0.004
	(0.002)	(0.002)	(0.002)
Black	0.087*	0.122*	0.041
	(0.028)	(0.030)	(0.025)
Hispanic	0.036	0.091*	−0.051
	(0.025)	(0.027)	(0.027)
Education	0.010*	−0.006	0.032*
	(0.005)	(0.004)	(0.006)
Age	0.000	−0.000	−0.001
	(0.000)	(0.000)	(0.001)
Intercept	0.160*	0.253*	0.250*
	(0.047)	(0.043)	(0.057)
Survey wave fixed effects	✓	✓	✓
Num. obs.	9,126	9,224	8,343

*$p < 0.05$

Note: Linear probability model with robust standard errors clustered on respondent.

judicial appointments, support declines by 0.16 and for unilateral agency implementation the decline is 0.24. Across the board, support for the rule of law is associated with statistically significant and substantively important declines in support for unilateral powers.

Table 4.2 also shows that presidential approval is a significant predictor of unilateral powers. Across the three models, presidential approval is associated with support for unilateral powers. For policymaking and judicial appointments, a one-unit increase in presidential approval (measured along a four-point scale) is associated with an increase in the probability of support by 0.11 points. For agency implementation, that associated increase in support is 0.17. Moving from strongly disapproving to strongly approving of the presidential office holder bolsters the probability of support for unilateral action by between 0.33 and 0.51.

4.4 RULE OF LAW AND POLITICAL CONTEXT

We now turn to examine whether the relationship between the rule of law and evaluations of presidential power diminish across various contexts. The public may have principled reasons for desiring unilateral actions from presidents. As we describe in Chapter 3, presidents turn to unilateral action in different contexts. They may evoke their strong personal feelings, blame congressional inaction, or invoke a national security imperative as the premise for their unilateral action. In the extreme, we might imagine that the relationship between support for the rule of law and unilateral policymaking approaches zero when national security is at stake. Such a finding would be akin to the rhetoric that often links presidents' use of power to matters of national security, when the rule of law is set aside in favor of empowering the president.

As we describe in Chapter 3, we embedded a survey experiment in a survey administered in September 2014 by Survey Sampling International (SSI). Each respondent was assigned to either the control group (who received the standard unilateral policymaking questions in Table 3.1) or one of three treatment groups. The treatments asked the respondents to consider unilateral policymaking in light of "when a president feels strongly about an issue," "when Congress will not act," or "in matters of national security."

To account for the differences in support for unilateral action that varies across conditions – described in Chapter 3 – we included indicators for each of the three treatment groups. We examine how support for the rule of law operates across contexts by estimating the relationship between it and unilateral policymaking for each of our treatments. To do so, we interact support for the rule of law with indicators for each of the treatment conditions. As in our previous models, we use a linear probability model and control for a host of individual-level characteristics.

To make the constituent terms of the interactions more easily understandable, we standardized the rule-of-law measure so that it has a mean of zero and a standard deviation of one. The results are shown in Table 4.3. Consistent with the earlier models, we find that presidential approval and belief in the rule of law are significantly related to support for unilateral power. Consistent with the aggregate analyses we report in Chapter 3, respondents granted stronger support for unilateral power in the context of congressional inaction and matters of national security. When presidents justify their unilateral actions on the basis of "feeling

TABLE 4.3 *Model of support for unilateral actions across context: Evidence from a survey experiment*

Constant	−0.047
	(0.050)
President feels strongly	−0.024
	(0.026)
Congress won't act	0.158*
	(0.026)
National security at issue	0.166*
	(0.026)
Support for rule of law	−0.112*
	(0.018)
Presidential approval	0.178*
	(0.009)
Hispanic	0.049
	(0.039)
Black	0.126*
	(0.039)
Age	−0.000
	(0.001)
Income	0.005
	(0.006)
Education	−0.003
	(0.007)
President feels strongly × Support for rule of law	−0.036
	(0.026)
Congress won't act × Support for rule of law	0.017
	(0.025)
National security at issue × Support for rule of law	0.014
	(0.025)
Num. obs.	2,011

$^*p < 0.05$
Note: Linear probability model.

strongly" about an issue, the public is unmoved when compared to the control condition.

More importantly, the base term for beliefs in the rule of law is negative and statistically significant. As we found in our analysis of TAPS data, this coefficient indicates that individuals with stronger beliefs in the rule of law are more likely to oppose unilateral policymaking. The interaction between support for rule of law and each of the treatment conditions is not statistically distinguishable from zero. This suggests that the rule of law does not operate differently as a constraint on support for unilateral power in contexts of presidents feeling strongly about a matter, legislative gridlock, or national security than when these details are omitted.

Attitudes towards unilateral action are neither ephemeral nor the sole result of issue framing. In fact, our evidence points sharply and consistently in a different direction. Across nine survey waves covering four years and two presidencies and in a survey experiment that invokes a range of political contexts, we find that beliefs in the rule of law consistently constrain public support for unilateral action. Moreover, beliefs in the rule of law remain a strong predictor of support for presidential power across several contextual conditions. Consistent with our argument, these results provide further evidence of the centrality of Americans' core democratic values in shaping their beliefs about the proper distribution of power across the political system.

4.5 THE ROBUSTNESS OF CORE VALUES ON VIEWS OF EXECUTIVE POWER

In the previous section, we show that core values towards the rule of law are strongly associated with views of unilateral power while controlling for a host of other variables, including presidential approval. In this section, we examine the durability of this relationship by examining potential moderators. We investigate whether other political contexts subsume the relationship between the rule of law and attitudes towards presidential power. We consider the extent to which this relationship is driven by particular types of individuals or specific moments in our survey, or whether it vanishes against the backdrop of additional political contexts.

4.5.1 Presidential Approval

First, we examine how the relationship varies by presidential approval. This analysis allows us to consider whether core democratic values are associated with attitudes towards presidential power among both presidential supporters and opponents. If the relationship is only present among opponents of the president, this would suggest that Americans set aside their beliefs in core democratic values when they are politically aligned with the current president. It also suggests a potential floor on the degree to which Americans' views on democratic values may operate to

TABLE 4.4 *Model of support for unilateral powers among presidential approvers*

	Policymaking	Judicial appointments	Agency implementation
Support for rule of law	−0.114*	−0.070*	−0.050*
	(0.016)	(0.014)	(0.013)
Male	0.028	−0.049*	0.021
	(0.024)	(0.022)	(0.020)
Income	0.000	−0.007*	0.004
	(0.004)	(0.003)	(0.003)
Black	0.130*	0.155*	0.100*
	(0.037)	(0.036)	(0.025)
Hispanic	0.027	0.111*	−0.024
	(0.038)	(0.041)	(0.035)
Education	0.005	−0.011	0.022*
	(0.009)	(0.008)	(0.007)
Age	0.003*	0.000	0.001
	(0.001)	(0.001)	(0.001)
Intercept	0.588*	0.788*	0.774*
	(0.080)	(0.072)	(0.062)
Survey wave fixed effects	✓	✓	✓
Num. obs.	3,824	3,968	3,668

$^*p < 0.05$

Note: Linear probability model with robust standard errors clustered on respondent.

constrain the president. If the president's supporters prioritize their political alignment with the president over their belief in the rule of law, then this core value matters little in turning erstwhile supporters against the president. If, on the other hand, supporters also bring democratic attitudes to questions of presidential power, public opinion may exert a vital influence on presidents' calculations about the use of power. Tables 4.4 and 4.5 present the same model as Table 4.2 but estimate the relationship separately for presidential approvers and presidential disapprovers. This allows us to compare the relative influence of support for rule of law across each group. Across all models, support for the rule of law is negative and statistically significant. Among both supporters and opponents of the president in office, high support for the rule of law is associated with lower levels of support for unilateral presidential power. For unilateral policymaking and judicial appointments, the coefficients are larger for approvers in Table 4.4.

TABLE 4.5 *Model of support for unilateral powers among presidential disapprovers*

	Policymaking	Judicial appointments	Agency implementation
Support for rule of law	−0.043*	−0.021*	−0.070*
	(0.008)	(0.009)	(0.015)
Male	0.021*	0.005	0.092*
	(0.010)	(0.012)	(0.022)
Income	−0.001	−0.005*	0.002
	(0.001)	(0.002)	(0.003)
Black	0.038	0.105*	−0.036
	(0.029)	(0.050)	(0.053)
Hispanic	0.039	0.074*	−0.076*
	(0.023)	(0.029)	(0.034)
Education	0.013*	−0.002	0.035*
	(0.004)	(0.004)	(0.007)
Age	−0.001*	−0.000	−0.002*
	(0.000)	(0.000)	(0.001)
Intercept	0.259*	0.287*	0.518*
	(0.044)	(0.044)	(0.077)
Survey wave fixed effects	✓	✓	✓
Num. obs.	5,302	5,256	4,675

*$p < 0.05$
Note: Linear probability model with robust standard errors clustered on respondent.

Since these models are again linear probability models, the coefficients are directly interpretable. For example, the coefficient for support for rule of law in column 1 of Table 4.4 indicates that a one-unit increase in support for the rule of law decreased the probability of supporting unilateral policymaking by 0.11. In Table 4.4 we see that a one-unit increase in support for the rule of law decreases support for unilateral actions among presidential approvers by between 0.05 and 0.11. In Table 4.5, the relationship ranges from −0.07 to −0.02. Since support for rule of law ranges from one to five, each coefficient can be multiplied by four to estimate the size of the shift from being least supporting to most supporting of the rule of law. Across presidential approvers and disapprovers, the relationship persists. For unilateral policymaking and judicial appointments, the estimated relationship with support for rule of law for approvers is somewhat stronger than for disapprovers. For unilateral agency implementation, the opposite is true.

The influence of the rule of law is not reduced as presidential approval increases. Support for the rule of law operates consistently across levels of presidential approval. This finding is evidence of the pervasiveness of the effect of support for the rule of law across political stripes. The application of the rule of law is not applied selectively only among those who already disapprove of the president. Instead, the president's supporters and opponents alike bring core democratic principles to bear as they evaluate questions of presidential power.

4.5.2 Political Knowledge

Second, we examine the role of political knowledge as a moderator. As we describe in Chapter 3, we designed our survey instruments so that respondents could easily understand them. In Chapter 2, we argue that issues of unilateral power are different from other questions of political process because of their centrality in American culture and education. High-knowledge individuals may be more likely to view our questions about unilateral action as having implications for the current president and bring those and other considerations to bear at the expense of democratic values. Core values may be most important for explaining attitudes among respondents who are less aware of day-to-day political goings-on. Low political information individuals may be less likely to bring other considerations to bear beyond their base deference to the rule of the law. If the rule of law is associated with attitudes towards presidential power even among respondents who are less politically sophisticated, it is consistent with our argument that political socialization imbues Americans with a constitutional veneration that broadly structures views towards political power. Therefore, we evaluate whether political knowledge significantly moderates the relationship between beliefs in the rule of law and attitudes towards presidential power.

Table 4.6 presents the same linear probability model as Table 4.2 but includes a measure of political knowledge and an interaction between political knowledge and support for the rule of law. We base our measure of political knowledge on a battery of questions asked in September 2015, which we include in the Appendix to Chapter 4. The resulting scale ranges from zero to one with a mean of 0.71 and a standard deviation of 0.23. We assign the measure from September 2015 to all observations of each respondent.

In each of the models, we find a positive and statistically significant interaction between support for the rule of law and political knowledge

TABLE 4.6 *Model of support for unilateral powers: Interaction between political knowledge and support for rule of law*

	Policymaking	Judicial appointments	Agency implementation
Presidential approval	0.117*	0.114*	0.173*
	(0.005)	(0.005)	(0.006)
Support for rule of law	−0.226*	−0.148*	−0.176*
	(0.029)	(0.027)	(0.034)
Political knowledge	−0.808*	−0.715*	−0.446*
	(0.155)	(0.144)	(0.181)
Knowledge × Rule of law	0.217*	0.157*	0.153*
	(0.038)	(0.035)	(0.047)
Male	0.021	−0.014	0.047*
	(0.014)	(0.014)	(0.018)
Income	−0.001	−0.004	0.003
	(0.002)	(0.002)	(0.003)
Black	0.075*	0.114*	0.051
	(0.030)	(0.034)	(0.027)
Hispanic	0.023	0.064*	−0.061*
	(0.028)	(0.030)	(0.029)
Education	0.010	−0.002	0.024*
	(0.005)	(0.005)	(0.007)
Age	0.000	−0.000	−0.001
	(0.000)	(0.000)	(0.001)
Intercept	0.730*	0.725*	0.626*
	(0.120)	(0.108)	(0.132)
Survey wave fixed effects	✓	✓	✓
Num. obs.	7,904	7,974	7,244

*$p < 0.05$

Note: Linear probability model with robust standard errors clustered on respondent.

for each of our three attitudes towards unilateral powers. Increasing levels of political knowledge, these findings show, weaken the relationship between core democratic principles and attitudes towards presidential power. Consider, for example, the results for unilateral policymaking in column one of Table 4.6. Since political knowledge ranges from zero to one, the constituent term for rule of law presents the relationship to unilateral policymaking when political knowledge is zero. The coefficient of −0.266 indicates that a one-unit increase in support for the rule of law among those with the lowest levels of political knowledge is associated with decreased probability of support for presidential power among respondents by nearly a quarter point. The coefficient on the interaction term, however, is 0.217, which indicates that the relationship between the rule of law and evaluations of presidential power approaches zero among respondents with the highest level of political knowledge. The results from the other two dependent variables exhibit similar relationships.

These results provide intriguing evidence that political knowledge moderates the relationship between core beliefs in the rule of law and attitudes towards presidential power. On the one hand, these results may be surprising. High-knowledge individuals are often presumed to be more politically sophisticated and to have greater facility with abstract political principles. But this is not what we find. Instead, the rule of law is most strongly associated with attitudes towards presidential power among respondents who have lower levels of political knowledge.

Our theoretical perspective helps make sense of this finding. Americans, we suggest, are politically socialized through their early educational experiences. These experiences often emphasize the nation's founding principles. For individuals who are relatively inattentive to politics, these principles are likely to be the dominant frames through which they view the political world. Higher-knowledge respondents, however, are likely to have other political commitments based on ideology, partisanship, and alignments with specific presidents. These political commitments may reduce the extent to which respondents apply core democratic principles in evaluating presidential action. To the extent that Americans' antipathy towards presidential power reflects their support for core democratic values, this relationship is driven substantially by individuals who have a more casual relationship with the political system.

Moreover, our findings suggest that political cues and elite discourse do not drive the aggregate relationship between the rule of law and attitudes towards presidential power. Critics of presidential power often base their criticism on principles such as the rule of law. If the views expressed by the respondents were reflections of elite discourse rather than deep-seated values towards the presidency, we would see support for the rule of law associated with views towards presidential power among more politically knowledgeable, aware, sophisticated, and interested respondents. If this were the case, we would not be able to distinguish individuals' beliefs from the content of elite messages to which these respondents may be more attuned. Instead, we find that rule of law exerts the most influential association among individuals who are mostly *not* attuned to elite daily discourse. These findings are consistent with our theoretical perspective that posits that attitudes towards presidential power originate with individuals. This bottom-up characterization weighs against alternative theoretical accounts that argue that constitutional considerations can be primed only through elite appeals.

4.5.3   Time

Third, we consider the role of time and political context. We estimate the dynamics between the rule of law and attitudes towards unilateral powers for each wave. This analysis allows us to assess whether a single wave or group of waves drives our results.

We test the durability of the relationship between support for the rule of law and attitudes towards unilateral action across time by estimating a cross-sectional model of support for each of our nine waves of surveys between January 2014 and January 2018. In addition to two presidential administrations, our waves come from election and nonelection years and a range of political contexts.

To examine how support for the rule of law varies over time, we estimate models for each wave, and we again include presidential approval and other individual-level covariates in the linear probability models. Figure 4.2 presents the estimated rule of law coefficients for unilateral policymaking (top), unilateral judicial appointments (middle), and agency implementation (bottom). Lines spanning the points indicate 95 percent confidence intervals based on standard errors. Each plotted coefficient represents the relationship between support for unilateral (1/14). Here, a one-unit increase in support for the rule of law is associated with a 0.30 decline in the probability of supporting unilateral policymaking.

Across waves and questions, we find a consistent relationship between support for the rule of law and attitudes towards presidential power. For unilateral policymaking, every coefficient we estimate is negative and statistically significant, meaning that strong supporters of the rule of law are consistently more negative towards unilateral actions than weak supporters of the rule of law. Coefficients range from -0.23 to -0.32, meaning that holding all other factors constant, a one-unit increase in support for the rule of law is associated with a decline in the probability of supporting unilateral policymaking by 0.32 to 0.23 across waves. There is no discernible trend in these estimated relationships. Given the confidence intervals, they are not statistically distinguishable from each other though they are all statistically distinguishable from zero. There is no evidence that a single wave is driving the results we observe in our analyses.

Policymaking

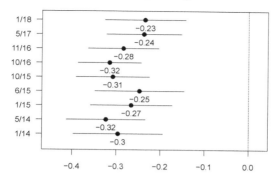

Change in probability of support

Judicial appointments

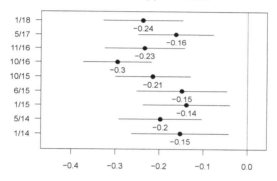

Change in probability of support

Agency implementation

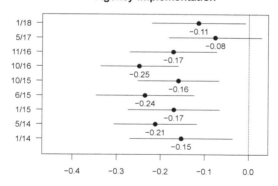

Change in probability of support

FIGURE 4.2 Support for rule of law and support for unilateral powers across nine survey waves, 2014 to 2018

Note: Each point represents the change in probability of supporting unilateral policymaking, judicial appointments, and agency implementation associated with a one-unit increase in support for the rule of law. Results are based on a linear probability model and are estimated for each survey wave from January 2014 to January 2018.

For judicial appointments and agency implementation, we see a similar dynamic. The estimated coefficients across each wave are negative, with only a single instance falling outside the conventional bounds of statistical significance. For judicial appointments, the coefficients range from -0.30 to -0.14, and for agency implementation, the range is -0.25 to -0.08. The overall picture is clear – the effects are consistently negative. Whether it be an election year (or even month) or the Trump or Obama administration, we find a consistent application of support for the rule of law and opposition to unilateral powers across our survey waves from 2014 to 2018.

4.6 DISCUSSION

In this chapter, we consider the relationship between support for the rule of law and attitudes towards unilateral action. We find support for the ideas we articulate in Chapter 2. Americans' support for the rule of law reflects a belief in the inviolability of the democratic processes that govern society. These core beliefs significantly constrain support for presidential power.

First, we analyze nearly 30,000 attitudes towards unilateral power from 1,700 individuals from nine survey waves between 2014 and 2018. We find a consistent and consequential negative relationship between support for the rule of law and support for unilateral acts, including policymaking, judicial appointments, and agency implementation. Second, we show that the relationship between support for the rule of law and unilateral action is consistent across each wave. Despite presidential and congressional elections, a transition from Obama to Trump, and a myriad of political contexts during the four years of our surveys, we find that support for the rule of law is a constant and consistent obstacle in supporting unilateral actions. Third, we evaluate this relationship over different substantive contexts in an additional survey experiment fielded in September 2014. Whether the president is invoking national security, congressional gridlock, or personal conviction, support for the rule of law exerts a consistently strong constraint on individuals' support for unilateral power.

5

Presidential Approval and Attitudes towards Power

More than thirty years ago, Theodore Lowi (1986) described the "plebiscitary presidency" as existing when a president has a free hand aside from being elected by the people or risking being impeached by Congress. This conception stems from assumptions that "the president should not and cannot be bound by normal legal restrictions" and that "deliberate barriers to presidential action must be considered tantamount to disloyalty" (Lowi 1986, 180–181).

Modern politics presents the plebiscitary presidency and mass partisan polarization as working in tandem. Partisanship powerfully shapes the attitudes and behaviors of the American public (Campbell et al. 1960; Gerber, Huber, and Washington 2010; Green, Palmquist, and Schickler 2002). Partisanship may even drive behaviors far afield from politics – like social behavior or decisions about leisure time (Gerber and Huber 2009; Iyengar, Sood, and Lelkes 2012). Our evidence from Chapter 4 shows that attitudes towards institutional power reflect, in part, the political support of the leader who is pursuing it.

Leaders can also drive attitudes and behaviors (Lenz 2012), and presidents can translate their public support into political outcomes (Canes-Wrone and Shotts 2004). The political relevance of President Donald Trump provides a clear example. During his time as a candidate and later as president, Trump reshaped Republican Party orthodoxies with relative ease. Attitudes towards subjects ranging from support for Vladimir Putin to Wikileaks seem to reverse on the basis of how parties perceive political events of the moment. The modern political arrangement – power-seeking presidents unencumbered by institutional constraints and claiming to be the one true representative of the country with a populace reflexively assuming any position their president favors – seems dangerous for democracy.

Building on this observation, commentators have sounded the alarm over democratic backsliding in the United States and elsewhere around the world. Appeals for power by popular leaders is a central threat to democratic stability and a cause of declining democracy (Levitsky and Ziblatt 2018). Political observers openly worry about mounting public support for authoritarianism (e.g., Edsall 2018), and political scientists have identified parallels between the United States and other countries that have experienced democratic declines (Levitsky and Ziblatt 2018; Mounk 2018). New academic initiatives are motivated by the belief that we are amidst a "time of potential danger to American democratic norms and institutions" ("Bright Line Watch" 2019) when "public support for democracy may be slipping" (Carey et al. 2019, 1). Though these perspectives are newly urgent in the United States, in recent years political developments have raised concerns about democratic backsliding around the globe, including in Eastern Europe (King 2017; Rohac 2018), Latin America (*Economist* 2018; Lynch 2018), central Asia (Schenkkan 2015), China and Southeast Asia (Heijmans 2017), and Africa (Temin 2017). These concerns are often rooted in the expansion of executive authority when elected leaders appeal to popular support to consolidate political power.

In Chapter 8, we return to the question of attitudes towards executive power and their consequences around the world. In this chapter, we examine, in three ways, the dynamics between support for the president and support for his institutional powers. As we show, an individual's political alignment with the president is associated with greater support for unilateral powers. But the effects are minimal. Instead, the dominant characteristics of attitudes towards presidential power are stability and opposition. Respondents infrequently change their minds about unilateral presidential power, and they are most often opposed to it.

First, we examine this question by leveraging within-respondent changes in attitudes towards unilateral power from our nine survey waves. This approach helps us identify the extent to which Obama and Trump can translate movements in public support into support for unilateral powers during their presidencies. As an individual comes to more strongly oppose or support a president, what happens to their views of the presidency?

Second, we use panel data to find what drives individual-level change in attitudes towards presidential power in times of transition. We focus on attitudes we gathered before the 2016 election in October 2016 and how they changed by May 2017 after Trump's inauguration and a few months into his presidency. This analysis provides a powerful lens through which to view the relationship between specific support and diffuse support. This analysis allows us to observe how attitudes towards presidential power change in the context of a change in the incumbent officeholder.

Finally, we consider how perceptions of a popular mandate affect individual-level assent for unilateral presidential power. In several survey experiments, we study whether the public grants greater support for unilateral powers when there is an impression that presidents are acting on a national mandate.

5.1 CHANGE AND CONTINUITY IN ATTITUDES TOWARDS UNILATERAL POWERS

Our analyses in Chapter 4 examine our data as nine waves of attitudes and mostly focused on cross-sectional, or between-respondent, differences. Since we surveyed the same individuals many times, we can also examine within-individual changes in support for unilateral powers. This approach allows us to examine the stability of individual attitudes towards presidential power over time, and also enables us to hold constant any individual-level attributes that may be associated with support for unilateral powers.

Figure 5.1 presents the average within-respondent change from one wave to the next in support for unilateral policymaking, judicial appointments, and agency implementation. For each response, we calculated the percentages of respondents who expressed more positive views towards unilateral power, more negative views towards unilateral power, or no attitudinal change. We omit the last wave of the Obama administration and the first wave of the Trump administration, which we address in detail later in this chapter. Between 76 and 83 percent of within-respondent attitudes remain constant across our measures of attitudes towards unilateral action. Among respondents who become either more positive or negative, moreover, there is a high degree of symmetry. For unilateral policymaking, for example, 8 percent of responses exhibited more negative attitudes, while 9 percent expressed more positive views. The pattern is similar for judicial appointments, with 82 percent of responses remaining constant and 9 percent each either more negative or more positive. For agency implementation, 76 percent of responses show no change,

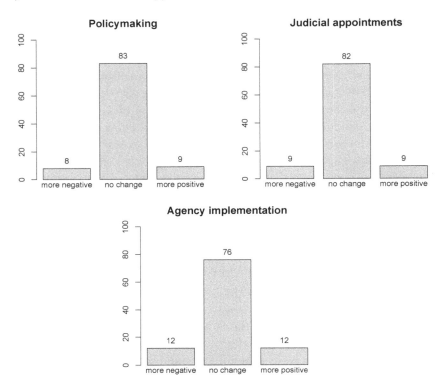

FIGURE 5.1 Within-respondent change in attitudes towards unilateral powers
Note: Changes are calculated based on respondent-level change in opinion from previous waves. We omit the Obama to Trump waves.

with 12 percent each either more negative or more positive. As we have previously documented, from January 2014 to January 2018, attitudes towards unilateral powers are very stable, which is a pattern that persists when looking at within-respondent change.

To what extent are the changes observed in Figure 5.1 a function of changing views of the president? To give us a sense of the magnitude in the changes in individual-level presidential approval, Figure 5.2 shows within-respondent change over monthly waves of TAPS from January 2014 to February 2018.[1] There is a high degree of stability in presidential approval. Of the nearly thirty thousand observations of presidential approval, 94 percent show no month-to-month change in respondents' approval of the president. The 6 percent that do change are equally

---

[1] Results are similar if we examine the difference between the last recorded response instead of monthly lags.

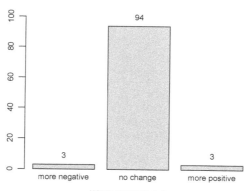

FIGURE 5.2 Within-respondent change in presidential approval
Note: From all (usually monthly) waves of TAPS starting in December 2013 through February 2018. We omit change from the last Obama to first Trump wave in January 2017.

divided among those who became more negative or more positive towards the president.

We use the data shown in Figure 5.1 to model the individual-level change in attitudes towards presidential power. The unit of analysis is a respondent's attitude towards unilateral power measured at each of the nine waves on which our unilateral powers questions appeared. We use a linear probability model and include fixed effects for individual respondents and survey waves. This specification accounts for time-invariant respondent characteristics that are associated with varying levels of support for the dependent variables.[2] We estimate separate models for each administration. The coefficients indicate the extent to which individual-level change in presidential approval drives opinions towards unilateral policymaking. The findings suggest that at the individual level, attitudes towards unilateral power are quite stable. Moreover, changes in support for each president do not translate into changes in views of unilateral power.

While we find no evidence that within-respondent changes in approval translate into changes in views of unilateral power, we approach these

---

[2] While we present a linear probability model in Table 5.1, the substantive results are the same as those from a logistic model, which we present in the Chapter Appendix in Table C.1.

TABLE 5.1 *Model of support for unilateral actions: Within-respondent change*

	Obama waves		
	Policymaking	Judicial appointments	Agency implementation
Presidential approval	−0.013	0.001	−0.004
	(0.012)	(0.014)	(0.015)
Intercept	0.214*	0.251*	0.547*
	(0.028)	(0.031)	(0.034)
Observations	8,267	8,288	7,506
Wave fixed effect	✓	✓	✓
Respondent fixed effects	✓	✓	✓
	Trump waves		
	Policymaking	Judicial appointments	Agency implementation
Presidential approval	−0.025	0.028	0.023
	(0.037)	(0.033)	(0.056)
Intercept	0.178*	0.096	0.390*
	(0.074)	(0.064)	(0.113)
Observations	2,779	2,892	2,568
Wave fixed effects	✓	✓	✓
Respondent fixed effects	✓	✓	✓

*$p < 0.05$
Note: Linear probability model with robust standard errors clustered on respondent.

findings with caution. As we have documented, there was only minimal variation either between- or within-respondents in presidential approval during the Obama and Trump waves. For the waves in which we measure attitudes towards unilateral powers, approval of Obama ranges from 42 to 52 percent. Presidential support by partisanship is even more stable. For Democrats, Obama's approval ranges from 74 to 82 percent. For Republicans, it ranges from 6 to 11 percent. During our two Trump waves, approval is nearly flat between the May 2017 and January 2018 waves. Aggregate approval increases from 35 to 36 percent. Approval among Democrats rises from 7 to 8 percent, and approval among Republicans increases from 72 to 74 percent. As Figure 5.2 shows, there is minimal within-respondent variation in presidential approval. This pattern is consistent with Gelman et al. (2016), which finds considerable stability in panel responses to presidential approval.

One issue that we have not addressed in this analysis is the seismic political shift from the Obama presidency to the Trump presidency. Because of the panel nature of our data, we can study within-respondent change in views of unilateral presidential power during this period where, as we describe, we see dramatic shifts in individual-level presidential approval.

5.2 LEARNING FROM THE TRUMP TRANSITION

In July 2012, private citizen Donald Trump was not pleased with how President Barack Obama was exercising unilateral power. Trump tweeted, "Why is @BarackObama constantly issuing executive orders that are major grabs of authority?" (Trump 2012). As a presidential candidate, Trump lambasted President Obama's "illegal and overreaching executive orders," but Trump himself "[began] his presidency with an unprecedented blizzard of executive action" (Korte 2017). Trump embraced unilateral action with aplomb by granting permits to private companies, establishing control of regulatory processes, and directing personnel decisions at the National Security Council meetings (Korte 2017). In the first weeks of the Trump presidency, the pace of executive action was so frenetic that the White House scheduled executive order signing ceremonies before they knew what the president would be signing and announced executive actions that would never come to be (Korte 2017). In this way, Trump's view on presidential power underwent a similar transformation as did the views of Barack Obama (Appelbaum and Shear 2016; Kessler 2014). As one retrospective on the Obama presidency noted, "Once a presidential candidate with deep misgivings about executive power, Mr. Obama will leave the White House as one of the most prolific authors of major regulations in presidential history" (Appelbaum and Shear 2016).

The transformation of views by Trump and Obama represents a common intuition about support for unilateral power. When individuals support the president (or, in Trump's and Obama's case, *become* the president), they favor presidents going it alone. When the president is of the other party, one will be critical of presidential power. This about-face represents a fundamental challenge in understanding attitudes towards institutions. If this is the broader state of public opinion on presidential power, then there are no values over how presidents exercise executive power. Any ideology over the use of power is a mirage for partisanship and presidential approval. As we describe in previous chapters, other studies find that, in different contexts, views of institutional power are indeed temporary and are mostly a function of who holds the office.

This hypocrisy is not limited to candidates for president. In the early 1970s, Arthur Schlesinger's *The Imperial Presidency* popularized the term for overreaching presidential authority. This phrase continues to scream from the headlines whenever a commentator asserts presidential overreach (e.g., Binder, Goldgeier, and Saunders 2020; Heer 2017; Kruse and Zelizer 2019). Though Schlesinger warned of a too-powerful presidency in the early 1970s as Nixon held office, this theme was absent in his previous endeavors in which he expressed admiration for Democratic presidents. One critic noted his change in tune and suggested Schlesinger had "furbishe[d] up an historical argument" in *The Imperial Presidency* to justify impeaching President Nixon, a Republican (Kirk 1974, 15). The critic pointed out that Schlesinger "showed little uneasiness" concerning presidential power as he advised President Kennedy or wrote his laudatory three-volume work, *The Age of Roosevelt* (Kirk 1974, 15). Another observer described Schlesinger's turnabout as "the most famous second thoughts expressed" by an erstwhile supporter of presidential power (Lowi 1986, 7). Schlesinger's critics assert he made an about-face in views of presidential power to accommodate his views of the president in power. Theodore Sorenson, an advisor to President Kennedy, noted the difficulty of viewing the office independent of the person. Writing in the aftermath of Watergate, he observed that, "Once when I thought of the Presidency I saw only Kennedy, and would have mistakenly enlarged the powers of the office accordingly. Today when some think of the Presidency they see only Nixon, and would mistakenly curb its powers accordingly" (Sorenson 1975, 23).

Examples of partisan hypocrisy – individuals changing their values to empower their partisan goals – seem rampant, but some stick to their principles. Consider conservative political commentator George Will, who has criticized the growth of presidential power under both Republican and Democratic chief executives. Whether the perceived expansions of presidential power for the line-item veto (Will 1997), changes in the legislative filibusters (Will 2005b), expansion of domestic surveillance (Will 2005a), or use of tariffs (Will 2018), Will has steadfastly attacked the growth of executive power and defended the prerogative of the legislative branch. Will himself seemed aware of the pervasiveness of partisan hypocrisy as, during the presidential campaign season, he ironically noted that, "If you liked President Obama's use of executive power, you're going to love President Trump" (Hains 2015). Will is, of course, taunting partisan hypocrites who were championing presidential power under Obama but would predictably bemoan it if Donald Trump were (as he would) to win the next election. While Schlesinger might be accused of being an about-facer in his views of presidential power, George Will has been a standpatter, who has expressed consistent views over decades.

We take advantage of two features of our research design that allow us to identify partisan hypocrites (i.e., about-facers) and ideologues (i.e., standpatters) in the electorate. The first feature is our repeated measures over time from TAPS respondents of their attitudes towards the president and presidency, which allows us to observe individual-level change in attitudes. These data are crucial for identifying the type of relationship we have described thus far (Lenz 2012). The second feature is that we study a period that witnesses a change in the presidency from Barack Obama to Donald Trump. If an individual uses the identity or partisanship of the president as a referent from which to express attitudes towards presidential power, we will see them change their minds with the inauguration of the Republican president. Our analysis is modeled after Key (1966, chapter 2), who identified "switchers" and "standpatters" in the electorate based on voting patterns across successive presidential election cycles. Rather than study vote choice, we examine change and continuity in public attitudes towards presidential power across successive presidential administrations.

5.2.1 Partisan and Ideological Views of Power

Imagine two worlds. The first world is one where the electorate is purely partisan. Like Arthur Schlesinger and his view of unilateral power, this electorate favors power if and only if it is exercised by someone they support to achieve goals they endorse. The other world is one where the electorate is purely ideological. This electorate, like George Will, has deep-seated views about the nature of the power of the president. The partisan electorate cares little for norms of forbearance or political culture that respects the rule of law. The ideological electorate ignores who holds the presidency because their attitudes towards the office are independent of the incumbent. The American electorate is neither one nor the other entirely, but identifying which conception most closely resembles the American public is one of the central questions this book seeks to answer.

Figure 5.3 depicts these two theoretical electorates in the context of changing presidencies. These Sankey diagrams show the flow of public

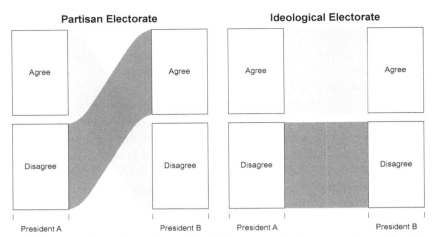

FIGURE 5.3 A hypothetical example of change in attitudes towards presidential power during political transitions

Note: The panel on the left depicts a partisan electorate in which citizens realign their views of presidential power when a new president comes to power. The panel on the right depicts an ideological electorate that holds durable views of unilateral powers, which remain the same under two different presidents.

opinion over two periods when leadership changes hands between two hypothetical presidents belonging to different political parties (President A to President B). The left panel represents a purely partisan electorate. They agree that presidents should have more power because they support President A, perhaps because they share President A's partisanship. There is an election and President B, from the other political party, comes to power. The public en masse switches their opinions on presidential power. When their preferred politician holds the reins of power, they will eagerly endorse executive power. When an out-partisan or an unfavored leader is president, they will oppose all varieties of presidential power.

The right panel of Figure 5.3 depicts an ideological electorate. While the partisan electorate adapts their views of executive power to who is in office, the ideological electorate remains steadfast. Despite a change in the party of the president, the ideological electorate, like George Will, maintains its view of presidential power. Just as Will critiqued the executive fiats of Presidents Bush through Obama, the ideological electorate remains eternally skeptical of presidential power regardless of who holds the reins of the executive branch.

This example also highlights the importance of panel data. In both examples, aggregate public opinion is identical: Half of the electorate supports executive power while the other half opposes it. In the case of the partisan electorate in the left panel, this stability belies substantial (indeed, total) individual-level change. In the case of the ideological electorate, aggregate stability mirrors individual-level stability.

We leverage the change in partisan control of the White House following a close election to study how Americans' political alignment with the president affects their attitudes towards the power its occupant should wield. We revisit the questions we fielded on TAPS throughout the Obama and Trump presidencies.

Using these data, we study several of the questions raised by our theoretical discussion. First, we investigate aggregate patterns of support for unilateral power. If the identity of the president affects Americans' views about the power of the presidency, then these patterns may vary across the two administrations that span the data. Alternatively, if Americans' attitudes about institutional arrangements persist across political regimes, we expect little change across time. Second, we investigate the predictors of unilateral power across the five waves of our data. To the degree that expressions of support for presidential power in surveys are non-attitudes, we expect that there will be no systematic relationship between the predictors of these beliefs across survey waves. But if underlying values and core principles structures these beliefs, we expect that they would consistently predict attitudes towards unilateral power. Third, we study individual-level stability in views towards presidential power and the predictors of attitude change. These data allow us to provide the most comprehensive study to date on individual-level changes and continuities in attitudes towards political institutions.

Figures 5.4 through 5.6 present changes in support for unilateral policymaking, judicial appointments, and agency implementation from October 2016 to May 2017. These Sankey diagrams depict the flow of respondents from each wave as a tributary. The dark gray represents those individuals who initially disapprove of the unilateral power in our first wave in October 2016. The bars, labeled "agree," "neither agree nor disagree [neither]," and "disagree," depict the proportions of respondents reporting each attitude in each wave.

Considering Figure 5.4, we see high levels of disapproval of unilateral policymaking from October 2016 to May 2017. Over half of all respondents – 53 percent – are standpatters who oppose unilateral policymaking both when Barack Obama is president as well as seven months and an inauguration later in May 2017 under President Donald Trump. While the data we present in Chapter 3 shows little aggregate change in support for unilateral power during this time period, the aggregate

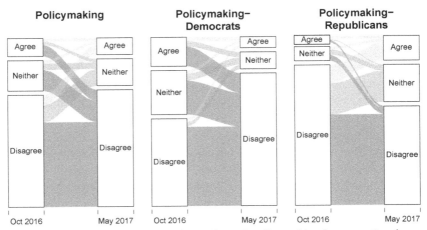

FIGURE 5.4 Change in support for unilateral policymaking between October 2016 and May 2017

data could have obscured individual-level change. At the individual level, Figure 5.4 makes clear that there was no mass reversal of public opinion on unilateral policymaking. Only about 13 percent of respondents are about-facers who reverse their support or opposition to unilateral policymaking between October and May during the transition from the Obama to the Trump presidency. We find 7 percent of respondents support unilateral powers in October and oppose them in May, while 6 percent oppose unilateral policymaking in October and support it in May. Among those who neither agree nor disagree with unilateral policymaking in October, most come to oppose it by May 2017.

When we look at the change in support within partisan groups, the story is consistent. Among Democrats, 50 percent of respondents are standpatters who oppose unilateral policymaking in both October and May. We also see that 21 percent of Democratic respondents move from being undecided to opposing unilateral policymaking upon the transition from Obama to Trump. Only 12 percent of Democrats are about-facers who support unilateral policymaking under Obama and switch to oppose it under Trump.

Among Republicans, 57 percent are standpatters who oppose unilateral policymaking in October and May. About the same share of our Republican respondents as our Democratic respondents are partisan about-facers. Just 11 percent oppose unilateral policymaking under Obama but come to support it under Trump. We see that about 19 percent of our sample move from disagreeing with unilateral policymaking

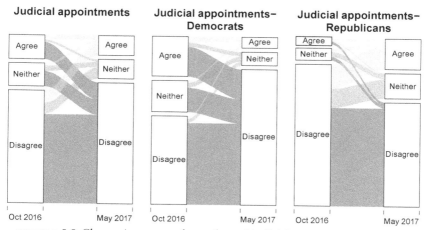

FIGURE 5.5 Change in support for unilateral judicial appointments between
October 2016 and May 2017

in October to becoming undecided in May 2017. Just as many Democrats
shift from undecided to opposition, a sizeable share of Republicans moves
from opposed to undecided in the same period.

We see a similar pattern with respect to unilateral judicial appointments. Figure 5.5 shows that a majority (55 percent) of respondents are
standpatters who oppose unilateral judicial appointments in both October and May. Some 19 percent of respondents are about-facers who
switch their views from support to opposition or opposition to support during the presidential transition. Majorities of Republicans and
Democrats – 51 and 61 percent, respectively – maintained their opposition to unilateral judicial appointments. Only 15 percent of Democrats
and 19 percent of Republicans switched their views to match their
co-partisanship with the president in office.

While the patterns of Figures 5.4 and 5.5 are largely consistent, there is
a different pattern with respect to agency implementation in Figure 5.6.
Most respondents (20 percent) agree with unilateral agency implementation in both October and May. Almost as many (18 percent) disagree
during both periods. Partisan about-facing is highest for agency implementation with 23 percent of Democrats and 22 percent of Republicans
realigning their views to match the partisanship of the president in office.

Table 5.2 summarizes the change in attitudes towards unilateral powers between October and May. The table reports the percentages of the
sample that were standpatters and opposed unilateral power in both periods. It also reports the percentages of the sample who were about-facers

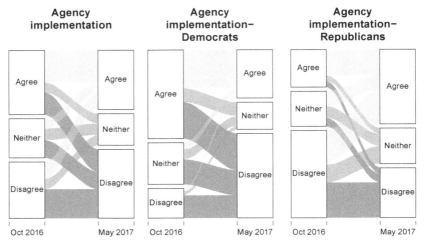

FIGURE 5.6 Change in support for unilateral agency implementation between
October 2016 and May 2017

and realigned their views of unilateral powers to match the change in the
partisanship of the presidency. For Democrats, this means they supported
the unilateral power in October under President Obama but opposed it
under President Trump. For Republicans, they opposed unilateral power
under Obama and supported it under Trump. This table tells much the
same story as Figures 5.4 to 5.6. For unilateral policymaking and judicial
appointments, at least 50 percent of the full sample, among both Republican and Democrats, were in opposition in both periods. Between 11 and
19 percent of partisans do an about-face.[3] Overall, Americans' attitudes
towards presidential power appear to be more like George Will's than
Arthur Schlesinger's.

5.2.2   Presidential Transition, Partisanship, and Evaluations
of Unilateral Power

These data suggest that most Americans hold relatively consistent and
stable views about presidential power. Yet Table 5.2 also shows that
not all Americans report the same evaluations of unilateral power across

---

[3] For unilateral policymaking, 13 percent of respondents were about-facers either shifting
from agreement to disagreement or disagreement to agreement. For unilateral judicial
appointments, 19 percent were about-facers, and for agency implementation, it is 25
percent.

TABLE 5.2 *Attitude change towards unilateral actions: Standpatters and about-facers, October 2016 and May 2017*

	Standpatters (Opposers)	About-facers (Partisan)
Policymaking		
All	53	
Democrats	50	12
Republicans	57	11
Judicial appointments		
All	55	
Democrats	51	19
Republicans	61	15
Agency implementation		
All	18	
Democrats	14	23
Republicans	22	22

Note: Entries show the percentage of respondents in each category based on survey responses in October 2016 and May 2017. We define standpatters as respondents who opposed powers in both October and May. Partisan about-facers are Republicans (Democrats) who oppose (support) power in October and support (oppose) it in May.

different presidential administrations. To what degree are public attitudes about presidential power dependent upon who holds office?

We study this question and leverage the fact that most of our survey respondents were asked their views on presidential power during both the Obama and the Trump presidencies. Using these data, we test whether respondents systematically changed their views about presidential power as party control of the White House changed from Democratic to Republican.[4] If, for example, Democratic identifiers are more likely to support presidential power when a Democrat occupies the White House, but are less supportive when a Republican moves in, and vice versa for Republican identifiers, we would expect to see these patterns reflected in the data.

---

[4] We use partisanship to study changes in attitudes towards presidential power for two main reasons. First, the funnel of causality developed by Campbell et al. (1960) posits that an individual's partisanship filters many of their downstream political evaluations, including evaluations of individual candidates and officeholders. Second, we follow previous work that has studied how changes in partisan control affect economic evaluations (e.g., Ang et al. 2022; Gerber and Huber 2010).

Our questions about presidential power were asked in October 2016, the month before the 2016 election; November 2016, immediately after the 2016 election outcome; and May 2017, several months into the Trump administration. Following research that studies how changes in partisan control of Congress and the presidency affect economic assessments (Ang et al. 2022; Gerber and Huber 2010), we examine how respondents' partisanship is associated with changing views of presidential power between the October 2016 wave and each of the two later waves. For each indicator of attitudes towards presidential power, we create a differenced measure that subtracts evaluations of presidential power (on a three-point scale) measured before the 2016 presidential election from evaluations reported in waves after the 2016 presidential election. For each dimension of presidential power, this approach creates a five-point measure of change. Positive numbers indicate more favorable evaluations in the postelection wave, negative numbers indicate less favorable evaluations in the postelection wave, and zero indicates no change.

We use these dependent variables to study the effect of partisanship on evaluations of presidential power. We measure partisanship with an instrument included in the May 2016 wave of TAPS. Because this variable is measured before the election outcome and subsequent change in presidential party, our measure of partisanship is not endogenous to the president currently in office. We use a five-point measure of partisan identification, where 2 = Strong Democrat, 1 = Weak or lean Democrat, 0 = Independent, −1 = Weak or lean Republican, and −2 = Strong Republican.

We use linear regression to model changes in evaluations of presidential power as a function of a five-point measure of respondent partisanship. We also estimate models that include beliefs in the rule of law and demographic controls, including age (in years), gender, racial/ethnic group membership, income, and education.[5] From these regressions, the coefficient for partisanship can be interpreted as the effect of learning that Republicans would control the presidency on respondents' evaluations of presidential power. If partisan alignment with the president causes more positive assessments of presidential power, we expect to find a negative coefficient for the partisanship variable. This would indicate that Republican identifiers were more supportive of presidential power and/or that Democratic identifiers were less supportive of presidential power after the election and presidency of Donald Trump compared with the attitudes they reported just weeks before the election.

---

[5] We used responses to the May 2016 TAPS wave to create the rule of law measure.

Table 5.3 shows the results. Panel A shows results for the unilateral policymaking measure, Panel B shows results for the judicial appointments measure, and Panel C shows results for the agency implementation measure. The labels at the top of the columns indicate when the postelection dependent variable was measured. The "November 2016" columns show results when we compared attitudes from the November 2016 wave to attitudes for the same respondents in the October 2016 (preelection) wave. The "May 2017" columns show results when we compared attitudes from the May 2017 wave to the October 2016 wave. For each dependent variable and postelection survey wave, we report results from two model specifications. The first model for each dependent variable omits controls while the second includes them. We limit the models to the respondents who completed each of the three waves (October 2016, November 2016, and May 2017) included in the analysis.

Panel A provides some evidence that partisanship affected attitudes towards presidential power following the 2016 presidential election and the inauguration of Donald Trump. Columns (1) and (2) compare evaluations of presidential power in the November 2016 postelection survey to respondents' preelection evaluations of presidential power. The coefficients for partisanship are negatively signed and statistically distinguishable from zero. These results provide evidence that, to the degree that public attitudes about unilateral power changed following the election of Donald Trump, they changed in ways that reflected respondents' partisan orientations. Our models indicate that respondents who identified as more strongly Democratic had more negative evaluations of presidential power while more strongly Republican respondents had more positive evaluations of presidential power. Based on the November 2016 postelection wave, a four-point increase in partisanship – which corresponds to the difference between a strong Republican and strong Democrat – is predicted to decrease evaluations of presidential power by about 0.22 units (0.056 × 4) relative to respondents' preelection attitudes. This is a relatively small change considering that the dependent variable is measured on a five-point scale and amounts to about one-third of a standard deviation of its values.

Panels B and C provide similar results when evaluating changes in attitudes towards presidential power before and after the election of Donald Trump. The coefficients for partisanship in columns (1) and (2) are consistently negative and statistically significant, indicating that Democratic respondents expressed more negative views towards presidential power after the election of Trump while Republican respondents

TABLE 5.3 *Changes in evaluations of presidential power*

Panel A: Policymaking	November 2016		May 2017	
	(1)	(2)	(3)	(4)
Partisanship	−0.078*	−0.056*	−0.281*	−0.256*
(+=Democratic)	(0.016)	(0.017)	(0.019)	(0.020)
Rule of law		0.063		0.060
		(0.037)		(0.044)
Intercept	−0.075*	−0.360*	0.013	−0.316
	(0.024)	(0.179)	(0.028)	(0.213)
Demographic controls	No	Yes	No	Yes
Observations	841	841	841	841
Panel B: Judicial appointments	(1)	(2)	(3)	(4)
Partisanship	−0.137*	−0.112*	−0.298*	−0.274*
(+=Democratic)	(0.019)	(0.020)	(0.021)	(0.022)
Rule of law		0.099*		0.071
		(0.044)		(0.047)
Intercept	−0.016	−0.457*	−0.012	−0.223
	(0.028)	(0.213)	(0.030)	(0.230)
Demographic controls	No	Yes	No	Yes
Observations	841	841	841	841
Panel C: Agency implementation	(1)	(2)	(3)	(4)
Partisanship	−0.153*	−0.131*	−0.356*	−0.325*
(+=Democratic)	(0.021)	(0.022)	(0.024)	(0.025)
Rule of law		0.046		0.105
		(0.048)		(0.054)
Intercept	−0.021	−0.479*	−0.033	−0.716*
	(0.031)	(0.235)	(0.035)	(0.266)
Demographic controls	No	Yes	No	Yes
Observations	841	841	841	841

*$p < 0.05$

Note: Entries are linear regression coefficients with standard errors in parentheses. The dependent variable is the change in approval of presidential power between the preelection period and the month listed at the top of the columns. Controls include indicators for age, sex, race/ethnicity, income, and education.

reported more positive views. The magnitudes of the relationships are somewhat larger for Panels B and C relative to Panel A. A four-point increase in partisanship is predicted to decrease evaluations of unilateral judicial appointments by about 0.45 units (0.112 × 4) and agency implementation by about 0.52 units (0.131 × 4). Each of these differences corresponds to about one-half of a standard deviation in the values of the dependent variables.

As columns (3) and (4) show, however, partisanship is more strongly associated with changes in attitudes towards presidential power once Trump was in office. In each panel, the magnitudes of the coefficients for partisanship are larger in columns (3) and (4) than they are in (1) and (2). A four-unit increase in partisanship from strong Republican to strong Democrat is associated with about a one standard deviation decrease in evaluations of presidential power.

Together, Tables 5.2 and 5.3 provide a nuanced view of public attitudes about presidential power. Table 5.2 shows that many Americans register consistent attitudes about presidential power despite changes in political context and the individual who serves as president. Yet not everyone is consistent, as between 13 and 25 percent of respondents shifted their views towards presidential power between October 2016 and May 2017. Table 5.3 shows that these "about-faces" occurred in ways that reflected respondents' partisan alignment with the president. Republicans who changed their views about presidential power were more enthusiastic about it following the election of Donald Trump, while Democrats who changed their views about power were less enthusiastic upon the election of Trump. For this slice of the electorate, partisanship is an important factor in determining views about presidential power. But for most of the electorate, stability is the dominant feature of Americans' attitudes towards presidential power.

5.2.3 Modeling Stability

Our theoretical argument suggests that this stability is associated with Americans' beliefs in the rule of law; specifically, we would expect that individuals with more substantial commitments to the rule of law are more likely to express consistent opinions across time. Individuals with weaker commitments to the rule of law, in contrast, are more likely to substitute shorter-term political considerations when evaluating presidential power.

We examine this expectation and conduct multivariate analyses to understand the sources of stability among our respondents. Table 5.4 presents a model of standpatter attitudes towards presidential power. As in our previous discussion, we designate individuals who held negative

TABLE 5.4 *Model of standpat opposition to unilateral actions: Transition from Obama to Trump*

	Policymaking	Judicial appointments	Agency implementation
Support for rule of law (May 2016)	0.842* (0.122)	0.955* (0.136)	0.955* (0.169)
Approval (Nov 2016)	−0.160* (0.065)	−0.085 (0.074)	−0.036 (0.086)
Education	0.159* (0.054)	0.251* (0.059)	−0.074 (0.070)
Male	−0.098 (0.149)	0.196 (0.165)	0.015 (0.201)
Income	0.001 (0.022)	0.055* (0.025)	0.046 (0.029)
Black	−0.474 (0.305)	−0.357 (0.331)	−0.295 (0.467)
Hispanic	0.433 (0.275)	−0.447 (0.295)	0.423 (0.362)
Age	−0.002 (0.005)	0.017* (0.005)	0.015* (0.007)
Intercept	−3.040* (0.553)	−5.159* (0.642)	−5.475* (0.824)
Observations	887	840	589

$^*p < 0.05$
Note: Logistic regression model with robust standard errors.

views of each of our unilateral powers in both October 2016 *and* May 2017 as standpatters. Table 5.4 presents a logistic regression model of standpatters for each of our three unilateral powers. Across the board, standpatters have higher levels of support for the rule of law. The coefficient for presidential approval is negatively signed in all three regression models. This finding indicates that individuals who reported higher levels of approval for Obama were less likely to report consistent attitudes towards presidential power for both presidents, but it is statistically significant for only the model (in column 1) of attitudes towards unilateral policymaking. For unilateral policymaking and judicial appointments, higher levels of education are also associated with firm opposition to unilateral actions. Additionally, age is associated with being a standpatter for unilateral judicial appointments and unilateral agency implementation, with older individuals more likely to report consistent attitudes across the two presidential administrations.

Across a range of analyses, the evidence provides little support for the notion that Americans view presidential power simply through partisan lenses, as the left plot in Figure 5.3 shows. There is no mass about-face by either Obama-opposers or Obama-supporters in views about presidential power upon the inauguration of Donald Trump. In the context of within-respondent change, we find limited evidence that attitudes towards presidential power reflect Americans' political orientations vis-à-vis the president. Instead, the evidence more closely corresponds to the ideological electorate portrayed by the right plot of the figure. Americans' attitudes towards presidential power are mostly stable across time and resistant to change even as the occupant of the White House changes. While a familiar roster of political characteristics shapes Americans' evaluations of the current president, these same characteristics are less relevant for characterizing the public's attitudes towards the office of the presidency.

5.3 MAJORITARIAN SUPPORT AND PUBLIC SUPPORT FOR UNILATERAL POWERS

In this section, we consider the relationship between public support for the president and support for unilateral powers in a different context. We examine if Americans' attitudes towards presidential power depend upon whether the president seeks to advance the majority's public opinion. We posit that Americans' desire democratic responsiveness and grant support for institutional arrangements that translate public preferences into policy outcomes. We suggest that an individual's support for the exercise of presidential power depends on the popularity of the president's preferred outcome. When the president and Congress are on opposite sides of a given issue, therefore, as higher proportions of the public support a specific policy of the president, we expect them to likewise be more supportive of the president using power to secure a preferred outcome.

In the context of bargaining, presidents can leverage public support for their desired policy outcomes to achieve greater legislative success with Congress (Canes-Wrone 2006; Canes-Wrone, Herron, and Shotts 2001). Likewise, presidents frequently invoke the conception of mandates to assert popular support for their chosen political agendas (e.g.,

Azari 2014). Attitudes towards the use of presidential power may depend on whether the president pursues policies in service of public opinion. This idea is consistent with "public constitutional sentiment" (Posner and Vermeule 2010, 77–78), which reflects the principle by which the public grants support for the exercise of power by a particular branch of government. As in these cases, we expect that public support for presidential agenda items translates into greater acceptance of his use of authority to achieve them.

From the perspective of democratic theory, understanding the public's attitudes about the use of presidential authority informs whether institutional arrangements reflect public opinion. Answering this question also clarifies the criteria citizens use to evaluate executive overreach. If voters oppose presidents' exercise of power no matter the public support for the specific policy, then presidents run the risk of mobilizing public opinion against them whenever they exercise authority. But if the public is supportive of the exercise of presidential power when the policy sees broad public support, the potential for public backlash is likely significantly reduced if not eliminated. Beyond an individual's own opinion over an issue, we expect that citizens will consider aggregate public support in determining whether to endorse unilateral presidential action.

Individual-level attitudes towards the exercise of presidential power may be contingent upon the level of aggregate public support for the president's desired policy outcome. Mass support for the president's policies may be especially influential in shaping individual-level assessments of whether presidents should exercise unilateral powers. Majoritarian and super-majoritarian support for a policy amplifies individual-level acceptance of the president using unilateral powers.

We assess our theoretical expectations by conducting and analyzing data from original survey experiments administered via MTurk. Our experiments contained short vignettes that described a policy proposal and asked respondents to indicate whether they supported the president's use of power to enact the policy. We also present respondents with information about aggregate public opinion on the issue at hand, whereby the treatment concerns the percentage of Americans who support the measure under consideration. This design allows us to hold constant the policy proposal and the means of implementation while varying only the level of aggregate public support for the otherwise identical policies.

We conducted our experiment in February 2016 with 999 respondents. We randomly assigned respondents to conditions in which we presented them with a short vignette that described a policy proposal

TABLE 5.5 *Majoritarian support survey experiment vignette wordings*

Issue area	Text
Environmental policy	Whoever is elected president in November 2016 is likely to propose new policies related to environmental regulations.
Trade policy	Whoever is elected president in November 2016 is likely to pursue new trade agreements with countries that compete with US manufacturing.
Travel policy	In recent years, contagious illnesses from other regions of the world have raised concerns about spreading disease in the United States. Whoever is elected president in November 2016 is likely to confront situations like these in the future and could consider restricting travel to the United States from people who live in countries that are affected by contagious epidemics.

under consideration. Our vignettes were short in length and used straightforward language to maximize external validity. As Mutz (2011, 65) notes, the "longer and more complex a treatment vignette is, the more one risks ineffective treatments."

Our vignettes omit partisan or political identifiers that the public often uses as cues when forming opinions. We also leave unspecified the specific policy proposal. These choices allow us to avoid deceiving respondents about aggregate levels of support for policy proposals they would be likely to recognize. The vignettes presented respondents with a policy proposal across each of three different domains: environmental policy, travel regulations, and foreign trade. These three issue areas invoke salient public debates, and the major parties have different approaches to addressing each of them. Consistent findings across all three issue areas would bolster confidence in the generalizability of our results. The experiments on unilateral powers told respondents that the next president is likely to propose new policies on each of these issues. The text from the first part of each vignette, which describes the policy area under consideration, is shown in Table 5.5.

Next, for each issue area, respondents were presented with information indicating disagreement between Congress and the president. This information evokes institutional conflict and asks respondents to evaluate the exercise of presidential power in this context. The treatment concerns the level of collective public support for the policy the president is considering implementing through unilateral means. Respondents were randomized to one of four conditions in which we told them that either a large majority, small majority, large minority, or small minority of the public supported the president's policy proposal.

The exact percentages of public support varied slightly across each vignette. In the environmental policy vignette, for instance, respondents in the large majority, the small majority, the large minority, and the small minority conditions were told that 80, 52, 48, and 20 percent of the public supported the president's position, respectively. We used similar patterns in characterizing public support in the other two vignettes. For the trade vignette, the percentage of public support for the proposal was characterized as 70, 55, 45, and 30 percent, respectively. For the travel vignette, the values of public support for the proposal were 75, 51, 49, and 25 percent, respectively. These percentages are consistent with our labeling of public support as large/small majority/minority, and, as we show, the exact percentages used did not produce substantively different patterns of results. Table 5.6 displays the text included in the vignettes across the four conditions.

Figure 5.7 displays the treatment effects from our experiments on support for the use of unilateral powers. For each policy area, the plot shows the differences in approving of unilateral action between the treatment condition shown on the *x*-axis and the baseline condition (small minority support for the president's policy position). Positive values along the *y*-axis indicate increased approval for unilateral action relative to the condition in which only a small minority of the public supports the president's position. The plotted points are the differences in proportions of approval, and the horizontal lines are the 95 percent confidence intervals. The dashed horizontal line at zero indicates the null hypothesis of no difference in approval of unilateral action relative to the baseline condition.

The results in Figure 5.7 show that collective opinion on the policy the president seeks to achieve affects support for unilateral power. Consider first the results in the context of environmental policy. Relative to the baseline (small minority) condition, the proportion of respondents who approved of unilateral action increases by 46 percentage points when a large majority of the public supports the president's policy objective. When a small majority of the public supports the president's position, approval of unilateral action increased by 28 points relative to

TABLE 5.6 *Majoritarian support survey experiment treatment condition wordings*

Condition	Text
Large majority	Please tell us whether you agree or disagree: If 80 percent of the public supports the president's proposal, the president should use his presidential powers to enact that policy if Congress is opposed to passing this as a new law.
Small majority	Please tell us whether you agree or disagree: If 52 percent of the public supports the president's proposal, the president should use his presidential powers to enact that policy if Congress is opposed to passing this as a new law.
Large minority	Please tell us whether you agree or disagree: If 48 percent of the public supports the president's proposal, the president should use his presidential powers to enact that policy if Congress is opposed to passing this as a new law.
Small minority	Please tell us whether you agree or disagree: If 20 percent of the public supports the president's proposal, the president should use his presidential powers to enact that policy if Congress is opposed to passing this as a new law.

the baseline condition. And when a large minority of the public shares the president's policy goal, the proportion of voters who approved of unilateral action increased by 10 points. Each of these treatment effects is statistically distinguishable from zero, indicating that voters grant significantly higher approval for the exercise of unilateral powers as public support increases for the president's policy position. Each of the treatment effects are also statistically distinguishable from each other. This shows that approval of unilateral powers monotonically increases as the public's policy preferences are more aligned with the president. While our analysis of TAPS data earlier in the chapter shows that individual-level change in attitudes towards presidential power is relatively uncommon – even in the context of the change from Obama to Trump – our experimental results show that the invocation of public backing for the president's policy proposals enhances their acceptance of unilateral powers.

We find substantively similar patterns of results for the experiments involving trade and travel policies. For both of these policy domains, we

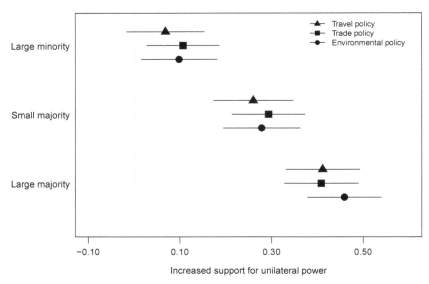

FIGURE 5.7 Collective public opinion and support for unilateral action
Note: Plotted points show the treatment effects relative to the baseline condition in which a *small minority* of the public shares the president's policy position. Positive estimates indicate greater support for unilateral action as larger shares of the public agree with the president's policy goal. The horizontal lines represent the 95 percent confidence intervals.

continue to find that increased public support for the president's position significantly increases approval of the use of unilateral powers. Moreover, the magnitudes of the treatment effects are similar to those in the environmental policy experiment. In the trade policy experiment, approval of unilateral action increases by 41, 30, and 11 percentage points relative to the baseline condition when a large majority, small majority, or large minority of the public, respectively, shared the president's policy position. Similarly, in the travel policy experiment, approval of unilateral action increased by 41, 26, and 6 percentage points relative to the baseline condition when a large majority, small majority, or large minority of the public, respectively, shared the president's view. Across three policy domains, our experiment identifies a consistent increase in approval of a president's use of unilateral power as the president's policy view is aligned with larger shares of Americans.

The results in Figure 5.7 indicate that public opposition to presidential power wanes as it is employed to advance collective policy goals. As larger shares of the public support the president's policy, Americans are more supportive of the president's use of unilateral authority. Concerns about tyranny loomed large in the design of the nation's political system and continue to shape attitudes about presidential power today. However, those concerns recede – but do not disappear – when presidents use their power to advance the public will. These results lend further support to our argument that Americans base their evaluations of presidential power on more fundamental concerns about the relationship between American democracy and executive power rather than on their approval of an individual president. Presidents can count on more significant support for using power not by enhancing their popularity, as suggested by Christenson and Kriner (2019) and Levitsky and Ziblatt (2018), but by advancing policies that large portions of the electorate support.

5.4 DISCUSSION

Public support is an essential determinant of the goals a president can accomplish. Presidential approval and partisanship are the dominant lenses through which most Americans view a wide range of political and nonpolitical phenomena (Gerber and Huber 2010; Lenz 2012). In this chapter, we consider how presidential approval shapes attitudes towards unilateral powers. Our analyses of within-respondent changes with a nationally representative panel of Americans found little evidence that changes in presidential approval affected attitudes towards unilateral power. From January 2014 to January 2018, we find no evidence that respondents who came to support or oppose Obama and then Trump systematically altered their views of presidential power.

We also focus on within-respondent changes as President Obama left office and President Trump became president. This dramatic change in the identity of the president invoked some changes in views towards unilateral presidential power but most respondents did not change their opinions. A majority of respondents opposed unilateral policymaking and judicial appointments regardless of whether Trump or Obama sat in the Oval Office. This pattern persisted across Republicans and Democrats, with most maintaining their views of presidential power.

When presidents drape themselves in the robes of public demand, they can magnify institutional powers. Writing as a political scientist, years before he would be elected president, Woodrow Wilson characterized the relationship between the public and the president accordingly: "[The president's] position takes the imagination of the country. He is the representative of no constituency, but of the whole people. When he speaks in his true character, he speaks for no special interest. If he rightly interpret the national thought and boldly insist upon it, he is irresistible" (Wilson

1908, 68). In an age when partisanship is said to influence every aspect of political and even nonpolitical life, it seems impossible that citizens would care about *how* a president gets the policies passed. But they do care. Wilson's observation is astute: the majoritarian features of the presidency, rather than presidential popularity in an age of partisanship, reflect the true force of the bully pulpit.

6

Public Cost of Unilateral Action

The previous chapters document Americans' antipathy towards executive power and explore the origins and predictors of these attitudes. But do these attitudes affect the public's evaluations of political outcomes and presidential behavior? Put differently, do Americans' attitudes towards the means affect how they evaluate the ends?

In this chapter, we test and present evidence that the public provides more negative evaluations of policies achieved through the use of unilateral power compared with those obtained through other means. We further find that the exercise of unilateral power reduces the president's public standing. These findings illuminate the political consequences of our theoretical argument. If Americans' attitudes towards executive power mirror their partisan preferences as they evaluate political outputs, the beliefs described by previous chapters may be of little consequence for shaping the politics of unilateral action. But we present evidence that Americans base their evaluations of policy outcomes on how they were fashioned and of presidents on how they deploy power. The studies in this chapter connect our study of attitudes towards unilateral powers to how public opinion provides incentives for, and places constraints on, presidential action.

6.1 PUBLIC RESPONSIVENESS TO PRESIDENTIAL ACTION

Legislation and executive action are not perfect substitutes. The reach of legislation is more expansive, and its impacts are more durable than unilateral action. Unilateral actions can be revoked or rescinded by future presidents (Thrower 2017b), whereas undoing congressional statutes requires supermajorities to pass new or amended legislation

(Ragusa and Birkhead 2020). The failure of Republican efforts to over-turn the Affordable Care Act in recent years offers a case in point.

Presidents may prefer to implement policies via legislation, but the contemporary legislative process is marked by polarization and razor-thin majorities, with Congress often blocking presidents' agendas. Under these conditions, executive action takes on a substantively different role (Cameron 2002). As Howell and Moe (2017) observe, "A big reason presidents have favored executive orders and other unilateral actions is that, with Congress such an institutional disaster, the legislative process is all but unavailable for solving problems." From the first day of their administrations, presidents face an uphill battle in enacting their priorities through legislation.

Given the background of legislative gridlock, unilateral action becomes an attractive option. Presidents may pursue unilateral approaches only after exhausting the possibility of securing legislation. Such was the case with President Obama's initiatives to reform immigration. But presidents may spurn plodding through imminently doomed legislative action to draw upon executive power from the start. They may calculate the prospects of congressional support and devise strategies for using unilateral powers accordingly. Presidents do not formulate legislative approaches for all of their policy agendas but instead assess the relative costs and benefits of avoiding or engaging Congress (Rudalevige 2002, chap. 8).

Presidents may even prioritize executive action over the legislative process. Because presidents must often make significant concessions when negotiating with Congress (Barrett and Eshbaugh-Soha 2007), unilateral action may allow the president to secure policies that better reflect his preferences. We observe this routinely in matters of international affairs, whereby presidents eschew treaties and prefer executive agreements, which are unilateral actions (Martin 2005). The first weeks of recent presidential administrations have revealed presidents eager to advance their policy goals on matters ranging from immigration to health care reform to pandemic relief through unilateral action rather than by first engaging Congress.

Existing scholarship has paid scant attention to how the public responds to the president's use of unilateral power. Most studies ignore or reject the potential for the public to evaluate presidents on the basis of how they achieve political outcomes. Instead, the public is presumed to base their evaluations of political outcomes on underlying policy preferences or partisan affiliation. Understanding how attitudes towards political processes affect attitudes about outcomes is crucial for identifying the potential for public opinion to affect presidents' decision-making processes.

6.2 STUDYING THE PUBLIC COSTS OF UNILATERAL POWER

How do voters respond when presidents use unilateral powers? While our research question is straightforward, answering it is less so. One method of inquiry would be to identify situations in which presidents achieved identical policy outcomes through different means: some through legislation and others through unilateral action. We could then compare the public responses to each. This approach fails, however, on both empirical and theoretical grounds. Empirically, this strategy is impractical, as it is impossible to identify real-world policy outcomes that were achieved through different means but were otherwise identical in every respect. Moreover, even if we could locate comparable cases, the political contexts would be sufficiently different between them that any comparisons would be problematic.

Even if the perfect set of comparable cases were to exist, there are good theoretical reasons to be skeptical of the results that such comparisons would produce. Unilateral actions are commonly understood as strategic actions by presidents to advance their policy goals, subject to potential constraints from other institutional actors (Howell 2003; Moe and Howell 1999b) – and, potentially, public opinion (Christenson and Kriner 2015; Posner and Vermeule 2010). Strategically minded presidents may thus avoid taking unilateral actions in precisely the situations in which public opinion would react harshly. This form of strategic selection bias is a common threat to inference when studying public responses to elite behavior. In the context of our research here, it could produce null findings regarding the relationship between unilateral action and public opinion when a better-specified counterfactual would provide evidence of a negative public response. This concern also applies to analyzing public responses to actual unilateral actions taken by presidents, which may explain the mostly null effects reported in Christenson and Kriner (2017a).

Instead, following recommendations on the design of survey experiments (Gaines et al. 2007; Mutz 2011), we modeled our study after research on the domestic politics of international relations (Chaudoin 2014; Tomz 2007). Similar to our own research questions, many of these studies examine how the public evaluates political leaders on the basis of their decisions related to either military intervention or the use of diplomacy with foreign states. In particular, research on audience costs typically employs experimental approaches in which respondents are randomized to receive information about whether a political leader issued a threat against a foreign country and whether the leader subsequently acted upon it. While the specifics vary depending on the nature of the research question, these studies identify potential audience costs by comparing respondents' evaluations of the leader based on whether the leader subsequently took action as threatened. A feature of these designs is that both the information as well as the political and strategic contexts are held constant across the various conditions. This approach enables sharp inferences about the effect of backing down relative to following through with the threat.

As part of our design, we ask respondents to evaluate hypothetical scenarios involving the potential use of unilateral action. We ask respondents to consider prospective instances of unilateral power. Three primary considerations motivated this choice. First, by presenting respondents with information about events that have not happened, we avoid contaminating the results of the experiment with the ideas about real-world events that respondents may bring with them. Second, our experiments invoke generic future presidents and hypothetical presidential candidates rather than actual presidents. This allows us to cleanly disentangle respondents' evaluations of policy actions from their attitudes towards a president. Third, by manufacturing cases of unilateral power, we can estimate the public costs for a variety of potential scenarios in which it may be employed. As we described in Section 6.1, presidents' unilateral actions reflect a range of strategic considerations including the potential public response. To understand the nature of latent public opinion, we study how respondents *would* evaluate unilateral power *if* a president had decided to use it. Therefore, our approach is similar to that used by Lowande and Gray (2017).

6.3 THE COSTS OF UNILATERAL ACTION VIS-À-VIS LEGISLATION

In our first set of experiments, we examine the costs of unilateral action relative to a legislative approach. We consider the public response to unilateral action using vignettes administered through a series of survey experiments. We conducted these experiments with a nationally representative sample of approximately 1,700 US adults on the October 2015 wave of TAPS, described in Chapter 3.

We study the effect of unilateral action on public opinion by administering information about a presidential candidate's policy goal and then randomizing the candidate's chosen strategy for achieving it. The design allows us to observe evaluations under counterfactual conditions in which presidential candidates propose to implement policies through legislative (rather than unilateral) means. We then compare respondents' assessment of the presidential contenders based on the information respondents received about how the candidates intended to accomplish their policies.

We fielded the survey in a context whereby candidates of both parties were campaigning for their party's nomination for the 2016 presidential election, during which time candidates announced some of the initiatives they promised to undertake via both legislation and unilateral action. For instance, Hillary Clinton announced that she would use unilateral power to achieve a variety of goals, from gun control to financial regulation (Allen 2015), while Marco Rubio pledged to use unilateral action to roll back actions taken by the Obama administration (Elliot 2016). The timing of our study, therefore, corresponds to a context in which many voters were considering both the substance of presidential candidates' policy proposals and how they would accomplish them.

The survey experiment consisted of vignettes about policy goals expressed by hypothetical presidential candidates, along with how the candidates intended to achieve them. The use of hypothetical candidates comes at the cost of reducing the real-world attributes of the experiment. This cost is offset by distancing respondents from their feelings about any actual politician, which could serve as confounders. We developed vignettes around three fictitious candidates with common last names ("Jones," "Davis," and "Smith"). We referred to each as "Candidate [last name]." No other personal information, including party affiliation, was provided. While these decisions limit the realism of our experimental setup, they allow us to establish the potential effects of unilateral action absent potential moderators such as partisanship and presidential approval. Our experimental approach thus focuses our attention on how public opinion reacts to how policy is made in circumstances in which presidents could plausibly consider unilateral action.

Following Mutz (2011), our vignettes were relatively short and employed straightforward language. Table 6.1 shows the vignette text across each experimental condition. Each candidate was associated with

TABLE 6.1 *Vignette wording for costs of unilateral action vis-à-vis legislation survey experiment*

Issue	Control condition	Legislative condition	Unilateral condition
Medical marijuana	Candidate Jones is running for president and has publicly voiced support for the legalization of marijuana for medical purposes. Jones said he supports allowing physicians in Veterans' hospitals to prescribe marijuana for their patients. He supports policies that will result in the federal legalization of medical marijuana.	Candidate Jones is running for president and has publicly voiced support for the legalization of marijuana for medical purposes. Jones said he would work with Congress to pass a bill that allows physicians in Veterans' hospitals to prescribe marijuana for their patients. This will result in the federal legalization of medical marijuana.	Candidate Jones is running for president and has publicly voiced support for the legalization of marijuana for medical purposes. Jones said he would act without Congress and use the powers of the presidency to allow physicians in Veterans' hospitals to prescribe marijuana for their patients. This will result in the federal legalization of medical marijuana.
Corporate taxes	Candidate Davis is running for president and has publicly voiced support for reducing taxes on corporations. Davis said he supports giving new tax breaks to qualifying corporations. These actions would result in a lower tax rate for many corporations.	Candidate Davis is running for president and has publicly voiced support for reducing taxes on corporations. Davis said he would work with Congress to pass a bill to give new tax breaks to qualifying corporations. These actions would result in a lower tax rate for many corporations.	Candidate Davis is running for president and has publicly voiced support for reducing taxes on corporations. Davis said he would act without Congress and use the powers of the presidency to give new tax breaks to qualifying corporations. These actions would result in a lower tax rate for many corporations.

TABLE 6.1 *(Continued)*

Issue	Control condition	Legislative condition	Unilateral condition
Deploy US troops	Candidate Smith is running for president and has publicly voiced support for defending America's allies abroad. Smith supports sending additional troops to Eastern Europe to protect those countries from a potential Russian invasion. This action will result in expanded US military efforts overseas.	Candidate Smith is running for president and has publicly voiced support for defending America's allies abroad. Smith said that he would work with Congress to pass a bill to send additional American troops to Eastern Europe to protect those countries from a potential Russian invasion. This action will result in expanded US military efforts overseas.	Candidate Smith is running for president and has publicly voiced support for defending America's allies abroad. Smith said that he would act without Congress and use the powers of the presidency to send additional American troops to Eastern Europe to protect those countries from a potential Russian invasion. This action will result in expanded US military efforts overseas.

a different issue area. Candidate Jones expressed support for legalizing medical marijuana, Candidate Davis supported reducing taxes for corporations, and Candidate Smith supported sending troops to Eastern Europe to protect that region from a potential Russian invasion. These three issues span the policy domains of social issues, economic policies, and foreign affairs. They also address salient policy debates in American politics. Our data confirm that public opinion varies considerably across these three policy proposals. To the extent we find similar patterns across policy areas, we have greater confidence of a general relationship between unilateral action and public response.

We randomly assigned respondents to one of three conditions relating to how the presidential candidates proposed achieving the desired policy. In the unilateral condition, the candidate promised to "act without Congress and use the powers of the presidency" to accomplish the policy. We avoided technical terms (e.g., "executive order," "memorandum," or "directive"). In the legislative condition, the candidate said he would "work with Congress to pass a bill" to accomplish the policy aim. In the control condition, we did not specify how the candidate would go about achieving the desired outcome. To avoid potential contamination from one vignette to the next, respondents received the same treatment assignment for each candidate and policy area. We also randomized the order in which we presented the candidates and issues.

Our vignettes abstract away from contextual circumstances that often accompany the use of unilateral action, such as elite debate surrounding the policy and characteristics of the leaders involved. Because these details were omitted, these features are essentially held constant, which avoids the challenges associated with potential confounding factors.

We evaluated two dependent variables. First, we examine support for the candidate in question. We asked respondents: "How likely would you be to support Candidate [name]?" The response options were on a four-point scale, ranging from "very unlikely" to "very likely." Second, we study respondents' approval of the candidate's proposed handling of the issue. The question wording was: "Do you approve or disapprove of Candidate [name]'s handling of [issue]?" This question was asked on a five-point scale, ranging from "strongly disapprove" to "strongly approve," with a middle option of "neither approve nor disapprove." For ease of presentation, we collapsed both measures into dichotomous indicators of evaluations of the candidates, though our results are nearly identical when using the original response scales. We present these results as robustness checks in Appendix D. Finally, in all our analyses, we report results using survey weights that are constructed based on national population parameters.

6.3.1   Results

We begin by examining whether respondents' evaluations of the presidential candidates are responsive to the means through which the candidates propose to enact their policy goals. Table 6.2 shows the proportions of respondents who reported supporting each candidate (top panel) and approving of the candidate's proposed handling of the issue (bottom panel). The entries in the table show, first, that the proportion of respondents supporting the candidates significantly varied across treatment groups in each policy domain. For instance, 62 percent of respondents in the control condition supported the candidate who wanted to legalize medical marijuana, compared with 58 percent of respondents in the

TABLE 6.2 *Summary of costs of unilateral action vis-à-vis legislation survey experiment*

	Legalize marijuana	Lower corporate taxes	Deploy US troops
Panel A	DV = Support candidate		
Control	0.62	0.24	0.35
	(0.02)	(0.02)	(0.02)
Observations	559	558	559
Legislative condition	0.58	0.28	0.31
	(0.02)	(0.02)	(0.02)
Observations	539	531	531
Unilateral condition	0.46	0.19	0.28
	(0.02)	(0.02)	(0.02)
Observations	535	527	526
F	14.85	5.42	2.91
p	< 0.01	< 0.01	0.05
Panel B	DV = Handling of issue		
Control	0.76	0.22	0.40
	(0.02)	(0.02)	(0.02)
Observations	404	418	365
Legislative condition	0.73	0.24	0.35
	(0.02)	(0.02)	(0.03)
Observations	395	378	347
Unilateral condition	0.54	0.11	0.29
	(0.02)	(0.02)	(0.02)
Observations	410	425	371
F	27.49	11.84	5.86
p	< 0.01	< 0.01	< 0.01

Note: Cell entries are the proportion of respondents who reported supporting the candidate (top panel) and approving of the candidate's handling of the issue (bottom panel). Standard errors in parentheses.

legislative condition and 46 percent of respondents in the unilateral condition. The hypothesis of no global differences can be rejected at $p < 0.01$ ($F = 14.85$). We find similar patterns for the candidates who supported reducing corporate taxes and deploying US troops to Eastern Europe.

Second, we find that the means by which presidential candidates proposed to achieve their policy goals led to significant differences in evaluations of the candidates' handling of the issues. For example, 22 percent of respondents in the control condition approved of the candidate's handling of corporate tax reductions, compared with 24 percent of respondents in the legislative condition and just 11 percent of respondents in the unilateral condition. These differences are significant at $p < 0.01$ ($F = 11.84$).

Third, the data suggest that Americans are most familiar, and perhaps comfortable, with policymaking that occurs through legislation. In contrast with other survey experiments (see, e.g., Gaines et al. 2007), we included the control condition – for which no additional information was provided about how the policies would be implemented – to benchmark the effect of the unilateral condition against the effect of informing respondents that the president intended to use the legislative route. The data indicate that the differences between the control condition and the legislative condition are considerably smaller than the difference between the control condition and the unilateral condition. For instance, as the first column of the top panel shows, the difference between the control condition and the legislative condition is 4 points for the proportion of respondents who supported the candidate on the issue of marijuana. In comparison, the difference is 16 points between the control condition and the unilateral condition for the same issue. We find this pattern for each of the other issues and both dependent variables. These data suggest that the absence of information about how policies are achieved leads respondents to infer that they are produced via the legislative route. The larger differences we find between the control group and the unilateral action condition suggest that respondents are less likely to consider policymaking as a function of executive action. Thus, an initial inspection of the data provides new evidence that the means by which political officials propose to achieve their policy goals affects how citizens evaluate those officials and their policies.

To test our expectation that the public reacts negatively to the unilateral action condition, we compare the average candidate evaluations among respondents in the unilateral action condition to those among respondents in the other two conditions. Figure 6.1 presents these comparisons and shows the treatment effects of unilateral action on support for the candidate. Each point represents the difference in mean support for the candidate between the unilateral treatment and one of the other two conditions. A triangle plots the difference between the unilateral and control conditions, and a circle plots the difference between the legislative condition.

These comparisons characterize different counterfactuals. While the former shows the effect of unilateral action relative to a condition in which respondents receive no information about how candidates propose to accomplish their goals, the latter identifies the effect of a unilateral approach relative to a legislative proposal. Negative numbers along the *x*-axis in Figure 6.1 indicate lower support among the unilateral condition, while positive values indicate stronger support among those in the unilateral condition. The vertical line at zero indicates the null hypothesis of no effect of unilateral action on candidate evaluations. The horizontal lines represent the 95 percent confidence intervals.

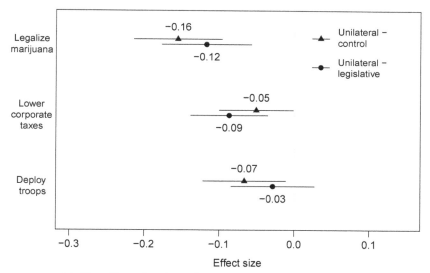

FIGURE 6.1 The effect of unilateral action vis-à-vis legislation on support for presidential candidates

Note: Triangles indicate differences between respondents in the control condition and the unilateral condition for each issue. Circles reflect the differences between respondents in the legislative condition and the unilateral condition for each issue. Negative values along the *x*-axis indicate that the unilateral treatment decreased candidate evaluations. The horizontal lines are the 95 percent confidence intervals associated with the differences in proportions. Across all issues, respondents in the unilateral condition expressed less support for candidates compared with respondents in the control and legislative conditions.

As Figure 6.1 shows, unilateral action significantly decreased support for the candidates. Compared to the control condition, the use of unilateral action to legalize marijuana decreased candidate support from 62 to 46 percent, or 16 percentage points. Similarly, respondents were 12 percentage points less supportive of a candidate who pledged to legalize marijuana via unilateral action rather than through the legislative process. Overall, respondents reacted in negative ways towards presidential candidates who proposed to change federal law regarding marijuana policies through unilateral action rather than through other means.

We find similar patterns for the other two issue areas, though the differences are somewhat smaller in magnitude. For the candidate who supported lowering corporate taxes, unilateral action reduced support by 5 percentage points relative to the control condition and 9 percentage points relative to the legislative route. Deploying troops via unilateral means reduced candidate support by 7 percentage points compared to the control condition and 3 percentage points compared to the legislative condition (the latter of which falls short of statistical significance at conventional levels). On the whole, the results in Figure 6.1 are consistent with our expectations and provide new evidence that the means by which politicians propose to achieve their policy objectives affect their levels of public support.

Figure 6.2 displays similar patterns for respondents' evaluations of the candidates' proposed handling of the issue. For the marijuana case, the pledge to use unilateral action decreased evaluations of the candidate's handling of the issue by 22 and 19 percentage points, respectively, compared to the control and legislative conditions. As with respondents' support for the candidates, the magnitude of the effect of unilateral action is strongest for marijuana but is consistently negative for the tax and troop deployment issues. Unilateral action reduced evaluations of the candidate's handling of the tax issue by 11 and 12 percentage points, respectively, compared to the control and legislative conditions. Similarly, unilateral action reduced evaluations of the candidate's handling of troop deployments by 12 and 6 percentage points, respectively, relative to assessments among respondents in the control and legislative conditions, though the latter result again falls short of statistical significance.

In all, we find that Americans evaluate policies – or, here, policy proposals – on the basis of how they are fashioned. Consistent with our evidence in the preceding chapters that documents Americans' opposition to presidential unilateralism in the abstract, our experimental findings indicate that the public provides systematically lower levels of support

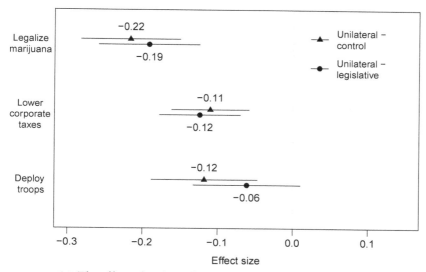

FIGURE 6.2 The effect of unilateral action vis-à-vis legislation on approval of
the candidates' handling of issues

Note: Triangles indicate differences between respondents in the control condition and the
unilateral condition for each issue. Circles reflect the differences between respondents in the
legislative condition and the unilateral condition for each issue. Negative values along the
x-axis indicate that the unilateral treatment decreased candidate evaluations. The horizontal
lines are the 95 percent confidence intervals associated with the differences in proportions.
Across all issues, respondents in the unilateral condition expressed less approval for the
candidates' handling of the issue compared with respondents in the control and legislative
conditions.

for executives who propose to deploy unilateral power to achieve their
policy goals. Across the three issues we examined, our findings suggest
that these reactions are most negative in the domain of social policy and
are smaller, though consistently negative, on economic issues and foreign
policy. Though we consider a small set of issues, the findings raise the
possibility that the public response to unilateral action could vary with
the politics or complexity of the particular issue area.

6.3.2 Leadership Traits and Potential Mechanisms

We further study the consequences of unilateral action by examining how
it affects respondents' assessments of the personality traits of the candidates. Our theoretical perspective posited in Chapter 2 and our results in
Chapter 4 demonstrate that Americans' evaluations of presidential power

reflect their commitments to the rule of law. We evaluate whether the public costs of unilateral power on candidate evaluations are consistent with
this proposed mechanism. After respondents received the vignette, we
measured respondent evaluations of the presidential candidates by asking
them to indicate whether they believed each candidate "respects the rule
of law." We measured responses to these questions on a four-point scale,
which we collapsed into a dichotomous indicator.

Figure 6.3 present the results. Consistent with our argument, we
find that unilateral action proposals significantly decreased respondents'
beliefs that the candidate respected the rule of law in each policy domain.
Compared to the control condition, unilateral action decreased respondents' beliefs that the candidate respected the rule of law by between
16 and 22 percentage points. We find nearly identical results when
comparing the unilateral condition to the legislative condition, where
respondents' evaluations of the candidate's respect for the rule of law were
reduced by between 19 and 24 percentage points. In sum, these results
suggest that the public applies its commitments to core democratic values – here, the rule of law – when evaluating proposals by presidents to
exercise unilateral powers.

We also evaluated whether the pledge to use unilateral action affected
other perceptions of the candidates. Elections provide voters with the
opportunity to elect officeholders on the basis of their competence (Alt,
Bueno de Mesquita, and Rose 2011; Ashworth 2012), and presidential
candidates have incentives to develop images that emphasize these qualities (Hayes 2005; Holian and Prysby 2014). It is possible, therefore, that a
candidate's intention to exercise unilateral powers could promote impressions of strong leadership. Perceptions of traits such as leadership can
lead to increased popular or electoral support (Fridkin and Kenney 2011;
Funk 1999; Miller, Moy, and Reeves 2018), and assessments of presidential leadership contribute to presidential approval ratings (Cohen 2015).
We thus investigated how unilateral action affected respondents' beliefs
that the candidate "provides strong leadership" and is "able to get things
done."

We present the results in Figure 6.4. If unilateral action increased perceptions of the candidates' leadership and ability to get things done, we
would expect to see positive values along the *x*-axes. We find no support
for this expectation, however. Looking first at the top panel of Figure
6.4, only in one of the six comparisons was unilateral action associated
with increased perceptions of leadership relative to a comparison scenario
(reducing corporate taxes via unilateral means increased perceptions of

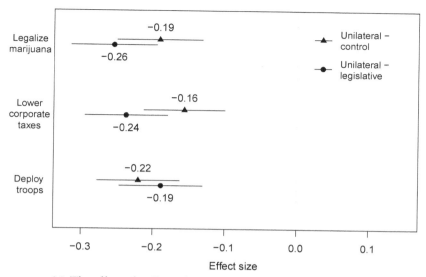

FIGURE 6.3 The effect of unilateral action vis-à-vis legislation on evaluations of
the candidates' commitment to the rule of law

Note: Triangles indicate differences between respondents in the control condition and
the unilateral condition for each issue. Circles reflect the differences between respondents
in the legislative condition and the unilateral condition for each issue. Negative values
along the *x*-axis indicate that the unilateral treatment decreased candidate evaluations. The
horizontal lines are the 95 percent confidence intervals associated with the differences in
proportions. Across all issues, respondents in the unilateral condition expressed significantly
lower evaluations of the candidates' commitments to the rule of law.

leadership by 1 percentage point relative to the control condition). This
difference is not statistically distinguishable from zero. The other comparisons show that unilateral action reduced perceptions of leadership
by between 3 and 12 percentage points. The bottom panel of the figure
reveals similar patterns. Rather than increasing perceptions of leadership
and accomplishment, our findings show that unilateral action decreased
respondents' assessments of these character traits. These results are generally consistent with a Neustadtian view of presidential leadership in
which effectiveness is gauged by a president's ability to secure support
from other key political actors rather than by going it alone.

The data reported here provide broad support that public evaluations
of presidents reflect not only what they do but also *how* they do it. The
public responds to how candidates propose to achieve their policy goals.
Proposals to use unilateral powers, in particular, decrease voters' assessments of the candidates. Contrary to suggestions that political leaders

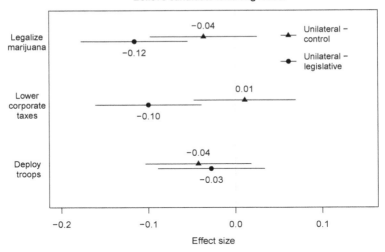

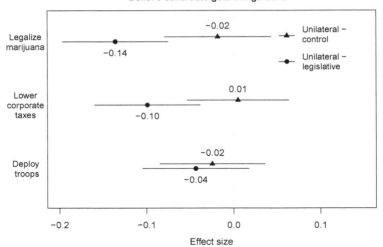

FIGURE 6.4 The effect of unilateral action vis-à-vis legislation on evaluations of candidate traits

Note: Triangles indicate differences between respondents in the control condition and the unilateral condition for each issue. Circles reflect the differences between respondents in the legislative condition and the unilateral condition for each issue. Negative values along the *x*-axes indicate that the unilateral treatment decreased candidate evaluations. The horizontal lines are the 95 percent confidence intervals associated with the differences. Unilateral action did not improve respondents' evaluations of the candidate for either dependent variable or for any issue area.

such as presidents can foment positive public images of leadership and accomplishment by acting alone (Howell 2013), our findings provide no evidence that unilateral action increases evaluations of candidates along these trait dimensions.

6.3.3 Unilateral Action and Issue Accountability

Our findings indicate that the public responds negatively to the use of unilateral power. One may wonder whether these patterns are sufficient for presidents to reconsider wielding power alone. Americans are increasingly divided in their evaluations of recent presidents. If the public costs of unilateral action are concentrated primarily among the president's partisan opponents, or among members of the public who oppose the president's policy goals, presidents may have little to lose by exercising unilateral power. But if unilateral action also reduces the president's standing among individuals who agree with the president, presidents may incur political costs from even their allies. This latter condition would provide suggestive evidence that presidents may need to think twice before pursuing unilateral means for accomplishing their policy goals.

We distinguish between these possibilities and investigate the potential for heterogeneous treatment effects. To do so, we study how preferences and procedures interact by evaluating whether the penalties for unilateral action vary depending on respondents' views on each of the three issues. Our primary focus is on whether the public costs of unilateral action vary on the basis of whether individuals agree or disagree with the president's policy position.

We measure respondents' views on each policy domain, in some instances leveraging previous panels of TAPS and using questions asked of the same respondents in earlier waves. The text of these questions is shown in Table D.1 in the Appendix to this chapter. Each question evaluates public opinion in the relevant policy domains, but there are varying degrees of correspondence with the specific policies advocated by the presidential candidates in our experimental vignettes and the wording of the survey instruments measuring policy preferences. The question wording for defense policy exhibits the greatest disparity with the policy outcome advocated by the presidential candidate. Opinions about marijuana were measured in March 2014, before some respondents joined the survey panel. Another of the measures (troop deployment) was asked in November 2015, and thus technically is a posttreatment variable. For ease of interpretation, we recoded each measure into binary variables indicating whether respondents agreed with the policy position advocated by the presidential candidates. Responses to these questions are contained in the variable *Policy agreement*.

Figure 6.5 shows the effects of unilateral action among respondents who support and oppose the presidential candidate's position for each issue. For this analysis, we calculate the effect of unilateral action relative to the legislative condition and omit respondents in the control group. As in Figure 6.4, negative numbers along the x-axes indicate that unilateral action reduced evaluations. The top figure shows that the effects were generally negative among respondents who supported the candidates' issue position. Five of the six treatment effects are negatively signed and four are statistically distinguishable from zero. The magnitudes were smallest for the tax issue and largest for deploying troops.

The bottom panel of Figure 6.5 shows results for respondents who oppose the candidate's position. The effects are negative and statistically significant for both dependent variables on the marijuana and tax issues. Interestingly, however, the results are positive for deploying troops. One potential explanation is that preferences for defense spending are relatively uncorrelated with attitudes towards deploying troops. However, we find similar patterns when distinguishing the effects based on self-reported partisanship and ideology, for which the effects of unilateral action are increasingly positive among individuals who identify as Democrats and express more liberal ideologies. Our results appear to reflect heterogeneity among respondents of varying political stripes in how they evaluate the use of unilateral power in the context of deploying military force.

We use linear regression to test more formally whether policy agreement moderates the effect of unilateral action on candidate evaluations. We regress each of the dependent variables for the three issue areas on an indicator for assignment to the unilateral (rather than legislative) condition, the binary indicator for policy agreement, and the interaction between them. The coefficient for the unilateral action condition provides an estimate of the treatment effect among individuals who oppose the candidate's policy position and the coefficient for the interaction term characterizes whether this effect differs for individuals who support the candidate's policy view.

Table 6.3 shows the results of these analyses. First, we find that the indicator for the unilateral condition is consistently negative and statistically significant for the marijuana legalization and corporate tax policy areas, indicating that respondents in this condition evaluated the presidential candidate more negatively than respondents in the legislative condition. The coefficients for the unilateral condition are positive, however, for

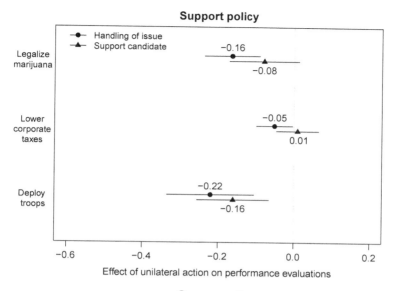

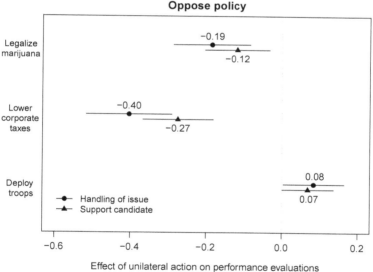

FIGURE 6.5 The effect of unilateral action vis-à-vis legislation on evaluations of presidential candidates

Note: Points represent the differences in aggregate evaluations of the presidential candidates based on whether they propose to achieve their policy goals via unilateral action or with legislation. The top plot shows effects among respondents who agree with the candidate's policy views and the bottom plot shows effects among respondents who disagree with the candidate's policy views. The plotted points show the differences in mean support, whereby negative values indicate public penalties for unilateral action relative to legislation. The horizontal lines represent the 95 percent confidence intervals.

the deploying troops policy. While this suggests that unilateral action increased candidate evaluations among respondents who oppose increasing spending for national defense, neither coefficient reaches standard levels of statistical significance.

Second, as one would expect, evaluations of the presidential candidates are more positive as respondents' policy preferences are aligned with the candidates' policy goals. The coefficients for *Policy agreement* are positive and statistically significant in each of the six models. Consistent with theories of issue accountability, respondents evaluated presidential candidates more favorably when the candidates shared respondents' policy views.

Third, and most importantly, while we find evidence that individuals' policy preferences moderate the effects of unilateral action, the results provide no evidence that the negative consequences of unilateral action are driven solely by individuals who oppose the presidential candidates' proposals. The coefficients for the interaction terms are negative and statistically significant in four of the six models, indicating that the effects of unilateral action were more negative for respondents whose policy views were aligned with those of the respective candidates. Neither interaction term is significant for the marijuana policy domain, indicating that the negative consequences of unilateral action applied to both supporters and opposers of the candidate's policy view.

The results in Table 6.3 highlight the interaction between substantive policies and procedural values in how Americans evaluate officeholders. The negative coefficients on most of the interaction terms indicate that policy agreement is a weaker predictor of candidate evaluations when the candidate pledges to use unilateral power. That is, while respondents generally provided more positive assessments of candidates who advocated issue positions shared by the respondents, policy agreement mattered less to respondents when candidates proposed to achieve their goals via unilateral actions rather than by working with Congress. These results suggest that the public's negative evaluations of unilateral power may undermine issue accountability by reducing support for candidates who otherwise promote popular policy agendas.

Together, our survey experiments demonstrate that a president's inclination to pursue policies through unilateral means may come at a public cost. Our data provide evidence of decreased public evaluations of presidential candidates who promise policies via unilateral action rather than by working with Congress. These effects are especially strong among respondents who agree with the candidate's policy position. Respondents who share officials' policy goals do not appear to be contented by their

TABLE 6.3 *Model of costs of unilateral action vis-à-vis legislation: Interaction with policy preferences*

Panel A	DV = Approve of handling		
	Marijuana	Taxes	Troops
Unilateral condition	−0.19*	−0.07*	0.08
	(0.04)	(0.03)	(0.04)
Policy agreement	0.46*	0.57*	0.38*
	(0.05)	(0.05)	(0.05)
Unilateral condition ×	0.02	−0.45*	−0.30*
Policy agreement	(0.07)	(0.07)	(0.07)
Observations	640	803	691

Panel B	DV = Support candidate		
	Marijuana	Taxes	Troops
Unilateral condition	−0.12*	−0.06*	0.07
	(0.04)	(0.03)	(0.04)
Policy agreement	0.37*	0.41*	0.23*
	(0.05)	(0.05)	(0.04)
Unilateral condition ×	0.04	−0.24*	−0.23*
Policy agreement	(0.07)	(0.07)	(0.06)
Observations	836	1,057	1,010

$^*p < 0.05$
Note: Entries are linear regression coefficients with standard errors in parentheses. The dependent variable is listed at the top of each panel. Respondents who received the legislative treatment condition are the omitted category. Data are weighted to national population parameters.

issue congruence, but instead downgrade their assessments of candidates who propose to achieve their objectives through means that respondents oppose. Presidents eager to curry favor with the public must consider not only the level of public support for their policy initiatives but also how the public may respond to the means through which they intend to achieve them. Advocating for popular initiatives may not be sufficient to boost an official's public standing if they implement such initiatives through unpopular means.

6.4 THE COSTS OF UNILATERAL ACTION VIS-À-VIS INACTION

Thus far, we have shown that the public does not uncritically accept when presidents use unilateral strategies. The public does not hold favorable views of presidential power, and our survey experiments indicate that the public penalizes leaders for the use of same. Instead, the public would prefer that presidents pursue their policy objectives through the legislative process.

Presidents, however, may not always have the luxury of considering the option of passing legislation in lieu of using unilateral powers. In our current era of heightened partisan disagreement and slim partisan majorities, many presidential policy initiatives may be dead on arrival to Congress. For these presidents, then, the choice is not whether they should pursue legislation rather than unilateral action; instead, these presidents must decide whether to take unilateral action or acquiesce to the status quo.

We conducted a second study to evaluate the public incentives for presidents to act when legislation is unlikely. Existing scholarship presents competing views about the nature of these incentives. Canonical accounts equate action with presidential leadership. For example, Howell (2013, 125) asserts that "opting not to act – indeed, merely being perceived as not acting – comes at a great political cost." Because presidents benefit from being perceived as strong leaders (Cohen 2015), unilateral action may also allow presidents to exhibit leadership in the face of legislative inaction.

There is sparse evidence that the mass public rewards presidents for taking action instead of accepting the status quo. The previous analyses in this chapter show that the public holds negative views of unilateral power and disapproves of presidents who exercise it. But these analyses do not adjudicate whether unilateral action is preferable to no action at all. Arbitrating between these competing expectations is essential for understanding presidents' public incentives for using unilateral power when congressional gridlock makes legislative action unlikely, a context increasingly familiar for recent presidents.

6.4.1 Public Opinion and Incentives for Unilateral Action

We examine the public reaction to unilateral action in the context of congressional inaction. Our primary interest is whether president's public standing is affected by exercising unilateral power when they would otherwise not achieve their policy goals. Identifying whether unilateral action provides benefits for the president, and among which voters, is essential for characterizing the president's public incentives during persistent gridlock.

6.4.2 Design

We embedded three experimental vignettes in a survey we conducted in March 2018. The survey was administered by YouGov, with a sample of approximately four thousand respondents designed to be demographically representative of the US population. The vignettes concerned salient political issues, including health care, immigration, and international sanctions. These issues addressed domestic and foreign policies on which Americans may have varying views about the desirability of unilateral action.

The vignettes presented all respondents with identical information about the president's policy goals, informed them that the president was unable to achieve these goals with legislation, and reported that the president criticized Congress for its inaction. This design ensures that all respondents were aware of the president's political views and disagreements with Congress. For each vignette, we randomly assigned respondents to one of two conditions. In the presidential inaction condition, we told respondents that the status quo remained unchanged. In the unilateral action condition, we told respondents that the president issued a unilateral directive to advance the policy goal. We present the full vignette wording in Table 6.4.

After each vignette, we measured respondents' evaluations of both the president's handling of the issue and job performance. The questions were asked as follows:

- Would you approve or disapprove of the way the president has handled [issue]?
- Would you approve or disapprove of the way the president has handled his job as president?

For simplicity, we collapsed the dependent variables into binary indicators for whether the respondent provided a positive evaluation of the president. Using these measures, we compared levels of support for the president across the two conditions. If the public prefers presidents to take direct action to achieve their goals rather than accept congressional inaction, we would expect to observe more positive presidential evaluations from respondents in the unilateral action condition. But if the public's opposition to unilateral power looms larger for respondents than the president's failure to achieve a policy goal, presidential evaluations would be more positive for the presidential inaction condition. Alternatively, if the

TABLE 6.4 *Vignette wording for costs of unilateral action vis-à-vis inaction*

Issue	Stasis condition	Unilateral condition
Immigration	Suppose a president would like to change policy to allow undocumented immigrants to become US citizens. Congress, however, is unwilling to take action on the president's proposal. In response to the stalemate, the president has harshly criticized the Congress's inaction. US immigration policy remains unchanged.	Suppose a president would like to change policy to allow undocumented immigrants to become US citizens. Congress, however, is unwilling to take action on the president's proposal. In response to the stalemate, the president has harshly criticized the Congress's inaction and acted unilaterally to allow some undocumented immigrants to become citizens if they meet certain criteria. US immigration policy is now changed.
Health care	A president would like to reform health care to reduce costs for small businesses. Congress has failed to pass legislation to make health insurance more competitive. In response, the president has complained about Congress's failure to make it more affordable for small businesses to provide health care. Health care policy remains unchanged.	A president would like to reform health care to reduce costs for small businesses. Congress has failed to pass legislation to make health insurance more competitive. In response, the president has complained about Congress's failure to make it more affordable for small businesses to provide health care. Instead, the president has acted without Congress and issued an executive order to loosen regulations on the insurance industry that would lower health care costs for small businesses. Health care policy is now changed.

TABLE 6.4 *(Continued)*

Issue	Stasis condition	Unilateral condition
Sanctions	A president has asked Congress to impose economic sanctions against a foreign nation known to be a state sponsor of terrorism, but Congress has refused to do so. In response to this stalemate, the president has angrily criticized Congress for their failure to act. There remain no sanctions against the foreign nation.	A president has asked Congress to impose economic sanctions against a foreign nation known to be a state sponsor of terrorism, but Congress has refused to do so. In response to this stalemate, the president has angrily criticized Congress for their failure to act. Additionally, the president has acted without Congress and used his unilateral powers to sanction the country. There are now sanctions against the foreign nation.

public evaluates presidents primarily on the basis of their policy views rather than their achievement of outcomes that reflect those views, we would expect to observe no difference between conditions.

In addition to testing the main effects of unilateral action on presidential evaluations, we also evaluate how the results vary among respondents who agree and disagree with the president's policy goals. Unilateral action may cultivate positive reactions among individuals who share the president's policy goals. If this were so, it would provide political cover for the president to take action even if groups who oppose the president's policy react negatively. Before respondents received the vignettes, they completed a battery of questions about their opinions on the three policy items referenced in the vignettes. The text of these questions is shown in Table D.2 in the Appendix to this chapter. Respondents answered each item using a four-point scale from "strongly support" to "strongly oppose," which we collapsed into a binary indicator of support. For each issue, we distinguished the treatment effects among respondents who shared and opposed the president's policy goal.

Comparing the effects of unilateral action among respondents who share and oppose the president's policy views allows us to put our hypothesis to an even stronger test. We expect that individuals who oppose the president's policy positions exhibit the most negative effects, as they may disagree with the president on both policy and procedural grounds. Individuals who share the president's policy goals, however, provide a more critical test. While they stand to realize policy gains when a president implements their preferred outcome via unilateral action, the result may violate their procedural preferences. If the former predominates, we will see positive effects among these respondents in the unilateral condition, which would suggest the public rewards presidents for implementing their preferred policy goals via unilateral power. But if respondents evaluate presidents on the basis not only of what they do but how they do it, we would expect that procedural preferences cancel out or outweigh their policy gains, in which case we would observe null or negative effects of the unilateral condition.

We test these hypotheses by comparing the mean levels of support across experimental conditions. We use survey weights in all analyses to estimate the population average treatment effects.

6.4.3 Results

Figure 6.6 shows the results across both dependent variables and each issue area. The points indicate the difference in the proportion of respondents who provided positive evaluations, and negative values indicate that presidential evaluations were lower among respondents in the unilateral condition. Across the three survey experiments, we find that the public penalizes presidents for pursuing unilateral action compared with accepting a status quo the president expressed interest in changing. Consider first the results for the immigration issue shown at the top of Figure 6.6. Overall, 52 percent of respondents in the inaction condition approved of the president's handling of this issue, compared with 43 percent of respondents in the unilateral condition. This difference of 9 percentage points is statistically significant ($p < 0.001$). Though the president expressed identical policy views in both conditions, respondents *penalized* the president for exercising unilateral power to achieve his goals rather than accepting the status quo. We find the same pattern across the other two issue areas, for which evaluations of the president's handling of the situation were 6 percentage points ($p < 0.001$) and 4 percentage points ($p < 0.01$) lower in the unilateral action condition compared to the inaction condition for immigration and economic sanctions, respectively.

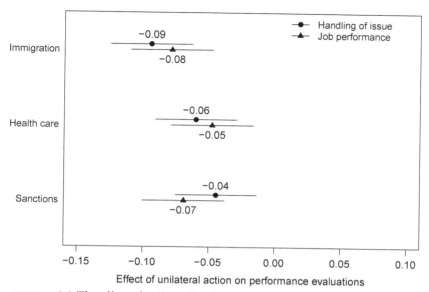

FIGURE 6.6 The effect of unilateral action vis-à-vis inaction on evaluations of the president

Note: Points represent the differences in aggregate evaluations of the president based on whether he exercises unilateral power to change existing policy or instead observes the status quo. The plotted points show the differences in mean support, where negative values indicate public penalties for unilateral action. The horizontal lines represent the 95 percent confidence intervals.

As Figure 6.6 shows, we find similar differences when evaluating approval of the president's job performance. Across each issue, we find that the president's approval rating is lower among respondents in the unilateral condition. The differences range from 5 to 8 percentage points and each is statistically significant ($p < 0.01$). These results provide striking and consistent evidence that presidents incur aggregate penalties for drawing upon unilateral action rather than retaining the status quo.

6.4.4 Policy Agreement and the Effects of Unilateral Action

We now examine how our treatment effects vary based on whether respondents support or oppose each of the president's policy beliefs. To do so, we estimate the treatment effects of the unilateral condition among respondents who either supported or opposed each of the president's policy goals. While we expect that individuals who opposed the president's policy goals provide the strongest negative reaction to the use of unilateral power, we are particularly interested in the effects among respondents who support the president's policy views. For these respondents, their support of the policy objectives pursued by presidents may conflict with their principled opposition to the use of unilateral power. The reactions among these respondents, therefore, is critical for characterizing the nature of the potential political costs of unilateral power. If individuals cast aside their views on presidential power when the president uses power to achieve policy ends they support, we would expect to observe positive treatment effects from the unilateral action condition. In this case, presidents hoping to maintain or increase their popular standing need only use unilateral actions to advance initiatives supported by the broader public. On the other hand, if individuals' views on power are at least as important in their evaluations of the president as their support for the president's policy accomplishments, then we would expect to observe null or negative effects of the unilateral power condition. Should this be the case, the results would suggest that presidents can expect to lose political support among the public even when pursuing popular policy goals.

The results are shown in Figure 6.7. Treatment effects of unilateral action among respondents who supported the president's policy goals are shown in the top plot; effects among respondents who opposed the president's policy goals are shown in the bottom plot. The treatment effects on the handling dependent variable are shown with a solid circle and the effects on the job approval dependent variable are shown with a solid triangle.

As the top plot shows, we find no evidence that unilateral action had positive effects on presidential evaluations among respondents who shared the president's policy beliefs. In the immigration vignette, for example, 51 percent of individuals who supported the president's position approved of the president's handling of the issue in the inaction condition, compared to 50 percent among respondents in the unilateral condition. Therefore, the exercise of unilateral power reduced the proportion of respondents who provided positive evaluations of the president by .01. We find similar patterns when evaluating the president's job performance evaluation. About 48 percent of the president's policy supporters approved of the president's job performance in the *inaction* condition compared to 44 percent of respondents in the *unilateral* condition. Neither of these differences is statistically distinguishable from zero; however, these findings provide no evidence that individuals who agree with the president's policy position express greater support for presidents who use unilateral power to implement it.

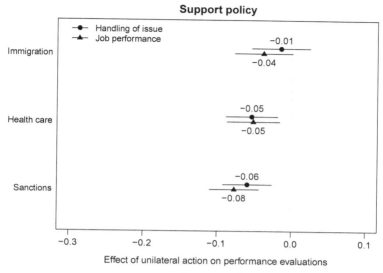

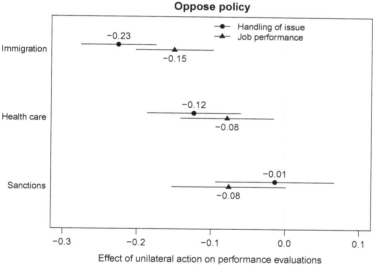

FIGURE 6.7 The effect of unilateral action vis-à-vis inaction on evaluations of the president by policy approval

Note: Points represent the differences in aggregate evaluations of the president based on whether he exercises unilateral power to change existing policy or instead observes the status quo. The top plot shows effects among respondents who share the president's policy views and the bottom plot shows effects among respondents who oppose the president's policy views. The plotted points show the differences in mean support, where negative values indicate public penalties for unilateral action. The horizontal lines represent the 95 percent confidence intervals.

The results are even starker for the other two policy issues. In the context of health care, the proportion of respondents who provided positive evaluations of the president was significantly lower in the unilateral condition. The unilateral condition reduced the proportion of respondents who approved of the president's handling of health care by 0.05 and reduced the proportion of respondents who approved of the president's job performance by a similar margin. For the issue of economic sanctions, the results are slightly larger in magnitude, where the unilateral condition reduced the proportion of respondents who approved of the president's handling by 0.06 and who approved of the president's job performance by 0.08. Overall, the evidence presented in the top plot indicates that individuals who agree with the president's policy positions do not provide any additional support for presidents who achieve them through unilateral power – in fact, the use of unilateral power may even decrease their evaluations of the president despite their agreement with his policy views.

As the bottom plot shows, we find that respondents who opposed the president's policy goals reacted consistently negatively to the use of unilateral power. The magnitude of the effects varied somewhat across policy areas. For example, on the issue of immigration, the proportion of respondents who approved of the president's handling of the issue was 0.23 lower and who approved of the president's job performance was 0.15 lower among respondents in the unilateral condition. The unilateral action condition also had consistently negative effects in the context of health care, though the magnitudes were about half as large as the effects for the immigration issue. Finally, the results were a bit more mixed for the economic sanctions issue. The proportion of respondents who approved of the president's handling of the issue was 0.01 lower in the unilateral condition, though this result is not statistically distinguishable from zero. The results were stronger for the job performance dependent variable, where the proportion of respondents who approved of the president's job performance was 0.08 lower in the unilateral condition. Overall, we find that respondents who opposed the president's policy views reported lower evaluations when the president achieves his policy goals through unilateral action.

While the plots in Figure 6.7 provide visual evidence that policy views moderated the effects of the president's use of unilateral power, we test these heterogeneous effects more formally. Using linear regression, we model the dependent variables as a function of whether respondents were in the unilateral treatment condition, their support for the president's policy view, and the interaction between them. If the effect of the unilateral condition varied on the basis of whether respondents agreed with the president's policy views, the coefficient on the interaction term would be statistically distinguishable from zero.

The results are shown in Table 6.5. The interaction terms are statistically significant in two of the six models, providing some limited evidence that respondents' policy views conditioned the effects of the unilateral action treatment. Perhaps more interestingly, the coefficients are occasionally positive, indicating that the negative effects of unilateral action are smaller among respondents who shared the president's policy views. Moreover, in no model do the results show that supporters of the president's policy views provided *more positive* assessments of the president for using unilateral action rather than accepting the status quo. Across each policy area and both dependent variables, respondents who opposed the president's policy position penalized the president for unilateral action and, strikingly, we find no evidence that unilateral action improved evaluations of the president among respondents who supported the president's policy views.

While these results may initially be unsurprising, closer consideration suggests that these findings provide new evidence about how accountability mechanisms operate. Americans do not simply evaluate politicians on the basis of whether those officials share the public's policy views. If that were the case, we would expect no difference in presidential evaluations between the unilateral and inaction conditions; after all, both conditions provided identical information to respondents about the president's policy views. Instead, our results indicate that the public – particularly those members of the public who disagree with the president – also penalizes presidents for taking action to advance their policy views. Accountability is not simply about issue congruence; it is also enforced by the public's response to the use of power.

6.4.5 Within-Respondent Results

Our results are between-respondent estimates in which we compared respondents' evaluations for each issue area based on whether we assigned them to the unilateral action or inaction conditions. Unlike the experiments using TAPS data presented earlier in this chapter, respondents' treatment assignments in the experiments administered via YouGov were randomized separately for each of the three issues. Thus, we can also evaluate the effect of the unilateral action treatment using a within-respondent

TABLE 6.5 *Model of costs of unilateral action vis-à-vis inaction: Interactions with policy preferences*

Panel A	DV = Approve of handling		
	Health care	Immigration	Sanctions
Unilateral action	−0.12*	−0.23*	−0.01
	(0.03)	(0.03)	(0.04)
Policy agreement	0.21*	−0.03	0.30*
	(0.02)	(0.02)	(0.03)
Unilateral action ×	0.07	0.21*	−0.05
Policy agreement	(0.04)	0.03)	(0.04)
Observations	3,903	3,916	3,905

Panel B	DV = Approve of job performance		
	Health care	Immigration	Sanctions
Unilateral action	−0.08*	−0.15*	−0.08*
	(0.03)	(0.03)	(0.04)
Policy agreement	0.23*	−0.11*	0.31*
	(0.03)	(0.02)	(0.03)
Unilateral action ×	0.03	0.11*	0.00
Policy agreement	(0.04)	(0.03)	(0.04)
Observations	3,874	3,891	3,884

$^*p < 0.05$

Note: Dependent variable is shown at the top of each panel. Estimates are linear regression coefficients with standard errors in parentheses.

analysis. To do so, we estimated linear regressions of our dependent variables on indicators for treatment assignment along with respondent and vignette fixed effects. This specification accounts for respondent- and vignette-specific factors that may affect respondents' evaluations of the president. Using this approach, our model identifies the effect of the *unilateral action* condition using within-respondent variation in treatment assignment.[1] In contrast with the between-respondent analysis, we estimate the effect of the unilateral condition by aggregating across issues rather than evaluating the effects separately for each of them.

Table 6.6 shows the results of the within-respondent analyses. The left two columns focus on the overall effects of the unilateral condition. The

---

[1] Overall, treatment assignments varied across vignettes for 76 percent of respondents.

coefficients for both dependent variables are negatively signed, statistically significant, and similar in magnitude. These results indicate that the unilateral condition reduced the probability that a respondent approved of the president's handling and the president's job performance by an average of 6 to 7 percentage points.

The results in the right two columns of Table 6.6 evaluate how these effects are moderated by respondents' policy views. *Policy agreement* is a binary indicator for whether respondents support the policy in the relevant issue area. The coefficients for *Unilateral condition* show the results for individuals who oppose the president's policy position and indicate that unilateral action reduced the probability of approving of the president's handling by about 13 percentage points and approving of the president's job performance by about 9 percentage points. The coefficient for *Policy agreement* shows how agreeing with the president's policy position affected respondents' presidential evaluations. On average, respondents were 16 percentage points more supportive of the president's handling of the issue and 14 percentage points more supportive of the president's job performance. The interaction terms, however, are both positive. Consistent with the between-respondent analyses reported earlier in the chapter, we find that the unilateral condition had a significantly smaller effect on evaluations of the president's issue handling among individuals who agreed with the president's policy views. However, the magnitude of the interaction term was smaller than the magnitude of the constituent term for the unilateral condition, indicating that policy agreement is not sufficient to overcome the penalties imposed on presidents for the use of unilateral action. The results for evaluations of the president's job performance are similar. Although the interaction term falls short of conventional levels of statistical significance, it is positively signed yet smaller in magnitude than the constituent term for unilateral action.

The results of these experiments contextualize the findings from previous research on the public cost of unilateral action and challenge accounts that argue that presidents have electoral incentives to push their agenda at all costs. Not only might presidents experience negative public reactions when pursuing unilateral action rather than legislation, but these negative public reactions also exist when the alternative to unilateral action is no policy change at all. Instead, our results suggest that the public does not view presidents as "policymakers-in-chief" but instead prefers them to respect traditional limits on the president's use of formal power.

TABLE 6.6 *Model of costs of unilateral action vis-à-vis inaction:*
Within-respondent estimates

	Handling	Approval	Handling	Approval
Unilateral condition	−0.07*	−0.06*	−0.13*	−0.09*
	(0.01)	(0.01)	(0.03)	(0.02)
Policy agreement			0.16*	0.14*
			(0.02)	(0.02)
Unilateral condition × Policy agreement			0.08*	0.04
			(0.03)	(0.02)
Individual fixed effects	✓	✓	✓	✓
Issue fixed effects	✓	✓	✓	✓
Observations	11,936	11,858	11,724	11,649
Respondents	3,999	3,997	3,964	3,961

*$p < 0.05$

Note: Robust standard errors clustered on respondent are in parentheses. Data are weighted to national population parameters. Dependent variables are shown at the top of each column.

6.4.6 Evaluating the Role of Constitutional Considerations

Our experimental results offer compelling evidence that Americans apply their negative attitudes towards unilateral power when evaluating both the presidents who exercise it and the policy outcomes that are achieved through its use. Even individuals who support the president's policy goals would sometimes prefer for the status quo to remain in place rather than for the president to create policy change with the stroke of a pen.

These findings are consistent with our theoretical argument. Here we examine the evidence for our proposed mechanism. Our experiment, like most, is not well-suited for directly estimating the effects of potential mediators (on this topic, see Green, Ha, and Bullock 2010). Instead, we use an indirect approach. If Americans' commitments to constitutional principles drive their skepticism of executive power, as we argue, then we would expect to find that respondents' beliefs in the rule of law will moderate the negative effects of the unilateral condition.

Before respondents received the experimental vignettes, we measured their support for the rule of law using a battery similar to that reported in Chapter 4. Respondents answered the first four items described in Table 4.1 along a four-point scale that ranged from "strongly disagree" to "strongly agree." The fifth item was not asked on the YouGov survey. These items were scaled to create an index of support for the rule of law, which ranged from zero to three.[2] As with our analyses in Chapter 4, larger values of this variable indicate respondents with stronger commitments to the rule of law. The mean value was 2.16, and the median was 2.25.

We evaluate whether the rule of law moderates the treatment effects of the unilateral condition using our within-respondent analyses. This analysis allows us to evaluate the overall relationship between the rule of law and our treatment effects for each dependent variable. We again use linear regression to model each dependent variable as a function of an indicator for assignment to the *Unilateral condition* and its interaction with respondents' support for the rule of law. Note that our regression model includes respondent-level fixed effects, and the rule of law varies between individuals but not between vignettes. Therefore, our model does not recover a constituent term for the *Rule of law* variable. Instead, the regressions estimate whether the effect of assignment to the *Unilateral condition* varies among respondents on the basis of their level of support for the rule of law. If our argument is correct, we would expect to find that the effects of unilateral action are more negative among individuals with stronger support for the rule of law. Therefore, we expect that the coefficients for the *Unilateral condition* are negative, indicating that the effects of the treatment are negative among individuals with the strongest support for the rule of law. We further expect that the coefficients for the interaction terms are positive, which would indicate that the magnitude of the effects attenuates among individuals with less support for the rule of law.

Table 6.7 shows the results and supports our expectations. The first column shows the results for the dependent variable that measures respondents' approval of the president's handling of the policy area. The coefficient for assignment to the *Unilateral condition* is positive yet not statistically significant, indicating that the unilateral action may have increased evaluations of the president among respondents with the least support for the rule of law, although the coefficient is not reliably estimated. The coefficient for the interaction term, however, is negative and statistically significant. It indicates that the treatment effects of the unilateral conditions among respondents with higher values on the rule of law scale – which, here, corresponds to weaker commitments to the rule of law – were increasingly negative. Given the magnitude of the interaction term, the results suggest that the treatment effect was approximately zero

---

[2] The Cronbach's alpha was 0.74.

TABLE 6.7 *Model of costs of unilateral action vis-à-vis inaction: How attitudes towards the rule of law moderate the effect of unilateral action*

	Handling	Approval
Unilateral condition	0.07	0.05
	(0.04)	(0.04)
Unilateral condition ×	−0.07*	−0.05*
Rule of law	(0.02)	(0.02)
Individual fixed effects	✓	✓
Issue fixed effects	✓	✓
Observations	11,884	11,809
Respondents	3,981	3,979

*$p < 0.05$

Note: Robust standard errors clustered on respondent are in parentheses. Data are weighted to national population parameters. Dependent variables are shown at the top of each column.

among people with a value of one on the rule of law scale (which applies to about 4 percent of respondents), and was negative among the 60 percent of respondents with values on the rule of law scale greater than that. The results for the approval-dependent variable are equivalent. The magnitude of the effect of the unilateral condition was increasingly negative among respondents with stronger commitments to the rule of law.

Consistent with our theoretical perspective, we find that Americans' commitments to the rule of law affect how they evaluate presidential power. Individuals with stronger commitments react more negatively to the use of power, while these effects attenuate among individuals who feel less strongly that the rule of law is inviolable. This pattern provides powerful evidence that Americans do not merely fall back on their partisan, ideological, or policy commitments when evaluating presidential power, but that their constitutional commitments also shape how they view the institution of the presidency.

6.5 DISCUSSION

Presidents are held accountable for an extraordinary range of outcomes and often assert their unilateral powers to achieve their goals. Extant scholarship focuses almost exclusively on the constraints provided by legislatures, courts, and bureaucrats on a president's decision to go it alone (Bolton and Thrower 2016; Howell 2003; Mayer 1999; Rudalevige 2012; Thrower 2017a). Using a framework that emphasizes political accountability, we study how the public reacts to unilateral action by presidents and establish how public opinion may affect a president's use of power.

We find that the public assesses presidents beyond mere partisanship and ideology. Citizens also judge how presidents govern while in office. We present evidence that, despite the certainty with which presidents may order and implement a unilateral action, it is "costly" to both "the aims in whose defense it is employed" as well as "objectives far afield" (Neustadt 1990, 28). Unilateral action is costly to a president's public standing, and the threat of public backlash may constrain a president in its use (Bruff 2015; Posner and Vermeule 2010). By addressing potential biases due to strategic selection in related empirical work (Christenson and Kriner 2017a, 2019), we provide new evidence that both means and ends affect how Americans evaluate their presidents.

Accounts of the modern presidency emphasize the need for presidents to exercise leadership and to take decisive action. Scholars frequently assert that the public expects presidents to attend to all issues (Neustadt 1990) because the political costs of failing to do so are too high (Howell 2013). We find little support for these claims. While legislative gridlock may offer opportunities for strategic presidents to advance their policy interests unilaterally, our survey evidence demonstrates that presidents suffer a public cost for doing so. This penalty exists even among segments of the public who support the president's position. Our findings suggest that, while it is important to the public for presidents to share their policy views, it is not necessary – and may even be detrimental – for presidents to take direct action to advance them. The public may instead prefer to forgo a policy they support rather than have it implemented via means they find inappropriate.

Our findings in this chapter illustrate the political consequences of Americans' political values on presidential power that we presented in earlier chapters. Americans have attitudes about the nature of presidential power, and they apply these attitudes when evaluating how presidents deploy those prerogatives. Despite claims that the public wants presidents to "break constitutional rules and find ways to exercise their will" (Howell 2013, 106), we find evidence that the public is concerned about how presidents exercise the powers of the office. The public wants presidents to endorse policy goals that they share, and they also have preferences about how presidents seek to achieve them. Americans' deference to the rule of law shapes their tolerance for presidents who abide by a limited understanding of presidential power as inherited from the founding.

The experiments we report in this chapter enable us to evaluate the effect of unilateral action relative to complementary counterfactuals. In the first experiment, we study how unilateral action affects presidential evaluations relative to a legislative initiative that accomplishes the same outcome. In the second, we study the effect of unilateral action relative to a scenario in which no policy change occurs. Together, the results characterize how the use of unilateral power interacts with the public's policy preferences to affect presidential evaluations. Among individuals who support the president's policy views, the penalty for pursuing policies via unilateral action rather than legislation are just as great – if not greater – than among individuals who oppose the president's policy goals. Supporters of the president's policy goals react less negatively to unilateral action when a policy would not be changed without its use. Even in this latter scenario, however, our results provide no evidence that presidents have incentives to wield unilateral powers to advance the policy goals shared by their supporters.

Our findings have implications for how voters exercise accountability with respect to the presidency. When presidents use unilateral power to achieve their policy goals, the public's policy views gain importance for how they evaluate the president. Conditional on the president's expressed policy goals, the public's evaluations of the president more strongly reflect their ideological agreement with the president when unilateral action is used to achieve those goals. This finding suggests at least two important implications. First, strategic presidents have incentives to consider public opinion when issuing unilateral directives. Our evidence indicates that unilateral action more strongly links presidents to their policy views in the minds of the public. The president's public standing is more likely to suffer when unilateral action is used to advance unpopular policy views, yet may be rewarded if unilateral power advances popular policy goals. Second, our respondents were provided with full information about the president's use (or not) of unilateral power. If presidents were to use unilateral power but at least some voters were uninformed about this action, the accountability relationship would be weaker than if all voters were fully informed. Therefore, presidents may have strategic incentives to obfuscate about using unilateral power depending on their expectations about the likely public response.

Our experimental approach helps to address biases associated with issues of strategic selection. But it also omits features of the real world that may have implications for the politics of unilateral action. While presidents may generally prefer legislative solutions, public response to unilateral action may depend on whether such actions are the president's first resort or are instead taken after legislative attempts have failed. The first weeks of the Trump administration provide evidence consistent with our findings. President Trump's unilateral approach to restricting entry to the United States from countries associated with terrorism was met with widespread disapproval and public protest – even though Trump had previously expressed support for similar positions while campaigning for president. The adverse reaction to President Trump is consistent with the findings presented in this chapter. While unilateral action may be a president's best opportunity to realize their policy goals, exercising it comes at a cost.

7

Public Assessments of Presidential Power from the Past

As we detail in previous chapters, much of our evidence abstracts away from real-world political figures and contexts. This approach has many advantages. We are able to design our own survey questions to measure precisely the concepts of interest. The survey data are from high-quality and nationally representative samples. We also have the same measures – answered by many of the same respondents – across two presidential administrations.

Though this approach has many advantages, it limits the range of questions we can answer with it. Do Americans show a similar disdain for unilateral powers in previous eras of American politics? Or do our findings reflect the political moment of the 2010s? The period we examine is characterized by historic levels of partisan polarization, persistent legislative gridlock, and relatively low levels of trust in institutions. Under these conditions, unilateral action may be uniquely employed by presidents, politicized by their opponents, and rejected by the public. Does the skepticism towards presidential power documented by our measures persist across time and presidents?

Likewise, how well do attitudes about unilateral power in the abstract relate to Americans' assessments of presidential power exercised in the real world? Though we address this concern in part in Chapter 6, we return to this question in this chapter. To what extent do Americans' attitudes towards unilateral power affect their evaluations of actions taken by presidents? And more generally, how do the patterns we identify correspond to public opinion towards other facets of presidential power?

Beyond allowing us to study the robustness of the findings presented in earlier chapters, addressing these issues has important implications for evaluating our theoretical argument. If, as we argued, public opinion is shaped by the skepticism of executive power expressed during the founding era and passed down through the intervening years, we would expect these attitudes to be expressed consistently over time. On the other hand, if beliefs about presidential power are driven more by political context and individual presidents, we would expect to observe variability across time. Extending our analysis across time further allows us to examine how accountability mechanisms may have operated vis-á-vis presidential power in periods during which partisan politics had a different character relative to today's polarization.

7.1 HISTORICAL POLLING DATA ON PRESIDENTIAL POWER

Addressing the above concerns is not straightforward, however. As we note in earlier chapters, aside from our work, neither pollsters nor scholars have dedicated much attention to survey questions addressing issues of presidential power. No time series of Americans' attitudes about unilateral power precedes our study. To make progress, we cast a wider net and study the public's evaluation of presidential power more generally.

We draw from the *iPoll* database housed at the Roper Center for Public Opinion Research, which makes available public polls conducted since polling began in the 1930s. Researchers have used polling data from as far back as the 1930s to study public opinion on major policy initiatives and evaluations of political figures (Berinsky 2006; Berinsky et al. 2011; Page and Shapiro 1992). Berinsky (2009), for instance, uses polling data during the Franklin Roosevelt administration to study foreign policy attitudes in the context of World War II. Baum and Kernell (2001) use historical polling data to examine how various constituencies evaluated President Roosevelt's job performance during his administration. And Caldeira (1987) uses a series of survey questions that appeared throughout 1937 to study how Americans evaluated President Roosevelt's court-packing proposal. However, apart from scholarship that uses presidential approval ratings (e.g., Erikson, MacKuen, and Stimson 2002; Page and Shapiro 1992), to our knowledge, researchers have not made use of the rich historical polling data to study the public's relationship to the presidency.

We study public opinion on issues of presidential power over the last eight decades. To do so, we conducted a comprehensive and exhaustive search of *iPoll* to identify every survey item on presidential power that has appeared on major surveys conducted by Gallup, Roper, Pew, Harris, and major news organizations since the presidency of Franklin Roosevelt. We identified these questions by initially searching for questions that referenced both "president" and "power." We read every question identified through this search and distinguished whether it concerned issues of presidential power. We identified 173 questions that met these criteria and that spanned the period from 1936 to 2020. These questions capture a range of politically salient issues over the last eight decades, including the following:

- Do you believe the President of the United States should have the power of a dictator over the country in time of war? (Gallup, 1938)
- Some people say the President should not be allowed to send troops overseas unless Congress approves it. Other people say the President should have the power to send troops overseas when he feels the situation calls for it. With which group do you agree? (Gallup, 1952)
- Some people have said that the only way to be sure that prices can be held down is to give the President the power to control prices when he feels it is necessary. Do you favor this power of presidential control or do you oppose it? (Harris, 1976)
- President Reagan would like the law changed to give presidents the right to reject individual items in large spending bills without having to reject the whole bill. Reagan says that would help him cut government spending and reduce the federal budget deficit. Critics say that would give the President too much power over how government money is spent. Do you favor or oppose giving the President the authority to reject individual items in spending bills without having to reject the entire bill? (ABC News, 1987)
- Do you think the president should or should not have the power to authorize the National Security Agency to monitor electronic communications of suspected terrorists without getting warrants, even if one end of the communication is in the United States? (Fox News, 2006)
- President (Donald) Trump says he has the absolute power to pardon himself, although he says he won't need to do that. Just your own best judgment, does a president have the power to pardon himself? (*USA Today*, 2018)

The full set of questions is shown in Tables E.1 through E.17 in the Appendix to this chapter.

The questions in our sample include many substantive issues and employ a wide range of response options. Rather than attempt to standardize the public's responses across these diverse issues with varying response options, we instead construct a measure that indexes *net support* for presidential power. *Net support* characterizes the pro-presidential power responses minus the anti-presidential power responses. Consider, for instance, the first question in our list. Thirty-one percent of respondents answered in the affirmative and 62 percent in the negative, with the remaining 7 percent reporting no opinion. Therefore, the net support for this question is negative 31. Likewise, for the last item in the list (Trump's power to pardon himself), 36 percent of respondents supported the president's use of emergency power to construct a border wall while 56 percent opposed it. The difference produces a net support score of negative 20. We calculate the net support for all the questions in our sample.

Using this measure, we study whether our findings on unilateral power in the contemporary era generalize to other aspects of presidential power in earlier years. As we show in Chapter 3, our survey data from 2014 to 2018 indicated that Americans expressed little support for unilateral power. For example, in January 2014, around 18 percent of our survey respondents approved of presidents making policy on their own, while 69 percent disapproved. Four years later, in January 2018, 12 percent of respondents approved, while 68 percent disapproved. Were we to construct a measure of net support for these measures, we would find that attitudes towards unilateral power were significantly underwater at negative 51 for the former and negative 56 for the latter. Do Americans view other dimensions of presidential power through a similarly negative lens? To what extent does public opinion about the presidency vary across time?

We note several limitations of our investigation. The questions we identify concern a range of topics related to presidential power, and neither the question content nor the response options are standardized across time. Because of these issues, we interpret the values of net support with some caution. Moreover, we would not expect to observe consistent values of net support across all the survey questions in our dataset because some of the questions invoke the concentration of presidential power to a greater degree than others. For example, citizens' views of unilateral powers may be starkly different when comparing congressionally authorized price controls with war powers. Likewise, we show in several chapters of this book that context may influence how the public evaluates unilateral power. Just as public opinion towards issues like environmental policy or foreign affairs would not show identical distributions of views across survey items, we do not expect to observe equal distributions of opinions across different questions related to presidential power. Instead, we focus on the aggregate patterns rather than the consistency of response patterns across questions.

7.2 ATTITUDES TOWARDS PRESIDENTIAL POWER, 1936 TO 2020

Figure 7.1 summarizes the results from this investigation. The plotted points indicate the net support for each survey question, which is listed in abbreviated form on the *y*-axis and can be cross-referenced with Tables E.1 through E.17 in the chapter appendix. Values further to the left on the *x*-axis indicate lower net support for presidential power, while values further to the right indicate greater net support. The vertical dashed line at zero indicates survey questions for which public opinion regarding presidential power was equally split. If the public consistently opposes presidential power, we expect to observe that the points fall to the left side of the dashed line. We plot the survey instruments along the *y*-axis from lowest to highest levels of net support.

Figure 7.1 reveals that net public opinion weighs strongly and consistently against presidential power. The average net support across all items is −16 and is statistically distinguishable from zero ($p < 0.01$). This pattern provides evidence that, on average, Americans oppose presidential power. In more than 70 percent of the cases – 123 of the 173 items – the public expresses a net negative sentiment towards presidential power. On the whole, therefore, Americans' deep-seated skepticism towards executive power is manifested in their attitudes towards specific proposals related to the exercise of presidential power over the last eighty years.

These patterns do not appear to be driven by any particular president, nor is there much evidence that public opposition to presidential power is confined to any particular historical period. We make these claims cautiously since there are large gaps in temporal coverage of the data. Yet net support for presidential power varies in magnitude for each president who appears in the sample multiple times. There is weak evidence of a linear time trend in attitudes, with a correlation of −0.23 ($p < 0.01$) between the year each poll was fielded and net support. We find some evidence of a cubic relationship across time in views about presidential power. When regressing net support on linear, quadratic, and cubic expressions of time, the coefficients for each term are statistically significant ($p < 0.01$, 0.02, and 0.05, respectively) and are positively, negatively, and positively signed, respectively. However, the coefficients are extremely small in magnitude for the higher-order terms. Given that different questions have been asked over time, moreover, we are reluctant to conclude that the evidence of temporal variation in attitudes towards presidential power is anything but weak. For the most part, then, Americans' opposition to an expansive view of presidential power – even in the context of specific presidents who would wield those powers – is a persistent feature of American politics.

We also use the historical polling questions described to extend analyses we present in Chapter 3, in which we show that Americans' attitudes about presidential power are distinct from their evaluations of presidents themselves. Here, we study the relationship between support for presidential powers and presidential approval at the time of the survey. We use data from Gallup to characterize the level of presidential approval that most closely preceded each of the polls shown in Figure 7.1. These figures are available for 145 of the 173 polling questions.[1]

The correlation between presidential evaluations and attitudes towards presidential power is displayed in Figure 7.2. The x-axis shows the percentage of respondents who approved of the president's job performance, and the y-axis shows net support for presidential power (also reported in Figure 7.1). If attitudes towards presidential power were mirrors of Americans' evaluations of the sitting president, we would observe that the points would line up on a diagonal forty-five-degree line from the bottom left to the top right.

As with our findings about the relationship between presidential approval and support for unilateral action in Chapter 3, we find a positive correlation between presidential approval and attitudes towards presidential power. Yet the correlation is noisy, weak, and not statistically distinguishable from zero. The public registered varying levels of net support for presidential power even when the sitting president had approval ratings around 70 percent. Overall, the correlation between the measures is 0.02, which implies that variation in presidential approval explains less than one-tenth of 1 percent of the variation in net support for presidential power. Consistent with our analyses of public opinion towards unilateral power during the Obama and Trump presidencies, our data show that Americans do not view the institution of the presidency through the same lens they use to evaluate incumbent presidents.

---

[1] The other twenty-five polling questions were asked prior to Gallup presidential approval ratings, before approval ratings had been surveyed for a new president, or in the transition period between presidents where the referent president was not clear.

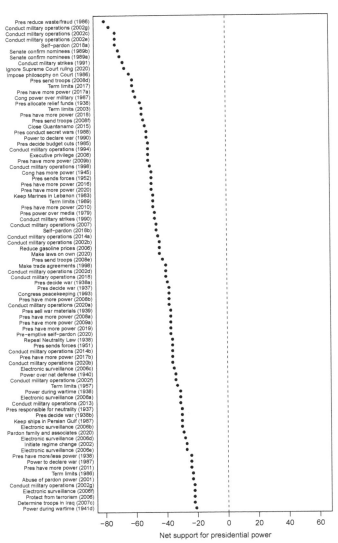

FIGURE 7.1 Americans' support for presidential power, 1936 to 2020 (continued to next page)

Note: The points represent Americans' net support for presidential power using data from *iPoll* on 173 survey questions related to presidential power. Each question was coded to distinguish support for from opposition to presidential power. Net support reflects difference between the percentage of respondents who supported presidential power and the percentage who opposed it. The zero mark on the *x*-axis indicates that as large a share of respondents opposed presidential power as supported it.

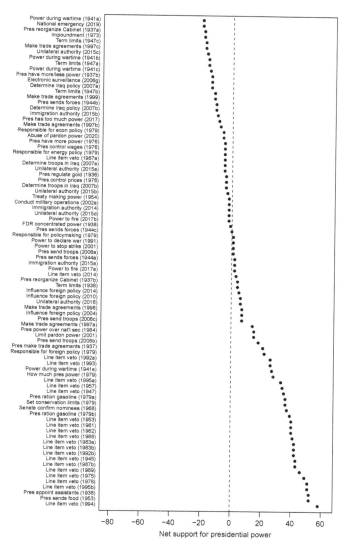

FIGURE 7.1 Americans' support for presidential power, 1936 to 2020 (continued from previous page)

Note: The points represent Americans' net support for presidential power using data from *iPoll* on 173 survey questions related to presidential power. Each question was coded to distinguish support for from opposition to presidential power. Net support reflects difference between the percentage of respondents who supported presidential power and the percentage who opposed it. The zero mark on the *x*-axis indicates that as large a share of respondents opposed presidential power as supported it.

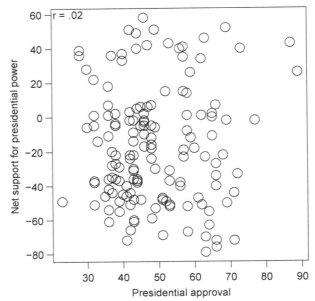

FIGURE 7.2 Presidential approval and support for presidential power, 1936 to 2020

Note: Figure shows data from *iPoll* surveys on presidential power and Gallup approval ratings from the beginning of the month in which each survey was conducted.

The patterns in Figure 7.1 suggest a potential question about sources of variation in aggregate attitudes towards presidential power. These data are not ideal for studying this question since the polling items invoke a range of aspects of presidential power and are not directly comparable across time. Consider, for example, that a 1936 Gallup poll asked respondents whether Congress should "renew the president's power to regulate the amount of gold in the dollar," which was supported by 35 percent of respondents and opposed by 39 percent. Likewise, a 2001 Fox News poll asked respondents whether the president "should have the power to stop a strike by a labor union," with which 44 percent agreed and 43 percent disagreed. How would responses to these questions have looked if they had been asked in 1953, or 1968, or 1989? We cannot say, and thus, we are reluctant to make comparisons across items that invoke qualitatively different aspects of presidential power and were asked in qualitatively different contexts.

We can say, however, that the data in Figure 7.1 provide evidence that Americans oppose presidential power in the context of military interventions. Some of the most negative values of *net support* were registered for questions about the president's war powers (1938 and 1987), power to send troops to Korea (1952), and the president's control over military conflict relative to Congress (1951, 1993, and 2002). These figures may be surprising given the influence of the two presidencies thesis (Canes-Wrone, Howell, and Lewis 2008; Wildavsky 1966). In a study of public support for the use of military force, Gelpi, Feaver, and Reifler (2009, 236) conclude that the public "does not give the president an unqualified blank check of support for costly military operations" but instead makes relatively rational decisions about the costs and benefits of conflict. Our data provide intriguing evidence for an even stronger conclusion: on balance, Americans oppose delegating warmaking power to the president. While the public may be more supportive of unilateral presidential action when national security is at stake, as we show in Chapter 3, this does not translate into unlimited support for the powers of the commander in chief.

Our reach back through the last eight decades of polling history provides evidence consistent with the survey data we have collected over the last several years. Americans generally do not support expansive views of presidential power and instead are likely to oppose them. These beliefs are not an artifact of recent political contestation – rather, they have been registered by the mass public at least back to the birth of modern polling. Moreover, the evidence suggests that these attitudes are distinct from Americans' evaluations of presidents themselves.

7.3 EVALUATING PRESIDENTIAL USES OF UNILATERAL ACTION

How do abstract attitudes towards unilateral power affect how Americans evaluate real-world outcomes that presidents have achieved on their own? In Chapter 6, we report experimental results that show survey respondents evaluate policies achieved through unilateral means less favorably than legislatively enacted outcomes. While these findings have a high level of internal validity due to our experimental design, questions remain about attitudes towards real-world policy outcomes implemented through unilateral action.

We can neither retroactively conduct experiments in times past nor manipulate how presidents have accomplished their policy goals. Instead, we study how attitudes towards unilateral action are associated with approval of policies that presidents have achieved through unilateral means. If the public's attitudes towards presidential power affect their evaluations of presidential initiatives, we expect to find a relationship between Americans' approval of unilateral power and their assessments of the policies presidents achieved with its use.

We study this question using data from three nationally representative surveys conducted by *The Economist/YouGov*. The surveys were conducted in February 2014, November 2014, and January 2016. The February 2014 and November 2014 surveys included one thousand respondents, and the January 2016 survey included two thousand respondents. Each of these surveys asked respondents whether they approved of a series of policies that presidents from Lincoln to Obama achieved through unilateral action. Twelve unique directives were included across the three surveys, with some of the presidential actions included on multiple surveys. Respondents were asked to evaluate "the executive order" that accomplished each of the following, with survey dates shown in parentheses:[2]

- Freed all slaves in the states that were in rebellion against the federal government (all three).
- Established the Works Progress Administration (February 2014).
- Created military exclusion zones during World War II and allowed for the forcible relocation of Americans of Japanese descent to internment camps (all three).
- Desegregated the US military (all three).
- Placed US steel mills facing a strike by union workers under federal control (February 2014, November 2014).
- Restricted all nongovernmental organizations that receive federal funding from performing or promoting abortion services as a method of family planning in foreign countries (February 2014, January 2016).
- Authorized enhanced interrogation techniques and established military tribunals to try foreign enemy combatants (February 2014, January 2016).
- Directed the Centers for Disease Control (CDC) to research the causes and prevention of gun violence (February 2014).
- Deferred deportation hearings for illegal immigrants who were brought into this country before they were sixteen years old, have lived in the United States for at least five years, must be younger than thirty,

---

[2] Although some of these actions were not executive orders, all of them were unilateral actions taken by a president.

and have graduated from high school in the United States or served in the US military (February 2014, January 2016).

- Require dealers who sell guns on the Internet and at gun shows to obtain a federal license and require those dealers to conduct background checks on potential buyers (January 2016).
- Require manufacturers and dealers to report to federal authorities if firearms were lost in transit between a manufacturer and a seller (January 2016).
- Instruct the FBI to hire 230 more additional examiners and other personnel to help process new background checks twenty-four hours a day, seven days a week (January 2016).

The questions were asked on a four-point scale that ranged from "approve strongly" to "disapprove strongly."

Figure 7.3 shows the distribution of evaluations across each of the items when collapsing "strongly" and "somewhat" evaluations. Support for these actions varied widely, from a low of 16 percent of respondents in the November 2014 survey who approved of Japanese internment to a high of 78 percent of respondents in the January 2016 survey who supported requiring gun manufacturers and dealers to report firearms that are lost in transit. Figure 7.3 also shows that the percentages of Americans who were unsure of their opinion varied across the items. While only 9 percent of respondents were unsure about their position with regard to conducting research on gun violence by the CDC, 30 percent of respondents on the November 2014 wave were unsure about their views on the nationalization of the steel industry. Overall, Figure 7.3 shows that Americans do not uniformly approve of or oppose unilateral actions but express varying levels of approval in ways that reflect, at least partly, their policy views. We study the degree to which Americans' views about executive power are also associated with these evaluations.

Importantly for our purposes, each survey also contained an item that evaluated respondents' support for presidential unilateral power. Before respondents were asked to evaluate the policies noted, they were asked whether they "approve or disapprove of presidents using executive orders." This variable was measured on a four-point scale ranging from "strongly approve" to "strongly disapprove," with an additional option for "not sure." Responses to this item are shown in Figure 7.4. For simplicity, we combined the "strongly" and "somewhat" response options. The patterns are consistent across each survey. For instance, 43 percent of respondents in the February 2014 survey "strongly approved"

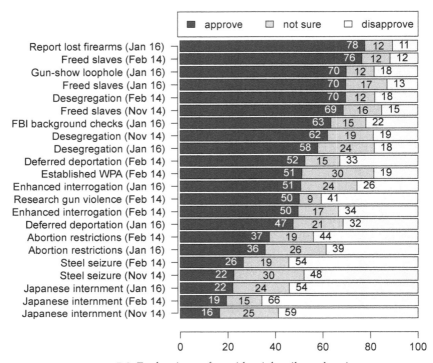

FIGURE 7.3 Evaluations of presidential unilateral actions
Note: Bars show the percentages of respondents who approved or disapproved of, or were unsure about, each presidential action.

or "somewhat approved" of presidents using executive orders, compared with 42 percent and 39 percent in the November 2014 and January 2016 surveys, respectively. The percentage of respondents who were "not sure" about their views was also consistent across time, ranging from 15 to 17 percent.

We note that the overall level of support for presidential power is higher than we document with our survey instrument in Chapter 3. While we cannot identify the source of the differences in levels of support between survey items, we can offer some speculations. First, it is unclear what comes to mind when Americans are asked about executive orders rather than – as our questions in Chapters 3 through 5 referenced – the use of presidential power to achieve policies without involving Congress. To the extent Americans know what an executive order is, they could envision anything from a mundane order amending the boundaries of a federally designated ecosystem reserve to the Emancipation Proclamation or the seizing of the steel industry. It is hard to say. Relatedly, it is unclear how many Americans know the details about executive orders. If many Americans do not know that executive orders can create policy outcomes without the involvement of Congress, these response patterns may over-state public support for presidential unilateralism. Second, our survey experiment in Chapter 3 shows that respondents were somewhat more supportive of unilateral power when the question wording included the term "executive order." The increase in support was approximately 6 per-centage points, though we do not want to overstate this finding because it was not statistically significant at conventional levels.

We use these data to study whether respondents who support pres-idents using executive orders provide more positive evaluations of uni-lateral policies relative to other respondents. To perform our analyses, we create a binary dependent variable that distinguishes whether respon-dents approved of each of the unilateral actions described above. Our key independent variable measures attitudes towards unilateral action using the data shown in Figure 7.4. We created a binary indicator for whether respondents approved of presidents using executive orders and excluded respondents who were "not sure." We note that this question appeared in the YouGov surveys before respondents were asked to evalu-ate each of the actions listed. The question order could prime respondents' attitudes towards each of the specific unilateral actions. For this reason, the observed magnitudes of the estimated relationships could overstate the true effects. However, we see variation *within individuals* in sup-port for the various unilateral actions. This pattern suggests that even those respondents who provided evaluations of individual directives that are consistent with their general approval of executive orders recog-nized that not all policies achieved through unilateral means are equally desirable.

We estimate a series of linear regressions for which approval of each unilateral policy is regressed on attitudes towards unilateral action. If the means through which policies are achieved affects how the public evaluates those policies, we expect to find a positive association between attitudes towards unilateral action and each of the policy outcomes listed. We also include respondents' ideological self-placements along a five-point scale ranging from "very conservative" (one) to "very liberal" (five) and their reported partisan affiliation along a seven-point scale from "strong Republican" (one) to "strong Democrat" (seven). Our substan-tive findings remain unchanged. We weight all our analyses to national population parameters.

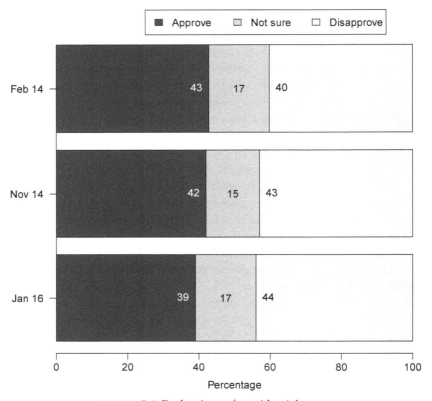

FIGURE 7.4 Evaluations of presidential power

Note: Bars show the percentages of respondents who approved or disapproved of, or were unsure about, presidents using executive orders.

This exercise constitutes a difficult test of the relationship between unilateral action and evaluations of policy outcomes. Our dependent variables measure attitudes towards high-profile historical events including the Emancipation Proclamation, Japanese internment during World War II, Truman's seizure of the steel industry that resulted in the *Youngstown Steel* case, and electronic surveillance conducted during the George W. Bush and Barack Obama presidencies. Given the significance of these actions, it may be surprising to find evidence of an association between respondents' contemporary attitudes towards unilateral action and their assessments of historical policy outcomes.

We emphasize, however, that this analysis falls squarely in the camp of observational research. Two primary limitations accompany this analysis. First, we did not (and could not) randomly assign respondents' attitudes towards unilateral power. The credibility of our analysis hinges on the selection on observables assumption. That is, if we omitted a variable that confounds the relationship between attitudes towards executive power and evaluations of presidential actions, our inferences regarding the nature of this relationship may be flawed. It is for this reason that we included respondents' partisanship and ideological self-identification, each of which could affect how they evaluate executive power and the policies achieved through its use. While it is not immediately obvious what other factors may serve as potential confounders, we acknowledge our vulnerability to this critique.

Second, it is worth considering the relevant counterfactual. Would our survey respondents have expressed higher levels of approval of the president's actions if the president had *not* issued a unilateral directive, or had instead worked with Congress to pass legislation? Our experimental analyses in Chapter 6 attempted to distinguish these possibilities, yet our analyses in the observational setting cannot.

7.4 EVALUATIONS OF EXECUTIVE ORDERS

We present the results from our analyses graphically in Figure 7.5; the full tables of coefficients are shown in Tables E.18 through E.20 in the Appendix to Chapter 7. The figure shows the differences in the estimated probability of supporting each unilateral directive based on whether respondents approved or disapproved of presidents using executive orders. The horizontal lines show the 95 percent confidence intervals.[3] Negative values along the x-axis indicate decreased support for the policy among respondents who disapprove of executive orders. The dashed vertical line shows the null hypothesis of no relationship between general attitudes about unilateral power and evaluations of specific presidential directives.

As Figure 7.5 shows, for each presidential action, we find that attitudes towards unilateral action are associated with evaluations of policies achieved through its use. Respondents who disapproved of executive orders were less supportive of twenty-one of the twenty-two policies we studied. The differences were statistically significant for seventeen of the twenty-two policies. Interestingly, of the five that were statistically insignificant, two concerned evaluations of Japanese internment and two

---

[3] The confidence intervals are generally smaller for estimates based on questions asked on the January 2016 survey, as the larger sample size reduces the uncertainty.

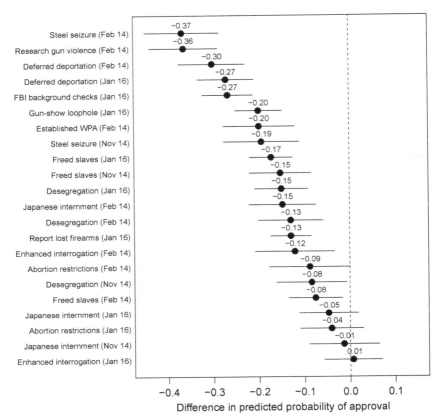

FIGURE 7.5 How attitudes towards unilateral action affect evaluations of previous executive actions

Note: The points represent the differences in the predicted probability of approving of each unilateral action between respondents who approve and disapprove of presidents issuing executive orders. The *x*-axis shows the decrease in estimated approval for the executive action among respondents who disapprove of presidents issuing executive orders. The horizontal lines represent the 95 percent confidence intervals. Estimates are based on linear regression models presented in Tables E.18 through E.20 in the Appendix to Chapter 7. The dashed vertical line shows the null hypothesis of no relationship between general attitudes about unilateral power and evaluations of specific presidential directives.

others concerned restrictions on the use of federal funds for abortion services. The estimate is also not statistically significant for the question about enhanced interrogation techniques that appeared on the January 2016 survey.

For the other questions about presidential directives, however, the reductions in support for the policy outcomes were statistically and substantively significant. For instance, the difference in the probability of approving of an executive order requiring the Centers for Disease Control and Prevention to research the causes of gun violence was 36 percentage points higher for a respondent who approved of presidents using executive orders relative to those who disapproved of presidents exercising that power. These patterns apply even among directives that are more publicly salient and/or politically controversial; for instance, the difference in supporting deportation deferrals was 30 percentage points in the February 2014 survey and 27 percentage points in the January 2016 survey.

The results shown in Figure 7.5 demonstrate that attitudes towards unilateral power in the abstract shape how voters evaluate specific policies that presidents have achieved through unilateral means. Not only do voters penalize presidential candidates for advocating policy change through unilateral rather than legislative means, as our experiment demonstrates in Chapter 6, but voters who express opposition to unilateral action are also less supportive of policies that are accomplished unilaterally. In addition, the survey results suggest that the insights from our experimental analysis generalize to current and past presidents and policy outcomes. Since we lack a true counterfactual policy outcome accomplished through non-unilateral means, as we note previously, we present these results with caution. Nevertheless, the results shown in Figure 7.5 provide evidence that the public judges presidents' policy accomplishments on the basis of their evaluations of not only the outcomes presidents achieved but also *how* those policies were achieved.

7.5 REVISITING PRESIDENTIAL CONTROVERSIES

Our evidence in this chapter portrays an American public that expresses skeptical views towards presidential power. The public registers these beliefs not just towards the use of unilateral directives but also in response to more general attempts to bolster presidential authority. Despite differences in presidents, political context, economic conditions, not to mention question wordings and response options, these patterns are consistent with what we show in our more controlled survey experimental results in previous chapters.

We explore how these findings provide new insight into political controversies over presidential power. Previous research has studied public reactions towards presidents' attempts to expand their power. As we mentioned in Section 7.1, Caldeira (1987) investigates public opinion towards Franklin Roosevelt's court-packing plan in 1937. The article makes a plausible argument that both judicial behavior and media coverage of the Supreme Court contributed to the public's eventual opposition to Roosevelt's plan. Our theoretical account, however, could suggest an alternative story. Namely, public opposition to additional power for Roosevelt vis-á-vis the courts was due to the skepticism towards presidential power that we document in this book. Unfortunately, data that would allow us to distinguish these two accounts do not exist, yet our explanation could provide new insight into how we understand this historical phenomenon.

We apply our argument to provide fresh perspective on four other historical cases in which presidential power was contested: the Brownlow Commission and Franklin Roosevelt's Reorganization Plan; Harry Truman's nationalization of steel mills; the Iran-Contra affair during Ronald Reagan's presidency; and George W. Bush's use of electronic surveillance during the global war on terror. Each of these cases is well known, and we do not provide a full historical accounting of their background details. Our intent is not to revise existing historical accounts of the politics that accompanied these events. Instead, we hope to show how debates over, and reactions to, each of these phenomena reflect the public's attitudes about presidential power.

7.5.1 Reorganizing the Executive Branch

It may be an understatement that the topic of administrative reform "lacks sex appeal" (Polenberg 1979, 45) for the American public. Yet administrative reform was the subject of salient debates between the president and Congress during Franklin Roosevelt's second term in office. Public opposition to Roosevelt's plans played a crucial role in curtailing President Roosevelt's efforts to centralize government administration in the White House.

The size and scope of the federal government expanded dramatically with the New Deal programs inaugurated in Roosevelt's first term. But as the administrative state grew, Roosevelt found it more challenging to control and oversee. To counteract these tendencies and bring about more effective administration, in 1936, Roosevelt appointed the President's Committee on Administrative Management to study the issue and propose a series of recommendations. In 1937, the committee issued the Brownlow Report (so named after its chair, Louis Brownlow), which contained five principal recommendations (for a summary, see Polenberg 1979, 36). Roosevelt submitted his reorganization plan to Congress in

February 1937 that reflected the measures recommended by the committee. Yet more than a year passed before the Senate passed a bill that substantially diluted the measures Roosevelt had sought. Later that spring, the Senate bill – and Roosevelt's reorganization plan – was killed by the House (for further discussion of congressional debates, see Dearborn 2019b). While Congress passed a revised reorganization plan in 1939, the bill was authored by members of Congress while ignoring the proposals of the Brownlow Committee and thus was much less sweeping in scope than Roosevelt had hoped.

Despite winning more than 60 percent of the vote along with an Electoral College landslide in 1936, Roosevelt's reorganization plan failed to generate much public support. Upon the plan's release, the public was generally cool to Roosevelt's proposal. A Gallup poll conducted in January 1937 (and reflected in Figure 7.1) showed that only 43 percent of Americans approved of "giv[ing] the President power to enlarge the cabinet and reorganize government offices which would be under his supervision" while 39 percent were opposed and 19 percent registered "no opinion." The public's unease with its constitutional implications may have contributed to the lack of support. According to the same poll, only 25 percent of respondents agreed that the reorganization plan was "in line with the powers the Founders of the Constitution meant the President to have." Forty-one percent said that the reorganization plan was inconsistent with the intentions of the Constitution while 31 percent had no opinion.

These numbers may have represented the high-water mark on this issue, as the president's opposition successfully mobilized the public to their cause. When the Brownlow Report was first released, the *Washington Post* criticized it for misappropriating powers reserved for Congress to the presidency (Arnold 2007, 1034). Other critics went further and cast the reorganization plan as tantamount to tyranny. According to Polenberg (1979, 37), "enemies of the Roosevelt administration succeeded in whipping up public hysteria by claiming that reorganization would mean one-man rule." The National Committee to Uphold Constitutional Government, along with state and national chapters of the Chamber of Commerce, launched campaigns opposing the bill. Father Coughlin made his opposition to the bill his "leading cause" on his radio shows (Ciepley 2006, 140–142). At Coughlin's urging (*New York Times* 1938a), demonstrators descended upon Washington the day before the House vote to protest the reorganization plan. Upon the bill's failure, the *New York Times* (1938b, 16) concluded that it was due to congressional "revolt against further concentration of personal authority in the office of the Presidency."

These actions appeared to register with the public. In March 1938, a month before the House vote, only 17 percent of Americans believed that the president "should have more power ... than he now has" compared with 42 percent who thought he should have "less power." And in May 1938, after opponents in the House defeated the bill, only 22 percent of Americans in a Roper/Fortune Survey reported supporting the president's reorganization plan – despite Roosevelt receiving a 55 percent approval rating in the same survey.

The American public pays little attention to administrative politics. Yet public interest can be piqued at the right moment. Roosevelt's reorganization plan – and the constitutional consternation that accompanied it – appeared to awaken the public to mobilize against the president. Despite the president's popular support, Americans seemed to be persuaded that the reorganization plan threatened the separation of powers and concentrated too much authority in the presidency. Members of Congress, including many of the president's fellow Democrats, thus had political cover to assert their own institutional prerogatives.

7.5.2   Steel Seizure

Executive Order 10340 looms large in the history of American politics. President Truman issued the directive in April 1952, and with it, federalized ten steelmakers to ensure that production of materials during the Korean War would be uninterrupted in the face of a threatened strike over wages. The steel owners sued Truman, and two months later, they prevailed as the Supreme Court handed down a landmark decision in jurisprudence on presidential authority. The concurring opinion issued by Justice Robert H. Jackson set forth the ingredients of a test for deciding questions of presidential power that is still influential today.

Part of the justification for Jackson's opinion provides an important context about the controversy over steel seizure. In 1947, the Republican-controlled Congress passed the Taft-Hartley Act (formally, the Labor Management Relations Act of 1947) over Truman's veto. The bill enacted new restrictions on labor union activity and received significant Democratic support at both its passage and the vote to override Truman's veto. Congressional debates over Taft-Hartley made clear that the bill did not authorize government seizure of property during labor disputes. In issuing his executive order, Truman bypassed several other sources of authority and instead claimed inherent power to ensure "a continuing and uninterrupted supply of steel" during a national emergency. In doing so, Truman rejected the constraints enumerated by legislation that had received supermajority support in Congress only five years earlier.

In this context of institutional conflict, the public's immediate response to Truman's action seemed to be ambivalence. A poll conducted by Opinion Research Corporation in the days following the executive order found that a slim majority (51 percent) approved of "the President [ordering] the government to seize, or take over, the steel companies," with 43 percent disapproving. Yet the public expressed more evident opposition to the government using the seizure to unilaterally increase workers' wages despite the steel companies' opposition. Only 28 percent believed that such a move would be "fair" while 62 percent said it would not be fair. As the month went on, however, public support for the directive itself waned. A Gallup poll of 1,319 Americans three weeks after the executive order showed that only 35 percent approved, with 43 percent disapproving.

Historical accounts argue that the nature of the administration's claims to presidential power mobilized public opposition to Truman's actions. According to Hah and Lindquist (1975, 595), Assistant Attorney General Holmes Baldridge, who presented the government's argument in district court, "laid claim to unlimited presidential power ... [and] severely discredit[ed] the administration's case before the public." Public opinion polls support this reading, with a growing disapproval of Truman's action reflecting, at least in part, Americans' opposition to Truman's exercise of power. The Opinion Research Corporation poll asked respondents what they believed were "the best arguments against government seizure (of the steel companies)." Nearly a quarter (24 percent) of respondents expressed concern that it interfered with "free enterprise." Yet a plurality of respondents (by 1 percentage point) indicated that the best argument against Truman's steel seizure directive was that it was an "undemocratic way to handle [the] situation." Another 6 percent said that the best argument was that "Government would have too much power," and 5 percent said that it was "unconstitutional." A poll conducted by Gallup later in April showed similar patterns. In response to a similarly worded question, about a fifth of respondents (21 percent) reported that the best argument against the action was that it was some version of "illegal," "unconstitutional," or that "[the] President exceeded [his] power." Another 11 percent of respondents indicated that it was "undemocratic" or "like a dictatorship, just like Russia." Fewer respondents focused on government interference with business (8 percent) or a generic concern about enlarged government power (8 percent).

At the end of April, Judge David Pine of the District Court for the District of Columbia issued an injunction that prohibited the federal government from occupying the steel mills it had seized. Many newspapers reacted favorably and reflected the sentiments apparent in public opinion polls. Editorial pages, for instance, "showered encomiums on [Judge Pine] for upholding the traditional concept of constitutional government" and viewed Pine's decision as the triumph of law over the president's attempt to "rule by fiat" (Marcus 1994, 130–133). The reaction in the public sphere appeared to be driven less by principled opposition to Truman's policy decision and more by the president's use of power outside of constitutionally prescribed and popularly accepted bounds.

The *Youngstown* decision is regarded as a "rare instance" in which the Supreme Court stepped in to "restore the executive-legislative balance arrived at in 1947 and required by the Constitution" (Matheson 2009, 79). This "restoration" was not only of concern to constitutional scholars. According to Stebbins (1971), as the Korean War grew more unpopular, the public had begun to lament the absence of constitutional restraints on presidential power. Therefore, the public "welcomed the decision in the Steel Case which they believed harkened back to older, more concrete, more comprehensible constitutional values" (Stebbins 1971, 21). The story of the steel seizure case lays bare the politics of power: not only must presidents be concerned with how their policy objectives will be received, but they also must consider the reaction to their use of authority.

7.5.3   Iran-Contra

In November 1986, news broke of a secret deal involving the United States, Iran, and rebels in Nicaragua. For most of the Reagan administration, American officials had sold arms to the Iranian government. The funds provided by Iran were subsequently diverted by Reagan administration officials to aid the Contras, a rebel group seeking to overthrow the socialist Nicaraguan government.

These transactions explicitly violated US policies. The arms sales to Iran occurred despite the embargo President Carter had imposed on Iran in November 1979 and that had continued as the stated policy under President Reagan. Under Reagan's administration, officials pressured other nations to do the same. In exchange for weapons, the Iranian government facilitated the release of seven Americans held hostage in Lebanon. In the case of the Contras, the Boland Amendment passed by Congress (and signed by President Reagan) had restricted the use of US funds in Nicaragua and explicitly outlawed funding the government's overthrow.

The revelation became arguably the biggest scandal of the Reagan presidency. Ten days after news initially broke, Reagan gave a prime-time address from the Oval Office, where he acknowledged the arms deals but denied that they were performed in exchange for American hostages. In a subsequent Oval Office address delivered in March 1987, Reagan acknowledged that arms had been traded for hostages but denied any knowledge that funds had been diverted to aid the Contras. Testimony of other senior officials, including National Security Council member Oliver North, confirmed that funds had been redirected to the Contra rebels, though whether Reagan had direct knowledge of, or involvement with, these efforts remain contested.

Even before the scandal became news, Americans strongly disapproved of both transactions implicated in it. In August 1983, a Roper poll found that only 6 percent of respondents supported selling arms to Iran, while 83 percent opposed it. An NBC News/*Wall Street Journal* survey in October 1986 found that only 31 percent of respondents believed "the Reagan Administration should make an exception to its policy of not negotiating with terrorists to help free the Americans held hostage in Lebanon" while 57 percent opposed this view. Americans had similarly dim opinions about supporting the Contras. A June 1986 ABC News/*Washington Post* poll showed that only 29 percent of Americans favored "the U.S. granting military and other aid" to the Contras while 62 percent opposed this measure.

Public opinion moved swiftly against Reagan upon news of the scandal. This reaction occurred on two fronts. First, public support for the administration's policies only worsened after the scandal came to light. An ABC News poll conducted the week after the scandal broke showed that only 17 percent of respondents approved "of the U.S. shipping arms to Iran (as authorized by President Reagan) as a way to get American hostages held in Lebanon released" while 79 percent disapproved it. Likewise, only 13 percent of Americans surveyed in November 1986 approved of using proceeds from the arms sales to fund the Contras. This number was virtually identical in a Gallup poll conducted in December 1986. According to a CBS News/*New York Times* poll in November 1986, an even smaller proportion of Americans (8 percent) believed that providing aid to the Contras was "so important" that "it should be done even without congressional approval."

Second, Reagan's popularity took a sharp hit in the polls. His approval ratings dropped 15 to 20 percentage points upon news of the affair (Brody and Shapiro 1989). According to Gallup, Reagan's approval rating at the end of October was 63 percent; by early December, this number had dropped to 47 percent, where it hovered for the next twenty months.

At least part of Americans' reactions to the Iran-Contra scandal may have reflected the belief that the president and his administration had exceeded their authority. For instance, a Gallup poll in December 1986 asked Americans to consider various aspects of the Iran-Contra scandal that bothered them. A significant majority (71 percent) of survey respondents reported that it bothered them "a lot" that that administration had "[gone] around the laws or will of Congress."[4] Similarly, an NBC News/*Wall Street Journal* poll in January 1987 showed that 60 percent of respondents believed that "officials in the Reagan administration broke ... laws when they sold arms to Iran" while only 19 percent thought they did not. And 59 percent of respondents in the same poll believed that Reagan officials broke laws when they supplied the Contras with military assistance.

Political elites also expressed these sentiments. In President Reagan's weekly radio address on November 29, 1986, he urged his colleagues and the nation to move past the Iran issue. Senator Daniel Patrick Moynihan took the unusual step of providing a Democratic response, in which he encouraged the president to address the Iran issue more thoroughly, asserting that "laws [had] been broken" (Boyd 1986). Around the same time, President Reagan convened a commission, chaired by former Senator John Tower, to investigate the administration's handling of the Iran-Contra affair. After the Tower Commission released its report in February 1987, Democrats and Republicans alike criticized the administration's actions and linked them to core constitutional principles. New York's Democratic Governor Mario Cuomo, for instance, responded that "our leaders have forfeited credibility and flouted the rule of law. No matter what else you say, it's sad and dangerous." Republican Elliot Richardson, who served in four cabinet positions during the Nixon and Ford administrations, likewise characterized Iran-Contra as "a White House operation carried out without an adequate sense of accountability to the American people and the Congress" (both quoted in *New*

---

4 Notably, this figure was substantially higher than the percentage of respondents (58) who were bothered "a lot" that the administration had "[failed] to consult and inform Congress and other officials" about their actions.

York Times 1987). Lawrence Walsh, a former assistant attorney general in the Eisenhower administration, was appointed independent counsel and oversaw the Iran-Contra investigation. In recounting his experiences in this role, Walsh (1997, 517) emphasized that "respect for the rule of law" was "the most important concept guiding [his] approach."

The "evasion hypothesis" (e.g., Deering and Maltzman 1999) posits that presidents will use unilateral actions to circumvent a Congress that opposes the president's policy preferences. In the case of both the arms-for-hostages deal and the diversion of funds to the Contras, Reagan officials pursued goals that directly contradicted existing US policy and ran contrary to laws passed by Congress. While public opinion generally opposed these policies, the negative response to the Iran-Contra affair also reflected their objections to the administration's use of power to achieve them. Presidents may not be able to "evade" Congress during periods of interbranch disagreement without courting public pushback precisely for attempting an end-run around Congress.

7.5.4 Wartime Presidents and the Limits of Power

The attacks of September 11, 2001, shocked the nation and the world. The Bush administration's response to the attacks reignited long-simmering debates about the nature of presidential power. While these debates focused in no small part on the content and goals of the Bush strategy, they were also fundamentally about questions of power. Yet public opinion figures relatively little in scholarship on presidential war powers. A large body of research considers the president's influence over warmaking vis-à-vis Congress (Howell and Pevehouse 2007; Kriner 2010) and debates the contributions of war to presidential power (Corwin 1947; Howell, Jackman, and Rogowski 2013; Rossiter 2005 [1948]; Schlesinger 1973). While scholars have studied public support for wartime efforts (Berinsky 2009; Mueller 1973; Zaller 1992), none of this research examines how Americans evaluate presidential wartime *powers*. In the case of the Afghanistan and Iraq wars, the available evidence suggests that the public's general views about war and peace were not the only factors that shaped their responses; *how* presidential administrations waged the wars played an important role.

Even after the 9/11 attacks, when President Bush's approval ratings reached historic heights, Americans did not grant carte blanche support for presidential war powers. In the summer and fall of 2002, as debate raged over military intervention in Iraq, the public did not believe that

President Bush alone should get to decide whether and how to undertake activity in Iraq. In a national poll conducted in August 2002, CBS News asked respondents whether "the President should have to get the approval of Congress before taking military action against Iraq to try and remove Saddam Hussein from power, or should he be able to make that decision himself?" Nearly three-quarters (71 percent) responded that Bush should have to receive congressional approval before intervening in Iraq while only 27 percent said that the decision should be the president's alone. Similar polls conducted by CBS/*New York Times*, Knowledge Networks, and Hart-Teeter Research Companies in September 2002 showed that at least 60 percent, and usually more, of respondents agreed that warmaking power should not be delegated solely to the president. And, in a September 2002 poll conducted by Gallup, respondents weighed in about the potential terms of congressional approval. More than half (51 percent) of respondents *opposed* Congress granting President Bush "unlimited authority to use military action against Iraq whenever he feels it is necessary." The reluctance to give Bush authority for conducting war was not merely a reflection of their opposition to military intervention. In the week after the 9/11 attacks, for example, Pew Research Center (2001) found that 82 percent of respondents supported military action against the 9/11 attackers, with 77 percent still supporting military action even if there would be "thousands of casualties." Despite high levels of presidential approval and the steps he was contemplating, Americans did not support delegating full authority for wartime decision-making to President Bush.

President Bush did not take the nation to war without congressional involvement. Though Bush did not secure a declaration of war from Congress, he did receive formal authorization to conduct military operations against the 9/11 perpetrators and, later, the government of Iraq. Bush used this authority to plunge the country into twin wars in Afghanistan and Iraq.

But domestic political trouble had not been far behind. At least as early as March 2003, large protests erupted against the Iraq war. The 2004 Republican National Convention in New York was the site of one of the largest demonstrations in US history and was also motivated by opposition to the war in Iraq. Revelations of the torture of detainees by Americans in the Abu Ghraib prison and the killing of Iraqi civilians by American contractors further inflamed public opinion against the war and Bush's administration of it.

Domestic political pressure further accelerated near the end of 2005. This time, at issue was not the administration's conduct of the war, but rather the president's assertion of authority. The *New York Times* revealed that the Bush administration had authorized the National Security Agency to monitor Americans' emails and phone calls without first receiving a warrant. According to the *New York Times*, official sources had "questioned whether the surveillance [had] stretched, if not crossed, constitutional limits on legal searches" (Risen and Lichtblau 2005, A1). Congress had not authorized the domestic surveillance program, and Bush officials declined to request it from Congress due to concerns they would not allow it.

As news reports revealed the extent of the Bush administration's secret surveillance program, the public largely rejected the president's authority to implement it. For context, consider that the public during this period supported security-oriented policies that would prevent terrorism and gave the administration fairly high marks for its work. A Pew Research Center survey in 2006 found that 55 percent of respondents believed that "the government had not gone far enough to protect the country" while only 26 percent thought that government had "gone too far restricting civil liberties." An October 2005 Pew Research Center survey, meanwhile, found that 67 percent of respondents – including majorities of both parties – believed that the Bush administration was doing "very well" or "fairly well" at reducing the threat of terrorism.

Against this backdrop, 53 percent of respondents in an NBC News/*Wall Street Journal* poll conducted in January 2006 said that the Bush administration "should be required to get a court order before conducting these wiretaps" while 41 percent believed the government "should be able to wiretap without a court order." Polls conducted in February found similar patterns for related items, with 41 percent of respondents in a CBS News poll agreeing that "the President has the legal authority to authorize wiretaps without a court warrant." In comparison, 52 percent believed he did not have the legal authority to do so. In response to a poll conducted by the Quinnipiac University Polling Institution, 55 percent expressed the view that a court order was required to "use wiretaps to listen to telephone calls and read emails between suspected terrorists in other countries and some people in the United States," while 42 percent said wiretaps could be used without a court order. Legal battles over the surveillance program directly referenced limits on presidential authority. In a district court ruling on *ACLU v. NSA* (493 F.3d 644), for instance, Judge Anna Diggs Taylor ordered that the surveillance program be discontinued, writing: "There are no hereditary Kings in America and no powers not created by the Constitution. So all 'inherent powers' must derive from that Constitution."

The program likewise attracted the attention of members of Congress. Representative John Conyers, Jr. (2007) included it as one of the two "high crimes" for which he believed the Bush administration should have been impeached. Others expressed similar views and specifically implicated President Bush's alleged abuses of power. For instance, former Representative Elizabeth Holtzman (2006) argued that: "The time has come to call for the impeachment of President Bush. Any President who maintains he is above the law – and acts repeatedly on that belief – seriously endangers our constitutional system of government."

Holtzman's arguments were supported by sizable majorities of the public. In August 2006, a CBS News/*New York Times* poll asked Americans whether it was "a good idea or a bad idea for the president to have the authority to make changes in the rights usually guaranteed by the Constitution." Only 36 percent replied that it was a "good idea" with 59 percent expressing the view that it was a "bad idea." Far from granting the president unaccountable authority to conduct wars abroad on his own terms, Americans recoiled at the notion that wars – specifically the Iraq war – fundamentally reshaped the bounds on presidential power.

The conduct of the war also left an impression on Americans' beliefs about the Bush administration's legacy concerning presidential war powers. In August 2007, The Parker Group asked respondents,

Bush will leave office having established precedents for new war powers unavailable to his predecessors and possibly attractive to his successors. These new war powers could be beyond control of both Congress and the Courts. How concerned are you that the developments after Bush leaves office will lead to the loss of our democracy?

A plurality of respondents (43 percent) said that they were "extremely concerned" with another 28 percent reporting that they were "somewhat concerned." Only 20 percent said that they were "not concerned."

The wars that began in the aftermath of 9/11 suggest several speculative conclusions. First, in survey after survey, Americans made clear their opposition to presidency-dominated war efforts. Even in matters of war, the public does not accept presidents' claims to dictator-like powers. Second, these attitudes appear to be linked to Americans' beliefs in the principles enshrined in the Constitution. Matters of war and peace, just like the domestic policy debates we have discussed throughout this book, should be decided through processes that give authority to both the president *and* Congress. Third, Americans can be mobilized in opposition to not just policies they oppose but also when officeholders – here, the president – use powers in ways they reject.

We cannot say how these data may have looked if history had taken a different path. But our theoretical perspective sheds light on the politics of presidential power and provides a new lens through which to interpret the post–9/11 wars and public evaluations of the authority claimed by President Bush to conduct them.

7.6 DISCUSSION

This chapter reinforces and extends the analyses from our earlier chapters. Using a wide range of polls from the 1930s to today, we show that Americans' skepticism towards executive power appears to extend back at least to the birth of the modern presidency under Franklin Roosevelt. Rather than being a product of our current political context, this skepticism seems to be a fundamental aspect of American political culture passed down from the nation's founding.

Moreover, we show that Americans apply these attitudes when holding presidents accountable for the policy outcomes presidents produce. Americans are more likely to disapprove of specific presidential directives when they disapprove of presidents' use of unilateral power in the abstract. These findings persist even when accounting for the public's political orientations vis-à-vis the partisan and ideological nature of the directives presidents have issued.

The findings presented in this chapter provide a comprehensive assessment of Americans' attitudes towards presidential power and its use. They also offer consistent and robust evidence that, far from exercising power free from the constraints of political accountability, presidents are routinely evaluated by the American public based not only on what they accomplish, but on how they accomplish it. The public does not have a high level of tolerance for the use of unilateral presidential directives. Nor does the public support measures that would result in a greater concentration of authority within the presidency. These attitudes as expressed through surveys are not random, ill-informed, or mirror reflections of popular support for the president; rather, they reflect the impressions of a public that is, and historically has been, readily mobilized to counter presidents who seek to push too far or too fast.

8

Attitudes towards Executive Power in a Comparative Context

Thus far, we have examined attitudes towards presidential power in the United States. In this chapter, we consider attitudes towards executive power around the world. In shifting to a cross-national analysis, we address several theoretical and empirical questions that we cannot answer by studying the United States alone. First, a cross-country approach allows us to situate Americans' orientations towards executive power within the range of opinions held by citizens of other countries, each with their distinct histories and institutional and political contexts. As Posner and Vermeule (2010, 188) suggest, resistance to unilateral power "might be a culturally specific phenomenon, unique to the United States."

Second, we study how these contextual features are associated with country-level variation in attitudes towards executive power. As we discuss in Chapter 4, if the aggregate distribution of Americans' support for the rule of law were different, we would expect to observe different patterns in aggregate attitudes towards presidential power. While we cannot run that experiment, we take advantage of variation in support for the rule of law across countries to evaluate how well this prediction is borne out.

Third, we evaluate how our findings about the individual-level predictors of support for executive power in the American context compare to the relationships found in other countries. This analysis allows us to characterize the generalizability of our findings and situate our results for the United States relative to other contexts.

Fourth, and finally, we relate attitudes about executive power to more fundamental questions about support for democratic governance. We focus particularly on evaluating the potential for mass publics to serve as a backstop against the erosion of democratic practices by power-seeking executives. A cross-national approach to studying this question is particularly helpful given the lack of institutional variation in the US context (as discussed by Cameron 2009). In addressing these research questions, we contribute to other scholarship on cross-national attitudes towards political institutions including the judiciary (e.g., Bartels and Kramon 2020; Driscoll and Nelson 2018; Gibson, Caldeira, and Baird 1998) and chief executives (e.g., Bratton 2007; Dulani and Tengatenga 2020).

8.1 VIEWS OF EXECUTIVE POWER AND DEMOCRACY

The election and presidency of Donald Trump prompted numerous indictments of the administration as engaging in nascent authoritarianism. These accounts portray the presidents' supporters as complicit in Trump's accumulation of power (a hypothesis we explore in Chapter 5). These critiques mostly ignore the possibility that mass publics might have meaningful attitudes towards executive power, which could be mobilized against the president by political parties and other organized groups. In previous chapters, we find evidence that takes issue with these pessimistic conclusions. We find that Americans view presidential power with skepticism, and that these attitudes persist even as their political alignment changes with respect to the president currently in office.

But the United States is not alone in being viewed as having a power-seeking chief executive who gives rise to fears over democratic stability. In places such as Turkey, Hungary, and Poland, elected executives have taken steps to consolidate their power and enact antidemocratic reforms. These actions have alarmed scholars and observers over concerns of democratic backsliding.

Democratic institutions are vulnerable to the political ambitions of would-be authoritarians. Subversion of democracy is perhaps most under threat from elected officials rather than through military coups. The most prominent version of this perspective expresses concern that citizens are ill-equipped to defend democratic institutions against erosion from within. Levitsky and Ziblatt (2018, 19) consider the possibility that "the fate of a government lies in the hands of its citizens. If people hold democratic values, democracy will be safe. If citizens are open to authoritarian appeals, then, sooner or later, democracy will be in trouble." But they conclude: "This view is wrong." Instead, political power is a mirror of popular support (Levitsky and Ziblatt 2018, 191). The implicit assumption is that voters make political decisions that reflect a leader's popularity. Like the partisan perspective outlined earlier, this view permits little room for voters to have meaningful preferences about political power and procedures – and if they do, these preferences play no role in voters' evaluations of political officials and the outcomes they produce.

We show that in the United States, Americans do not reflexively support greater presidential power as their presidents' popularity rises. In this context, at least, the claims in Levitsky and Ziblatt (2018) are not well-supported by our analyses. But what of the rest of the world? Are attitudes about executive prerogative a pure reflection of individual support for the president or prime minister in power? Is the United States unique in having low levels of support for executive power that reflect core values about the rule of law?

8.2 ATTITUDES TOWARDS EXECUTIVE POWER AROUND THE WORLD

Many studies of presidentialism begin with a consideration of the stability and duration of presidential systems vis-à-vis parliamentary systems (Carey and Shugart 1998; Cheibub 2007; Linz 1990; Mainwaring and Shugart 1997a; Przeworski et al. 2000; Stepan and Skach 1994). One of the central tenets of presidential systems is that chief executives possess a "strong claim to democratic, even plebiscitarian, legitimacy" (Linz 1990, 53). This legitimacy may "bring on a refusal to acknowledge the limits of the mandate that even a majority – to say nothing of a mere plurality – can claim as democratic justification for the enactment of its agenda" (Linz 1990, 61). As a result of the nature of presidential representation, "compromise, negotiation, and power-sharing" occur only as "necessary antinomies – deviations from the rules of the system" (Linz 1990, 68). Though not the only critique of presidentialism, fear of executive overreach is one of the primary wellsprings of concern in the debate over the merits of executive systems.

As with studies of the American presidency, one dominant strand of comparative research on executive power considers the institutional conditions under which presidents exercise unilateral powers, especially as it relates to the legislative branch (Carey and Shugart 1998; Cheibub 2007; Cheibub, Przeworski, and Saiegh 2004; Mainwaring and Shugart 1997b; Palanza 2019). Often, these analyses probe whether executive actions better reflect a seizure of power from or delegation of authority by the legislature (Carey and Shugart 1998) and the specific conditions under which conflicts emerge (Shugart and Carey 1992).

Despite a large literature on public attitudes towards governing institutions in comparative context (e.g., Inglehart 2003), studies on presidentialism often minimize the role of public opinion. In summarizing the literature on inter-institutional dynamics between legislatures and presidents, Calvo (2014, 150–151) notes that:

> [M]ost comparative research on legislatures concentrates on explaining the effect of relatively stable institutional rules such as decrees, vetoes, committee rules, and amendments ... There is little comparative research, therefore, integrating these different contextual and institutional sources of presidential legislative strength.

Chief among these contextual sources of presidential power, Calvo (2014) notes, is presidential approval. Like studies that focus on the American presidency, to the extent comparative studies focus on presidential approval, they conceptualize it as a currency with which to bargain with the executive branch (Calvo 2014; Helmke 2017; Palanza 2019; Pereira, Power, and Rennó 2005; Reich 2002). As with studies of the American presidency, there is little acknowledgment that public opinion may operate as an influence on presidents beyond popular support.[1]

We contribute to this scholarship by identifying contextual and individual-level sources of attitudes towards executive power in a comparative context. To conduct our analysis, we use several existing sources of survey data from around the world. The "traditional focus" of studies of presidentialism is the United States and Latin America (Chaisty, Cheeseman, and Power 2014), but we also study our question in the context of countries in Africa. This decision, based in part on data availability, allows us to examine the durability of the relationships in regions with distinct experiences with executive power (see Prempeh 2008, for an overview).

To measure diffuse support for executive power by the mass public, we rely on survey data from respondents from countries of the Americas and Africa. For the Americas, we rely on the AmericasBarometer by the Latin American Public Opinion Project (LAPOP). This series of surveys "is the only scientifically rigorous comparative survey that covers thirty-four nations including all of North, Central, and South America,

---

[1] See Hassan (2015) for an example of a study that considers how presidential power is conditioned by public views of legitimacy concerning the bureaucracy.

as well as a significant number of countries in the Caribbean." Our analysis of respondents from the Americas includes survey responses from twenty-six countries from 2010 to 2019. For Africa, we utilize survey data from the Afrobarometer series. Afrobarometer is a "non-partisan, non-partisan, pan-African research institution conducting public attitude surveys on democracy, governance, the economy and society in 30+ countries repeated on a regular cycle." Our analysis of surveys from Afrobarometer includes respondents from thirty-seven countries from 2000 to 2019.

8.2.1 Measuring Support for Executive Power

We study attitudes towards executive power using several questions from both the AmericasBarometer and Afrobarometer surveys. In previous chapters, we mostly relied on survey instruments that we developed. Our questions about unilateral policymaking, unilateral judicial appointments, and unilateral agency implementation measure support for executive fiat relative to other branches of the US government. In this chapter, we rely on questions crafted by others to measure attitudes towards the concentration of executive power. We utilize a variety of questions that, like ours, ask about executive power in the context of other political institutions. Each of these questions asks about the expansion of executive power as it relates to either the courts or the legislative branch. To preview, as we find with our unilateral action questions from previous chapters, support for executive power around the world is quite low and constrained by beliefs over core democratic principles.

Support for Executive Power, the Americas. From the AmericasBarometer, we analyze two questions that ask whether it is justifiable for the president to suspend either the legislative or judicial bodies and govern without them. Each item allows respondents a choice of whether they believe the act is justified. As it is in the United States, support for executive power is low throughout the Americas. Overall, only 17 percent of respondents agreed that the executive would be justified to "close Parliament [Congress] during difficult times." Across time, this figure ranged from 14 percent in 2010 and 2012 to 25 percent in 2019. Similarly, support for closing the supreme court or constitutional tribunal range from 11 percent in 2012 to 30 percent in 2019.

Attitudes towards executive power vary across countries. Aggregating responses to the country level, the mean and median levels of support for governing without parliament are 16 percent, with no country reporting more than a third of respondent support.[2] Support for governing without courts is even lower, with the mean and median country-level support at 14 percent and with no country reporting support for governing without them from more than a quarter of respondents. Notably, citizens from the United States are not exceptional among their fellow respondents from the Americas, with 16 percent believing the presidential shuttering of the legislative branch is justified and 12 percent believing the same concerning the Supreme Court. These values fall just below the median values observed by each country across all waves.[3]

Support for Executive Power, Africa. We use four measures of attitudes towards executive power included in the Afrobarometer surveys. The first survey instrument queries whether respondents approve of abolishing elections and parliament in favor of presidential rule. The question asks:

- "There are many ways to govern a country. Would you disapprove or approve of the following alternatives? Elections and Parliament are abolished so that the president can decide everything."

We refer to this question as *decides everything*. For ease of interpretation, we collapse the five-point scale of agreement to a binary indicator of support and provide additional analyses of alternative coding in Appendix F. We again find substantial opposition to executive authority among respondents from countries of Africa. Overall, 88 percent of respondents disapprove of presidents governing unilaterally, and only 12 percent approve. Aggregated by country, median support for abolishing elections and parliament in favor of presidential rule stands at 10 percent.

Three additional questions evaluate related dimensions of respondents' attitudes towards executive power. In each, respondents were presented with two statements about executive power and asked to choose one that best reflected their beliefs. The pairs of statements were:

- "Since the President was elected to lead the country, he should not be bound by laws or court decisions that he thinks are wrong." OR "The

---

[2] Support for this question is highest in Peru. In particular, respondents from the 2018 survey expressed extremely high support for executive rule vis-á-vis both parliament and the court with 59 and 50 percent support, respectively. Substantial and long-running political turmoil and dysfunction in Peru during this time culminated with President Vizcarra dissolving Congress in 2019 amid a prolonged corruption crisis (Kurmanaev and Zarate 2019).

[3] For additional descriptive analyses, see Zechmeister and Lupu (2019a).

President must always obey the laws and the courts, even if he thinks they are wrong."
- "Parliament should ensure that the President explains to it on a regular basis how his government spends taxpayers' money." OR "The President should be able to devote his full attention to developing the country rather than wasting time justifying his actions."
- "Members of Parliament represent the people; therefore they should make laws for this country, even if the President does not agree." OR "Since the President represents all of us, he should pass laws without worrying about what Parliament thinks."

After reading each pair of statements, respondents selected a response option and indicated whether they "agree strongly with" or "agree with" it. For each question, we create measures of support for executive power by creating a binary indicator for agreeing or strongly agreeing with the pro-executive power statement.[4] We refer to these questions as *not bound by laws*, *doesn't have to justify*, and *pass laws without Congress*, respectively. Across the survey instruments, we again find low levels of support for presidential power with support for the pro-executive power statement ranging from 12 percent (not bound by laws) to 34 percent (doesn't have to justify).

8.2.2 Measuring Core Values

As in our previous analyses, we wish to examine the extent to which core values structure attitudes towards executive power. For the Americas-Barometer surveys, no question asks specifically about support for the rule of law. Instead, we rely on a survey instrument that asks more broadly about support for democracy. This measure is based on a conception of democracy from Dahl (1971), which focuses on respondents' views of democracy as the best form of government.

---

[4] In the appendix, we explore alternative approaches to this coding. It is tempting to scale these measures together to create a single index of support for executive power, but this is difficult to justify. Though the measures are positively correlated with each other, their Cronbach's alpha is 0.4 indicating that they are not each reliably measuring the same underlying concept. Conducting a principal component analysis yields similar findings. The first dimension explains just 38 percent of the variance with each additional dimension explaining between 18 and 24 percent of the variance. These concepts appear to be measuring somewhat different conceptions of executive power and so we analyze them separately.

In political systems, democracy and the rule of law are closely related. Though not perfect mirrors, "the rule of law is among the essential pillars upon which any high-quality democracy rests" (O'Donnell 2004, 32). Gibson (2007, 593) notes that the "rule of law and democracy are not equivalent, nor are they inextricably connected, but most believe successful democracies must rule through law." The connection between attitudes towards democracy and support for the rule of law has also been documented in public opinion. In a study examining how individuals' democratic values condition the ability of elites to buy votes of the mass electorate, Carlin and Moseley (2014) note that views of executive authority are a component of support for democracy. Views of democracy consist of several distinct values, which include beliefs about how elections should be conducted and also how politicians should exercise power.

The survey instrument we use asks respondents whether they think the most preferable form of government is either democracy, a nondemocratic government, or if the type of government does not matter to them. The AmericasBarometer survey has asked respondents about their support for democracy since 2004, during which time support has ranged from 58 to 69 percent.[5] In Latin America and the Caribbean region, support never varied year-over-year by more than 1.6 points from 2004 to 2014, but support dropped in the 2016/2017 wave from 66 to 58 percent (Zechmeister and Lupu 2019b). From 2010 to 2019, the average score for respondents from the United States ranges from a high of 5.7 in 2010 to a low of 5.4 in 2014 and 2017. That translates to 64 percent approval in 2010 and 57 percent and 56 percent support in 2014 and 2017, respectively. The survey also asks respondents to rate the job performance of the current administration of the president or prime minister, which allows us to include a measure of specific support of the chief executive in modeling support for executive power. The full question wordings and choice sets are presented in Table 8.1.

The Afrobarometer surveys ask about support for democracy as well as support for the rule of law. To measure support for the rule of law, we utilize a question that asks respondents whether they think it is important to obey the government regardless of who they voted for or if they think it is not necessary to obey the laws if they did not vote for the government. This question is similar to one of the five questions we used in the rule

---

[5] Based on responses of six or seven on the seven-point ladder, for which only the extreme values are labeled.

TABLE 8.1 *Question wording for survey instruments from AmericasBarometer*

Question	Choice set
Support for Executive Power. Do you believe that when the country is facing very difficult times it is justifiable for the president of the country to close the Congress/Parliament and govern without Congress/Parliament?	yes, it is justified; no, it is not justified
Support for Executive Power. Do you believe that when the country is facing very difficult times it is justifiable for the president of the country to dissolve the Supreme Court/Constitutional Tribunal and govern without the Supreme Court/Constitutional Tribunal?	
Support for Democracy. Changing the subject again, democracy may have problems, but it is better than any other form of government. To what extent do you agree or disagree with this statement?	Now we will use a ladder where 1 means "strongly disagree" and 7 means "strongly agree." A number in between 1 and 7 represents an intermediate score.
Executive Approval. Speaking in general of the current administration, how would you rate the job performance of [Prime Minister or President] [Name]?	very good; good; neither good nor bad (fair); bad; very bad

of law battery in Chapter 4 that asks respondents whether they believed it is necessary to obey laws of a government that they did not vote for. As with several of the executive power questions from the Afrobarometer, respondents were asked which of the two statements they agreed or strongly agreed with. The result is a four-point scale of support for the rule of law ranging from 1 (i.e., strongly agree with the anti-democratic statement) to 4 (i.e., strongly agree with the democratic statement). Overall, a majority of all respondents (56 percent) strongly agree that it is important to obey the government in power no matter who they voted for, with an additional 32 percent of respondents agreeing (though not strongly). Only about 12 percent of respondents agreed or strongly agreed that it is not necessary to do so.

Afrobarometer also provides a measure of support for democracy, which allows for a more direct comparison to the results from the AmericasBarometer analyses. To measure support for democracy, respondents are asked to select one of three statements about democracy that most closely reflects their opinions. Similar to the AmericasBarometer question, the first statement is "democracy is preferable to any other kind of government." The second statement is "In some circumstances, a nondemocratic government can be preferable," and the third statement is "For someone like me, it doesn't matter what kind of government we have." We code *support for democracy* as a three-point measure where preferring a nondemocratic government is coded as 1 seeing no difference is coded as 2, and preferring democracy is 3. Overall, 73 percent of respondents – nearly three-quarters – identify democracy as preferable to any other kind of government with 14 percent and 13 percent viewing other forms of government as potentially preferable or not believing it matters, respectively.

We present the full question wordings and response set in Table 8.1 (for the AmericasBarometer) and Table 8.2 (for the Afrobarometer).

8.3 COUNTRY-LEVEL EVALUATIONS OF EXECUTIVE POWER

First, we evaluate the relationship between core values and support for executive power at the national level. Do countries that express greater support for democracy and the rule of law also report greater opposition towards executive power? In our previous analysis, our data were entirely from the United States from the 2010s. By turning to comparative data, we can explore whether the relationship between core values and executive power is a general relationship that exists beyond the United States or whether it is a case of American exceptionalism. To preview, we find that across the countries of the Americas and Africa, higher levels of support for core values (i.e., support for democracy and the rule of law) is associated with lower levels of support for executive power.

Figure 8.1 plots the relationship for the AmericasBarometer surveys. For each country and wave, we calculate mean levels of support for core values, which we plot on the *x*-axis, and support for executive power, which we plot on the *y*-axis. The two questions that measure support for executive power are binary indicators. Along the *y*-axis, we present the percent of respondents by country/wave who believe it is acceptable for the president or prime minister to close the legislature (left panel) or dissolve the high court (right panel). Along the *x*-axis, we plot the average level of support for democracy along a seven-point scale for each country/wave combination. We include a local polynomial regression line and indicate the correlations in the upper right-hand corners of each plot. The

TABLE 8.2 *Question wording for survey instruments from Afrobarometer*

Question	Choice set
Support for Executive Power. There are many ways to govern a country. Would you disapprove or approve of the following alternatives?: Elections and Parliament are abolished so that the president can decide everything.	strongly disapprove, disapprove, neither approve nor disapprove, approve, strongly approve
Support for Executive Power. Statement 1: Since the President was elected to lead the country, he should not be bound by laws or court decisions that he thinks are wrong. Statement 2: The President must always obey the law and the courts, even if he thinks they are wrong.	
Support for Executive Power. Statement 1: Parliament should ensure that the President explains to it on a regular basis how his government spends taxpayers' money. Statement 2: The President should be able to devote his full attention to developing the country rather than wasting time justifying his actions.	Which of the following statements is closest to your view? Agree very strongly with statement 1; agree with statement 1; agree with statement 2; agree very strongly with statement 2
Support for Executive Power. Statement 1: Members of Parliament represent the people; therefore they should make laws for this country, even if the President does not agree. Statement 2: Since the President represents all of us, he should pass laws without worrying about what Parliament thinks.	
Support for Rule of Law. Statement 1: It is important to obey the government in power, no matter who you voted for. Statement 2: It is not necessary to obey the laws of a government that you did not vote for.	
Support for Democracy. Statement 1: Democracy is preferable to any other kind of government. Statement 2: In some circumstances, a nondemocratic government can be preferable. Statement 3: For someone like me, it doesn't matter what kind of government we have.	Which of these three statements is closest to your own opinion?
Executive Approval. Do you approve or disapprove of the way that the following people have performed their jobs over the past twelve months, or haven't you heard enough about them to say?: [Name of President]	strongly disapprove, disapprove, approve, strongly approve

figure shows a strong negative relationship between support for democracy and the two measures of support for executive power. Even though support for democracy is relatively high, with all country/wave scores

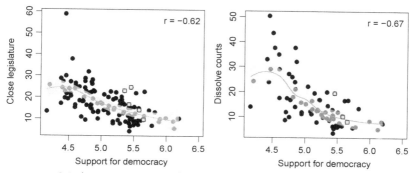

FIGURE 8.1 Aggregate support for democracy and support for presidential power, the Americas

Note: Points are mean scores for each country survey wave. United States indicated by gray squares. Support for democracy is measured along a seven-point scale.

falling between 4.2 and 6.5, the pattern is clear. Every one-point increase in national support for democracy is associated with a decline of about ten points in support for closing parliament and about fourteen points in support for dissolving courts and allowing presidential rule.

The surveys from the AmericasBarometer allow us to directly compare the United States to other countries in the Americas. In Figure 8.1, averages for the United States are plotted as gray squares in each plot. In both panels of Figure 8.1, the United States scores low on support for executive power and high on support for democracy, but it is not an outlier on either dimension. The relationship between core values and executive power is in line with the overall trend we observed with the data we collected in the United States.

Figure 8.2 presents the relationship between support for the rule of law and support for executive power at the country/wave level among countries represented in the Afrobarometer surveys. Along the x-axis is the average support score for the rule of law at the country/wave level. The y-axis displays the average levels of support for executive power based on the four measures described in Table 8.2. We see the same patterns as in Figure 8.1. At the country/wave level, support for the rule of law is again negatively correlated with views of an array of measures of support for executive power. Correlations for support for the rule of law and the four measures of support for executive power range from −0.46 to −0.33. Regressing executive power on rule of law shows that a one-point increase in support for the rule of law along the four-point scale is associated with a nineteen-point decline in support for executives governing without elections and parliament. Regressions for the remaining

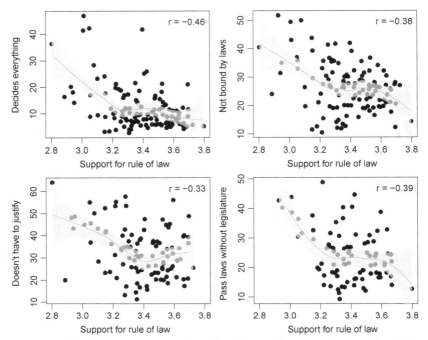

FIGURE 8.2 Aggregate support for rule of law and support for presidential power, countries of Africa

Note: Points are mean scores for each country survey wave. Support for the rule of law is measured along a four-point scale.

three questions show that a one-point increase in national support for the rule of law is associated with a decline in support for executive power of between sixteen and nineteen points.

We present the same analysis using support for democracy in Figure 8.3. Although we believe the measure of support for the rule of law is a more direct measure of the concept we present in Chapter 4, we use support for democracy since we have a similar measure from the AmericasBarometer surveys. Country/wave mean scores of support for rule of law and democracy are correlated at 0.35. When we consider the relationship between support for democracy and support for executive power, we see the same negative relationship. All correlations are negative and range from −0.58 to −0.22.

Taken together, these results demonstrate that across the Americas and Africa, countries with stronger beliefs in core democratic values also report lower levels of support for executive authority. Even incremental increases in core beliefs about the conduct of government are associated

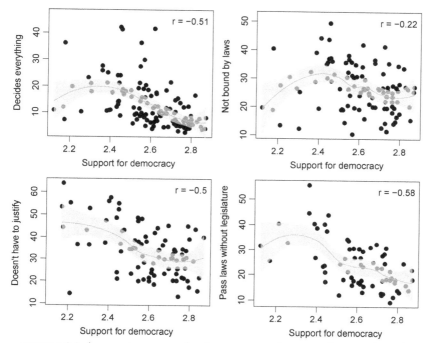

FIGURE 8.3 Aggregate support for democracy and support for presidential power, countries of Africa

Note: Points are mean scores for each country survey wave. Support for democracy is measured along a three-point scale.

with changing aggregate support for executive power. From our analysis of the AmericasBarometer, we also see that the United States is not exceptional in either its low levels of support for executive power or its high levels of support for democracy or the relationship between these two factors.

8.4 INDIVIDUAL ANALYSES

Next, we examine the relationship between core values and support for executive power at the individual level across the Afrobarometer and AmericasBarometer samples. As with the aggregate analyses, we explore whether core beliefs about democracy or the rule of law structure attitudes about the bounds of power of executives. As in Chapter 4, we also evaluate an alternative hypothesis, which holds that views of executive power merely reflect whether an individual supports the person who holds executive office.

While we see correlations at the aggregate level across countries in the previous sections, this analysis burrows deeper to examine whether these same dynamics exist at the individual level. These analyses are *within-country* and examine whether respondents' assessments of executive power in a given country vary according to their core values and evaluations of the sitting government.

We conduct our individual-level analyses by regressing each measure of attitude towards executive power on respondents' core democratic beliefs. For each of the AmericasBarometer and Afrobarometer surveys, we use their respective measures of support for democracy to model the variety of attitudes towards executive powers we previously described. All models also include the measure of *executive approval* as previously described. To better grasp the strength of relationships across analyses, we standardize some of our measures. We measure approval of the executive officeholder with a binary indicator. All of our measures of executive power are also included as binary indicators of support. For the two measures of support for democracy (i.e., the seven-point scale for the AmericasBarometer and the three-point scale for the Afrobarometer), we rescale each measure so that it ranges from zero to one. The estimated coefficients can therefore be interpreted across models as a shift from the lowest level of support for democracy to the highest.

To account for variation in political context and institutions across country and time, and which could confound the relationship between individual characteristics and views towards executive power, we include country/wave fixed effects in all models.[6] Additionally, we control for other individual characteristics, as we will describe. With this specification, we estimate linear probability models and cluster standard errors on country/wave. Therefore, our coefficients of interest are identified with variation in executive approval and core values among respondents from the same country and survey wave. Given the perspectives outlined above, we test the hypotheses that executive approval is positively associated with and democratic values are negatively associated with support for executive power.

---

[6] Cross-national differences in evaluations of executive power could reflect differences in formal powers enshrined in countries' constitutions. The country/wave fixed effects account for baseline differences in attitudes towards executive power that could reflect these country-level sources of variation. Future research could evaluate how constitutional differences affect public opinion towards political institutions.

Individual Results, the Americas. Table 8.3 presents our individual-level analysis of the AmericasBarometer surveys. The first column shows results for whether respondents believe it is justifiable for the president to close the legislature during difficult times (i.e., *close legislature*), and the second column shows analogous results for closing the courts (i.e., *dissolve courts*). We include demographic variables including age, gender, education, income, and marital status to account for individual-level factors that may influence political attitudes and whose distributions are likely to vary across countries.

We find similar results for both models in Table 8.3. Consistent with results from the United States in previous chapters, *executive approval* is positively related to support for executive power, as the coefficients are statistically significant in both models. Approving of the presidential officeholder is associated with an increase of 0.04 in the probability of support for executive power to close the legislature and of 0.06 to dissolve the courts. We also find that *support for democracy* is negatively associated with views towards executive power, and these coefficients are also statistically distinguishable from zero. Moving from the lowest to the highest level of support for democracy is associated with a 0.05 decline in the probability of supporting a president's power to close the legislature and a 0.06 decline in the probability of supporting a president's prerogative to dissolve the courts. Across the Americas, support for democracy is related to more restrained views of executive power vis-à-vis legislatures and the courts.

These patterns are robust to several alternative specifications reported in Appendix F. Here, we employ logistic regression models and use survey weights in lieu of controlling for individual-level covariates. Our substantive conclusions remain. We also distinguish parliamentary versus presidential systems using data from Cruz, Keefer, and Scartascini (2018) and include an indicator for whether the country is a parliamentary system.[7] Because these characteristics tend to be fixed within countries over long periods of time, we estimate a variety of models that alternately include and omit country fixed effects. The inclusion of this term does not materially affect our conclusions from Table 8.3. Even when

---

[7] Based on the coding in Cruz, Keefer, and Scartascini (2018), 15 percent of respondents in the AmericasBarometer sample are from parliamentary systems (i.e., Belize, Canada, Jamaica, Suriname, Trinidad and Tobago) and 2 percent are from Guyana, the lone semi-presidential system in the data.

TABLE 8.3 *Model of support for executive powers and support for democracy, the Americas*

	Close legislature	Dissolve courts
Executive approval	0.040*	0.061*
	(0.012)	(0.010)
Support for democracy	−0.054*	−0.060*
	(0.007)	(0.009)
Intercept	0.204*	0.176*
	(0.010)	(0.015)
Country × Year fixed Effects	✓	✓
Demographic controls	✓	✓
Num. obs.	72,602	47,355

$^*p < 0.05$.
Note: Linear regression with robust standard errors clustered on country/wave.

accounting for a country's political system, *executive approval* and *support for democracy* continue to be significantly associated with attitudes towards executive power.

Individual Results, Africa. Tables 8.4 and 8.5 present individual-level models for respondents from the Afrobarometer surveys. The dependent variables are binary indicators of support for executive power – *president decides everything, president not bound by laws, president doesn't have to justify*, and *pass laws without Congress*. For each of these indicators, a one indicates support for executive power. As in the previous section, we rescale our measures of core democratic values (i.e., support for democracy and support for the rule of law) from zero to one and employ linear probability models. We follow Bartels and Kramon (2020) and include measures of gender, education, poverty, age, and whether their locale is urban or rural to account for individual-level factors that could be associated with views toward executive power.

In Table 8.4, the coefficients for *support for rule of law* indicates the change in probability of support for executive power associated with an increase from the lowest level to highest level of support for rule of law. Across the four models, support for rule of law is associated with between a 0.04 and 0.02 decline in support for executive power. Additionally, we see that support for the person holding the office is associated with an increase in support for executive power from between 0.03 and 0.06. Notably, our findings for *support for rule of law* persist even when accounting for evaluations of the current president. When considering

TABLE 8.4 *Model of support for executive powers and support for rule of law, African countries*

	Decide	Not bound	Justify	Pass laws
Executive approval	0.035*	0.033*	0.034*	0.061*
	(0.002)	(0.003)	(0.003)	(0.003)
Support for rule of law	−0.026*	−0.019*	−0.038*	−0.044*
	(0.001)	(0.001)	(0.002)	(0.002)
Intercept	0.357*	0.437*	0.586*	0.532*
	(0.012)	(0.017)	(0.018)	(0.018)
Country × Wave fixed effect	✓	✓	✓	✓
Demographic controls	✓	✓	✓	✓
Num. obs.	140,670	145,648	128,494	104,932

*$p < 0.05$.

Note: Linear regressions with robust standard errors clustered on country/wave.

TABLE 8.5 *Model of support for executive powers and support for democracy, African countries*

	Decide	Not bound	Justify	Pass laws
Executive approval	0.027*	0.026*	0.030*	0.052*
	(0.004)	(0.005)	(0.007)	(0.009)
Support for democracy	−0.094*	−0.044*	−0.113*	−0.097*
	(0.007)	(0.007)	(0.008)	(0.009)
Intercept	0.322*	0.414*	0.538*	0.467*
	(0.009)	(0.011)	(0.012)	(0.015)
Country × Wave fixed effect	✓	✓	✓	✓
Demographic controls	✓	✓	✓	✓
Num. obs.	144,365	118,223	103,468	75,419

*$p < 0.05$.

Note: Linear regressions with robust standard errors clustered on country/wave.

support for democracy in Table 8.5, the magnitude of these relationships is comparable to those observed in our analysis of the AmericasBarometer surveys. Across the four models, support for democracy is associated with between a 0.11 and 0.04 decline in support for executive power.

As with our analysis of AmericasBarometer data, we conducted a number of robustness checks, which we present in Appendix F. Using logistic regression models and survey weights in lieu of controlling for individual-level covariates again yields substantively similar results. We also run models using alternative four-point or five-point codings for the dependent variables. Again, our substantive results remain.

We also estimated models with the Afrobarometer that accounted for differences in views of executive power by political systems. Based on the coding from Cruz, Keefer, and Scartascini (2018), 84 percent of the Afrobarometer respondents are from presidential systems with 10 percent from parliamentary systems (i.e., Botswana, Lesotho, Mauritius) and the remainder from hybrid systems (i.e., South Africa and Togo). Our findings are robust to accounting for a country's political system and across model specifications. The results suggest that individuals in parliamentary systems report more negative evaluations of executive power than individuals in presidential or hybrid systems. While these results are perhaps a function of affinity for one's own political system, we do not wish to overinterpret this finding and note that it raises interesting possibilities for future research.

Our results provide strong evidence that American public opinion towards executive power is hardly unique, at least in comparison with attitudes in Africa and the Americas. At the national level, we document strong negative associations between core democratic values and support for executive power. These aggregate cross-country relationships also persist at the individual level within countries. Overall, these patterns offer consistent support for the generalizability of our findings across more than sixty countries.

8.4.1 Presidential Approval and Support for Executive Power

One possibility is that support for democracy operates unevenly across approvers and disapprovers of the person holding the office when it comes to views of executive power. Rather than act as an independent influence, democratic principles might only depress support for executive power among those who already disapprove of the presidential officeholder. For support for democracy and support for rule of law to constrain executive power, it would need to operate among both supporters and opponents of the person in office.

To explore this possibility, we examine the interaction between executive support and support for democracy and support for rule of law. Our analyses are the same as in the previous section with the addition of an interaction term between executive support and support for democracy. These results are presented in Tables 8.6, 8.7, and 8.8.

TABLE 8.6 *Model of support for executive powers and support for democracy, the Americas: Interaction between support for democracy and executive approval*

	Close legislature	Dissolve courts
Executive approval	0.013	0.065*
	(0.014)	(0.015)
Support for democracy	−0.077*	−0.056*
	(0.011)	(0.012)
Exec. approval ×	0.039*	−0.006
Support for democracy	(0.014)	(0.015)
Intercept	0.148*	0.175*
	(0.017)	(0.024)
Country × Year fixed effect	✓	✓
Demographic controls	✓	✓
Num. obs.	72,602	47,355

*$p < 0.05$.
Note: Linear regressions with robust standard errors clustered on country/wave.

TABLE 8.7 *Model of support for executive powers and support for rule of law, African countries: Interaction between support for rule of law and executive approval*

	Decide	Not bound	Justify	Pass laws
Executive approval	0.066*	0.030*	0.042*	0.045*
	(0.005)	(0.007)	(0.008)	(0.008)
Support for rule of law	−0.054*	−0.058*	−0.108*	−0.144*
	(0.005)	(0.007)	(0.007)	(0.008)
Exec. approval ×	−0.039*	0.003	−0.010	0.020*
Support for rule of law	(0.006)	(0.008)	(0.010)	(0.010)
Intercept	0.313*	0.420*	0.543*	0.497*
	(0.012)	(0.017)	(0.018)	(0.018)
Country × Wave fixed effect	✓	✓	✓	✓
Demographic controls	✓	✓	✓	✓
Num. obs.	140,670	145,648	128,494	104,932

*$p < 0.05$.
Note: Linear regressions with robust standard errors clustered on country/wave.

Across the ten models in Tables 8.6, 8.7, and 8.8, most of the interaction terms are statistically indistinguishable from zero, meaning that presidential approvers do not weigh democratic principles any differently than disapprovers when it comes to translating core values into views of

TABLE 8.8 *Model of support for executive powers and support for democracy, African countries: Interaction between support for democracy and executive approval*

	Decide	Not bound	Justify	Pass laws
Executive approval	0.048*	0.025*	0.032*	0.064*
	(0.004)	(0.007)	(0.008)	(0.008)
Support for democracy	−0.076*	−0.045*	−0.111*	−0.086*
	(0.004)	(0.006)	(0.007)	(0.007)
Exec. approval ×	−0.027*	0.001	−0.003	−0.016
Support for democracy	(0.005)	(0.008)	(0.009)	(0.009)
Intercept	0.308*	0.414*	0.536*	0.459*
	(0.012)	(0.017)	(0.018)	(0.018)
Country × Wave fixed effect	✓	✓	✓	✓
Demographic controls	✓	✓	✓	✓
Num. obs.	144,365	118,223	103,468	75,419

$^*p < 0.05$.
Note: Linear regressions with robust standard errors clustered on country/wave.

executive power. Substantively, support for democratic values is associated with depressed views of unilateral power among both approvers and disapprovers of the executive office holder.

In the AmericasBarometer analyses in Table 8.6, the interaction is statistically significant and positive for the *close legislature* model. Among disapprovers of the executive in office, *support for democracy* is associated with a 0.08 decline in the probability of supporting closing the legislature and allowing presidential rule. That relationship is weaker among presidential approvers, with support for democracy being associated with a 0.04 decline in support for presidential rule ($−0.077 + 0.039$). While the size of the relationship is reduced, support for democracy is still negatively associated with views towards executive power even among individuals who approve of the current president.

In the Afrobarometer analyses in Table 8.7, interactions for support for rule of law and executive approval are significant for two models. In the *decide* model, the interaction is statistically significant and negative. Among those who oppose the individual in office, support for democracy is associated with a decline of 0.05 in support for abolishing elections and parliament and allowing the president to decide everything. Among approvers of the president, democratic values are even more strongly brought to bear. Support for democracy is associated with a decline of 0.09 ($−0.054 + −0.039$). In the *pass laws* model, we see an interaction that is statistically significant and positive. Among opposers of the president, support for the rule of law is associated with a decline of 0.14 in the probability in supporting the power of the president to pass laws without worrying about the legislative body. Among presidential approvers, that probability falls by 0.02 points to −0.12.

In the Afrobarometer analyses in Table 8.8, we present the results for the interaction between support for democracy and executive approval. We again see that the interaction is statistically significant and negative for the *decide* model. Among those who oppose the individual in office, support for democracy is associated with a decline of 0.08 in support for abolishing elections and parliament and allowing the president to decide everything. Among approvers of the president, democratic values are even more strongly brought to bear. Support for democracy is associated with a decline of 0.10 (−0.076+−0.027) in the probability of supporting an executive being allowed to decide everything. While we observe a statistically significant interaction, the substantive conclusions remain.

Taken together, we do not find systematic evidence that support for democracy operates differently between presidential approvers and disapprovers. The relationship between support for democracy and endorsing executive power is not conditioned on support of the person holding the office.

8.5 A COMPARATIVE ANALYSIS OF ATTITUDES

We now turn to examine how the individual-level dynamics we observe in Section 8.4 vary across countries. This analysis allows us to study whether core values translate into skepticism of executive power in a uniform way across countries. Establishing and investigating the nature of this relationship is an essential contribution to the understanding of attitudes towards governance around the world. Because of our focus, we highlight the relative place of the United States in terms of these relationships.

To conduct this analysis, we again focus on individuals and how their core values and support for the executive in their respective countries shape support for executive power. In the previous section, we account for differences across countries and waves by including indicator variables in our statistical models. We now leverage those differences by estimating relationships for each country that we observe. Citizens of different countries may show systematic differences in how they bring core values to bear on their views of executive power on the basis of deep-seated geographic or cultural differences (Almond and Verba 1963; Fischer

1989; McClosky and Zaller 1984). Differences may also reflect political circumstances and contexts. While the political system of the United States has remained relatively stable, other countries have experienced more recent changes and greater volatility in their political institutions.

Because one of our goals is to understand US attitudes in context, we focus on the surveys from the AmericasBarometer, which, unlike Afrobarometer, includes respondents from the United States. As dependent variables, we focus on the two items that measure whether respondents support executives suspending the legislative body or the courts and ruling in their stead. We again model these attitudes as a function of beliefs about democracy and specific support for the president or prime minister in power.

In these analyses, we conduct twenty-six separate regressions, one for each country contained in the AmericasBarometer surveys. In each model, we also include an indicator variable for each survey wave for each respective country along with the same demographic controls we previously used for the pooled analyses. Our focus is on how support for democracy (again standardized along a zero to one scale) is related to the probability of support for executive power while controlling for the aforementioned factors especially *executive approval*. Negative values indicate that support for democracy is associated with opposition to executive power. We again employ linear probability models.

Figure 8.4 presents the results from the AmericasBarometer surveys sorted by magnitude of the coefficient on *support for democracy*. Consider the results for Argentina in the left panel, which examines support for a president's ability to close the legislature and govern alone. Moving from the lowest to highest level of support for democracy is associated with a decrease of 0.12 in supporting this measure of executive power. The error bars present the 95 percent confidence interval around the estimate and, in the case of Argentina, ranges from −0.17 to −0.08.

Our goal here is not to interpret the findings for each individual country but rather to understand the overall patterns across them. In our analysis of support for the president closing the legislature and governing without them (i.e., *close legislature*, left panel), twenty-two of the twenty-six estimated relationships are negative. For fourteen, the 95 percent confidence interval does not include zero. These results suggest that the relationship between core values and support for executive power is not fleeting or particular to only certain countries. Instead, it applies across most countries of the Americas.

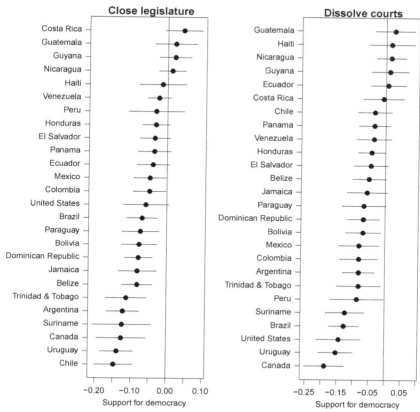

FIGURE 8.4 Support for executive powers and support for democracy:
Differences across the countries of the Americas

Notes: Estimates are from linear models estimated separately for respondents from each country. We control for executive approval along with a host of demographic variables, and include indicators for the survey wave when applicable. Each point is the change in support for executive power associated with a change in support for democracy from the lowest to highest value.

The magnitude of the association varies to some degree, however. For example, in the right panel of Table 8.4, we see the relationship between *support for democracy* and support for allowing an executive to dissolve the courts and govern without them. Among Hondurans, *support for democracy* is associated with a decline in support of executive power of 4 percentage points (i.e., a reduction in the probability of 0.04). In contrast, the same change is associated with a 19-point decline in Canada.

For respondents from the United States, moving from strongly disagreeing to strongly agreeing with democracy is associated with a decline of five points in supporting presidential rule over Congress. This relationship is comparable to the estimates for Brazil and Colombia yet significantly weaker than what we estimate among Canadians, Uruguayans, and Chileans. Americans more strongly bring core beliefs over democracy when they consider executive power over the judiciary. Here, we see support for democracy translate into a fourteen-point decrease in support for executive power.

From these results, we see familiar patterns. Core values structure beliefs about the nature of executive power. The relationship is consistent across the countries of the Americas albeit not entirely universal. Though beyond the scope of our analyses here, further research should consider the economic, institutional, contextual, and cultural factors that drive this dynamic. While variation exists, the relationship is durable. These results, in particular, help contextualize the findings from the previous chapters of this book. Is the United States exceptional in how its citizens translate support for the rule of law into opposition of executive power? It is clear from these results that this is not a case of American exceptionalism. All over the world, when citizens value the process of democratic politics, they cast a skeptical eye towards executive authority.

8.6 REGIME CHARACTERISTICS AND ATTITUDES TOWARDS EXECUTIVE POWER

In a final set of analyses, we consider the relationship between regime characteristics and support for executive power. Our results have established a consistent and robust link at both the individual and aggregate levels between beliefs in the rule of law and support for executive power. Here, we ask whether attitudes towards executive power reflect the characteristics of the political systems in which individuals live.

Identifying the connection between regime characteristics and attitudes towards executive power clarifies the stakes of our results. Posner and Vermeule (2010, 187) describe these stakes as "a central feature of American political psychology – fear of executive power – serves as a constraint on the executive every bit as important as the separation of powers and other institutional constraints." If attitudes towards executive power safeguard against the concentration of executive authority, skepticism or opposition towards executive power could serve as "a bulwark" (Posner and Vermeule 2010, 187) against the rise of dictatorship.

Testing the strongest version of this hypothesis requires data on attitudes towards executive power and the incidence of dictatorship, and a research design that allows us to credibly associate the two. Lacking both appropriate data and research design, we test a weaker version of this hypothesis: are mass attitudes towards executive power correlated with a political regime's commitment to the rule of law? Our theoretical perspective emphasizes the rule of law as a constraint against the concentration of executive authority. Based on our argument, we expect that countries have stronger commitments to the rule of law as more of their citizens oppose executive power.

We use data from the Varieties of Democracy (2020) project (V-DEM), which utilizes administrative data combined with expert assessments to measure democracy around the world. Specifically, we rely on V-DEM to characterize country-level commitments to the rule of law.[8] V-DEM describes this measure as an index of "[t]o what extent are laws transparently, independently, predictably, impartially, and equally enforced, and to what extent do the actions of government officials comply with the law?" It is comprised of indicators regarding judicial independence, impartial public administration, corruption, and, most importantly, executives' respect for the constitution. This variable ranges between zero and one where larger values indicate that the rule of law is more strongly observed. We use the values of this measure for 1999, 2005, 2010, and 2015.

Our independent variable characterizes aggregate attitudes towards executive power. We use data from waves three through six from the World Values Survey (2015). These data complement our analyses of the AmericasBarometer and Afrobarometer by providing more extensive coverage of countries in Europe, the Middle East, and Central and East Asia. These surveys include an item that asks respondents whether it would be "very good," "fairly good," "fairly bad," or "very bad" to "[have] a strong leader who does not have to bother with parliament and elections." This measure provides a direct assessment of how respondents in a large number of countries evaluate the desirability of executive power. Following Posner and Vermeule (2010), we calculate the proportion of respondents in each country who reported it would be "very bad" to have "a strong leader" to provide a measure of *oppose executive power*. The mean proportion of support for "strong leader[s]" was 30 percent.

We regress the country-level measure of the rule of law on aggregate attitudes towards executive power. The four waves of the World Values Survey were conducted between, respectively, 1995 and 1998, 1999 and

---

[8] This variable is v2x_rule.

TABLE 8.9 *Model of regime responsiveness to public opinion*

	(1)	(2)	(3)
Oppose executive power	0.32*	0.25*	0.34*
	(0.15)	(0.11)	(0.15)
Gross domestic product (per capita, ln)		0.20*	
		(0.02)	
Gross domestic product (growth)			0.47
			(0.41)
Intercept	0.56*	−1.23*	0.55*
	(0.06)	(0.29)	(0.06)
Observations	193	193	193
Clusters	87	87	87
Wave fixed effects	✓	✓	✓

Note: Coefficients from linear regression with robust standard errors clustered on country in parentheses. Dependent variable is a measure of a country's support for the rule of law. * $p < 0.05$.

2004, 2005 and 2009, and 2010 and 2014. Therefore, each measurement of a country's aggregate attitudes regarding executive power temporally precedes the V-DEM measure of the rule of law. We have a total of 193 country-year observations – with 47 from 1999, 34 for 2005, 55 for 2010, and 57 for 2015 – that represent 87 unique countries. In some models, we include controls for logged GDP per capita and, alternatively, GDP growth, to account for the possibility that governing systems are more responsive to economic and demographic factors than the attitudes of their citizenry (see Posner and Vermeule 2010, 189–192). Finally, we include indicators for the year in which the dependent variable was measured to account for secular trends in observance of the rule of law and cluster standard errors on country.

Table 8.9 shows the results. We find consistent evidence of an association between public attitudes towards executive power and a regime's observance of the rule of law. Across each model, the coefficient for *oppose executive power* is positive and statistically significant, indicating that respect for the rule of law is observed to a greater degree in countries where larger proportions of respondents expressed opposition to executive power. This relationship persists while accounting for a country's economic output, which itself is positively associated with the observance of the rule of law.

Our findings provide evidence of an association between the values held by a citizenry and a country's governing regime. Countries where larger shares of their citizens oppose executive power exhibit greater respect for the rule of law through their institutional arrangements. Posner and Vermeule (2010, 198), in contrast, use similar survey data to conclude that opposition to executive power "probably does not constitute a safeguard against dictatorship, in the United States or elsewhere." Our analyses suggest instead that a "tyrannophobic public" is more likely to live in countries with stronger support for the rule of law, which may be a prerequisite for constraining the ambitions of authoritarian-minded rulers.

Of course, our analyses are not dispositive, for the reasons we describe. Nonetheless, they provide evidence to suggest that a country's orientation vis-à-vis executive power may be able to prevent democratic backsliding at the hands of a would-be autocrat. Our findings are also consistent with related research that shows evidence of a similar link at the elite level. For example, Meijers and van der Veer (2019) show that members of the European Parliament who represented national parties with authoritarian ties were less likely to raise questions about breaches of the rule of law by governments in Hungary and Poland. Across a variety of contexts, therefore, public attitudes about executive power appear to be associated with elite behavior and governing practices.

8.7 DISCUSSION

Our cross-national analyses provide evidence that is strikingly consistent with what we have found for the United States. Citizens from across much of the globe exhibit similar levels of skepticism towards powerful leaders. Across a large number of countries, each with their own histories, traditions, and contexts, core democratic values are strongly associated with beliefs about executive power.

On the one hand, these findings suggest that Americans' skepticism about executive power is unexceptional. Rather, opposition to executive power appears to be a persistent pattern in survey respondents around the world. On the other hand, our cross-national data do not allow us to study the political origins of these attitudes. Our theoretical account in Chapter 2 points to the importance of political socialization in the United States based upon colonial experiences and founding-era orientations vis-à-vis executive power. Of course, these experiences were not common to other countries. Nevertheless, the variation we observe in support for executive power across countries suggests the importance of country-level factors for shaping these attitudes.

Our perspective has more sanguine implications about the potential for mass publics to constrain the power-seeking ambitions of their leaders. The threat of potential public consequences may induce political leaders to exhibit restraint when contemplating changes to democratic institutions. The democratic-demise literature understates the potential for citizens to have durable attitudes about democratic institutions and procedures and to bring them to bear when evaluating policies and office-holders. To the extent that citizens will rise up to resist leaders' efforts to consolidate their power, our perspective suggests that these attitudes reduce the potential for democratic backsliding.

9

Conclusion

By acting on their own, presidents can single-handedly recast the national political agenda and reshape the nation's public policies. The capacity for presidents to pursue their objectives through unilateral action rather than in consultation with Congress "virtually defines what is distinctively modern about the modern American presidency" (Moe and Howell 1999b, 851). These powers bear on every significant presidential initiative, as "[t]here is virtually no significant policy area in which presidents operate that has not been shaped to one degree or another by the use or abuse of [unilateral] tools" (Cooper 2002, ix).

How presidents develop and deploy their powers affects not only the characterization of the presidency's role in American democracy but also the relationship between Americans and their government. While previous scholarship had established "[n]o consensus on the role of public opinion in unilateral action" (Lowande 2014, 729), we provide new evidence about how the public evaluates unilateral power and its use by presidents.

Throughout this book, we show that citizens do not provide a blank check for presidents to exercise power as they see fit. The public also does not support presidents' power to act in proportion to their popularity. Instead, public opposition to executive power is an enduring characteristic of American democracy. While elite discourse around presidential power may reflect those elites' own political motivations, these discussions resonate with many Americans' core commitments to democratic processes. More speculatively, the threat of negative public reactions may provide an important check against presidents acting beyond the proper bounds of the US Constitution.

In this concluding chapter, we discuss the implications of our findings. First, we consider one of the most important implications of our book: the institutional lessons for considering when presidents deploy unilateral action. Then, we consider a number of broader implications and avenues for further research.

9.1 INSTITUTIONAL LESSONS

What insight does our evidence provide about presidential behavior? Our results suggest that presidents have fewer incentives to exercise unilateral power than previous accounts have recognized. To the extent that strategic presidents are concerned about the implications of their behavior for their approval ratings and electoral performance, we would expect to observe that presidents make use of unilateral action at lower rates than they might prefer, given their policy preferences.

Systematically testing this expectation is more difficult, however, than it may initially seem. We do not observe the unilateral directives presidents would have liked to issue but ultimately shelved due to their concerns about the political consequences. Nor do we observe the complete menu of options that presidents had before them as they pursued their policy goals. The difficulty in accounting for these counterfactuals complicates efforts to credibly identify the effect of public opinion on presidential behavior.

This challenge is not unique to our research. Scholarship in related areas has also recognized the difficulties in establishing how various political constraints affect presidential decision-making. Other research advances arguments about how factors such as public opinion, the media, and formal political institutions affect leaders' decisions to make foreign policy (Milner and Tingley 2015), use military force (Baum and Potter 2015; Howell and Pevehouse 2007; Kriner 2010; Tomz, Weeks, and Yarhi-Milo 2020), and exercise unilateral powers (Bolton and Thrower 2016; Chiou and Rothenberg 2014; Christenson and Kriner 2019; Howell 2003; Mayer 2002; Thrower 2017b). The evidence offered to assess these claims typically (though not always) comes from time-series analyses that document how presidential behavior varies with characteristics of the political environment. While the empirical patterns shown in these accounts are often consistent with the authors' claims, interpreting the findings as evidence of the causal effect of the hypothesized factor on presidential behavior requires strong assumptions about how presidents would have behaved in a different political environment. Our intention is not to diminish the contributions from this literature. Rather, we point out only that the challenges of establishing credible evidence about proposed constraints on decision-makers are common in empirical research on political institutions.

To illustrate the institutional lessons of our book, we instead present a pair of case studies that discuss President Obama's and Trump's ultimate decisions to use unilateral action in the context of immigration. Then, we relate our findings to these presidents' experiences with deciding to go it alone to achieve major policy promises. Finally, we take a step back and consider what our account provides that has been omitted or overlooked by existing models of unilateral action.

9.1.1 DREAMing of Obama Action on Immigration

Barack Obama made immigration a centerpiece of his 2008 campaign. In the Democratic primary, for example, Hillary Clinton expressed her opposition to issuing driver's licenses to undocumented immigrants. Obama seized the opportunity to declare his support for such a policy and touted his position when speaking with Latino voters on the campaign trail (Hamburger and Wallsten 2008).

After securing the Democratic presidential nomination, Obama advocated for comprehensive immigration reform. In early summer 2008, he delivered one of the most consequential speeches on the subject to the National Council of La Raza (since renamed UnidosUS), the nation's largest Latino advocacy organization. In his remarks, Obama promised to "finally enact comprehensive immigration reform" and assured the audience that he would be a president "who won't walk away from something as important as comprehensive reform when it becomes politically unpopular – because we have to finally bring those 12 million [undocumented immigrants] out of the shadows" (Obama 2008). Obama went on to victory in the 2008 election with record Latino support. The number of Latino voters increased by 25 percent over the 2004 presidential election, and exit polls indicated that Latino voters supported Obama over John McCain at a rate of two to one (*New York Times* 2008). Just four years earlier, in contrast, Democratic presidential candidate John Kerry received a bare majority (53 percent) of the Latino vote in the 2004 presidential election.

Upon Obama's inauguration, his presidency immediately confronted challenges posed by the Great Recession (Hendricks 2008). Yet as the first hundred days of Obama's presidency came and went without legislative progress on immigration reform, a growing chorus of doubters began questioning Obama's commitment to the issue (Board 2009). In a White House news conference on April 29, Obama was asked whether he still anticipated accomplishing immigration reform in the first year of his presidency. After describing a number of immigration enforcement issues that the Department of Homeland Security was considering, Obama hedged on whether comprehensive legislative efforts would be possible, noting that, "Ultimately, I don't have control of the legislative calendar. And so we're going to work with legislative leaders to see what we can do" (Office of the Press Secretary 2009).

Obama's hesitation in committing to legislative efforts on immigration reform may have reflected his calculation that congressional opposition was more profound than he initially anticipated. The struggle to pass health care legislation led him to reconsider the wisdom of also prioritizing immigration legislation so early in his presidency. By August, Obama announced that no legislative action on immigration would take place until 2010 due to the need to act on other issues, including energy and financial regulation (Thompson and Booth 2009). Obama instead announced a series of measures undertaken by the Department of Homeland Security to reform the ways immigration violators were detained (Bernstein 2009), to hold employers accountable for hiring undocumented workers (Thompson 2009), and to end the ban on travel and emigration to the United States by people infected with HIV/AIDS (Preston 2009).

As the calendar turned to 2010, activist groups became increasingly frustrated and impatient with the Obama administration. On March 8, representatives from the Fair Immigration Reform Movement lambasted the increased number of deportations under the Obama administration, and argued that Obama had failed to live up to his promise to enact meaningful reform in his first year in office (see also Hoyt 2010). Two days later, Obama met with many of these advocates and emphasized the necessity of securing Republican support for a legislative solution (Preston 2010). The lame-duck 111th Congress that met after the 2010 midterm elections took up a component of immigration reform efforts when it voted on the Development, Relief and Education for Alien Minors (DREAM) Act. Though the measure passed the House, it failed to secure the sixty votes for cloture in the Senate and thus was killed by filibuster (CNN Wire Staff 2010).

As the legislative path for immigration reform seemed to close, many activists began to encourage President Obama to use executive authority to change the country's immigration policies. Their efforts eventually paid off. On June 15, 2012, Obama announced his first significant executive action on immigration in creating the Deferred Action for Childhood Arrivals (DACA) program, which allowed certain undocumented immigrants brought to the United States as children to work in the United States without fear of deportation (Preston and Cushman 2012). Though some analysts believed the move was risky, the reaction was relatively positive. Perhaps just as importantly, Obama's action helped shore up Latino support. "To Latino voters, almost as significant as the policy was the fact that the president had taken a political risk for their sake. And the fact that it had paid off was even better news" (Ball 2014).

Despite the potential impact of DACA, the policy fell short of the comprehensive immigration reform package that Obama had hoped to achieve. During the 2012 presidential campaign, Obama cited the failure to enact comprehensive reform as the biggest failure of his first term. Fresh off re-election, in January 2013 Obama urged Congress to take up his immigration plan if its members could not agree to their own plan (Goldfarb and Helderman 2013). Immigration reform again languished in the Senate, however, and persistent legislative gridlock renewed pressure on Obama to use executive authority to change immigration policy. For instance, in a November 25 speech in San Francisco, Obama was interrupted by an audience member who yelled from the audience, "Mr. President, please use your executive order to halt deportations for all 11.5 million undocumented immigrants in this country right now." When the protester shouted to Obama that "you have a power to stop deportation for all undocumented immigrants in this country," the president responded, "Actually, I don't." Obama then made a surprising articulation of the weakness of the presidency and explained why he lacked the power to stop deportations:

Now, what you need to know, when I'm speaking, as President of the United States, and I come to this community, is that, if, in fact, I could solve all these problems without passing this through Congress, then I would do so. We're also a nation of laws. That's part of our tradition. And so, the easy way out is to try to yell and pretend like I can do something by violating our laws, and what I'm proposing is the harder path: to use our democratic processes to achieve the same goal you want to achieve. But it won't be as easy as just shouting, it requires us lobbying and getting it done. (Obama 2013)

As Obama had done throughout his presidency, he emphasized that changing immigration policies required congressional action. However, his pronouncement that he could not take executive action to halt deportations was perplexing given that DACA had done just that. Perhaps more revealing, Obama's description of executive action as tantamount to "violating our laws" seems congruent with many Americans' perceptions of unilateral power, as we documented in Chapter 4.

Just seven months later, the president reversed course when he spoke from the Rose Garden in June 2014 and promised to take executive action to ease the threat of deportation. The president argued that he could take executive action "only when we have a serious problem, a serious issue, and Congress chooses to do nothing" (Obama 2014b). In the speech, Obama announced that he had directed the Attorney General and Secretary of Homeland Security to recommend unilateral measures for his consideration by the end of the summer and promised that he would adopt them "without delay." But when Labor Day signaled the end of summer, Obama backed off his pledge. Responding to concerns that executive action could jeopardize Democrats' performance in that fall's midterm elections, Obama announced that he would delay executive action until later in the year (Shear 2014b). The decision to delay taking action reflects a theme of this book: unilateral action, particularly when used to address controversial issues, can generate public backlash. By putting off the new directives, the Obama administration seemed to acknowledge the political costs that could accompany them.

A few weeks after the 2014 midterms, President Obama gave a prime-time address in which he announced new executive actions that changed immigration law enforcement. The most controversial of these would protect undocumented immigrants from deportation for people who have lived in the United States for more than five years, have children who are American citizens or legal residents, and meet certain other requirements. Obama was keenly aware of the possibility that his opponents would question the legal basis of his actions, and he justified them accordingly:

The actions I'm taking are not only lawful, they're the kinds of actions taken by every single Republican President and every single Democratic President for the past half century. And to those members of Congress who question my authority to make our immigration system work better, or question the wisdom of me acting where Congress has failed, I have one answer: Pass a bill. (Obama 2014a)

The reaction to Obama's immigration measures was swift. Critics challenged that President Obama's use of executive action was an acknowledgment of his inability or unwillingness to negotiate effectively with

Congress. Some argued that Obama's use of executive authority "should absolutely not pass muster in terms of constitutionality" and suggested that Obama "certainly could be impeached" for it (Flynn 2019). But though Donald Trump provided similarly fierce criticism of Obama's use of unilateral power while he was a private citizen (e.g., @realDonaldTrump 2012), as president he found himself in similar territory when addressing immigration priorities of his own.

9.1.2 Trump's Wall

Border security was the most prominent issue priority of Donald Trump's campaign for president. From the day he announced his candidacy in June 2015, Trump repeatedly emphasized his commitment to constructing a wall along the country's border with Mexico. In his announcement speech, Trump promised to "build a great, great wall on our southern border" (Time Staff 2015). As Trump appeared increasingly likely to win the Republican Party's presidential nomination, he elaborated on his plan to have Mexico contribute financially to the construction of the wall. A memorandum issued by his campaign in March 2016 indicated that Trump would cut off remittances sent to Mexico unless it contributed $5 to $10 billion towards the border wall (Trump 2016b; Woodward and Costa 2016). And in the final presidential debate before the November 2016 election, Trump again reasserted his commitment to the wall: "I want to build the wall. We need the wall. The border patrol, ICE, they all want the wall" (Politico Staff 2016).

Despite Trump's criticism of Obama's use of executive action, he was not shy about his intention to use unilateral power to build a border wall. In making this assertion, Trump suggested exercising emergency powers to claim executive authority that would allow him to modify federal regulations about the flow of transfer payments into Mexico. Days after winning the presidential election, Trump advisers argued that he could draw upon existing statutory authority to construct a border wall without involving Congress (Raju, Walsh, and Barrett 2016), though such action would require appropriations passed by Congress if Mexico refused to pay for it. And by the end of Trump's first week in office, he signed Executive Order 13767 to direct the secretary of the Department of Homeland Security to "take all appropriate steps to immediately plan, design, and construct a physical wall along the southern border, using appropriate materials and technology to most effectively achieve complete operational control of the southern border." Hoping to encourage Congress to provide appropriations for the construction of a border wall, Trump asserted to a joint session of Congress in February 2017 that "we will soon begin the construction of a great, great wall along our southern border" (Trump 2017).

But funding for the wall was in short supply. Later in the spring of 2017, a government shutdown loomed as Democrats united in opposition to Trump's request for $1.5 billion in wall funding. Opposition also came from Senate Republicans, including those who represented border states. Instead, Congress and Trump agreed on a short-term spending bill that funded the government through September 30. Yet Trump resolved to revisit wall funding in future negotiations with Congress. The next attempt was in October 2017 when the Trump administration reasserted its demand for border wall funding and linked it to renewing the DACA program. President Trump threatened to rescind the DACA program (Nakamura 2017) if Congress refused to meet his appropriations request. By the close of 2017, a government shutdown again loomed on the horizon. This time, Democrats sought to use their leverage to insist that "Dreamers" would be protected from deportation if they were to agree to a budget deal with the president. President Trump countered with a threat to veto such a bill unless it also contained funding for the border wall (Nelson 2017). This time, Trump requested, but did not receive, $25 billion in wall funding in exchange for renewing DACA; after a shutdown, however, both Trump and congressional Democrats dropped their immigration-related demands and promised, yet again, to revisit the immigration issue. In his State of the Union address delivered at the end of January 2018, Trump reemphasized his commitment to building a border wall (Trump 2018). In March, Trump officials began to float the idea that Trump could fund the wall without involving Congress in the process by diverting military funding to help build it (Dawsey and DeBonis 2018).

The debate over the border wall came to a head in December 2018. Two years after being elected, Trump had little to show for his promise to construct a wall. Funding for the government was set to run out on December 21, and Trump had requested $5.7 billion in wall funding. The Senate unanimously passed a continuing resolution that would keep the government open but did not contain wall funding, which seemed likely to pass the House and receive the president's signature. However, Trump threatened to veto any measure that did not contain wall funding. While the House passed a bill that contained this funding, Senate Democrats threatened a filibuster and kept the measure from receiving a vote. The government shutdown began on December 22 and lasted until January 25, 2019 – the longest government shutdown in US history. Trump and congressional Democrats reached an agreement on a three-week funding plan to keep the government open until February 15. Trump again insisted that a subsequent budget bill contain funding for a border wall, and more publicly discussed using unilateral power to do so if Congress refused (Costa, Sonmez, and Miroff 2019).

As the February 15 deadline approached, Trump signed a new budget resolution to fund the government through September 30, 2019. The agreement passed by Congress and signed by Trump, however, provided far less funding for border security ($1.375 billion) than he had requested. On the same day, Trump invoked the National Emergencies Act of 1976 to declare an emergency on the Mexican border (Baker 2019). The action allowed the president to divert $3.6 billion from military projects and an additional $3 billion from other appropriations to spend on wall construction. Trump's action immediately prompted criticism from Democrats and some Republicans, who argued that the president's action to reappropriate funds to circumvent Congress amounted to a "power grab" and an "unconstitutional abuse of his authority" (Baker 2019).

9.1.3 Lessons on Presidential Decision-Making

For all their differences, the Obama and Trump experiences with immigration and border security reveal two similarities in how the politics of presidential power shaped their behavior. First, both presidents expressed commitments to these issues while campaigning for office but encountered sustained legislative resistance to them. In both cases, Congress refused to pass legislation that would have allowed both presidents to achieve their publicly stated goals and signature campaign promises. Eventually, both Obama and Trump drew upon executive powers to do what Congress would not. Though they could not accomplish their goals through legislation, they used unilateral action to make progress towards achieving them.

What stands out is not that they eventually exercised those powers, but how long it took them to do so. Obama's and Trump's reluctance to exercise unilateral powers contrasts with common depictions of contemporary presidents as imperial tyrants. If presidents can make new policies on their own, and have neither the courts nor Congress to fear, why wouldn't they do so?

The answer, we suggest, is consistent with the account we have offered in this book. The reactions to both presidents' actions highlight the political liabilities of unilateral power. Presidents Obama and Trump had clear priorities and ultimately pursued them via unilateral action. They did so because they had incentives to show activist groups and party loyalists that they would keep their word. But taking unilateral action was also a political liability – and not because the public uniformly opposed these policies. On the contrary, the measures Obama and Trump ultimately took had relatively strong public support. Polls conducted as Obama took office showed that large majorities of Americans supported a path to citizenship for immigrants meeting certain conditions (Hook 2007; *Washington Post* 2007). And, with respect to Trump's policy stance, a 2015 poll conducted by the Monmouth University Polling Institute showed that Americans supported a border wall with Mexico by a 5-percentage-point margin, 48 to 43. In both cases, Congress was gridlocked and internally fragmented while the public was at least tacitly supportive of the president's policy goal. Conventional models of interbranch bargaining indicate that presidents have the greatest latitude to act unilaterally in these circumstances.

We suggest that the public's skepticism towards presidential power makes presidents more reluctant to issue unilateral directives. These costs, we argue, play an unappreciated role in shaping the politics that accompany the exercise of executive power. Moreover, few political issues have bedeviled recent presidents as much as immigration policies; to the degree that presidents anticipate public pushback on issues that are central to their agendas, these considerations may be even more likely to affect presidential decision-making on issues lower on their priority lists.

Second, the responses to Obama's and Trump's actions demonstrate the political salience of and the politics around presidential power. Some of the presidents' critics took issue with the policy objectives of the presidents' actions. But, consistent with our argument, many critics expressed opposition to the means through which the presidents achieved these policies. Even some political allies – including those who supported the presidents' policy objectives – registered unease with the presidents' use of power. On this score, the Obama and Trump presidencies are not anomalies. As examples throughout the book indicate, Republican and Democratic presidents alike have long been criticized for claiming and using authority that served as an affront to the separation of powers. The rhetoric that accompanies these debates highlights at least some of the terms on which presidential power is contested, and suggest that claims of presidential overreach are predictable yet potent means of countering presidents' bold assertions of authority.

9.2 REVISITING MODELS OF UNILATERAL ACTION

As the previous chapters of this book along with Trump's and Obama's experiences with immigration make clear, the public's skepticism towards unilateral power shapes its reaction to its use. Yet existing theories largely overlook how presidents anticipate the potential public response when considering unilateral action. Most scholarship in this area emphasizes how other political institutions constrain presidents' exercise of power. These studies posit that congressional opposition to the president's policy preferences is an especially important factor. Howell (2003) and Chiou and Rothenberg (2017), for example, emphasize that Congress restrains presidential action through its ability to enact legislation that supersedes presidential directives. Likewise, judicial review raises the possibility that the courts will strike down exercises of presidential power as unconstitutional or in violation of statutory authority (Fox and Stephenson 2011; Howell 2003; Thrower 2017a). A smaller body of scholarship suggests that concerns over bureaucratic implementation may similarly constrain presidential decision-making (Kennedy 2015; Lowande 2018; Rudalevige 2021; Turner 2020).

To the extent that existing models allow for the public to affect presidential calculations, it is through the public's elected officials in Congress. That is, electorally motivated legislators are theorized to possess incentives to represent their constituents' beliefs when deciding how to render judgment on presidential actions, and thus congressional constraints on presidential behavior are imposed by legislators' electorally induced preferences. As we discuss in Chapter 2, this characterization is reflected in related empirical research on public opinion and unilateral power (Christenson and Kriner 2020), in which the public evaluates presidential action negatively only when prompted to do so by their representatives in Congress.

This perspective, though, does not ascribe a particularly robust role to the public for holding presidents accountable for the use of power. How might the public serve as a direct influence on presidential behavior outside of their representatives in Congress? First, legislators are imperfect agents of their constituents. If legislators are unaware of (Broockman and Skovron 2018) or unresponsive to (Ahler and Broockman 2018) constituent opinion on high-profile policy issues, members of Congress may not be ideal vehicles for transmitting constituent opinion on issues involving presidential power. Second, our current era of partisan polarization and presidentialized parties (Jacobson 2019) suggests that legislators from the president's party will be especially reluctant to criticize the president no matter how brazen the action. Constituents represented by presidential copartisans may be especially poorly represented in debates over presidential behavior given the findings we present in Chapter 3 that documents low levels of support for presidential power among even Americans who share the president's partisanship. Third, other scholarship describes how public opinion can have an independent effect on presidential activity outside of legislative channels. For example, constituents have often contacted presidential administrations directly to request presidential action (Lee 2003), and presidential rhetoric and patterns of unilateral activity have been responsive to public opinion expressed through protest activity (Gillion 2013, chap. 4). While we do not claim that Congress cannot represent public opinion in its interbranch disputes with the president, we instead suggest that public opinion occupies a more central role in the politics of presidential power than existing accounts permit.

We briefly sketch what we see as the key components of a theory of unilateral power in the shadow of public opinion. Presidents enter office motivated to advance their policy goals. They look for opportunities to shift status quo policies in their preferred ideological direction. Presidents also seek to maintain public support. High approval ratings not only can facilitate congressional support for the president's legislative program, making it easier for presidents to achieve more of their policy goals (Canes-Wrone 2006), but they also bolster the president's subsequent reelection chances (Abramowitz 2016). The public evaluates the president both on the basis of their agreement with the president's policies and the means by which those policies were enacted (for a related specification of voter decision-making, see Svolik 2020). Though the emphasis placed on these two factors may vary across both individuals and contexts (as the results in Chapters 3 and 4 suggest), positive weight on the latter factor indicates that a president benefits less from enacting popular policies through means of which the public disapproves.

Under these circumstances, presidents consider whether the benefits of exercising their power exceed the political costs they may incur for doing so. If a president anticipates substantial backlash for exercising power in a way that violates the public's procedural sensibilities, he or she may calculate that the policy gains are not sufficiently large to justify presidential action. Alternatively, if public demand for policy change is sufficiently great, the president may decide that the benefits from using unilateral power to advance those goals exceed any potential procedural penalties. Presidents may also be differently responsive to the potential public reaction depending on their current level of public support, commitment to their own policy goals, and the electoral calendar.

This framework speaks to some recent theoretical work that links public opinion more directly to unilateral power. Judd (2017) develops a model in which presidents may use unilateral power to demonstrate their competence to the electorate even though such actions may produce inferior policies. In this model, presidents' electoral concerns motivate them to create policies that may reduce voter welfare, which could suggest that presidents overproduce unilateral activities. Kang (2020), in contrast, models a scenario in which the public's democratic values, very much of the flavor we describe, interact with the president's use of unilateral power to mobilize supporters through the provision of expressive benefits. Along with both of these models, our findings highlight public opinion as a source of presidential accountability and contribute a set of normative standards that can be used for evaluating unilateral power.

9.3 LIMITS, EXTENSIONS, AND TRADE-OFFS

This book focuses on understanding the politics of presidential power when others contest the president's claim to authority. Public opinion can arbitrate disputes over competing claims to power. We have presented a wide range of evidence that documents the public's resistance to executive authority and demonstrates how mass publics hold executives accountable for its use. Yet our account does not hold that demands for policy change never focus on presidential action, or that Americans reflexively oppose expressions of presidential power in any context or form. In some circumstances, members of the president's political constituency may demand policy change through unilateral action, as the urgency of policy change outweighs potential concerns about how that change is implemented. In other cases, presidents may draw upon unilateral powers when specifically authorized to do so by Congress. The political dynamics surrounding unilateral power in these settings may differ from the account we have offered. We discuss two such instances next. In the first, organized groups motivated presidents to exercise rather than retreat from unilateral action; in the second, the absence of conflict between a president and Congress enabled a president to reap political benefits from using unilateral power.

9.3.1 "The Fierce Urgency of Now": Organized Interests and Demands for Presidential Action

Our book focuses on public opinion and how the mass public receives and processes unilateral presidential action. But the mass public is only one audience with whom the president engages. While the public writ large may express dissatisfaction with the exercise of presidential power, presidential action sometimes may come with a dividend of support from organized interest groups. Since interest groups have a high demand for policy, unilateral directives may offer presidents opportunities to satisfy groups' policy goals. Interest groups are an oft-neglected actor in presidential politics (Miller 2020), and their focus on policy change may exhibit less concern for the means through which those changes occur.

Civil rights is illustrative of this point. Presidents have often struggled to balance the policy demands of civil rights groups with their own political ambitions. With a general public which is often apathetic – and sometimes intensely opposed – to the cause of civil rights, many presidents have resorted instead to unilateral action to bring about policy change. We briefly outline two cases of Democratic presidents resorting to unilateral action to satisfy the demands of civil rights organizations that are generally aligned with their party.

Consider first the case of President Franklin Roosevelt. As the economy began to ramp up during the early stages of World War II, many union leaders reiterated their resistance to Blacks in the workforce. A. Philip Randolph, the head of the Brotherhood of Sleeping Car Porters, a Black labor organization, threatened a march on Washington to express outrage over the exclusion of Blacks from employment in defense-related jobs (Morgan 1970, 36–38). Randolph and the other leaders were not naive and knew that any legislative efforts to integrate the workforce would be killed by Southern Democrats in Congress. Randolph and fellow leaders "wanted the president to act through an executive order" (Urofsky 2020, 15). In an attempt to placate their interests, President Roosevelt sent a letter to the cochairs of the government office in charge of defense contracts, which "reiterat[ed] the administration's opposition to discrimination" (Urofsky 2020, 15). This effort did not satisfy Black leaders, who refused to call off the march. Roosevelt relented and scheduled another meeting with Randolph. On June 25, 1941, less than a week before the planned march, Roosevelt issued Executive Order 8802, which declared that "there shall be no discrimination in the employment of works in defense industries or government because of race, creed, color or national origin." Wanting to avoid a massive protest, Roosevelt was eventually compelled to take executive action after first attempting weaker and unsatisfactory implements to signal a commitment to civil rights in government employment (Milkis and Tichenor 2019). Randolph and representatives from other mass organizations, perhaps anticipating that legislative attempts to integrate the workforce would be futile, explicitly sought unilateral action from President Roosevelt as a means of addressing their policy demands.

President John F. Kennedy faced similar pressures from activists and organized interests. Despite mostly avoiding civil rights issues during the 1960 campaign, Kennedy stirred the hopes of civil rights organizers when he criticized the outgoing Eisenhower administration for its inaction on civil rights issues. After Kennedy won the election with strong support from Black voters, the National Association for the Advancement of Colored People (NAACP) proposed a "sweeping executive order" on civil rights issues to the new president (Urofsky 2020, 32–33). But Kennedy perceived no public appetite writ large for the action and showed no willingness to pursue it (Urofsky 2020, 32). Despite Kennedy's reluctance, civil rights leaders did not relent in their call for action. Upon Kennedy's inauguration, Martin Luther King, Jr. called on him to "give segregation its death blow through the stroke of a pen" (quoted in Schlesinger 1965, 930). King noted that

Historically the Executive has promulgated orders of extraordinary range and significance. ... Executive orders could require the immediate end to all discrimination in any housing accommodations financed with federal aid. Executive orders could prohibit any contractor dealing with any federal agency from practicing discrimination in employment. (King 1961)

Kennedy initially eschewed legislation and major executive action, but pursued a number of smaller gestures including personnel appointments. He appointed Black Americans to top posts in his administration, nominated five Black federal judges, and admitted the first Black reporter to the White House press pool (Urofsky 2020, 33–34). His first major directive on civil rights came in March 1961. Though most executive orders came with little fanfare or attention, Kennedy signed Executive Order 10925 in March 1961 "at a highly publicized ceremony in the White House" (Urofsky 2020, 35). The order created the President's Committee on Equal Employment Opportunity to study employment discrimination within the federal government. Still, the effect of the order was "modest"

(Urofsky 2020, 35), and civil rights groups continued to press Kennedy to honor commitments he made while campaigning for the presidency. On one presidential visit to Los Angeles, a local chapter of the Congress of Racial Equality greeted him with placards that urged him to "Pick up the pen, Mr. President" (*TIME* 1962). Finally, President Kennedy picked up his pen late in 1962 after the midterm elections and issued Executive Order 11063. The order forbade discrimination in the sale or lease of housing owned by the federal government and was "the most significant change in federal fair housing policy initiated between the Truman and Johnson administrations" (Lamb, Boston, and Nieheisel 2019). While Kennedy's initial efforts were mild relative to his private commitments to civil rights leaders, he followed up on these effects and ultimately introduced a civil rights bill to Congress in June 1963 after making a televised address to the American people outlining the moral necessity of civil rights. For civil rights groups, policy change via unilateral action was far preferable to a continuation of the status quo.

Roosevelt's and Kennedy's experiences illustrate some scope conditions of our analysis. While groups like the NAACP may be "normally oriented towards legislative and judicial action" (Urofsky 2020, 34), they, unlike the mass public, may strongly prefer unilateral action over nothing at all. These groups' incentives to achieve policy change take precedence over any hesitation about procedural concerns. Policy demanders thus may not penalize – and may even reward – presidents for addressing their priorities via unilateral action.

9.3.2   Politics of Delegated Powers

As we show in this book, unilateral action triggers citizens' procedural values that, in turn, cause the public to sanction unilateral policies and the presidents who create them. Yet presidents do not always create unilateral policies in the face of congressional opposition or legislative gridlock. Sometimes, they do so with the explicit authorization of Congress. One implication of delegating power to the executive branch, however, is that it forecloses an effective avenue of criticism by other political actors. When legislatures allocate power to executives, it limits the former's ability to invoke this set of critiques. Complaints about the president's use of power are much less credible when Congress has encouraged the president to do exactly that.

When Congress delegates to the executive branch, the president exercises power on the basis of the authority that Congress has explicitly transferred. While members of Congress may be able to evade account-ability for difficult decisions delegated to the executive (Fox and Jordan 2011), delegating in this context comes with the trade-off of waiving their claims to procedural criticism of the president. When the president is per-ceived to be exercising power that is within his purview, it is more difficult to mobilize opposition to the president for using power.

Richard Nixon's imposition of price and wage controls illustrates this point. On August 15, 1971, President Nixon interrupted the popular Sun-day evening show *Bonanza* to announce a series of new economic policies in response to unemployment and inflation rates that had each hovered around 6 percent. Among the policies he announced was the issuance of Executive Order 11615, which ordered a ninety-day freeze on prices and wages. The announcement of this "radical plan" (Clark 1985, 113) followed a weekend-long meeting with advisers at Camp David, which Stein (1988, 176) describes as "one of the most exciting and dramatic events in the history of economic policy." Today, some regard the eve-ning of Nixon's announcement as "A Date Which Has Lived in Infamy" (Domitrovic 2011).

Yet public backlash to Nixon's actions never materialized. Quite the contrary, as Jacobs (2016, 33) describes:

No single act of Nixon's first term was as popular as the adoption of price controls. The president's standing in public opinion polls got a boost; the vast majority of Americans approved of his action. ... [T]he public saw him as a courageous leader, in the mold of Franklin Roosevelt, who did what needed to be done.

This characterization is reflected in public opinion polls following Nixon's actions. A national poll conducted by Louis Harris & Associates in the days following Nixon's announcement showed that 73 percent of respon-dents supported the wage and price freeze, compared with only 15 percent who opposed it. A Gallup poll conducted during the same time period showed similar levels of support, with 68 percent approving and only 11 percent disapproving. Even as Nixon's opponents had the opportunity to mobilize the public against his orders, support faded only incremen-tally in the months to follow. A poll from the Roper Organization in October 1971 showed that 62 percent approved while 25 percent disap-proved, and a November 1971 poll from Harris showed that 67 percent of respondents approved of Nixon's actions.

What accounts for the broad public support for Nixon's exercise of unilateral power? Earlier in his administration, it bears noting, Nixon had rejected wage or price controls. He believed that they both were likely to be ineffective and inconsistent with his worldview. Nixon outlined these views during a radio address delivered on June 17, 1970, where he pressured Congress to pass a series of legislative initiatives that he argued would provide more permanent solutions to the nation's temporary economic malaise. "Controls and rationing ... are an easy way into more trouble," he argued, and would "only postpone a day of reckoning." As the *New York Times* (1970, 1) summarized his address, "None of the new devices announced by the President would involve 'jawboning' as commonly understood – that is, the firm use of the moral authority of the Presidency to prevent excessive wage-price increases."

In contrast with the examples we cited earlier in the book, in this instance, there was no opportunity for members of Congress and other political elites to question Nixon's authority. The Economic Stabilization Act passed by the Democratic-controlled Congress in 1970 explicitly gave Nixon the power he subsequently exercised in August 1971. This grant of authority was, by all accounts, "a political dare" (Shultz and Dam 1978, 141), as "Democrats did not believe that a Republican would use them, and certainly not Richard Nixon ... who had spent much of his first years in the Oval Office resisting controls" (Jacobs 2016, 30). This was no ordinary instance of delegation from Congress to the president. In the face of mounting public pressure for action, "[w]hat Congress decided to do was put the problem on the president's plate.... [t]he only thing Congress didn't give Nixon was a cape and a pair of tights" (Eggers and O'Leary 2009, 21–22). Through an extraordinary grant of power to the president, "Congress could make absolutely clear that the Republican executive, not the Congress, was responsible for the state of the economy" (Sundquist 2002, 87).

Once Congress explicitly gave Nixon the power to implement price and wage controls, Nixon had little to fear from exercising unilateral power. By the end of summer 1971, Nixon had his eye on the 1972 presidential election. The state of the economy had cost Nixon's party additional seats in the 1970 midterm elections, further shrinking the party's representation in the House. Nixon was determined not to let the same thing happen to his reelection in 1972. And because Nixon "could not claim lack of authority" to set price and wage controls (Stein 1988, 161), the decision was entirely his. With his announcement in August 1971, Nixon received sole policy credit for his initiatives and had the security of knowing that his partisan opponents could not criticize his use of power. The lesson from this case is clear: when presidents advance popular policies with authority given to them by Congress, the mechanisms we identify throughout this book are unlikely to materialize.

Nixon's unprecedented economic interventions also help illustrate the scope of our theoretical perspective. We examine public evaluations of presidential power under circumstances in which it is contested. We do not claim that these attitudes are reflexively activated and mechanically registered when the public evaluates presidential behavior. Indeed, as we show in Chapters 3, 4, and 6, the public provides varying levels of approval of presidential action across policy domains. And as we suggest here, the public is less inclined to weigh in against the use of presidential power when presidents exercise authority that has been granted to them. In these circumstances, executive power does not awaken the same constitutional considerations that accompany presidents' use of power as when claims to authority are contested.

9.4 PRESIDENTIAL POWER AND AMERICAN DEMOCRACY

We began our empirical investigation by studying how Americans view the institution of the presidency rather than individual presidents. Through a similar lens, our book illuminates Americans' views of the president as an agent of the state.

Understanding how Americans view presidential power has implications for applying normative theories of representation to the presidency. For example, public support for presidential power may indicate the degree to which citizens authorize the president to act on their behalf (see, e.g., Pitkin 1967). To the extent the public endorses the use of presidential power, these evaluations provide evidence to assess voters' judgments that the presidency "stands in" for them to take action on their behalf (Rehfeld 2006, 2).

This relationship is assumed by much of the historiography on the growth of the presidency over the last century. According to this conventional wisdom, major crises such as World War I, the Great Depression, and World War II highlighted the need for vigorous presidential leadership, and Presidents Wilson and Roosevelt were up to the task. In turn, these accounts argue, the public began to place their faith in presidents as being the particular embodiment of the federal government best able to serve their interests. This has produced a vicious cycle in which the public is perceived to ask more from their presidents and presidents claim more authority in order to meet these expectations.

Yet, to use the parlance of Easton (1965), the evidence we provide suggests it is a mistake to ascribe high levels of legitimacy to presidential claims to authority. In survey after survey, we show that the public routinely offers high levels of support for presidents themselves while simultaneously withholding broad grants of authority for the office of the presidency. While the absence of major protests and other acts of rebellion against presidential action may be interpreted as evidence of Americans' acceptance of, or at least acquiescence to, unilateral authority, it may be a mistake to interpret these non-findings as evidence of Americans' embrace of executive power.

To the extent political leadership involves bold claims to presidential authority, our account also suggests that the constraints imposed by public opinion complicate presidents' incentives to exercise leadership. The fear of political backlash may instead encourage presidents to resist the temptations of power grabs. Though as a political leader in the United States the president is without peer, decades of scholarship has presented limited evidence, at best, to support the notion that the public endorses expanded presidential prerogative even against ever-expanding public expectations.

More generally, our account also provides evidence about how Americans' procedural commitments structure their relationship to the state. Americans do not base their views about policy outcomes and officeholders simply on whether they share ideologies or preferences. Americans do not view policy outcomes and officeholders simply on their ideological agreement with them. The public also strongly prefers that the rules are followed and that policies are crafted in ways that respect them. To the extent we consider a minimalist definition of democracy, meaning "rule by the people," Americans' commitments to the rule of law suggest a view of representation that goes beyond more narrow partisan and ideological interests. Instead, our findings are consistent with the public's endorsement of a "proceduralist vision" in which "modern democratic procedure ... is the best way of respecting equal liberty in a context of pluralism and dissent" (Saffon and Urbinati 2013, 442).

Even more broadly, we provide evidence for the relevance of Americans' views about political power. The public, our data show, holds views about who ought to have power and what are appropriate uses for it. The presidency, of course, is not the only institution or setting in which power is contested. Many questions central to American democracy revolve around questions of power, for instance: How does money shape political outcomes? Is the judiciary too involved in policy debates? To what degree can states regulate access to the ballot box? When does home rule apply to municipal government? Who gets to draw the boundaries of legislative districts? Can the president remove executive branch officers? How can Congress exercise oversight of the bureaucracy? Answering each of these questions, and many others, involves reckoning with normative assessments of power allocation.

9.5 THINKING ABOUT AND BEYOND THE PRESIDENCY

Even in an age of partisan rancor, Americans – like citizens around the world – rely on democratic values to inform attitudes about their government. Our inquiry makes clear that the exercise of power affects how the public views policies and the actors who advance them. Partisanship helps explain these attitudes but does not account for the full story. While scholars should not ignore the role of partisan identification in driving a wide array of behaviors and beliefs, we should not assume that nothing else matters. Even in an era with strong partisanship and a highly polarized electorate, our evidence shows that Americans make policy evaluations that reflect not only whether policies were made by their preferred politicians. The public also assesses policies based on how they were enacted.

Presidents undoubtedly weigh the potential public costs of executive action with decisions about whether bold action is warranted. Creating and securing long-term legacies through unilateral action may come with short-term penalties by the public. Our research suggests that presidents should not merely justify the policy merits of their unilateral actions, they should also emphasize their commitment to defend the US Constitution. Likewise, opponents of a president's agenda may expand the scope of conflict or bolster disagreement with presidential prerogatives by appealing to process over, or in addition to, policy.

The underpinning of resistance to undemocratic uses of power is, we suggest, civic education. Americans learn in school as children the values that compel resistance to unilateral action. Political culture, formal education, and childhood socialization instill mechanisms that make America less resistant to democratic collapse than others acknowledge. Yet scholars and public interest groups have expressed concern over the decline of civics education in the United States (Allen 2019; Levine and Kawashima-Ginsberg 2017; Shapiro and Brown 2018). Our argument suggests that revitalizing civic education is an important step towards further mobilizing the public around issues of sound governance.

Ours is not the first inquiry into how procedures affect the public's view of policy, but there is ample room for more scholarship in this vein. Under what conditions does the nature of the process change views about the desirability of the policy? As Carey and Shugart (1998) remind us, the shape of executive power ranges from rolling out tanks to filling out forms. Presidents are not the only ones engaged in unorthodox policymaking that may appear to distort the process imagined at the Constitutional Convention. Executives, legislators, bureaucrats, and jurists turn to inventive and sometimes arbitrary uses of process to accomplish their goals. At their core, complaints about judicial activism and opaque bureaucratic regulatory processes, for example, are rooted in ideas about the proper use of power and channels of policymaking. In an era of partisan polarization, discord, and rancor, and when trust in many of the nation's core institutions is at historically low levels, these untraditional mechanisms of policymaking may increasingly substitute for the School House Rock version. We hope our investigation paves the way for additional research on how the American public understands these and other means of policymaking and the factors that shape their assessments.

Appendix A

Appendix to Chapter 3

TABLE A.1 *Survey response patterns for unilateral policymaking*

Survey date	Refused	Strongly agree	Somewhat agree	Neither	Somewhat disagree	Strongly disagree	Don't know
January 2014	29	53	252		620	535	186
	(2)	(3)	(15)		(37)	(32)	(11)
May 2014	25	66	303		601	493	132
	(2)	(4)	(19)		(37)	(30)	(8)
January 2015	15	53	303		552	429	137
	(1)	(4)	(20)		(37)	(29)	(9)
June 2015	11	51	277		579	396	135
	(1)	(4)	(19)		(40)	(27)	(9)
October 2015	13	41	203	378	563	456	
	(1)	(2)	(12)	(23)	(34)	(28)	
October 2016	13	20	148	280	676	331	102
	(1)	(1)	(9)	(18)	(43)	(21)	(6)
November 2016	11	18	106	226	648	428	105
	(1)	(1)	(7)	(15)	(42)	(28)	(7)
May 2017	4	44	178	327	882	617	113
	(0)	(2)	(8)	(15)	(41)	(28)	(5)
January 2018	4	37	189	292	768	557	116
	(0)	(2)	(10)	(15)	(39)	(28)	(6)

Note: Each row shows the unweighted response frequency to the question measuring support for unilateral policymaking. The month and year in which the survey was fielded is shown in the leftmost column. Numbers in parentheses show the percentage of respondents who provided each response (numbers may not sum to 100 due to rounding).

TABLE A.2 *Survey response patterns for unilateral judicial appointments*

Survey date	Refused	Strongly agree	Somewhat agree	Neither	Somewhat disagree	Strongly disagree	Don't know
January 2014	23	95	303		608	424	222
	(1)	(6)	(18)		(36)	(25)	(13)
May 2014	17	78	293		662	416	154
	(1)	(5)	(18)		(41)	(26)	(10)
January 2015	6	67	281		533	442	160
	(0)	(4)	(19)		(36)	(30)	(11)
June 2015	13	57	278		554	404	143
	(1)	(4)	(19)		(38)	(28)	(10)
October 2015	15	44	205	371	608	411	
	(1)	(3)	(12)	(22)	(37)	(25)	
October 2016	9	39	188	233	651	349	101
	(1)	(2)	(12)	(15)	(41)	(22)	(6)
November 2016	11	39	160	209	605	403	115
	(1)	(3)	(10)	(14)	(39)	(26)	(7)
May 2017	4	55	218	251	896	646	95
	(0)	(3)	(10)	(12)	(41)	(30)	(4)
January 2018	5	63	199	262	729	596	109
	(0)	(3)	(10)	(13)	(37)	(30)	(6)

Note: Each row shows the unweighted response frequency to the question measuring support for unilateral judicial appointments. The month and year in which the survey was fielded is shown in the leftmost column. Numbers in parentheses show the percentage of respondents who provided each response (numbers may not sum to 100 due to rounding).

TABLE A.3 *Survey response patterns for unilateral agency implementation*

Survey date	Refused	Strongly agree	Somewhat agree	Neither	Somewhat disagree	Strongly disagree	Don't know
January 2014	29	107	609		409	193	328
	(2)	(6)	(36)		(24)	(12)	(20)
May 2014	21	108	658		433	183	217
	(1)	(7)	(41)		(27)	(11)	(13)
January 2015	13	116	566		388	163	243
	(1)	(8)	(38)		(26)	(11)	(16)
June 2015	16	114	522		392	159	246
	(1)	(8)	(36)		(27)	(11)	(17)
October 2015	10	91	491	490	333	239	
	(1)	(6)	(30)	(30)	(20)	(14)	
October 2016	16	59	483	353	350	149	159
	(1)	(4)	(31)	(22)	(22)	(9)	(10)
November 2016	13	61	451	336	353	157	170
	(0)	(4)	(29)	(22)	(23)	(10)	(11)
May 2017	6	89	578	411	586	321	174
	(0)	(4)	(27)	(19)	(27)	(15)	(8)
January 2018	5	104	592	359	481	256	166
	(0)	(5)	(30)	(18)	(25)	(13)	(8)

Note: Each row shows the unweighted response frequency to the question measuring support for unilateral agency implementation. The month and year in which the survey was fielded is shown in the leftmost column. Numbers in parentheses show the percentage of respondents who provided each response (numbers may not sum to 100 due to rounding).

TABLE A.4 *Respondent demographics, The American Panel Survey (TAPS)*

Category	Jan 2014	May 2014	Jan 2015	June 2015	Oct 2015	Oct 2016	Nov 2016	May 2017	Jan 2018
Gender									
Men	49	49	49	50	50	49	49	48	48
Women	51	51	51	50	50	51	51	52	52
Race/ethnicity									
White, non-Hispanic	74	74	75	75	76	77	77	76	77
Black, non-Hispanic	8	9	8	8	8	7	7	7	7
Other, non-Hispanic	5	5	5	5	5	5	5	4	4
Hispanic	11	11	10	10	10	9	9	11	10
2+ racial groups, non-Hispanic	2	2	2	2	2	2	2	2	
Education									
No high school diploma	3	3	3	3	2	2	2	3	3
High school diploma	14	13	13	12	13	12	12	14	12
Some college	32	32	32	32	31	31	31	31	30
Bachelor's degree or higher	51	51	52	53	54	54	55	52	54
Income									
Under $10,000	5	5	4	5	4	4	4	4	4
$10,000 to $29,999	18	18	17	17	17	18	18	17	11
$30,000 to $49,999	20	20	21	20	19	18	19	18	18
$50,000 to $79,999	23	23	24	23	24	24	23	24	25
$80,000 to $99,999	11	11	11	12	11	11	11	12	14
$100,000 or more	23	22	23	23	24	25	25	22	29
Age									
18–29	9	9	8	7	9	7	7	10	7
30–44	21	20	20	20	20	20	20	21	18
45–64	32	32	33	33	32	33	33	30	38
65 or older	38	39	39	40	39	39	39	38	37

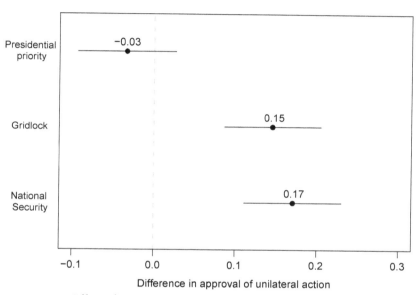

FIGURE A.1 Effect of context on approval of unilateral policymaking: Sample average treatment effects

Note: Data from an experiment conducted in September 2014 by Survey Sampling International (SSI). Points show the sample average treatment effects of each condition relative to the control condition where no context was provided. Positive values along the x-axis indicate greater support for unilateral power for the context shown along the y-axis. Horizontal lines are the 95 percent confidence intervals associated with the mean differences in support.

TABLE A.5 *Respondent demographics, MTurk sample*

Demographic	Percentage
Gender	
Women	48
Men	52
Age	
18–29	42
30–49	46
50–64	10
65+	2
Education	
Some HS	1
HS degree/GED	9
Some college	34
College degree	42
Post-graduate degree	15
Race/ethnicity	
Black	5
Hispanic	5
White	78
Asian American	9
Other	2
Income	
Below 25K	20
25–50K	29
50–75K	23
75–100K	14
100–200K	12
200K+	1
Ideology	
Very liberal	20
Somewhat liberal	32
Moderate	25
Somewhat conservative	18
Very conservative	5
Partisanship	
Democrat	41
Republican	19
Independent	35
Other	5

Appendix B

Appendix to Chapter 4

TABLE B.1 *Model of support for unilateral powers: Logistic models*

	Policymaking	Judicial appointments	Agency implementation
Presidential approval	0.808*	0.740*	0.773*
	(0.036)	(0.034)	(0.028)
Support for rule of law	−0.546*	−0.270*	−0.299*
	(0.064)	(0.056)	(0.057)
Male	0.193*	−0.100	0.298*
	(0.093)	(0.086)	(0.081)
Income	0.001	−0.038*	0.018
	(0.014)	(0.013)	(0.012)
Black	0.367*	0.508*	0.250
	(0.145)	(0.154)	(0.137)
Hispanic	0.207	0.491*	−0.256
	(0.159)	(0.147)	(0.131)
Education	0.086*	−0.037	0.153*
	(0.035)	(0.030)	(0.028)
Age	0.002	−0.003	−0.002
	(0.003)	(0.003)	(0.003)
Intercept	−1.875*	−1.141*	−1.095*
	(0.326)	(0.279)	(0.282)
Survey wave fixed effects	✓	✓	✓
Num. obs.	9126	9224	8343

*$p < 0.05$.
Note: Logistic model with robust standard errors clustered on respondent.

TABLE B.2 *Model of support for unilateral powers: Five-point dependent variables*

	Policymaking	Judicial appointments	Agency implementation
Presidential approval	0.389*	0.383*	0.412*
	(0.011)	(0.012)	(0.013)
Support for rule of law	−0.281*	−0.191*	−0.176*
	(0.023)	(0.023)	(0.027)
Male	0.048	−0.064	0.122*
	(0.032)	(0.033)	(0.038)
Income	0.001	−0.016*	0.010
	(0.005)	(0.005)	(0.006)
Black	0.192*	0.227*	0.140*
	(0.063)	(0.074)	(0.059)
Hispanic	0.066	0.204*	−0.084
	(0.064)	(0.069)	(0.064)
Education	0.008	−0.031*	0.067*
	(0.012)	(0.012)	(0.013)
Age	0.001	−0.003*	−0.001
	(0.001)	(0.001)	(0.001)
Intercept	−0.767*	−0.355*	−0.552*
	(0.121)	(0.115)	(0.137)
Survey wave fixed effects	✓	✓	✓
Num. obs.	10129	10097	9627

$^*p < 0.05$.
Note: Linear regressions with robust standard errors clustered on survey wave.

TABLE B.3 *Model of support for unilateral powers: Presidential copartisanship*

	Policymaking	Judicial appointments	Agency implementation
Pres. copartisan	0.209*	0.215*	0.345*
	(0.011)	(0.011)	(0.014)
Support for rule of law	−0.076*	−0.044*	−0.064*
	(0.009)	(0.009)	(0.011)
Male	0.025*	−0.013	0.058*
	(0.013)	(0.013)	(0.017)
Income	−0.000	−0.006*	0.003
	(0.002)	(0.002)	(0.003)
Black	0.131*	0.161*	0.093*
	(0.029)	(0.030)	(0.025)
Hispanic	0.044	0.101*	−0.048
	(0.026)	(0.028)	(0.030)
Education	0.012*	−0.003	0.033*
	(0.005)	(0.005)	(0.006)
Age	0.001	0.000	−0.000
	(0.000)	(0.000)	(0.001)
Intercept	0.278*	0.372*	0.427*
	(0.047)	(0.044)	(0.058)
Survey wave fixed effects	✓	✓	✓
Num. obs.	9434	9514	8602

$^*p < 0.05$.

Note: Linear probability model with robust standard errors clustered on respondent.

TABLE B.4 *Model of support for unilateral policymaking: By wave from October 2015 to January 2018, least squares model*

	1/14	5/14	1/15	6/15	10/15	10/16	11/16	5/17	1/18
Presidential approval	0.43*	0.47*	0.56*	0.47*	0.50*	0.32*	0.15*	0.37*	0.29*
	(0.03)	(0.03)	(0.03)	(0.03)	(0.02)	(0.02)	(0.02)	(0.02)	(0.03)
Support for rule of law	−0.30*	−0.32*	−0.27*	−0.25*	−0.31*	−0.32*	−0.28*	−0.24*	−0.23*
	(0.05)	(0.05)	(0.05)	(0.05)	(0.04)	(0.04)	(0.04)	(0.04)	(0.05)
Male	−0.02	0.04	0.03	0.15*	−0.05	−0.03	0.14*	0.13*	0.08
	(0.06)	(0.06)	(0.06)	(0.07)	(0.05)	(0.05)	(0.05)	(0.06)	(0.06)
Income	−0.01	0.01	0.02	−0.00	0.00	0.00	0.00	−0.01	−0.01
	(0.01)	(0.01)	(0.01)	(0.01)	(0.01)	(0.01)	(0.01)	(0.01)	(0.01)
Black	0.06	0.26*	0.12	0.12	−0.07	0.36*	0.25*	0.09	0.15
	(0.13)	(0.11)	(0.12)	(0.13)	(0.10)	(0.09)	(0.10)	(0.11)	(0.11)
Hispanic	0.23*	0.12	0.03	−0.02	0.14	0.02	0.04	−0.09	−0.06
	(0.11)	(0.11)	(0.11)	(0.12)	(0.10)	(0.09)	(0.10)	(0.10)	(0.11)
Education	0.02	0.02	0.01	0.07*	0.02	−0.04*	−0.03	−0.00	−0.00
	(0.02)	(0.02)	(0.02)	(0.02)	(0.02)	(0.02)	(0.02)	(0.02)	(0.02)
Age	0.00	0.00	−0.00	0.00	0.00	−0.00	0.00*	0.00	−0.00
	(0.00)	(0.00)	(0.00)	(0.00)	(0.00)	(0.00)	(0.00)	(0.00)	(0.00)
Intercept	−0.75*	−0.81*	−0.99*	−1.29*	−0.82*	−0.17	−0.40*	−0.79*	−0.46*
	(0.25)	(0.22)	(0.23)	(0.24)	(0.20)	(0.17)	(0.19)	(0.19)	(0.21)
Num. obs.	1062	1265	1117	1075	1121	1195	1198	1057	1039

*$p < 0.05$

TABLE B.5 *Model of support for unilateral judicial appointments: By wave from October 2015 to January 2018, least squares model*

	1/14	5/14	1/15	6/15	10/15	10/16	11/16	5/17	1/18
Presidential approval	0.49*	0.42*	0.47*	0.46*	0.41*	0.33*	0.11*	0.42*	0.39*
	(0.03)	(0.03)	(0.03)	(0.03)	(0.03)	(0.02)	(0.03)	(0.02)	(0.03)
Support for rule of law	−0.15*	−0.20*	−0.14*	−0.15*	−0.21*	−0.30*	−0.23*	−0.16*	−0.24*
	(0.06)	(0.05)	(0.05)	(0.05)	(0.04)	(0.04)	(0.05)	(0.04)	(0.05)
Male	−0.14*	−0.08	−0.15*	0.01	−0.09	−0.12*	0.02	−0.04	−0.02
	(0.07)	(0.06)	(0.07)	(0.07)	(0.06)	(0.05)	(0.06)	(0.06)	(0.06)
Income	−0.02*	−0.00	0.00	−0.02	−0.02*	−0.02*	−0.02*	−0.03*	−0.01
	(0.01)	(0.01)	(0.01)	(0.01)	(0.01)	(0.01)	(0.01)	(0.01)	(0.01)
Black	0.01	0.21	0.25	0.38*	0.26*	0.44*	0.32*	0.05	0.07
	(0.14)	(0.12)	(0.13)	(0.13)	(0.10)	(0.10)	(0.12)	(0.11)	(0.11)
Hispanic	0.28*	0.34*	0.29*	0.09	0.23*	0.15	0.03	0.16	0.26*
	(0.12)	(0.11)	(0.12)	(0.12)	(0.10)	(0.09)	(0.11)	(0.10)	(0.11)
Education	−0.01	−0.01	−0.03	0.02	0.02	−0.04*	−0.08*	−0.05*	−0.07*
	(0.03)	(0.02)	(0.02)	(0.02)	(0.02)	(0.02)	(0.02)	(0.02)	(0.02)
Age	−0.01*	0.00	−0.00	−0.00	−0.00	−0.00*	−0.00	−0.00	−0.00
	(0.00)	(0.00)	(0.00)	(0.00)	(0.00)	(0.00)	(0.00)	(0.00)	(0.00)
Intercept	−0.51	−0.91*	−0.98*	−1.01*	−0.58*	0.25	0.36	−0.62*	−0.16
	(0.27)	(0.23)	(0.25)	(0.24)	(0.20)	(0.18)	(0.21)	(0.19)	(0.21)
Num. obs.	1038	1244	1108	1071	1117	1205	1196	1069	1049

*$p < 0.05$

TABLE B.6 *Model of support for unilateral agency implementation: By wave from October 2015 to January 2018, least squares model*

	1/14	5/14	1/15	6/15	10/15	10/16	11/16	5/17	1/18
Presidential approval	0.55*	0.54*	0.52*	0.52*	0.50*	0.36*	0.13*	0.35*	0.30*
	(0.04)	(0.03)	(0.03)	(0.04)	(0.03)	(0.03)	(0.03)	(0.03)	(0.03)
Support for rule of law	−0.15*	−0.21*	−0.17*	−0.24*	−0.16*	−0.25*	−0.17*	−0.08	−0.11*
	(0.06)	(0.05)	(0.05)	(0.06)	(0.05)	(0.04)	(0.05)	(0.05)	(0.05)
Male	0.06	0.06	0.09	0.17*	0.17*	0.10	0.12	0.20*	0.18*
	(0.08)	(0.07)	(0.07)	(0.07)	(0.06)	(0.06)	(0.07)	(0.07)	(0.07)
Income	−0.01	0.01	0.01	0.01	0.02	0.01	0.02	0.01	0.02
	(0.01)	(0.01)	(0.01)	(0.01)	(0.01)	(0.01)	(0.01)	(0.01)	(0.01)
Black	0.09	0.22	0.07	0.29*	−0.04	0.22*	0.13	−0.17	−0.10
	(0.14)	(0.12)	(0.14)	(0.14)	(0.11)	(0.11)	(0.13)	(0.13)	(0.13)
Hispanic	−0.02	−0.07	−0.03	−0.08	0.03	−0.12	−0.30*	−0.23	−0.14
	(0.13)	(0.11)	(0.13)	(0.13)	(0.11)	(0.11)	(0.12)	(0.13)	(0.13)
Education	0.02	0.02	0.07*	0.08*	0.07*	0.07*	0.06*	0.09*	0.11*
	(0.03)	(0.02)	(0.03)	(0.03)	(0.02)	(0.02)	(0.02)	(0.03)	(0.03)
Age	−0.01*	−0.00	−0.00	−0.00	0.00*	−0.00	0.00	−0.00	−0.00
	(0.00)	(0.00)	(0.00)	(0.00)	(0.00)	(0.00)	(0.00)	(0.00)	(0.00)
Intercept	−0.33	−0.40	−0.65*	−0.63*	−1.29*	−0.16	−0.31	−1.10*	−0.86*
	(0.29)	(0.23)	(0.26)	(0.27)	(0.22)	(0.21)	(0.23)	(0.24)	(0.24)
Num. obs.	960	1194	1033	981	1123	1151	1147	1023	1015

$^* p < 0.05$

Appendix C

Appendix to Chapter 5

TABLE C.1 *Model of support for unilateral actions: Within-respondent change*

	Obama waves		
	Policymaking	Judicial appointments	Agency implementation
Presidential approval	−0.056	0.039	−0.039
	(0.102)	(0.090)	(0.087)
Observations	3069	3582	3839
Wave fixed effect	✓	✓	✓
Respondent fixed effects	✓	✓	✓
	Trump waves		
	Policymaking	Judicial appointments	Agency implementation
Presidential approval	−0.520	0.577	0.152
	(0.378)	(0.437)	(0.372)
Observations	250	256	346
Wave fixed effects	✓	✓	✓
Respondent fixed effects	✓	✓	✓

$^{*}p < 0.05.$

Note: Logistic model with robust standard errors clustered on respondent.

TABLE C.2 *Change in support for unilateral powers from October 2016 to May 2017*

Support October '16	Support May '17		
	Disagree	Neither	Agree
	Policymaking		
Disagree	75.9	14.9	9.1
Neither agree nor disagree	68.7	21.0	10.3
Agree	62.7	19.0	18.3
	Judicial appointments		
Disagree	78.7	10.1	11.2
Neither	65.1	23.5	11.4
Agree	70.7	10.3	19.0
	Agency implementation		
Disagree	51.2	18.4	30.4
Neither	44.5	29.8	25.7
Agree	35.1	15.3	49.5

TABLE C.3 *Change in support for unilateral powers from October 2016 to May 2017 (Democrats Only)*

Support October '16	Support May '17		
	Disagree	Neither agree nor disagree	Agree
	Policymaking		
Disagree	90.8	4.9	4.3
Neither	76.5	16.0	7.4
Agree	67.9	18.9	13.2
	Judicial appointments		
Disagree	92.2	4.8	3.0
Neither	77.3	16.0	6.7
Agree	74.3	10.5	15.1
	Bureaucratic implementation		
Disagree	76.9	12.5	10.6
Neither	60.1	23.6	16.2
Agree	41.5	15.7	42.8

TABLE C.4 *Change in support for unilateral powers from October 2016 to May 2017 (Republicans only)*

Support October '16	Support May '17		
	Disagree	Neither agree nor disagree	Agree
	Policymaking		
Disagree	64.9	22.1	13.1
Neither	40.9	36.4	22.7
Agree	36.8	15.8	47.4
	Judicial appointments		
Disagree	69.2	13.4	17.4
Neither	28.2	43.6	28.2
Agree	42.1	10.5	47.4
	Bureaucratic implementation		
Disagree	40.1	20.6	39.3
Neither	24.5	34.0	41.5
Agree	16.2	15.3	68.5

Appendix D

Appendix to Chapter 6

TABLE D.1 *Question wording for policy preference (TAPS instruments)*

Issue	Wording
Marijuana	Marijuana use should be legal in all states.
Taxes	Large business corporations pay less than their fair share in taxes.
Defense	The federal government should spend more money on national defense.

TABLE D.2 *Question wording for policy preference (YouGov instruments)*

Issue	Wording
Immigration	Do you support or oppose a proposal to allow undocumented immigrants to legally continue living in the United States if they meet certain criteria?
Health care	Do you support or oppose a proposal to reform the Affordable Care Act to reduce health care costs for small businesses?
Sanctions	Do you support or oppose imposing sanctions on foreign nations that are sponsoring terrorist acts, even if it hurts the economy by reducing opportunities for trade?

Appendix E

Appendix to Chapter 7

TABLE E.1 *Catalog of historical polls (1936–40)*

Date	Source	Question wording
Nov 1936	Gallup	Should Congress renew the president's power to regulate the amount of gold in the dollar?
Jan 1937	Gallup	Should Congress or the President be mainly responsible for America's neutrality policy?
Jan 1937	Gallup	Do you think such a change (giving the President power to enlarge the cabinet and reorganize government offices which would be under his supervision) is in line with the powers the founders of the Constitution meant the President to have?
Jan 1937	Gallup	Should Congress give the President power to enlarge the cabinet and reorganize government offices which would be under his supervision?
Jan 1937	Gallup	Should Congress renew the President's power to make trade agreements abroad?
Jul 1937	Gallup	Do you think the President of the United States should have more power or less power than he now has?
Sep 1937	Gallup	Which plan for keeping out of war do you have more faith in – having Congress pass stricter neutrality laws, or leaving the job up to the President?
Feb 1938	Gallup	Do you believe the President of the United States should have the power of a dictator over the country in time of war?
Mar 1938	Gallup	Would you favor the repeal of the Neutrality Law in order to give the President a freer hand in dealing with foreign nations?
Mar 1938	Gallup	Which of these plans for keeping out of war do you have more faith in – have Congress pass stricter neutrality laws or leave the job to the president?
Mar 1938	Gallup	Do you think the President of the United States should have more power or less power than he now has?
May 1938	Roper/ Fortune	Do you think President Roosevelt has concentrated too much power in his own hands?
Aug 1938	Gallup	Would you favor a constitutional amendment prohibiting any President of the United States from serving a third term?
Sep 1938	Gallup	Which plan for keeping out of war do you put more faith in – having Congress pass stricter neutrality laws, or leaving the job up to the President?
Oct 1938	Gallup	In deciding where and how to spend federal money for relief and recovery, who should have the greater say, Congress or the President?
Jan 1939	Gallup	Should Congress give the President power to appoint six executive assistants with a salary of $10,000 a year each?
Sep 1939	Roper/ Fortune Survey	Do you think the recent Congress was right or wrong in refusing to grant the President the power to decide what countries we would sell war materials to in case of a war abroad?
Dec 1940	Roper	Do you think we should or should not give the President more power and Congress less power in matters of national defense now?

TABLE E.2 *Catalog of historical polls (1941–4)*

Date	Source	Question wording
Jan 1941	Office of Public Opinion Research	The bill (President Franklin D. Roosevelt's Lend-Lease Bill now before Congress) would give the President power to lend to England or any other country warplanes or any other war supplies now belonging to our Army or Navy, if the President thought that this would help the defense of the United States. Do you approve or disapprove of this part of the bill?
Jan 1941	Office of Public Opinion Research	If Congress does pass the (lease-lend) bill, should the powers which it grants to the President be given to him for as long as the war lasts, or for only a limited period of time, such as 2 years?
Jan 1941	Office of Public Opinion Research	If Congress does pass this bill (the lend-lease bill regarding aid to England and other countries), should the powers which it grants to the President be given to him for as long as the war lasts, or for only a limited period of time, such as 2 years?
Jan 1941	Office of Public Opinion Research	If Congress does pass this bill (President Franklin D. Roosevelt's Lend-Lease Bill now before Congress), should the powers which it grants to the President be given to him for as long as the war lasts, or for only a limited period of time, such as 2 years?
Jan 1941	Office of Public Opinion Research	If Congress does pass this (lease-lend) bill, should the powers which it grants to the President be given to him for as long as the war lasts, or for only a limited period of time, such as 2 years?
Oct 1944	Office of Public Opinion Research	If two thirds of the United States Senate approves so that the United States does join such an international organization (in an effort to prevent future wars) how would you feel about the following question? The international organization may recommend that we use part of our armed forces to cooperate with others in stopping any war that may arise. Do you think that the United States should wait for a vote of approval in Congress in each case when war starts before the President can send a part of our armed forces to help stop the war, or do you think the President by himself should have the power to send some of our armed forces if he approves of the request of the international organization?
Oct 1944	Office of Public Opinion Research	If two-thirds of the United States Senate approves so that the United States does join such an international organization, how would you feel about the following question? The international organization may recommend that we use part of our armed forces to cooperate with others in stopping any war that may arise. Do you think that the United States should wait for a vote of approval in Congress in each case when war starts before the President can send a part of our armed forces to help stop the war, or do you think the President by himself should have the power send some of our armed forces if he approves of the request of the international organization?

TABLE E.3 *Catalog of historical polls (1944–53)*

Date	Source	Question wording
Oct 1944	Office of Public Opinion Research	Suppose an international organization is set up to prevent war by the use of military force, if necessary. Some people argue that before United States forces could be used in helping to prevent war, approval by Congress in addition to recommendation by the President should be required. Other people argue that if we have to wait for approval by Congress after the President has authorized the use of our forces, there would be so much delay that a big war might get started before we had a chance to stop it. How do you feel–do you think approval by congress should be required, even if there is some delay, or do you think our armed forces should be used is such a case at the request of the President alone?
May 1945	Gallup	Some writers believe that with Harry Truman as President, Congress will have more importance and power than it had under Franklin Roosevelt. Do you think this would be a good thing or a bad thing for the country?
Sep 1945	Gallup	At the present time when Congress passes a bill to spend money, the President cannot veto parts of that bill but must accept it in full or veto it. Do you think this should be changed so that the President can veto some items in a bill to spend money without vetoing the entire bill?
Feb 1947	Gallup	Do you favor adding a law to the Constitution to prevent any President of the United States from serving more than two terms?
Feb 1947	Gallup	Would you favor adding a law to the Consitution to prevent any President of the United States from serving more than two terms?
Mar 1947	Gallup	Do you favor adding a law to the Constitution to prevent any President of the United States from serving more than two terms?
May 1947	Gallup	At the present time, when Congress passes a bill, the President cannot veto parts of that bill, but must accept it in full or veto it. Do you think this should be changed so that the President can veto some items in a bill without vetoing the entire bill?
Jan 1951	Gallup	Some people say that the president should not be allowed to send United States soldiers overseas unless the Congress first approves it. Other people say that the president should have the power to send soldiers overseas when he feels the situation calls for it. With which group do you, yourself, agree?
Jan 1952	Gallup	Some people say the President should not be allowed to send troops overseas unless Congress approves it. Other people say the President should have the power to send troops overseas when he feels the situation calls for it. With which group do you agree?
Jul 1953	Gallup	President Eisenhower has asked the right to give or lend Government owned surplus grain to nations faced with famine. Should Congress give President Eisenhower this power, or not?
Aug 1953	Gallup	At present, when Congress passes a law to spend money, the president cannot approve just parts of that law, but must approve it in full, or turn it down in full. Should this be changed so that he can turn down some parts of the law without turning down the entire law?

TABLE E.4 *Catalog of historical polls (1955–78)*

Date	Source	Question wording
Jan 1955	Gallup	Generally speaking, do you approve or disapprove of the Bricker Amendment, which would curb the treaty making power of the president?
Mar 1957	Roper	Here are a few questions about matters that may come up before Congress this session. As you know, a law was passed a few years ago so that a President of the US (United States) can not serve more than two terms. Recently there has been some talk of changing back to the way it used to be, when there was no two-term limit. Do you think there should be a two-term limit, or should not be?
Jun 1957	Gallup	At present, when Congress passes a law to spend money, the president cannot approve just parts of that law, but must approve it in full, or turn it down in full. Should this be changed so that he can turn down some parts of the law without turning down the entire law?
Jul 1968	Harris	Here is a series of statements which have been made about the U.S. (United States) Supreme Court and about the nomination of Abe Fortas as Chief Justice. For each, tell me if you agree or disagree … If the President appoints a qualified man, the Senate should confirm his choice.
Apr 1973	Harris	Congress has passed a bill that says it will agree to a $268 billion ceiling on all federal spending, but would not allow President Nixon to refuse to spend monies Congress appropriates. Do you tend to agree or disagree with Congress on this matter?
Apr 1975	Gallup	At present, when Congress passes a bill, the president cannot veto parts of that bill, but must accept it in full or veto it. Do you think this should be changed so that the president can veto some items in a bill without vetoing the entire bill?
Jul 1976	Gallup	Are there any of them (on this list of types of government leaders and groups) that you would like to see have more power than they now have? [yes='President']
Dec 1976	Harris	Would you favor giving the President the power to control wages if he should think they are rising too fast for the good of the economy or would you oppose wage controls?
Dec 1976	Harris	Some people have said that the only way to be sure that prices can be held down is to give the President the power to control prices when he feels it is necessary. Do you favor this power of presidential control or do you oppose it?
Nov 1978	Gallup	At the present time, when Congress passes a bill, the president cannot veto parts of that bill, but must accept it in full or veto it. Do you think this should be changed so that the president can veto some items in a bill without vetoing the entire bill?

TABLE E.5 *Catalog of historical polls (1979–82)*

Date	Source	Question wording
May 1979	*Los Angeles Times*	Do you think the President should or should not have the power to ration gasoline if he decides there is a severe shortage?
Jul 1979	ABC News/Harris	(Now let me read you some specific things President Carter proposed in his (recent energy) speech. For each, tell me if you tend to favor or oppose it.) Giving the president the power to set mandatory conservation targets on the use of energy for every state to meet.
Jul 1979	ABC News/Harris	(Now let me read you some specific things President Carter proposed in his (recent energy) speech. For each, tell me if you tend to favor or oppose it.) Giving the president the power to put into effect a system of gasoline rationing if there is a nationwide shortage.
Sep 1979	Gallup	(Now I would like to ask you some questions about the president and Congress. Some people think that the president ought to have the major responsibility for making policy, while other people think that Congress ought to have the major responsibility. In general, which do you think should have the major responsibility for setting policy?
Sep 1979	Gallup	More specifically which do you think should have the major responsibility for setting energy policies?
Sep 1979	Gallup	Which do you think should have the major responsibility for setting economic policy?
Sep 1979	Gallup	Do you think the President has: too much power, too little power, or just about the right amount today?
Dec 1979	Public Agenda Foundation	(So far we've talked about newspapers and television, but now I'd like to talk about the broader areas of freedom of speech and freedom of the press or what I'll combine and call freedom of expression. Freedom of expression means different things to different people, now I'm interested in what it means to you. I'll read you some statements about the right of freedom of expression, about what it protects and how far it goes. For each one, tell me whether you agree that this is a freedom of expression right or not. If you're not sure, just say so.) ... the president has a right to close down a newspaper that prints stories that he feels are biased or inaccurate. Agree or disagree?
Oct 1981	Gallup	At the present time, when Congress passes a bill, the president cannot veto parts of that bill, but must accept it in full or veto it. Do you think this should be changed so that the president can veto some items in a bill without vetoing the entire bill?
May 1982	Gallup	At the present time, when Congress passes a bill, the president cannot veto parts of that bill, but must accept it in full or veto it. Do you think this should be changed so that the president can veto some items in a bill without vetoing the entire bill?

TABLE E.6 *Catalog of historical polls (1983–7)*

Date	Source	Question wording
Sep 1983	Gallup	Do you think the president should have to get the approval of Congress in order to keep the marines in Lebanon, or should he be able to make that decision himself?
Oct 1983	Gallup	At the present time, when Congress passes a bill, the president cannot veto parts of that bill, but must accept it in full or veto it. Do you think this should be changed so that the president can veto some items in a bill without vetoing the entire bill?
May 1984	Public Agenda Foundation	(There is debate among American policymakers about the best way to deal with the Soviet Union, and I want to read you some of the arguments in that debate. In a moment, I'll ask you about arguments made by people with a different point of view, but now I'd like to know how you feel about the following statements and arguments. For each of the following, please tell me whether you agree or disagree.) ... When it comes to America's national security, the president has access to secret information and we should go along with what he decides.
Nov 1985	*New York Times*	Who should have the most say about what cuts should be made to balance the budget – the president or Congress?
Jan 1986	President's Blue Ribbon Commission on Defense Management	Who do you think should have the main responsibility for reducing waste and fraud in defense spending?
Jul 1986	Hart	Under our system of checks and balances, it would be wrong to give a president too much power to impose his philosophy on the Supreme Court.
Aug 1986	Gallup	Would you favor or oppose such a proposal (to repeal the 22nd amendment to the Constitution to enable a president to serve more than two four-year terms)?
May 1987	Gallup/ *Newsweek*	Under the War Powers Resolution of 1973, a president must withdraw US troops from any hostile situation after two months unless the Congress has declared war. Do you think this gives Congress too much power over the president as US Commander-in-Chief, or do you think it is necessary to keep Congress involved in the war-making policies of the country?
May 1987	CBS News/ *New York Times*	Who should have the power to declare war – the president or Congress?

TABLE E.7 *Catalog of historical polls (1987–89)*

Date	Source	Question wording
Jun 1987	ABC News/ *Washington Post*	President Reagan would like the law changed to give presidents the right to reject individual items in large spending bills without having to reject the whole bill. Reagan says that would help him cut government spending and reduce the federal budget deficit. Critics say that would give the president too much power over how government money is spent. Do you favor or oppose giving the president the authority to reject individual items in spending bills without having to reject the entire bill?
Jul 1987	Gallup	At the present time, when Congress passes a bill, the president cannot veto parts of that bill, but must accept it in full or veto it. Do you think this should be changed so that the president can veto some items in a bill without vetoing the entire bill?
Sep 1987	CBS News/ *New York Times*	Do you think the president should get the approval of Congress in order to keep the ships in the Persian Gulf, or should he be able to make that decision himself?
Sep 1988	Market Opinion Research	(Here are some other ideas that people have had about dealing with wars in the third world. for each, please tell me if you think it is a good idea or a bad idea.) If our president and military are involved, they should keep their assistance to these countries secret, even if it means withholding information from Congress, the media, and the public?
Dec 1988	Roper	At the present time, when Congress passes a budget bill, the president must either sign the bill or reject it. Some people believe the president should be allowed to approve some expenditures in a budget bill and reduce or reject others that he disapproves of or thinks are too high. This would be what is called the line-item veto. Do you think the present all-or-nothing system is better, or that the line-item veto would be better?
Jan 1989	Gallup	At the present time, when Congress passes a bill, the president cannot veto parts of that bill, but must accept or veto it in full. Do you think this should or should not be changed so that the president can veto some items in a bill without vetoing the entire bill?
Feb 1989	ABC News/ *Washington Post*	Do you think the president should be able to pick whomever he wants for his cabinet without the approval of the Senate or do you think the president should have to have his cabinet choices approved by the Senate?
Feb 1989	Gallup	Would you favor or oppose repealing the 22nd amendment to the Constitution so that United States presidents could serve for more than 4-year terms?
Mar 1989	*Los Angeles Times*	Do you think the president should be able to pick whomever he wants for his cabinet without the approval of the Senate or do you think the president should have to have his cabinet choices approved by the Senate?

TABLE E.8 *Catalog of historical polls (1990–3)*

Date	Source	Question wording
Nov 1990	Gallup	Which of the following comes closest to your own view: the president should be able to go to war against Iraq without getting approval from Congress, or the president should be able to go to war against Iraq only if Congress approves of the decision?
Dec 1990	NBC News/ Wall Street Journal	Do you think President Bush should or should not be required to receive approval from Congress before taking offensive military action against Iraq?
Jan 1991	Gallup	How important do you think it is that President Bush first get the approval of Congress before taking military action against Iraq? Is it very important, somewhat important, not too important or not at all important?
Jan 1991	ABC News/ Washington Post	If (President) Bush decided to go to war with Iraq do you think he should ask permission from Congress before launching an attack, or not?
Mar 1992	Gordon S. Black	A line-item veto is an existing power in most states that permits the governors to veto only part of a bill, allowing the rest of the bill to become law. Some people are proposing that the president be granted this power, which could be used to veto some parts of bills that a president considers wasteful. others feel that the line-item veto would give the president too much power. Do you favor or oppose giving the president the line-item veto?
Dec 1992	NBC News/ Wall Street Journal	I would like to read you two statements about the proposal to give the President use of a line-item veto. The proposal would allow him to reject individual parts of spending programs that are included in a larger bill without having to veto the entire bill. Please tell me which one of the statements about this issue comes closer to your point of view. Statement A: Those in favor of giving the President the line-item veto say that this would make it easier for him to cut wasteful spending, and that most governors already have this power. Or Statement B: Those opposed to giving the President the line-item veto say that it would give too much power to the President and allow him to use this power for partisan purposes.
Mar 1993	Political Reform Study	A line-item veto is an existing power in most states that permits the governors to veto only part of a bill, allowing the rest of the bill to become law. Some people are proposing that the President be granted this power, which could be used to veto some parts of bills that a President considers wasteful. Others feel that the line-item veto would give the President too much power. Do you favor or oppose giving the President the line-item veto?
Oct 1993	ABC News Poll	Do you think Congress should have the power to prevent a president from sending US (United States) troops to participate in United Nations peacekeeping missions?

TABLE E.9 *Catalog of historical polls (1994–8)*

Date	Source	Question wording
Aug 1994	Gallup	Some members of Congress maintain that the Constitution of the United States requires President (Bill) Clinton to 'obtain prior express congressional authorization before he may order United States armed forces to make war in Haiti.' Do you favor or oppose President Clinton having to get congressional authorization before he takes any military action in Haiti?
Nov 1994	Gallup	(Here are some of the proposals in the Contract with America which the Republicans pledged to bring to a vote in the House of Representatives within the first 100 days of 1995. For each one, please tell me whether you favor or oppose it.) ... legislation which would allow the president to veto individual parts of a proposed spending bill, rather than having to accept or veto the entire bill.
Jan 1995	ABC News	Do you think the President of the United States should or should not have the authority to veto individual items in the federal budget, something known as the line-item veto?
Mar 1995	*Time*/ CNN	Please tell me whether you favor or oppose each of the following proposals ... giving the president a line-item veto, allowing him to veto one part of a spending bill passed by Congress without vetoing the whole measure.
Aug 1997	Gallup	Would you favor or oppose a proposal which would make it easier for the president to make trade agreements with other countries similar to the North American Free Trade Agreement between the United States and Mexico – also known as NAFTA?
Aug 1997	Penn, Schoen, & Berland	Presidents since 1974 have had trade negotiating authority known as fast track, which means the trade agreements the president negotiated are considered in Congress within 90 days and put to a simple yes or no vote without any additions that could upset the agreement. The authority to do this expired in 1994, and President (Bill) Clinton no longer has such authority. Do you strongly support renewing President Clinton's fast track trade authority, somewhat support, somewhat oppose, or strongly oppose it?
Sep 1997	Harris	President (Bill) Clinton is asking Congress to renew 'fast track' authority to him, to negotiate trade deals with other countries. Should Congress renew fast track authority to the president, or not?
Jan 1998	Pew	President (Bill) Clinton has asked Congress for authority to negotiate trade agreements. This would mean that once negotiations are completed, Congress would vote yes or no on the agreement as a whole, but could not make any amendments or changes. Do you favor or oppose giving the president this so-called fast track authority to negotiate free trade agreements?

Date	Source	Question wording
Feb 1998	Gallup	Some members of Congress maintain that the Constitution of the united states requires President (Bill) Clinton "to obtain prior express congressional authorization before he may order United States armed forces to make war in Iraq." Do you favor or oppose President Clinton having to get congressional authorization before he takes any military action in Iraq?
Apr 1998	Women in International Trade	Presidents since 1974 have had negotiating authority known as fast-track, which means that trade agreements the president negotiated are considered in Congress within 90 days and put to a simple yes or no vote without any additions that could upset the agreements. The authority to do this expired in 1994, and President (Bill) Clinton no longer has such an authority. Do you strongly support renewing President Clinton's fast track authority, somewhat support, somewhat oppose, or strongly oppose it?
Oct 1999	Program on International Policy Attitudes	Presidents since 1974 have had trade negotiating authority known as "fast track," which means the trade agreements the president negotiated are considered in Congress within 90 days and put to a simple yes or no vote, without any additions that could upset the agreement. The authority to do this expired in 1994, and President (Bill) Clinton no longer has such authority. do you strongly support renewing President Clinton's fast track trade authority, somewhat support, somewhat oppose, or strongly oppose it?
Feb 2001	Fox News/ Opinion Dynamics	Would you favor or oppose changing the Constitution to limit future presidents' right to grant pardons?
Feb 2001	Fox News/ Opinion Dynamics	Do you think that some of the pardons former President (Bill) Clinton issued on his last day in office were an abuse of the presidential pardon power or were they fairly typical of presidential pardons?
Mar 2001	Fox News/ Opinion Dynamics	Do you think the President of the United States should have the power to stop a strike by a labor union?
Jun 2002	CBS News	Do you think the president should have to get the approval of Congress in order to take military action against a nation that is planning to use weapons against U.S. (United States) or should he be able to make that decision himself?
Aug 2002	CBS News	Do you think the President should have to get the approval of Congress before taking military action against Iraq to try and remove Saddam Hussein from power, or should he be able to make that decision himself?
Aug 2002	*Newsweek*	How important do you think it is that President (George W.) Bush first get ... the approval of Congress before taking military action against Iraq? is it very important, somewhat important, not too important or not at all important?
Sep 2002	CBS News/ *New York Times*	Do you think the President should have to get the approval of Congress before taking military action against Iraq to try and remove Saddam Hussein from power, or should he be able to make that decision himself?

TABLE E.11 *Catalog of historical polls (2002–6)*

Date	Source	Question wording
Sep 2002	*Newsweek*	How important do you think it is that President (George W.) Bush first get ... the approval of Congress before taking military action against Iraq? is it very important, somewhat important, not too important or not at all important?
Sep 2002	NBC News/ *Wall Street Journal*	Which of the following positions do you agree with more? Statement A: the president should get congressional approval before taking any action against Saddam Hussein because Congress should have a role in the decision. Or Statement B: the president should take actions necessary to remove Saddam Hussein without getting congressional approval because a congressional debate might take it more difficult to achieve the objectives.
Sep 2002	*Newsweek*	How important do you think it is that President (George W.) Bush first get ... the approval of Congress before taking military action against Iraq? is it very important, somewhat important, not too important or not at all important?
Oct 2002	PIPA/ Knowledge Networks	Currently there is a debate in Congress about whether to grant the President's (George W. Bush's) request to let him decide whether the US (United States) should go to war with Iraq. Do you think Congress should give the President the power to decide whether the US should go to war with Iraq or Congress should retain the right to vote on whether the US should go to war with Iraq?
Jun 2003	Fox News/ Opinion Dynamics	Do you support or oppose changing the Constitution to allow a president to serve more than two years?
Jul 2004	Chicago Council	(How much influence do you think the following should have on US (United States) foreign policy? ... the president?
Jan 2006	Fox News/ Opinion Dynamics	Do you think the president should or should not have the power to authorize the National Security Agency to monitor electronic communications of suspected terrorists without getting warrants, even if one end of the communication is in the United States?
Feb 2006	Fox News/ Opinion Dynamics	Do you think the president should or should not have the power to authorize the National Security Agency to monitor electronic communications of suspected terrorists without getting warrants, even if one end of the communication is in the United States?
Feb 2006	ACLU	With whom do you agree more? Those who say the president needs the ability to eavesdrop on Americans without a court warrant in order to fight against terrorism, or those who say the president can just as effectively combat terrorism by following the law and getting court warrants to spy on Americans?

TABLE E.12 *Catalog of historical polls (2006–7)*

Date	Source	Question wording
Feb 2006	ACLU	With whom do you agree more? Those who say the president needs the ability to eavesdrop on Americans without a court warrant in order to fight against terrorism, or those who say no one is above the law, not even the president. President (George W.) bush should get court warrants to spy on Americans?
Feb 2006	ACLU	With whom do you agree more? Those who say the President (George W. Bush) should have the power to take whatever actions he believes are necessary to protect the country from terrorists, or those who say the President should not be acting on his own in deciding how to fight terrorism without the checks and balances of the courts or Congress.
Apr 2006	CBS News	Who do you think should take the lead responsibility in dealing with rising gasoline prices – the president, the Congress, or the Secretary of Energy?
Jul 2006	Harris	(Now, regardless of whether you favor or oppose each of the following powers of investigation, do you think this use of investigative powers by the president should be done under his executive authority without needing congressional authorization, or should this use of investigative power by the president be done only with congressional authorization?) ... monitoring of the content of internet discussions in chat rooms and other forums.
Jul 2006	Harris	(Now, regardless of whether you favor or oppose each of the following powers of investigation, do you think this use of investigative powers by the president should be done under his executive authority without needing congressional authorization, or should this use of investigative power by the president be done only with congressional authorization?) ... monitoring of international financial transactions to trace terrorist funding sources.
Jul 2006	Harris	(Now, regardless of whether you favor or oppose each of the following powers of investigation, do you think this use of investigative powers by the president should be done under his executive authority without needing congressional authorization, or should this use of investigative power by the president be done only with congressional authorization?) ... monitoring of cell phones and e-mail to intercept the content of communications of people suspected of terrorist activity.
Jan 2007	CBS	Do you think the president should have to get the approval of Congress before increasing the number of US (United States) troops in Iraq, or should he be able to make that decision himself?
Mar 2007	CNN	Who do you think should be primarily responsible for setting US (United States) policy in Iraq, Congress or the president?
Apr 2007	CBS/ *New York Times*	Currently, President (George W.) Bush and Congress disagree about what to do about U.S. (United States) troop levels in Iraq. Who do you think should have the final say about troop levels in Iraq, the president or Congress?

TABLE E.13 *Catalog of historical polls (2007–8)*

Date	Source	Question wording
Apr 2007	CBS	Currently, President (George W.) Bush and Congress disagree about what to do about US (United States) troop levels in Iraq. Who do you think should have the final say about troop levels in Iraq, the president or Congress?
Apr 2007	Fox News/ Opinion Dynamics	Who do you think should decide when US (United States) troops leave Iraq – the president or members of Congress?
May 2007	CNN	Who do you think should be primarily responsible for setting US (United States) policy in Iraq, Congress or the president?
May 2008	Gallup	Do you think the president should or should not be required to get the approval of Congress before sending United States armed forces into action outside the United States?
May 2008	Gallup	(Do you think the president should or should not be required to get the approval of Congress before sending US (United States) armed forces into action under each of the following circumstances?) how about ... if the president did not expect a combat operation to last a long time?
May 2008	Gallup	(Do you think the president should or should not be required to get the approval of Congress before sending US (United States) armed forces into action under each of the following circumstances?) how about ... if the president wanted to use air force or navy planes to bomb suspected terrorists?
May 2008	Gallup	(Do you think the president should or should not be required to get the approval of Congress before sending US (United States) armed forces into action under each of the following circumstances?) how about ... in order to conduct a humanitarian mission in response to a natural disaster?
May 2008	Gallup	Do you think the president should or should not be required to get the approval of Congress before sending US (United States) armed forces into action under each of the following circumstances? how about ... if the United States were attacked?
May 2008	Gallup	(Do you think the president should or should not be required to get the approval of Congress before sending US (United States) armed forces into action under each of the following circumstances?) how about ... if American citizens were in danger or in need of rescue abroad?
Sep 2008	Associated Press/ National Constitution Center	Do you think the Congress should have the power to force the president's closest advisors to testify before congressional committees, or do you think the president's closest advisors should be protected from having to testify before congressional committees?
Sep 2008	Associated Press/ National Constitution Center	If you thought it would help improve the economy, would you favor or oppose giving the president more power at the expense of the power of Congress and the courts?

TABLE E.14 *Catalog of historical polls (2008–14)*

Date	Source	Question wording
Sep 2008	Associated Press/ National Constitution Center	If you thought it would help improve national security, would you favor or oppose giving the president more power at the expense of the power of Congress and the courts?
Sep 2009	Associated Press/ National Constitution Center	If you thought it would help improve the economy would you favor or oppose giving the President more power at the expense of the power of Congress and the courts?
Jun 2010	Chicago Council	How much influence do you think the following should have on US (United States) foreign policy? ... the president?
Sep 2010	Associated Press/ National Constitution Center/GfK	If you thought it would help improve the economy would you favor or oppose giving the President more power at the expense of power of Congress and the courts?
Sep 2011	Associated Press/ National Constitution Center/GfK	If you thought it would help improve the economy would you favor or oppose giving the president more power at the expense of the power of Congress and the courts?
Feb 2013	Fox News	Do you think the president of the United States, on his own, should be able to authorize the use of deadly force, such as a drone strike, to kill a suspected terrorist who is a US citizen on US soil?
May 2014	Chicago Council	How much influence do you think the following should have on US (United States) foreign policy? ... the president?
Aug 2014	Reason Foundation/ Rupe Foundation	Would you favor or oppose a constitutional amendment to allow the president to veto certain parts of a bill, including spending, without vetoing everything in the bill, also known as a line-item veto?
Sep 2014	CNN	Do you think President (Barack) Obama should ask Congress for the authority to use additional military force against ISIS, or do you think he should have the option of using additional military force against ISIS without authorization from Congress?
Dec 2014	CNN	Do you think President (Barack) Obama should ask Congress for the authority to continue to use military force against ISIS (Islamic militants operating in Iraq and Syria), or do you think he should have the option of continuing to use military force against ISIS without authorization from Congress?
Dec 2014	ABC News/ *Washington Post*	Regardless of what you think of the program (executive action on undocumented immigrants), in taking this action do you think (Barack) Obama acted within his authority as president, or do you think he went beyond his authority as president?

TABLE E.15 *Catalog of historical polls (2015–16)*

Date	Source	Question wording
Jan 2015	Fox News	(President (Barack) Obama has used his executive authority to enact several policies without consulting Congress. For each of the following, please tell me whether you think Obama exceeded his authority as president, or not.) ... transferring suspected terrorists out of the detention center at Guantanamo Bay.
Jan 2015	Fox News	(President (Barack) Obama has used his executive authority to enact several policies without consulting Congress. For each of the following, please tell me whether you think Obama exceeded his authority as president, or not.) ... postponing some penalties under Obamacare.
Jan 2015	Fox News	(President (Barack) Obama has used his executive authority to enact several policies without consulting Congress. For each of the following, please tell me whether you think Obama exceeded his authority as president, or not.) ... reaching a climate-change deal with China.
Jan 2015	Fox News	(President (Barack) Obama has used his executive authority to enact several policies without consulting Congress. For each of the following, please tell me whether you think Obama exceeded his authority as president, or not.) ... ending the trade embargo and normalizing diplomatic relations with Cuba.
Jan 2015	Fox News	Regardless of what you think of this immigration policy, do you think Barack Obama acted within his authority as president when he issued this executive order, or do you think his actions went beyond his authority as president?
Feb 2015	Quinnipiac University Polling Institute	Regardless of what you think of this immigration policy, do you think Barack Obama acted within his authority as president when he issued this executive order, or do you think his actions went beyond his authority as president?
Nov 2015	Fox News	Would you favor or oppose President (Barack) Obama bypassing Congress and using executive action to close the Guantanamo Bay detention center?
Jan 2016	CBS News/ *New York Times*	Regardless of what you think of this gun policy (expanding background checks and strengthening federal enforcement of gun laws), do you think Barack Obama acted within his authority as president when he issued this executive action, or do you think his actions went beyond his authority as president?
Aug 2016	Pew Research Center	(Which comes closer to your view – even if neither is exactly right?) ... Many of the country's problems could be dealt with more effectively if US presidents didn't worry so much about Congress or the Supreme Court; it would be too risky to give US presidents more power to deal directly with many of the country's problems?

TABLE E.16 *Catalog of historical polls (2017–18)*

Date	Source	Question wording
Feb 2017	Pew Research Center	(Which comes closer to your view – even if neither is exactly right?) ... Many of the country's problems could be dealt with more effectively if US presidents didn't worry so much about Congress or the Supreme Court; it would be too risky to give US presidents more power to deal directly with many of the country's problems?
Feb 2017	Pew Research Center	As you may know, the Twenty-Second Amendment to the Constitution limits a United States President to two terms in office. Do you think US presidents should be allowed to serve for more than two terms, or do you think US presidents should be limited to only two terms?
Mar 2017	Winning the Issues	... It is just as founders intended it to be; it has shifted too much towards the president; it has shifted too much towards Congress.
May 2017	Quinnipiac University Polling Institute	Do you consider President (Donald) Trump's decision to fire former FBI (Federal Bureau of Investigation) Director James Comey an abuse of power, or not?
Jun 2017	Quinnipiac University Polling Institute	Do you consider President (Donald) Trump's decision to fire former FBI (Federal Bureau of Investigation) Director James Comey an abuse of power, or not?
Jun 2017	Associated Press-NORC Attitudes on Climate Change	If you thought it would help solve the country's problems, would you favor or oppose giving the president more power at the expense of the power of Congress and the courts?
Mar 2018	Pew Research Center	(As I read some pairs of statements, please tell me whether the first statement or the second statement comes closer to your own views – even if neither is exactly right.) ... Many of the country's problems could be dealt with more effectively if US presidents didn't have to worry so much about Congress or the courts, it would be too risky to give US presidents more power to deal directly with many of the country's problems.
Apr 2018	Fox News	In general, do you think President (Donald) Trump should – or should not – get the consent of Congress before authorizing US military action?
Jun 2018	AP-NORC	Do you think it would be acceptable or unacceptable for presidents to pardon themselves if charged with a crime?
Jun 2018	USA Today	President (Donald) Trump says he has the absolute power to pardon himself, although he says he won't need to do that. Just your own best judgment, does a president have the power to pardon himself?

TABLE E.17 *Catalog of historical polls (2019–20)*

Date	Source	Question wording
Jan 2019	Fox News	If Congress does not approve funding for a wall (on the border with Mexico), would you support or oppose the president (Donald Trump) bypassing Congress and declaring a national emergency on the nation's southern border that would give him the executive power to construct a border wall without congressional approval?
Jul 2019	Pew Research Center	As I read some pairs of statements, please tell me whether the first statement or the second statement comes closer to your own views – even if neither is exactly right ... Many of the country's problems could be dealt with more effectively if United States presidents didn't have to worry so much about Congress or the courts. It would be too risky to give US presidents more power to deal directly with many of the country's problems.
Jan 2020	Fox News	In general, do you think President (Donald) Trump should – or should not – get the consent of Congress before authorizing United States military action?
Jan 2020	Quinnipiac University Polling Institute	Do you think President (Donald) Trump should consult with Congress if he plans to launch more military strikes in the Middle East or not?
Feb 2020	Fox News	Do you think some of the recent pardons President (Donald) Trump issued were an abuse of the presidential pardon power or were they fairly typical of presidential pardons?
Jun 2020	Pew Research Center	Which of the following statements comes closer to your own view – even if neither is exactly right? ... Many of the country's problems could be dealt with more effectively if United States presidents didn't have to worry so much about Congress or the courts, it would be too risky to give US presidents more power to deal directly with many of the country's problems.
Sep 2020	Marquette Law School	When Congress fails to act, should the president have the power to make laws on his own?
Sep 2020	Marquette Law School	If the Supreme Court rules against the president in a case, does the president have the power to ignore that ruling, or is the president required to do as the ruling says?
Dec 2020	USA Today	President (Donald) Trump is reportedly considering issuing a significant number of pardons for his children, top aides and others before leaving office. Which comes closer to your view? ... This would be an appropriate use of the president's pardon power, this would be an abuse of the president's pardon power.
Dec 2020	USA Today	President (Donald) Trump is reportedly considering whether to issue a preemptive pardon for himself before leaving office. Which comes closer to your view? ... This would be an appropriate use of the president's pardon power, this would be an abuse of the president's pardon power.

TABLE E.18 *Attitudes towards unilateral action and evaluations of policy outcomes (February 2014)*

Independent Variables	Freed slaves	Established WPA	Japanese internment	Desegreg ation	Steel seizure	Abortion restrictions	Enhanced interrogation violence	Research gun	DACA
Approve of unilateral action	0.08*	0.20*	0.15*	0.13*	0.37*	0.09	0.12*	0.36*	0.30*
	(0.03)	(0.04)	(0.04)	(0.04)	(0.04)	(0.05)	(0.04)	(0.04)	(0.04)
Ideology (+=liberal)	0.00	0.03	−0.07*	0.01	−0.05*	−0.11*	−0.14*	0.04*	0.06*
	(0.02)	(0.02)	(0.02)	(0.02)	(0.02)	(0.02)	(0.02)	(0.02)	(0.02)
Partisanship (+=Democrat)	0.02*	0.06*	0.00	0.01	−0.01	−0.03*	−0.03*	0.04*	0.05*
	(0.01)	(0.01)	(0.01)	(0.01)	(0.01)	(0.01)	(0.01)	(0.01)	(0.01)
Intercept	0.70*	0.29*	0.34*	0.65*	0.33*	0.85*	1.06*	0.05	0.07
	(0.04)	(0.05)	(0.05)	(0.04)	(0.05)	(0.05)	(0.05)	(0.04)	(0.05)
N	744	572	725	724	678	682	690	738	739

* $p < 0.05$

Note: Entries are linear regression coefficients with standard errors in parentheses. The dependent variable is an indicator for whether respondents approve of the executive action which accomplished each policy outcome described at the top of each column. Data are weighted to national population parameters.

TABLE E.19 *Attitudes towards unilateral action and evaluations of policy outcomes (November 2014)*

Independent Variables	Freed slaves	Japanese internment	Desegregation	Steel seizure
Approve of	0.15*	0.01	0.08*	0.19*
unilateral action	(0.03)	(0.04)	(0.04)	(0.04)
Ideology	0.05*	−0.06*	0.06*	−0.03
(+=liberal)	(0.02)	(0.02)	(0.02)	(0.02)
Partisanship	0.00	0.02*	−0.01	0.04*
(+=Democrat)	(0.01)	(0.01)	(0.01)	(0.01)
Intercept	0.57*	0.29*	0.57*	0.16*
	(0.04)	(0.04)	(0.05)	(0.05)
N	735	692	727	641

$^*p < 0.05$

Note: Entries are linear regression coefficients with standard errors in parentheses. The dependent variable is an indicator for whether respondents approve of the executive action which accomplished each policy outcome described at the top of each column. Data are weighted to national population parameters.

TABLE E.20 *Attitudes towards unilateral action and evaluations of policy outcomes (January 2016)*

Independent variables	Freed slaves	Japanese internment	Desegregation	Abortion restrictions	Enhanced interrogation	DACA	Gun show loophole	Report lost guns	Background checks
Approve of unilateral action	0.17*	0.05	0.15*	0.04	−0.01	0.27*	0.20*	0.13*	0.27*
	(0.02)	(0.03)	(0.03)	(0.04)	(0.03)	(0.03)	(0.03)	(0.02)	(0.03)
Ideology (+=liberal)	0.04*	−0.04*	0.05*	−0.10*	−0.11*	0.08*	0.06*	0.03*	0.03*
	(0.01)	(0.02)	(0.01)	(0.02)	(0.02)	(0.02)	(0.01)	(0.01)	(0.01)
Partisanship (+=Democrat)	−0.01	−0.01	0.00	−0.03*	−0.03*	0.02*	0.02*	0.01	0.02*
	(0.01)	(0.01)	(0.01)	(0.01)	(0.01)	(0.01)	(0.01)	(0.01)	(0.01)
Intercept	0.68*	0.42*	0.55*	0.83*	1.07*	0.15*	0.41*	0.67*	0.42*
	(0.03)	(0.04)	(0.03)	(0.04)	(0.04)	(0.04)	(0.03)	(0.03)	(0.03)
N	1,363	1,274	1,308	1,244	1,311	1,334	1,438	1,388	1,403

$^*p < 0.05$

Note: Entries are linear regression coefficients with standard errors in parentheses. The dependent variable is an indicator for whether respondents approve of the executive action which accomplished each policy outcome described at the top of each column. Data are weighted to national population parameters.

Appendix F

Appendix to Chapter 8

TABLE F.1 *Model of support for executive powers and support for democracy, the Americas: Logistic regression models*

	Close legislature	Dissolve courts
Executive approval	0.298*	0.524*
	(0.094)	(0.088)
Support for democracy	−0.393*	−0.480*
	(0.052)	(0.072)
Intercept	−2.095*	−1.905*
	(0.106)	(0.162)
Country × Year fixed effects	✓	✓
Demographic controls	✓	✓
Num. obs.	72,602	47,355

*$p < 0.05$.
Note: Logistic regressions with robust standard errors clustered on country/wave.

TABLE F.2 *Model of support for executive powers and support for rule of law, African countries: Logistic regression models*

	Decide	Not bound	Justify	Pass laws
Executive approval	0.391*	0.178*	0.164*	0.367*
	(0.052)	(0.027)	(0.030)	(0.047)
Support for rule of law	−0.682*	−0.289*	−0.522*	−0.710*
	(0.056)	(0.054)	(0.048)	(0.066)
Intercept	−0.356*	−0.273*	0.279*	0.141
	(0.096)	(0.062)	(0.068)	(0.092)
Country × Wave fixed effect	✓	✓	✓	✓
Demographic controls	✓	✓	✓	✓
Num. obs.	140,670	145,648	128,494	104,932

*$p < 0.05$.
Note: Logistic regressions with robust standard errors clustered on country/wave.

TABLE F.3 *Model of support for executive powers and support for democracy, African countries: Logistic regression models*

	Decide	Not bound	Justify	Pass laws
Executive approval	0.288*	0.144*	0.145*	0.324*
	(0.049)	(0.030)	(0.032)	(0.056)
Support for democracy	−0.788*	−0.227*	−0.512*	−0.522*
	(0.049)	(0.037)	(0.038)	(0.049)
Intercept	−0.390*	−0.296*	0.215*	0.038
	(0.084)	(0.056)	(0.057)	(0.097)
Country × Wave fixed effect	✓	✓	✓	✓
Demographic controls	✓	✓	✓	✓
Num. obs.	144,365	118,223	103,468	75,419

*$p < 0.05$.

Note: Logistic regressions with robust standard errors clustered on country/wave.

TABLE F.4 *Model of support for executive powers and support for democracy, the Americas: Using survey weights*

	Close legislature	Dissolve courts
Executive approval	0.042*	0.059*
	(0.003)	(0.004)
Support for democracy	−0.065*	−0.073*
	(0.005)	(0.006)
Intercept	0.108*	0.092*
	(0.010)	(0.009)
Country × Wave fixed effects	✓	✓
Num. obs.	96,745	55,033

*$p < 0.05$.

Note: Survey design is explicitly declared including weights as advised by AmericasBarometer documentation.

TABLE F.5 *Model of support for executive powers and support for rule of law, African countries: Using survey weights*

	Decide	Not bound	Justify	Pass laws
Executive approval	0.036*	0.035*	0.036*	0.063*
	(0.005)	(0.005)	(0.006)	(0.007)
Support for rule of law	−0.080*	−0.056*	−0.125*	−0.135*
	(0.007)	(0.010)	(0.011)	(0.013)
Intercept	0.289*	0.380*	0.514*	0.432*
	(0.007)	(0.010)	(0.011)	(0.014)
Country × Wave fixed effects	✓	✓	✓	✓
Num. obs.	141,919	147,035	129,595	105,990

*$p < 0.05$.

Note: Linear regressions with survey weights. Robust standard errors clustered on country/wave. Demographic variables are not included in the model.

TABLE F.6 *Model of support for executive powers and support for democracy, African countries: Using survey weights*

	Decide	Not bound	Justify	Pass laws
Executive approval	0.027*	0.030*	0.032*	0.055*
	(0.004)	(0.006)	(0.006)	(0.009)
Support for democracy	−0.099*	−0.043*	−0.116*	−0.107*
	(0.007)	(0.007)	(0.009)	(0.010)
Intercept	0.282*	0.378*	0.514*	0.419*
	(0.007)	(0.007)	(0.008)	(0.010)
Country × Wave fixed effects	✓	✓	✓	✓
Num. obs.	148,207	119,363	104,388	76,382

*$p < 0.05$.

Note: Linear regressions with survey weights. Robust standard errors clustered on country/wave. Demographic variables are not included in the model.

TABLE F.7 *Model of support for executive powers and support for democracy, the Americas: Controlling for political system*

	Close legislature	Dissolve courts
Executive approval	0.040*	0.061*
	(0.003)	(0.004)
Support for democracy	−0.054*	−0.060*
	(0.005)	(0.006)
Parliamentary system	0.047*	0.076*
	(0.020)	(0.022)
Intercept	0.132*	0.178*
	(0.019)	(0.019)
Country × Year fixed effects	✓	✓
Demographic controls	✓	✓
R^2	0.041	0.068
Adj. R^2	0.039	0.066
Num. obs.	72,602	47,355

$^*p < 0.05$.
Note: Linear regression with robust standard errors clustered on country/wave.

TABLE F.8 *Model of support for executive powers and support for rule of law, African countries: Controlling for political system*

	Decide	Not bound	Justify	Pass laws
Executive approval	0.035*	0.033*	0.033*	0.058*
	(0.005)	(0.005)	(0.006)	(0.008)
Support for rule of law	−0.077*	−0.056*	−0.115*	−0.134*
	(0.006)	(0.011)	(0.011)	(0.013)
Parliamentary system	−0.190*	−0.203*	−0.179*	−0.108*
	(0.003)	(0.003)	(0.004)	(0.004)
Intercept	0.331*	0.418*	0.549*	0.495*
	(0.009)	(0.012)	(0.015)	(0.016)
Country × Wave fixed effect	✓	✓	✓	✓
Demographic controls	✓	✓	✓	✓
Num. obs.	140,670	143,602	125,403	103,070

$^*p < 0.05$.
Note: Linear regressions with robust standard errors clustered on country/wave.

TABLE F.9 *Model of support for executive powers and support for democracy, African countries: Controlling for political system*

	Decide	Not bound	Justify	Pass laws
Executive approval	0.027*	0.026*	0.030*	0.049*
	(0.004)	(0.005)	(0.007)	(0.009)
Support for democracy	−0.094*	−0.044*	−0.114*	−0.096*
	(0.007)	(0.007)	(0.008)	(0.009)
Parliamentary system	−0.154*	−0.204*	−0.169*	−0.138*
	(0.002)	(0.003)	(0.004)	(0.003)
Intercept	0.322*	0.414*	0.537*	0.472*
	(0.009)	(0.011)	(0.012)	(0.015)
Country × Wave fixed effect	✓	✓	✓	✓
Demographic controls	✓	✓	✓	✓
Num. obs.	144,365	117,245	101,500	74,601

*$p < 0.05$.

Note: Linear regressions with robust standard errors clustered on country/wave.

TABLE F.10 *Model of support for executive powers and support for democracy, African countries: Using four-/five-point scales with dependent variables*

	Decide (4-pt)	Not bound (5-pt)	Justify (5-pt)	Pass laws (5-pt)
Executive approval	0.105*	0.073*	0.075*	0.112*
	(0.006)	(0.007)	(0.008)	(0.008)
Support for democracy	−0.360*	−0.105*	−0.280*	−0.214*
	(0.008)	(0.009)	(0.010)	(0.010)
Intercept	2.755*	2.500*	2.697*	2.584*
	(0.035)	(0.038)	(0.041)	(0.038)
Country × Wave fixed effect	✓	✓	✓	✓
Demographic controls	✓	✓	✓	✓
Num. obs.	152,466	118,223	103,468	75,419

*$p < 0.05$.

Note: Linear regressions with robust standard errors clustered on country/wave.

TABLE F.11 *Model of support for executive powers and support for rule of law, African countries: Using four-/five-point scales with dependent variables*

	Decide (4-pt)	Not bound (5-pt)	Justify (5-pt)	Pass laws (5-pt)
Executive approval	0.151*	0.091*	0.090*	0.150*
	(0.006)	(0.006)	(0.007)	(0.006)
Support for rule of law	−0.425*	−0.227*	−0.424*	−0.517*
	(0.010)	(0.010)	(0.011)	(0.011)
Intercept	2.846*	2.579*	2.805*	2.778*
	(0.036)	(0.038)	(0.042)	(0.038)
Country × Wave fixed effect	✓	✓	✓	✓
Demographic controls	✓	✓	✓	✓
Num. obs.	148,178	145,648	128,494	104,932

*$p < 0.05$.

Note: Linear regressions with robust standard errors clustered on country/wave.

Bibliography

Aberbach, Joel D., Mark A. Peterson, and Paul J. Quirk. 2007. "Who Wants Presidential Supremacy? Findings from the Institutions of American Democracy Project." *Presidential Studies Quarterly* 37: 515–530.

Abramowitz, Alan I. 2016. "Will Time for Change Mean Time for Trump?" *PS: Political Science & Politics* 49 (4): 659–660.

Adams, James, Erik Engstrom, Danielle Joesten, Walt Stone, Jon C. Rogowski, and Boris Shor. 2017. "Do Moderate Voters Weigh Candidates' Ideologies? Voters' Decision Rules in the 2010 Congressional Elections." *Political Behavior* 39: 205–227.

Ahler, Douglas J., and David E. Broockman. 2018. "The Delegate Paradox: Why Polarized Politicians Can Represent Citizens Best." *Journal of Politics* 80(4): 1117–1133.

Allen, Danielle. 2019. "Here's One More Question Parents Should Think about during Back-to-School Season." *Washington Post* September 5.

Allen, Jonathan. 2015. "Hillary Clinton's Sweeping Executive Power Agenda is Unprecedented." *Vox* October 8. http://www.vox.com/2015/10/8/9480589/hillary-clinton-executive-action.

Almond, Gabriel Abraham, and Sidney Verba. 1963. *The Civic Culture: Political Attitudes and Democracy in Five Nations.* Princeton, NJ: Princeton University Press.

Alt, James, Ethan Bueno de Mesquita, and Shanna Rose. 2011. "Disentangling Accountability and Competence in Elections: Evidence from U.S. Term Limits." *Journal of Politics* 73 (1): 171–186.

Alvarez, R. Michael, and John Brehm. 2002. *Hard Choices, Easy Answers.* Princeton, NJ: Princeton University Press.

Ang, Zoe, Andrew Reeves, Jon C. Rogowski, and Arjun Vishwanath. 2022. "Partisanship, Economic Assessments, and Presidential Accountability." *American Journal of Political Science* 66 (2): 468–484.

Annenberg Public Policy Center of the University of Pennsylvania. 2018. "Civics Knowledge Predicts Willingness to Protect Supreme Court." September 13. https://cdn.annenbergpublicpolicycenter.org/wp-content/uploads/2018/09/Appendix_2018_Annenberg_civics_survey.pdf.

Ansolabehere, Stephen D., and Philip E. Jones. 2010. "Constituents' Responses to Congressional Roll-Call Voting." *American Journal of Political Science* 54: 583–597.

Ansolabehere, Stephen D., and Jon C. Rogowski. 2020. "Unilateral Action and Presidential Accountability." *Presidential Studies Quarterly* 50 (1): 129–145.

Ansolabehere, Stephen D., and Ariel White. 2020. "Policy, Politics, and Public Attitudes toward the Supreme Court." *American Politics Research* 48 (3): 365–376.

Appelbaum, Binyamin, and Michael D. Shear. 2016. "Once Skeptical of Executive Power, Obama Has Come to Embrace It." *New York Times* August 13. www.nytimes.com/2016/08/14/us/politics/obama-era-legacy-regulation.html.

Arnold, Peri E. 2007. "The Brownlow Committee, Regulation, and the Presidency: Seventy Years Later." *Public Administration Review* 67 (6): 1030–1040.

Ashworth, Scott. 2012. "Electoral Accountability: Recent Theoretical and Empirical Work." *Annual Review of Political Science* 15: 183–201.

Azari, Julia R. 2014. *Delivering the People's Message*. New York: Cornell University Press.

Baker, Peter. 2019. "Trump Declares a National Emergency, and Provokes a Constitutional Clash." *New York Times* February 15. www.nytimes.com/2019/02/15/us/politics/national-emergency-trump.html.

Ball, Molly. 2014. "Obama's Long Immigration Betrayal." *The Atlantic* September 9. www.theatlantic.com/politics/archive/2014/09/obamas-long-immigration-betrayal/379839/.

Barrett, Andrew W., and Matthew Eshbaugh-Soha. 2007. "Presidential Success on the Substance of Legislation." *Political Research Quarterly* 60 (1): 100–112.

Bartels, Brandon L., and Christopher D. Johnston. 2013. "On the Ideological Foundations of Supreme Court Legitimacy in the American Public." *American Journal of Political Science* 57 (1): 184–199.

Bartels, Brandon L., and Eric Kramon. 2020. "Does Public Support for Judicial Power Depend on Who Is in Political Power? Testing a Theory of Partisan Alignment in Africa." *American Political Science Review* 114 (1): 144–163.

Baum, Matthew A., and Samuel Kernell. 2001. "Economic Class and Popular Support for Franklin Roosevelt in War and Peace." *Public Opinion Quarterly* 65 (2): 198–229.

Baum, Matthew A., and Philip B. K. Potter. 2015. *War and Democratic Constraint: How the Public Influences Foreign Policy*. Princeton, NJ: Princeton University Press.

Bechtel, Michael, Jens Hainmueller, Dominik Hangartner, and Marc Helbling. 2015. "Reality Bites: The Limits of Framing Effects for Salient and Contested Policy Issues." *Political Science Research & Methods* 3 (3): 683–695.

Benen, Steve. 2017. "Trump's Views on the 'Executive-Order Concept' Have Evolved." *MSNBC* October 16. www.msnbc.com/rachel-maddow-show/trumps-views-the-executive-order-concept-have-evolved-msna1029421.

Berelson, Bernard R., Paul F. Lazarsfeld, and William N. McPhee. 1954. *Voting: A Study of Opinion Formation in a Presidential Campaign.* Chicago, IL: University of Chicago Press.

Berinsky, Adam J. 2009. *In Time of War: Understanding Public Opinion, from World War II to Iraq.* Chicago, IL: University of Chicago Press.

2006. "Public Opinion in the 1930s and 1940s: The Analysis of Quota Controlled Sample Survey Data." *Public Opinion Quarterly* 70 (4): 530–564.

Berinsky, Adam J., Gregory A. Huber, and Gabriel S. Lenz. 2012. "Evaluating Online Labor Markets for Experimental Research: Amazon.com's Mechanical Turk." *Political Analysis* 20 (3): 351–368.

Berinsky, Adam J., Eleanor Neff Powell, Eric Schickler, and Ian Brett Yohai. 2011. "Revisiting Public Opinion in the 1930s and 1940s." *PS: Political Science and Politics* 44 (2): 515–520.

Bernstein, Nina. 2009. "U.S. to Reform Policy on Detention for Immigrants." *New York Times* August 5. www.nytimes.com/2009/08/06us/politics/06detain.html.

Bewetherick, Michael, Rebecca Lieberman, Mikayla Bouchard, and Amy Fiscus. 2019. "Potential Post-Trump Reforms." *New York Times* September 9. www.nytimes.com/interactive/2019/us/politics/post-trump-reforms-executive-power.html.

Binder, Sarah, James Goldgeier, and Elizabeth N. Saunders. 2020. "The Imperial Presidency Is Alive and Well." *Foreign Affairs* January 21. www.foreignaffairs.com/articles/2020-01-21/imperial-presidency-alive-and-well.

Biskupic, Joan. 2020. "Trump's Unbroken Pattern of Disdain for the Rule of Law." *New York Times* February 22. www.cnn.com/2020/02/22/politics/trump-justice-barr-rule-of-law/index.html.

Black, Ryan C., Anthony J. Madonna, Ryan J. Owens, and Michael S. Lynch. 2007. "Adding Recess Appointments to the President's 'Tool Chest' of Unilateral Powers." *Political Research Quarterly* 60: 645–654.

Board, Editorial. 2009. "Immigration Reform and Hard Times." *New York Times* April 13:Op–ed. www.nytimes.com/2009/04/14/opinion/14tue1.html.

Boehner, John. 2014. "Boehner: Why We Must Now Sue the President." *CNN* November 21. www.cnn.com/2014/07/06/opinion/boehner-obama-lawsuit/index.html.

Bolton, Alexander, and Sharece Thrower. 2016. "Legislative Capacity and Executive Unilateralism." *American Journal of Political Science* 60: 49–663.

Bombadieri, Marcella. 2007. "Clinton Vows to Check Executive Power." *Boston Globe* October 11. http://archive.boston.com/news/nation/articles/2007/10/11/clinton_vows_to_check_executive_power/.

Boyd, Gerald M. 1986. "Reagan Tells U.S. Not to Overlook Issues beyond Iran." *New York Times* November 30.

Bratton, Michael. 2007. "The Democracy Barometers (Part I): Formal Versus Informal Institutions in Africa." *Journal of Democracy* 18 (3): 96–110.

"Bright Line Watch." 2019. http://brightlinewatch.org.

Brody, Richard A. 1991. *Assessing the President: The Media, Elite Opinion, and Public Support.* Palo Alto, CA: Stanford University Press.

Brody, Richard A., and Catherine R. Shapiro. 1989. "Policy Failure and Public Support: The Iran-Contra Affair and Public Assessment of President Reagan." *Political Behavior* 11 (4): 353–369.

Broockman, David E., and Christopher Skovron. 2018. "Bias in Perceptions of Public Opinion among Political Elites." *American Political Science Review* 112(3): 542–563.

Brown, Adam R., and Jeremy C. Pope. 2019. "Measuring and Manipulating Constitutional Evaluations in the States: Legitimacy Versus Veneration." *American Politics Research* 47 (5): 1135–1161.

Brownlow, Louis. 1955. *A Passion for Politics: The Autobiography of Louis Brownlow (First Half).* Chicago, IL: University of Chicago Press.

Bruff, Harold H. 2015. *Untrodden Ground: How Presidents Interpret the Constitution.* Chicago, IL: University of Chicago Press.

Bryce, James. 1995 [1888]. *The American Commonwealth.* Indianapolis, IN: Liberty Fund.

Bush, George W. 2001. "Homeland Security Presidential Directive 1: Directive on Organization and Operation of the Homeland Security Council." *Weekly Compilation of Presidential Documents* 37 (44): 1568–1570.

Caldeira, Gregory A. 1987. "Public Opinion and the U.S. Supreme Court: FDR's Court-Packing Plan." *American Political Science Review* 81 (4): 1139–1153.

Caldeira, Gregory A., and James L. Gibson. 1992. "The Etiology of Public Support for the Supreme Court." *American Journal of Political Science* 36: 635–664.

Calvo, Ernesto. 2014. *Legislator Success in Fragmented Congresses in Argentina.* New York: Cambridge University Press.

Cameron, Charles M. 2000. *Veto Bargaining: Presidents and the Politics of Negative Power.* New York: Cambridge.

2002. "Studying the Polarized Presidency." *Presidential Studies Quarterly* 32 (4): 647–663.

2009. "The Presidential Veto." In *Oxford Handbook of the American Presidency,* ed. by George Edwards III and William G. Howell, 361–382. New York: Oxford University Press.

Campbell, Angus, Philip E. Converse, Warren E. Miller, and Donald E. Stokes. 1960. *The American Voter.* New York: Wiley.

Campbell, Karlyn Kohrs, and Kathleen Hall Jamieson. 1990. *Deeds Done in Words: Presidential Rhetoric and the Genres of Governance.* Chicago: University of Chicago Press.

2008. *Presidents Creating the Presidency: Deeds Done in Words.* Chicago, IL: University of Chicago Press.

Canes-Wrone, Brandice. 2006. *Who's Leading Whom?* Chicago, IL: University of Chicago Press.

Canes-Wrone, Brandice, and Kenneth W. Shotts. 2004. "The Conditional Nature of Presidential Responsiveness to Public Opinion." *American Journal of Political Science* 48: 690–706.

Canes-Wrone, Brandice, David W. Brady, and John F. Cogan. 2002. "Out of Step, Out of Office: Electoral Accountability and House Members' Voting." *American Political Science Review* 96: 127–140.

Canes-Wrone, Brandice, Michael C. Herron, and Kenneth W. Shotts. 2001. "Leadership and Pandering: A Theory of Executive Policymaking." *American Journal of Political Science* 45: 532–550.

Canes-Wrone, Brandice, William G. Howell, and David E. Lewis. 2008. "Toward a Broader Understanding of Presidential Power: A Reevaluation of the Two Presidencies Thesis." *Journal of Politics* 70: 1–16.

Carey, John M., Gretchen Helmke, Brendan Nyhan, Mitchell Sanders, and Susan Stokes. 2019. "Searching for Bright Lines in the Trump Presidency." *Perspectives on Politics* 17 (3): 699–718.

Carey, John M., and Matthew Soberg Shugart, eds. 1998. *Executive Degree Authority*. New York: Cambridge University Press.

Carlin, Ryan E., and Mason Moseley. 2014. "Good Democrats, Bad Targets: Democratic Values and Clientelistic Vote Buying." *Journal of Politics* 77 (1): 14–26.

Carmines, Edward G., and James A. Stimson. 1980. "The Two Faces of Issue Voting." *American Political Science Review* 74: 78–91.

Carter, Amy, and Ryan L. Teten. 2002. "Assessing Changing Views of the President: Revisiting Greenstein's 'Children and Politics.'" *Presidential Studies Quarterly* 32 (3).

Carter, John R., and David Schap. 1987. "Executive Veto, Legislative Override, and Structure-Induced Equilibrium." *Public Choice* 52: 227–244.

Chaisty, Paul, Nic Cheeseman, and Timothy Power. 2014. "Rethinking the 'Presidentialism Debate': Conceptualizing Coalitional Politics in Cross-Regional Perspective." *Democratization* 21 (1): 72–94.

Chaudoin, Stephen. 2014. "Promises or Policies? An Experimental Analysis of International Agreements and Audience Reactions." *International Organization* 68 (1): 235–256.

Cheibub, José Antonio. 2007. *Presidentialism, Parliamentarism, and Democracy*. New York: Cambridge University Press.

Cheibub, José Antonio, Adam Przeworski, and Sebastian M. Saiegh. 2004. "Government Coalitions and Legislative Success Under Presidentialism and Parliamentarism." *British Journal of Political Science* 34: 565–587.

Chen, Lanhee J. 2015. "Undoing the Unilateral Presidency." *The Wall Street Journal* August 31. www.wsj.com/articles/undoing-the-unilateral-presidency-1441062753.

Chernow, Ron. 2017. *Grant*. New York: Penguin Books.

Chiou, Fang-Yi, and Lawrence S. Rothenberg. 2014. "The Elusive Search for Presidential Power." *American Journal of Political Science* 58: 653–668.

2017. *The Enigma of Presidential Power: Parties, Policies and Strategic Uses of Unilateral Action*. New York: Cambridge University Press.

Chong, Dennis, and James N. Druckman. 2007. "Framing Theory." *Annual Review of Political Science* 10: 103–126.

Christenson, Dino P., and David M. Glick. 2015. "Chief Justice Roberts's Health Care Decision Disrobed: The Microfoundations of the Supreme Court's Legitimacy." *American Journal of Political Science* 59 (2): 403–418.

Christenson, Dino P., and Douglas L. Kriner. 2017a. "Constitutional Qualms or Politics as Usual? The Factors Shaping Public Support for Unilateral Action." *American Journal of Political Science* 61 (2): 335–349.

2019. "Does Public Opinion Constrain Presidential Unilateralism?" *American Political Science Review* 113 (4): 1071–1077.

2017b. "Mobilizing the Public against the President: The Political Costs of Unilateral Action." *American Journal of Political Science* 61: 769–785.

2015. "Political Constraints on Presidential Unilateral Action." *Case Western Reserve Law Review* 65: 897–932.

2020. *The Myth of the Imperial Presidency: How Public Opinion Checks the Unilateral Executive.* Chicago, IL: University of Chicago Press.

Ciepley, David. 2006. *Liberalism in the Shadow of Totalitarianism.* Cambridge, MA: Harvard University Press.

Clark, Gordon L. 1985. "The Spatial Division of Labor and Wage and Price Controls of the Nixon Administration." *Economic Geography* 61 (2): 113–128.

CNN Wire Staff. 2010. "Procedural Vote on DREAM Act Fails in Senate." *CNN Politics* Dec 18.

Cohen, Jeffery E. 1999. *Presidential Responsiveness and Public Policy-Making.* Ann Arbor: University of Michigan Press.

2015. *Presidential Leadership in Public Opinion.* New York: Cambridge University Press.

2017. "The Promise of Experiments for Studying the Presidency." *Presidential Studies Quarterly* 47 (3): 414–431.

Converse, Philip E. 1970. "Attitudes and Nonattitudes: Continuation of a Dialogue." In *The Quantitative Analysis of Social Problems,* ed. by Edward R. Tufte, 168–189. Reading, MA: Addison-Wesley.

1964. "The Nature of Belief Systems in Mass Publics." In *Ideology and Discontent,* ed. by David E. Apter. Ann Arbor: University of Michigan Press.

Conyers, John C. 2007. *The Constitution in Crisis: The High Crimes of the Bush Administration and a Blueprint for Impeachment.* New York: Sky-horse.

Cooper, Phillip J. 2002. *By Order of the President: The Use and Abuse of Executive Direct Action.* Lawrence: University of Press of Kansas.

Coppedge, Michael, John Gerring, Carl Henrik Knutsen et al. 2020. "V-Dem Codebook v10." *Varieties of Democracy (V-Dem) Project.* V-Dem Institute, University of Gothenberg.

Coppock, Alexander. 2019. "Generalizing from Survey Experiments Conducted on Mechanical Turk: A Replication Approach." *Political Science Research and Methods* 7 (3): 613–628.

Corwin, Edward. 1947. *Total War and the Constitution.* New York: Alfred A. Knopf.

Costa, Robert, Felicia Sonmez, and Nick Miroff. 2019. "Trump Sticks to Demand for Border Wall Funding as Shutdown Drags On." *Washington*

Post January 6. www.washingtonpost.com/politics/president-trump-heads-to-camp-david-as-shutdown-enters-third-week/2019/01/06/22af03c0-11c3-11e9-b6ad-9cfd62dbb0a8_story.html.

Crisp, Brian F., Santiago Olivella, and Guillermo Rosas. 2020. *The Chain of Representation: Preferences, Institutions, and Policy across Presidential Systems*. New York: Cambridge University Press.

Cruz, Cesi, Philip Keefer, and Carlos Scartascini. 2018. *The Database of Political Institutions 2017*. Washington, DC: Inter-American Development Bank.

Dahl, Robert A. 1990. "Myth of the Presidential Mandate." *Political Science Quarterly* 105:355–372.

———. 1971. *Polyarchy: Participation and Opposition*. New Haven, CT: Yale University Press.

Dawsey, Josh, and Mike DeBonis. 2018. "Trump Privately Presses for Military to Pay for Border Wall." *Washington Post* March 27. www.washingtonpost.com/politics/trump-privately-presses-for-military-to-pay-for-border-wall/2018/03/27/d79907a2-31c9-11e8-9759-56e51591e250_story.html.

Dearborn, John A. 2019a. "The 'Proper Organs' for Presidential Representation: A Fresh Look at the Budget and Accounting Act of 1921." *Journal of Policy History* 31 (1): 185–203.

———. 2019b. "The Foundations of the Modern Presidency: Presidential Representation, the Unitary Executive Theory, and the Reorganization Act of 1939." *Presidential Studies Quarterly* 49 (1): 185–203.

de Benedictis-Kessner, Justin, and Christopher Warshaw. 2020. "Accountability for the Economy at All Levels of Government in United States Elections." *American Political Science Review* 114 (3): 660–676.

Deering, Christopher J., and Forrest Maltzman. 1999. "The Politics of Executive Orders: Legislative Constraints on Presidential Power." *Political Research Quarterly* 52: 767–783.

Delli Carpini, Michael X., and Scott Keeter. 1996. *What Americans Know about Politics and Why It Matters*. New Haven, CT: Yale University Press.

Denning, Steve. 2019. "How Trump's Cabinet Now Undermines the Rule of Law." *Forbes Magazine* May 19. www.forbes.com/sites/stevedenning/2019/05/19/how-trumps-cabinet-now-undermines-the-rule-of-law/#10e02fe31dea.

Dennis, Jack, and Carol Webster. 1975. "Children's Images of the President and of Government in 1962 and 1974." *American Politics Quarterly* 3 (4): 386–405.

Doherty, David. 2015. "How Policy and Procedure Shape Citizens' Evaluations of Senators." *Legislative Studies Quarterly* 40 (2): 241–272.

Doherty, David, and Jennifer Wolak. 2012. "When Do the Ends Justify the Means? Evaluating Procedural Fairness." *Political Behavior* 34: 301–323.

Domitrovic, Brian. 2011. "August 15, 1971: A Date Which Has Lived in Infamy." *Forbes* August 14. www.forbes.com/sites/briandomitrovic/2011/08/14/august-15-1971-a-date-which-has-lived-in-infamy/#9c3121858a6.

Donald, David Herbert. 2011. *Lincoln*. New York: Simon & Schuster Paperbacks.

Downs, Anthony. 1957. *An Economic Theory of Democracy*. New York: Harper/Row.

Driscoll, Amanda, and Michael J. Nelson. 2018. "There Is No Legitimacy Crisis: Support for Judicial Institutions in Modern Latin America." *Revista de la Sociedad Argentina de Análisis Político* 12 (2): 361–377.

Druckman, James N. 2001. "The Implications of Framing Effects for Citizen Competence." *Political Behavior* 23 (3): 225–256.

Druckman, James N., and Justin W. Holmes. 2004. "Does Presidential Rhetoric Matter? Priming and Presidential Approval." *Presidential Studies Quarterly* 34 (4): 755–778.

Druckman, James N., and Lawrence R. Jacobs. 2015. *Who Governs? Presidents, Public Opinion, and Manipulation.* Chicago, IL: University of Chicago Press.

Druckman, James N., Erik Peterson, and Rune Slothuus. 2013. "How Elite Partisan Polarization Affects Public Opinion Formation." *American Political Science Review* 107:57–79.

Dulani, Boniface, and John Tengatenga. 2020. "Big Man Rule in Africa: Are Africans Getting the Leadership They Want?" *The African Review* 46 (2): 275–291.

Easton, David. 1965. *A Systems Analysis of Political Life.* New York: Wiley.

Easton, David, and Jack Dennis. 1969. *Children in the Political System.* New York: McGraw Hill.

Economist. 2020. "Americans' View of Black–White Race Relations Hits a 20-Year Low." September 8.

Economist/YouGov. 2014a. November 22–24; http://d25d2506sfb94s .cloudfront.net/cumulus_uploads/document/c3szg5n2qi/econTabReport. pdf.

    2014b. February 1–3; http://d25d2506sfb94s.cloudfront.net/cumulus_ uploads/document/rqhac97mko/econTabReport_update.pdf.

    2016. January 15–19; https://d25d2506sfb94s.cloudfront.net/cumulus_ uploads/document/ps6zskmuwy/econTabReport.pdf.

Editorial Board. 2021. "Ease Up on the Executive Actions, Joe." *New York Times* January 27.

    2020. "Elect Joe Biden, America." *New York Times* October 6.

    2015. "Obama's Lawless Labor Board." *Wall Street Journal* August 11. www.wsj.com/articles/obamas-lawless-labor-board-1439336842.

Edsall, Thomas B. 2018. "The Contract with Authoritarianism." *New York Times* April 5. www.nytimes.com/2018/04/05/opinion/trump-authoritarianism-republicans-contract.html.

Edwards, III, George C. 1989. *At the Margins: Presidential Leadership of Congress.* New Haven, CT: Yale University Press.

    1983. *The Public Presidency: The Pursuit of Popular Support.* New York: St. Martins.

Edwards, III, George C., William Mitchell, and Reed Welch. 1995. "Explaining Presidential Approval: The Significance of Issue Salience." *American Journal of Political Science* 39 (1): 108–134.

Eggers, William D., and John O'Leary. 2009. *If We Can Put a Man on the Moon: Getting Big Things Done in Government.* Boston, MA: Harvard Business Review Press.

Elliot, Philip. 2016. "Marco Rubio Promises to Reverse Obama's Planned Gun Limits." *Time* January 3. https://time.com/4165730/marco-rubio-gun-control/.

Erikson, Robert S., Michael B. MacKuen, and James A. Stimson. 2002. *The Macro Polity*. New York: Cambridge University Press.

Eshbaugh-Soha, Matthew. 2013. "Presidential Influence of the News Media: The Case of the Press Conference." *Political Communication* 30 (4): 548–564.

Fatovic, Clement. 2004. "Constitutionalism and Presidential Prerogative: Jeffersonian and Hamiltonian Perspectives." *American Journal of Political Science* 48: 429–444.

Feldman, Stanley. 1988. "Structure and Consistency in Public Opinion: The Role of Core Beliefs and Values." *American Journal of Political Science* 32: 416–440.

Fischer, David Hackett. 1989. *Albion's Seed: Four British Folkways in America*. Oxford: Oxford University Press.

Fisher, Louis. 2010. "When Wars Begin: Misleading Statements by Presidents." *Presidential Studies Quarterly* 40: 171–184.

Flynn, Meagan. 2019. "'Subvert the Constitution': Trump's 2014 Remarks on Obama's Executive Actions Show 'Hypocrisy,' Critics Say." *Washington Post* February 15. www.washingtonpost.com/nation/2019/02/15/subvert-constitution-trumps-remarks-obamas-executive-actions-show-hypocrisy-critics-say/.

Forbes, J. Randy. 2015. "Executive Action and the Rule of Law." *Website of Congressman J. Randy Forbes* [archive] Februray 26. http://webarchive.loc.gov/all/20150304194839/http://forbes.house.gov/news/documentsingle.aspx?DocumentID=398057.

Ford, Henry Jones. 1898. *The Rise and Growth of American Politics*. New York: Macmillan.

Fox and Friends. 2016. Fox News Channel.

Fox, Justin, and Stuart V. Jordan. 2011. "Delegation and Accountability." *Journal of Politics* 73 (3): 831–844.

Fox, Justin, and Matthew C. Stephenson. 2011. "Judicial Review as a Response to Political Posturing." *American Political Science Review* 105 (2): 397–414.

Fridkin, Kim L., and Patrick J. Kenney. 2011. "The Role of Candidate Traits in Campaigns." *Journal of Politics* 73: 61–73.

Friedman, Lawrence M. 1998. *American Law: An Introduction*. New York: W. W. Norton & Company.

Funk, Carolyn L. 1999. "Bringing the Candidate into Models of Candidate Evaluation." *Journal of Politics* 61: 700–720.

Gaines, Brian J., James H. Kuklinski, Paul J. Quirk, Buddy Peyton, and Jay Verkuilen. 2007. "Same Facts, Different Interpretations: Partisan Motivation and Opinion on Iraq." *Journal of Politics* 69: 957–974.

Gallup. 2019. "Most Admired Man and Woman." https://news.gallup.com/poll/1678/most-admired-man-woman.aspx.

Gamio, Lazaro, and Lauren Leatherby. 2021. "How 450,000 Coronavirus Deaths Added Up." *New York Times* February 3.

Gasper, John T., and Andrew Reeves. 2011. "Make It Rain? Retrospection and the Attentive Electorate in the Context of Natural Disasters." *American Journal of Political Science* 55: 340–355.

Gelman, Andrew, Sharad Goel, Douglas Rivers, and David Rothschild. 2016. "The Mythical Swing Voter." *Quarterly Journal of Political Science* 11: 103–130.

Gelpi, Christopher, Peter D. Feaver, and Jason Reifler. 2009. *Paying the Human Costs of War: American Public Opinion and Casualties in Military Conflicts.* Princeton, NJ: Princeton University Press.

Gerber, Alan S., and Gregory A. Huber. 2009. "Partisanship and Economic Behavior: Do Partisan Differences in Economic Forecasts Predict Real Economic Behavior?" *American Political Science Review* 103 (3): 407–426.

2010. "Partisanship, Political Control, and Economic Assessments." *American Journal of Political Science* 54: 153–173.

Gerber, Alan S., Gregory A. Huber, and Ebonya Washington. 2010. "Party Affiliation, Partisanship, and Political Beliefs: A Field Experiment." *American Political Science Review* 104: 720–744.

Gibson, James L. 2007. "Changes in American Veneration for the Rule of Law." *DePaul Law Review* 56: 593–614.

2012. *Electing Judges: The Surprising Effects of Campaigning on Judicial Legitimacy.* Chicago, IL: University of Chicago Press.

2004. *Overcoming Apartheid: Can Truth Reconcile a Divided Nation?* New York: Russell Sage Foundation.

1989. "Understandings of Justice: Institutional Legitimacy, Procedural Justice, and Political Tolerance." *Law and Society Review* 23: 469–496.

Gibson, James L., and Gregory A. Caldeira. 2009. *Citizens, Courts, and Confirmations: Positivity Theory and the Judgments of the American People.* Princeton, NJ: Princeton University Press.

Gibson, James L., and Michael J. Nelson. 2015. "Is the U.S. Supreme Court's Legitimacy Grounded in Performance Satisfaction and Ideology?" *American Journal of Political Science* 59: 162–174.

2018. *Black and Blue: How African Americans Judge the U.S. Legal System.* New York: Oxford University Press.

Gibson, James L., Gregory A. Caldeira, and Vanessa A. Baird. 1998. "On the Legitimacy of National High Courts." *The American Political Science Review* 92 (2): 343–358.

Gibson, James L., Gregory A. Caldeira, and Lester Kenyatta Spence. 2003. "Measuring Attitudes toward the United States Supreme Court." *American Journal of Political Science* 47: 354–367.

Gillion, Daniel Q. 2013. *The Political Power of Protest: Minority Activism and Shifts in Public Policy.* Cambridge: Cambridge University Press.

Ginsberg, Benjamin, and Kathryn Wagner Hill. 2019. *Congress: The First Branch.* New Haven, CT: Yale University Press.

Goldfarb, Zachary A. 2014. "Obama to Raise Minimum Wage for Federal Contract Workers." *Washington Post* January 28. www.washingtonpost.com/

politics/obama-to-raise-minimum-wage-for-government-contract-workers/
2014/01/27/f7994b34-87cd-11e3-916e-e01534b1e132_story.html.

Goldfarb, Zachary A., and Juliet Eilperin. 2014. "Obama to Sign Order Barring US Contractors from Job Bias Based on Sexual Orientation." *Washington Post* June 16. www.washingtonpost.com/politics/obama-to-sign-order-prohibiting-contractors-from-discriminating-against-lgbt-people/2014/06/16/4a83726c-f573-11e3-a606-946fd632f9f1_story.html.

Goldfarb, Zachary A., and Rosalind Helderman. 2013. "Obama Makes His Immigration Push." *Washington Post* January 28. www.washingtonpost.com/politics/obama-unveils-his-own-proposal-for-immigration-reform/2013/01/29/b27dcb78-6a47-11e2-95b3-272d604a10a3_story.html.

Goldstein, Jared A. 2014. "The American Liberty League and the Rise of Constitutional Nationalism." *Temple Law Review* 85: 281–330.

Gordon, Sanford C. 2011. "Politicizing Agency Spending Authority: Lessons from a Bush-Era Scandal." *American Political Science Review* 105 (4): 717–734.

Goren, Paul. 2001. "Core Principles and Policy Reasoning in Mass Publics: A Test of Two Theories." *British Journal of Political Science* 31: 159–177.

Green, Donald P., Shang E. Ha, and John G. Bullock. 2010. "Enough Already about 'Black Box' Experiments: Studying Mediation Is More Difficult than Most Scholars Suppose." *The ANNALS of the American Academy of Political and Social Science* 628 (1): 200–208.

Green, Donald P., Bradley Palmquist, and Eric Schickler. 2002. *Partisan Hearts and Minds.* New Haven, C.: Yale University Press.

Greenstein, Fred I. 1965. *Children and Politics.* New Haven, CT: Yale University Press.

1969. *Children and Politics.* Rev. ed. New Haven, CT: Yale University Press.

1975. "The Benevolent Leader Revisited: Children's Images of Political Leaders in Three Democracies." *American Political Science Review* 69 (4): 1371–1398.

Grim, Ryan. 2020. "Inside Biden's Meeting with Civil Rights Leaders." *Intercept* December 10.

Gronke, Paul, and Brian Newman. 2003. "FDR to Clinton, Mueller to?: A Field Essay on Presidential Approval." *Political Research Quarterly* 56 (4): 501–512.

Groseclose, Tim, and Nolan McCarty. 2001. "The Politics of Blame: Bargaining before an Audience." *American Journal of Political Science* 45: 100–119.

Hah, Chong-do, and Robert M. Lindquist. 1975. "The 1952 Steel Seizure Revisited: A Systematic Study in Presidential Decision Making." *Administrative Science Quarterly* 20 (4): 587–605.

Hains, Tim. 2015. "George Will: 'If You Liked President Obama's Use Of Executive Power, You'll Love President Trump.'" *RealClearPolitics* [post from Fox News Sunday] December 13. www.realclearpolitics.com/video/2015/12/13/george_will_if_you_liked_president_obamas_use_of_executive_power_youll_love_president_trump.html.

Hamburger, Tom, and Peter Wallsten. 2008. "Obama's Grass-Roots Latino Strategy." *Los Angeles Times* February 2. http://articles.latimes.com/2008/feb/02/nation/na-latinos2.

Harbridge, Laurel, and Neil Malhotra. 2011. "Electoral Incentives and Partisan Conflict in Congress: Evidence from Survey Experiments." *American Journal of Political Science* 55 (3): 494–510.

Harrison, Brian F. 2015. "Bully Pulpit or Partisan Bully? Partisanship, Elite Polarization, and U.S. Presidential Communication." *Social Science Quarterly* 97 (2): 418–438.

Hartz, Louis. 1955. *The Liberal Tradition in America*. New York: Harcourt, Brace & World.

Harwood, John. 2010. "Obama Notwithstanding, Democrats Defend 'Messy' Lawmaking." *New York Times* January 31. www.nytimes.com/2010/02/01/us/politics/01caucus.html.

Hassan, Mai. 2015. "Continuity Despite Change: Kenya's New Constitution and Executive Power." *Democratization* 22 (4): 587–609.

Hayes, Danny. 2005. "Candidate Qualities through a Partisan Lens: A Theory of Trait Ownership." *American Journal of Political Science* 49: 908–923.

Healy, Andrew, and Gabriel S. Lenz. 2017. "Presidential Voting and the Local Economy: Evidence from Two Population-Based Data Sets." *Journal of Politics* 79 (4): 1419–1432.

Healy, Andrew, Neil Malhotra, and Cecilia Mo. 2010. "Irrelevant Events Affect Voters' Evaluations of Government Performance." *Proceedings of the National Academy of Sciences* 107: 12804–12809.

Heer, Jeet. 2017. "Don't Just Impeach Trump. End the Imperial Presidency." *The New Republic* August 12. https://newrepublic.com/article/144297/dont-just-impeach-trump-end-imperial-presidency.

Heijmans, Philip. 2017. "Strongman Worries in Southeast Asia." *U.S. News* November 1. www.usnews.com/news/best-countries/articles/2017-11-01/new-concerns-over-southeast-asian-countries-backsliding-from-democracy.

Helmke, Gretchen. 2017. *Institutions on the Edge: Inter-Branch Crises in Latin America*. New York. Cambridge University Press.

Hendricks, Tyche. 2008. "Economy May Trump Obama's Pledge on Immigration." *San Francisco Chronicle* December 10. www.sfgate.com/news/article/Economy-may-trump-Obama-s-pledge-on-immigration-3181646.php.

Hess, Robert D., and David Easton. 1960. "The Child's Changing Image of the President." *Public Opinion Quarterly* 24 (4): 632–644.

Hibbing, John R., and Elizabeth Theiss-Morse. 1996. *Congress as Public Enemy*. Cambridge: Cambridge University Press.

2001. "Process Preferences and American Politics: What the People Want Government to Be." *American Political Science Review* 95 (1): 145–153.

2002. *Stealth Democracy: Americans' Beliefs about How Government Should Work*. New York: Cambridge University Press.

Hochschild, Jennifer L. 1981. *What's Fair? American Beliefs about Distributive Justice*. Cambridge, MA: Harvard University Press.

Hofstadter, Richard. [1948] 1989. *The American Political Tradition and the Men Who Made It*. New York: Vintage Books.

Hogue, Henry B. 2004. "Recess Appointments to Article III Courts." *Presidential Studies Quarterly* 34: 656–673.

Holian, David B., and Charles Prysby. 2014. "Candidate Character Traits in the 2012 Presidential Election." *Presidential Studies Quarterly* 44 (3): 484–505.

Holsti, Ole R. 1992. "Public Opinion and Foreign Policy: Challenges to the Almond-Lippmann Consensus." *International Studies Quarterly* 36 (4): 439–466.

Holtzman, Elizabeth. 2006. "The Impeachment of George W. Bush." January 11. www.thenation.com/article/archive/impeachment-george-w-bush/.

Hook, Janet. 2007. "Legalization of Immigrants Widely Backed." *Los Angeles Times* June 13.

Howell, William G. 2003. *Power without Persuasion: The Politics of Direct Presidential Action.* Princeton, NJ: Princeton University Press.

2015. "Results of President Obama's Race to the Top." *Education Next* 15 (4): 58–66.

2013. *Thinking about the Presidency.* Princeton, NJ: Princeton University Press.

Howell, William G., Saul P. Jackman, and Jon C. Rogowski. 2013. *The Wartime President: Executive Influence and the Nationalizing Politics of Threat.* Chicago, IL: University of Chicago Press.

Howell, William G., and Terry M. Moe. 2017. "American's Antiquated Constitution." *Prospect* February 2. www.prospectmagazine.co.uk/world/americas-antiquated-constitution-united-states-constitution-donald-trump-electoral-college.

2016. *Relic: How Our Constitution Undermines Effective Government and Why We Need a More Powerful Presidency.* New York: Basic Books.

Howell, William G., and Jon C. Pevehouse. 2007. *While Dangers Gather: Congressional Checks on Presidential War Powers.* Princeton, NJ: Princeton University Press.

Hoyt, Joshua. 2010. "Obama Risks Alienating Latinos with Lack of Immigration Reform." *Washington Post* March 5. www.washingtonpost.com/wp-dyn/content/article/2010/03/04/AR2010030404037.html.

Huber, Gregory A., and Neil Malhotra. 2017. "Political Homophily in Social Relationships: Evidence from Online Dating Behavior." *Journal of Politics* 79 (1): 269–283.

Huddy, Leonie, Lilliana Mason, and Lene Aarøe. 2015. "Expressive Partisanship: Campaign Involvement, Political Emotion, and Partisan Identity." *American Political Science Review* 109(1): 1–17.

Inglehart, Ronald. 2003. "How Solid Is Mass Support for Democracy – And How Can We Measure It?" *PS: Political Science & Politics* 36 (1): 51–57.

Iyengar, Shanto, Gaurav Sood, and Yphtach Lelkes. 2012. "Affect, Not Ideology: A Social Identity Perspective on Polarization." *Public Opinion Quarterly* 76 (3): 405–431.

Jacobs, Lawrence R., and Robert Y. Shapiro. 2000. *Politicians Don't Pander: Political Manipulation and the Loss of Democratic Responsiveness.* Chicago, IL: University of Chicago Press.

Jacobs, Meg. 2016. *Panic at the Pump: The Energy Crisis and the Transformation of American Politics in the 1970s*. New York: Hill/Wang.

Jacobson, Gary. 2019. *Presidents and Parties in the Public Mind*. Chicago, IL: University of Chicago Press.

Jessee, Stephen A. 2012. *Ideology and Spatial Voting in American Elections*. New York: Cambridge University Press.

2010. "Partisan Bias, Political Information and Spatial Voting in the 2008 Presidential Election." *Journal of Politics* 72: 327–340.

2009. "Spatial Voting in the 2004 Presidential Election." *American Political Science Review* 103: 59–81.

Jones, Jeffrey D. 2019. "Subgroup Differences in Trump Approval Mostly Party-Based." *Gallup Organization* March 29. https://news.gallup.com/poll/248135/subgroup-differences-trump-approval-mostly-party-based.aspx.

Judd, Gleason. 2017. "Showing Off: Promise and Peril in Unilateral Policy-Making." *Quarterly Journal of Political Science* 12: 241–268.

Kagan, Elena. 2001. "Presidential Administration." *Harvard Law Review* 114: 2245–2385.

Kang, Myunghoon. 2020. "Presidential Unilateral Action as a Tool of Voter Mobilization." *Presidential Studies Quarterly* 50 (1): 107–128.

Karl, Jonathan. 2014. "Obama's Long Lost Campaign Promise." *ABC News* February 17. https://abcnews.go.com/blogs/politics/2014/02/obamas-long-lost-campaign-promise.

Karol, David, and Edward Miguel. 2007. "The Electoral Cost of War: Iraq Casualties and the 2004 U.S. Presidential Election." *Journal of Politics* 69:633–648.

Keith, Bruce E., David B. Magleby, Candice J. Nelson, Elizabeth Orr, Mark C. Westlye, and Raymond E. Wolfinger. 1992. *The Myth of the Independent Voter*. Berkeley: University of California Press.

Kennedy, Joshua B. 2015. "'Do This! Do That! And Nothing Will Happen': Executive Orders and Bureaucratic Responsiveness." *American Politics Research* 43: 59–82.

Kernell, Samuel. 2006. *Going Public: New Strategies of Presidential Leadership*. Washington, DC: CQ Press.

Kessler, Glenn. 2014. "Obama's Royal Flip-Flop on Using Executive Action on Illegal Immigration." *Washington Post* November 18. www.washingtonpost.com/news/fact-checker/wp/2014/11/18/obamas-flip-flop-on-using-executive-action-on-illegal-immigration/.

Key, V.O. Jr. 1966. *The Responsible Electorate*. Cambridge: Harvard University Press.

1949. *Southern Politics in State and Nation*. New York: A. Knopf.

Kinder, Donald R., and Nathan P. Kalmoe. 2017. *Neither Liberal nor Conservative: Ideological Innocence in the American Public*. Chicago, IL: University of Chicago Press.

Kinder, Donald R., Mark D. Peters, Robert P. Abelson, and Susan T. Fiske. 1980. "Presidential Prototypes." *Political Behavior* 2 (4): 315–337.

King, Esther. 2017. "Democratic Backsliding Threatens International Order: Report." *Politico* January 31. www.politico.eu/article/democratic-backsliding-threatens-international-order-report/.

King, Martin Luther. Jr. 1961. "The President Has the Power: Equality Now." *The Nation* February 4.

Kirk, Russell. 1974. "A Plebiscitary Emperor?" *Center House Bulletin* 4 (1): 15.

Kitrosser, Heidi. 2015. *Reclaiming Accountability: Transparency, Executive Power, and the U.S. Constitution.* Chicago, IL: University of Chicago Press.

Klar, Samara, and Yanna Krupnikov. 2016. *Independent Politics: How American Disdain for Political Parties Leads to Inaction.* New York: Cambridge University Press.

Klein, Ezra. 2016. "Partisanship is a helluva drug." *Vox* December 23. www.vox.com/policy-and-politics/2016/12/23/14062616/republicans-trump-ideology-conservatives.

Kleinerman, Benjamin A. 2007. "Can the Prince Really Be Tamed? Executive Prerogative, Popular Apathy, and the Constitutional Frame in Locke's 'Second Treatise.'" *American Political Science Review* 101 (2): 209–222.

Korte, Gregory. 2014. "Obama Issues 'Executive Orders by Another Name.'" *USA Today* December 16. www.usatoday.com/story/news/politics/2014/12/16/obama-presidential-memoranda-executive-orders/20191805/.

———. 2017. "Trump's Executive Actions Come Faster and in Different Forms than Before." *USA Today* January 30. www.usatoday.com/story/news/politics/2017/01/30/trumps-executive-actions-come-faster-and-different-forms-than-before/97255592/.

Krause, George A., and David B. Cohen. 1997. "Presidential Use of Executive Orders, 1953–1994." *American Politics Research* 25 (4): 458–481.

Krieg, Gregory. 2016. "Donald Trump Predicts 'You Won't Be Able to Get Guns'." *CNN* January 4. www.cnn.com/2016/01/04/politics/donald-trump-guns-obama-executive-action/index.html.

Kriner, Douglas. 2010. *After the Rubicon: Congress, Presidents, and the Politics of Waging War.* Chicago, IL: University of Chicago Press.

Kriner, Douglas L., and Andrew Reeves. 2015. *The Particularistic President: Executive Branch Politics and Political Inequality.* New York: Cambridge University Press.

Krosnick, Jon A. 1990. "Americans' Perceptions of Presidential Candidates: A Test of the Projection Hypothesis." *Journal of Social Issues* 42 (2): 159–182.

Kruse, Kevin M., and Julian E. Zelizer. 2019. "Have We Had Enough of the Imperial Presidency Yet?" *New York Times* January 9. www.nytimes.com/2019/01/09/opinion/president-trump-border-wall-weak.html.

Kurmanaev, Anatoly, and Andrea Zarate. 2019. "Peru's President Dissolves Congress, and Lawmakers Suspend Him." *New York Times* September 30.

Lamb, Charles M., Joshua Boston, and Jacob R. Nieheisel. 2019. "Power Plus Persuasion: The Anatomy of Kennedy's Housing Order." *Congress & the Presidency* 46 (1): 109–134.

Landler, Mark, and Megal Thee-Brenan. 2013. "Survey Shows Scant Support for Syria Strike." *New York Times* September 9. www.nytimes.com/2013/09/10/world/middleeast/poll-majority-of-americans-oppose-military-strike.html.

Lee, Frances E. 2003. "Geographic Politics in the U.S. House of Representatives: Coalition Building and Distribution of Benefits." *American Journal of Political Science* 47 (4): 714–728. http://doi.org/10.1111/1540-5907.00050.

Lee, Mike. 2016. "The Incredible Shirking Congress." *National Review* July 11. www.nationalreview.com/magazine/2016/07/11/legislative-judicial-branch-powers-warped/.

Lee, M. J. 2012. "Santorum: Obama arrogant." *Politico* June 28. www.politico.com/story/2012/06/santorum-obama-arrogance-historic-077993.

Lemire, Jonathan, and Jill Colvin. 2017. "Trump Touts Executive Orders He Once Lambasted." *AP* April 25. https://apnews.com/e9f75e03bb7a41c1a44e9512d4990832/Trump-touts-executive-orders-he-once-lambasted.

Lenz, Gabriel S. 2012. *Follow the Leader? How Voters Respond to Politicians' Policies and Performance.* Chicago, IL: University of Chicago Press.

Levay, Kevin E., Jeremy Freese, and James N. Druckman. 2016. "The Demographic and Political Composition of Mechanical Turk Samples." *Sage Open* January–March: 1–17.

Levine, Peter, and Kei Kawashima-Ginsberg. 2017. "The Republic Is (Still) at Risk – and Civics Is Part of the Solution." Jonathan M. Tisch College of Civic Life, Tufts University. https://civxnow.org/sites/default/files/resources/SummitWhitePaper.pdf.

Levinson, Sanford. 2006. *Our Undemocratic Constitution.* New York: Oxford University Press.

Levitsky, Steven, and Daniel Ziblatt. 2018. *How Democracies Die.* New York: Penguin.

Lind, E. Allan, and Tom R. Tyler. 1988. *The Social Psychology of Procedural Justice.* New York: Plenum Press.

Linz, Juan J. 1990. "The Perils of Presidentialism." *Journal of Democracy* 1: 51–69.

Litman, Harry. 2018. "President Trump Thinks He Is a King." *New York Times* June 3. www.nytimes.com/2018/06/03/opinion/mueller-trump-executive-power.html.

Locke, John. 2003 [1690]. *Two Treatises of Government,* ed. by Peter Laslett. Cambridge: Cambridge University Press.

Lowande, Kenneth S. 2014. "After the Orders: Presidential Memoranda and Unilateral Action." *Presidential Studies Quarterly* 44: 724–741.

2021. "Presidents and the Status Quo." *Quarterly Journal of Political Science* 16 (2): 215–244.

Lowande, Kenneth S., and Thomas Gray. 2017. "Public Perception of the Presidential Toolkit." *Presidential Studies Quarterly* 47 (3): 432–447.

Lowande, Kenneth S., and Sidney M. Milkis. 2014. "'We Can't Wait': Barack Obama, Partisan Polarization and the Administrative Presidency." *The Forum* 12: 3–27.

Lowande, Kenneth S., Jeffery A. Jenkins, and Andrew J. Clarke. 2018. "Presidential Particularism and US Trade Politics." *Political Science Research and Methods* 6: 265–281.

Lowi, Theodore J. 1986. *The Personal President: Power Invested, Promise Unfulfilled.* Ithaca, NY: Cornell University Press.

Lupia, Arthur. 1994. "Shortcuts versus Encyclopedias: Information and Voting Behavior in California Insurance Reform." *American Political Science Review* 88: 63–76.

Lupia, Arthur, and Mathew D. McCubbins. 1998. *The Democratic Dilemma: Can Citizens Learn What They Need to Know?* Cambridge: Cambridge University Press.

Lynch, Edward. 2018. "Latin American Democracy is Crumbling Under Corruption." *The Hill* March 28. https://thehill.com/opinion/international/380482-latin-american-democracy-is-crumbling-under-corruption.

Mahler, Jonathan. 2008. "After America's Imperial Presidency." *New York Times* Nov 10. www.nytimes.com/2008/11/10/news/10iht-09powert.17670887 .html.

Mainwaring, Scott, and Matthew S. Shugart. 1997a. "Juan Linz, Presidentialism, and Democracy: A Critical Appraisal." *Comparative Politics* 29 (4): 449–471.

Mainwaring, Scott, and Matthew Soberg Shugart, eds. 1997b. *Presidentialism and Democracy in Latin America.* New York: Cambridge University Press.

Mansfield, Harvey C. 1989. *Taming the Prince: The Ambivalence of Modern Executive Power.* New York: The Free Press.

Marcus, Maeva. 1994. *Truman and the Steel Seizure Case: The Limits of Presidential Power.* Durham, NC: Duke University Press.

Margalit, Yotam. 2011. "Costly Jobs: Trade-Related Layoffs, Government Compensation, and Voting in U.S. Elections." *American Political Science Review* 105 (1): 166–188.

Martin, Lisa L. 2005. "The President and International Commitments: Treaties as Signaling Devices." *Presidential Studies Quarterly* 35 (3): 440–465.

Matheson, Scott M. 2009. *Presidential Constitutionalism in Perilous Times.* Cambridge, MA: Harvard University Press.

Mayer, Kenneth R. 1999. "Executive Orders and Presidential Power." *Journal of Politics* 61 (2): 445–466.

2002. *With the Stroke of a Pen.* Princeton, NJ: Princeton University Press.

McCarty, Nolan M. 2009. "Presidential Vetoes in the Early Republic: Changing Constitutional Norms or Electoral Reform?" *Journal of Politics* 71 (2): 369–384.

McClosky, Herbert. 1964. "Consensus and Ideology in American Politics." *American Political Science Review* 58: 361–381.

McClosky, Herbert, and John R. Zaller. 1984. *The American Ethos: Public Attitudes toward Capitalism and Democracy.* Cambridge, MA: Harvard University Press.

McConnell, Christopher, Yotam Margalit, Neil Malhotra, and Matthew Levendusky. 2018. "The Economic Consequences of Partisanship in a Polarized Era." *American Journal of Political Science* 62 (1): 5–18.

McManus, Doyle. 2019. "Trump's War on the Rule of Law." *Los Angeles Times* November 27. www.latimes.com/politics/story/2019-11-27/trump-wages-war-on-the-rule-of-law.

Meacham, Jon. 2008. *American Lion: Andrew Jackson in the White House.* New York: Random House.

Meijers, Maurits J., and Harmen van der Veer. 2019. "MEP Responses to Democratic Backsliding in Hungary and Poland: An Analysis of Agenda-Setting and Voting Behaviour." *Journal of Common Market Studies* 57 (4): 838–856.

Mellman, Mark. 2017. "Partisanship: A Powerful Drug." *The Hill* April 11. http://thehill.com/opinion/mark-mellman/328384-mellman-partisanship-a-powerful-drug.

Milkis, Sidney M., and Daniel J. Tichenor. 2019. *Rivalry and Reform: Presidents, Social Movements, and the Transformation of American Politics.* Chicago, IL: University of Chicago Press.

Miller, David Ryan. 2020. "All the President's Organized Interests." Ph. D. thesis, Washington University in St. Louis.

Miller, David, Bryant Moy, and Andrew Reeves. 2018. "U.S. Presidential Campaigns and Their Impact." In *Oxford Bibliographies in Political Science,* ed. by L. Sandy Maisel. New York: Oxford University Press.

Milner, Helen, and Dustin Tingley. 2015. *Sailing the Water's Edge: The Domestic Politics of American Foreign Policy.* Princeton, NJ: Princeton University Press.

Miratrix, Luke W., Jasjeet S. Sekhon, Alexander G. Theodoridis, and Luis F. Campos. 2018. "Worth Weighting? How to Think about and Use Weights in Survey Experiments." *Political Analysis* 26 (3): 275–291.

Moe, Terry M. 1985. "The Politicized Presidency." In *The New Direction in American Politics,* ed. by Paul E. Peterson and John B. Chubb, 235–271. Washington, DC: The Brookings Institution Press.

Moe, Terry M., and William G. Howell. 1999a. "Unilateral Action and Presidential Power: A Theory." *Presidential Studies Quarterly* 29: 850–873.

1999b. "The Presidential Power of Unilateral Action." *Journal of Law, Economics, and Organization* 15: 132–179.

Monmouth University Polling Institute. 2015. "Split Decision on Mexico Border Wall." September 10. www.monmouth.edu/polling-institute/reports/monmouthpoll_us_091015/.

Montagnes, B. Pablo, Zachary Peskowitz, and Joshua McCrain. 2019. "Bounding Partisan Approval Rates under Endogenous Partisanship: Why High Presidential Partisan Approval May Not Be What It Seems." *Journal of Politics* 81 (1): 321–326.

Moore, David W. 1995. *The Superpollsters.* New York: Four Walls Eight Windows.

Moore, Elena. 2020. "Biden's First 100 Days: Here's What to Expect." *National Public Radio* November 8.

Morgan, Ruth P. 1970. *The President and Civil Rights: Policy Making by Executive Order.* New York: St. Martin's Press.

Mounk, Yasha. 2018. *The People versus Democracy: Why Our Freedom Is in Danger and How to Save It.* Cambridge, MA: Harvard University Press.

Mueller, John. 1970. "Presidential Popularity from Truman to Johnson." *American Political Science Review* 65: 18–34.

1973. *War, Presidents and Public Opinion.* New York: Wiley.

Murray, Mark. 2013. "NBC Poll: Nearly 80 Percent Want Congressional Approval on Syria." *NBC News* August 30. www.nbcnews.com/news/other/nbc-poll-nearly-80-percent-want-congressional-approval-syria-f8C11038428.

Mutz, Diana C. 2011. *Population-Based Survey Experiments.* Princeton, NJ: Princeton University Press.

Nakamura, David. 2017. "Trump Administration Releases Hard-Line Immigration Principles, Threatening Deal on 'Dreamers'." *Washington Post* October 8. www.washingtonpost.com/news/post-politics/wp/2017/10/08/trump-administration-releases-hard-line-immigration-principles-threatening-deal-on-dreamers/.

Napolitano, Andrew. 2013. "President Obama Puts Politics above the Rule of Law." *reason* July 11. https://reason.com/archives/2013/07/11/is-barack-obama-above-the-law.

Nelson, Louis. 2017. "Trump to Dems: No DACA Deal without the Border Wall." *Politico* December 29. www.politico.com/story/2017/12/29/trump-dreamers-daca-deal-border-wall-319627.

Nelson, Thomas E., Rosalee A. Clawson, and Zoe M. Oxley. 1997. "Media Framing of a Civil Liberties Conflict and Its Effect on Tolerance." *American Political Science Review* 91 (3): 567–583.

Neustadt, Richard E. 1990. *Presidential Power and the Modern Presidents: The Politics of Leadership from Roosevelt to Reagan.* New York: John Wiley/Sons.

"New Day [Transcript]." 2020. *CNN* January 21. http://transcripts.cnn.com/TRANSCRIPTS/2001/21/nday.05.html.

New York Times. 1938a. "Father Coughlin Urges Group Protest." April 4: 8.

1938b. "The Administration Loses." April 9: 16.

1987. "Drawing Conclusions from the Tower Findings." March 1.

2008. "Election Results 2008. National Exit Polls Table." November 5. www.nytimes.com/elections/2008/results/president/national-exit-polls.html.

2011. "The Candidates on Executive Power." December 29. http://archive.nytimes.com/www.nytimes.com/interactive/2011/12/29/us/election-news/candidates-on-executive-power.html.

Nicholson, Stephen P. 2012. "Polarizing Cues." *American Journal of Political Science* 56: 52–66.

O'Donnell, Guillermo. 2004. "The Quality of Democracy: Why the Rule of Law Matters." *Journal of Democracy* 15 (4): 32–46.

2006. "Why the Rule of Law Matters." In *Assessing the Quality of Democracy,* ed. by Larry Diamond and Leonardo Morlino, 3–17. Baltimore, MD: Johns Hopkins University Press.

Obama, Barack. 2008. "Obama Addresses the National Council of La Raza [Transcript]." *Washington Post* July 15. www.washingtonpost.com/wp-dyn/content/article/2008/07/15/AR2008071501138.html.

———. 2010. "Remarks by President in State of the Union Address," *The White House: Office of the Press Secretary* January 27. https://obamawhite house.archives.gov/the-press-office/remarks-president-state-union-address.

———. 2014a. "Remarks by the President in Address to the Nation on Immigration." *The White House: Office of the Press Secretary* November 20. https://obamawhitehouse.archives.gov/the-press-office/2014/11/20/remarks-president-address-nation-immigration.

———. 2014b. "Remarks by the President on Border Security and Immigration Reform." *The White House: Office of the Press Secretary* June 30. https://obamawhitehouse.archives.gov/realitycheck/the-press-office/2014/06/30/remarks-president-border-security-and-immigration-reform.

———. 2013. "Remarks by the President on Immigration Reform." *The White House: Office of the Press Secretary* November 25. https://obamawhitehouse.archives.gov/the-press-office/2013/11/25/remarks-president-immigration-reform-san-francisco-ca.

———. 2014c. "Weekly Address: Working When Congress Won't Act." *The White House: Office of the Press Secretary* May 17. https://obamawhitehouse.archives.gov/the-press-office/2014/05/17/weekly-address-working-when-congress-won-t-act.

Office of the Press Secretary. 2009. "News Conference by the President." *The White House* April 29. https://obamawhitehouse.archives.gov/the-press-office/news-conference-president-4292009.

Oneal, John R., and Anna Lillian Bryan. 1995. "The Rally 'Round the Flag Effect in U.S. Foreign Policy Crises, 1950–1985." *Political Behavior* 17: 379–401.

Oxley, Zoe M., Mirya R. Holman, Jill S. Greenlee, Angela L. Bos, and J. Celeste Lay. 2020. "Children's Views of the American Presidency." *Public Opinion Quarterly* 84 (1): 141–157.

Page, Benjamin I., and Robert Y. Shapiro. 1992. *The Rational Public: Fifty Years of Trends in Americans' Policy Preferences.* Chicago, IL: University of Chicago Press.

Palanza, Valeria. 2019. *Checking Presidential Power: Executive Decrees and the Legislative Process in New Democracies.* New York: Cambridge University Press.

Paolacci, Gabriele, and Jesse Chandler. 2014. "Inside the Turk: Understanding Mechanical Turk as a Participant Pool." *Current Directions in Psychological Science* 23 (3): 184–188.

Park, Taeyong, and Andrew Reeves. 2020. "Local Unemployment and Voting for President: Uncovering Causal Mechanisms." *Political Behavior* 42 (2): 443–463.

Paxton, Ken. 2015. "The President Must Respect the Rule of Law." *National Review* March 11. www.nationalreview.com/2015/03/president-must-respect-rule-law-ken-paxton/.

Paz, Christian. 2019. "Read Adam Schiff's Opening Statement in the First Impeachment Hearing." *The Atlantic* November 13. www.theatlantic.com/

politics/archive/2019/11/adam-schiffs-impeachment-opening-statement/
601915/.

Pelosi, Nancy. 2020. "McConnell and the GOP Senate are Accomplices to Trump's Wrongdoing." *Washington Post* February 7. www.washingtonpost.com/opinions/nancy-pelosi-mcconnell-and-the-gop-senate-are-accomplices-to-trumps-wrongdoing/2020/02/07/d06582be-49e4-11ea-9164-d3154ad8a5cd_story.html.

Pereira, Carlos, Timothy J. Power, and Lucio Rennó. 2005. "Under What Conditions Do Presidents Resort to Decree Power? Theory and Evidence from the Brazilian Case." *Journal of Politics* 67 (1): 178–200.

Peterson, David A. M., Lawrence J. Grossback, James A. Stimson, and Amy Gangl. 2003. "Congressional Response to Mandate Elections." *American Journal of Political Science* 47: 411–426.

Pew Research Center. 2001. "American Psyche Reeling from Terror Attacks." September 19.

2016. "Clinton, Trump Supporters Have Starkly Different Views of a Changing Nation." August 18. www.people-press.org/wp-content/uploads/sites/4/2016/08/08-18-2016-August-political-release.pdf.

2017a. "In First Month, Views of Trump Are Already Strongly Felt, Deeply Polarized." February 16. www.people-press.org/wp-content/uploads/sites/4/2017/02/02-16-17-Political-release.pdf.

2006. "Iran a Growing Danger, Bush Gaining on Spy Issue." February 7.

2017b. "Large Majorities See Checks and Balances, Right to Protest as Essential for Democracy." March 2. www.people-press.org/wp-content/uploads/sites/4/2017/03/03-02-2017-Democratic-values-release2.pdf.

2005. "Opinion Leaders Turn Cautious, Public Looks Homeward." November 17. www.pewresearch.org/politics/2005/11/17/opinion-leaders-turn-cautious-public-looks-homeward/.

2018. "The Public, the Political System and American Democracy." April 26. www.people-press.org/wp-content/uploads/sites/4/2018/04/4-26-2018-Democracy-release-1.pdf.

2020. "U.S. Image Plummets Internationally as Most Say Country Has Handled Coronavirus Badly." September 15. www.pewresearch.org/global/2020/09/15/us-image-plummets-internationally-as-most-say-country-has-handled-coronavirus-badly/.

Pew Research Center for the People & the Press. 2013. "Majority Views NSA Phone Tracking as Acceptable Anti-terror Tactic." June 10. www.people-press.org/2013/06/10/majority-views-nsa-phone-tracking-as-acceptable-anti-terror-tactic/.

2010. *Political Knowledge Update: Senate Legislative Process a Mystery to Many*. Tech. rep. www.people-press.org/2010/01/28/senate-legislative-process-a-mystery-to-many/.

Pious, Richard M., and Christopher H. Pyle. 1984. *The President, Congress, and the Constitution: Power and Legitimacy in American Politics*. New York: Free Press.

Pitkin, Hanna F. 1967. *The Concept of Representation*. Berkeley: University of California Press.

Polenberg, Richard. 1979. "Roosevelt, Carter, and Executive Reorganization: Lessons of the 1930s." *Presidential Studies Quarterly* 9 (1): 35–46.

Politico Staff. 2016. "Full transcript: Third 2016 Presidential Debate." *Politico* October 20. www.politico.com/story/2016/10/full-transcript-third-2016-presidential-debate-230063.

Popkin, Samuel L. 1994. *The Reasoning Voter: Communication and Persuasion in Presidential Campaigns*. Second. Chicago, IL: University of Chicago Press.

Posner, Eric A., and Adrian Vermeule. 2010. *The Executive Unbound: After the Madisonian Republic*. New York: Oxford University Press.

Prempeh, H. Kwasi. 2008. "Progress and Retreat in Africa: Presidents Untamed." *Democracy* 19 (2): 109–123.

Preston, Julia. 2009. "Obama Lifts a Ban on Entry into U.S. by HIV-Positive People." *New York Times* October 30. www.nytimes.com/2009/10/31/us/politics/31travel.html.

———. 2010. "Obama Links Immigration Overhaul to G.O.P. Backing." *New York Times* March 11. www.nytimes.com/2010/03/12/us/politics/12immig.html.

Preston, Julia, and John H. Cushman Jr. 2012. "Obama to Permit Young Migrants to Remain in U.S." *New York Times* June 15. www.nytimes.com/2012/06/16/us/us-to-stop-deporting-some-illegal-immigrants.html?pagewanted=all&_r=0.

Przeworski, Adam, Michael Alvarez, Jose A. Cheibub, and Fernando Limongi. 2000. *Democracy and Development: Political Institutions and Material Well-being in the World, 1950–1990*. New York: Cambridge University Press.

Ragusa, Jordan M., and Nate Birkhead. 2020. *Congress in Reverse: Repeals from Reconstruction to the Present*. Chicago: University of Chicago Press.

Raju, Manu, Deirdre Walsh, and Ted Barrett. 2016. "Can Trump Build a Wall without Congress' Approval?" *CNN Politics* November 11. www.cnn.com/2016/11/11/politics/donald-trump-wall-congress/index.html.

Rakove, Jack N., ed. 2009. *The Annotated U.S. Constitution and Declaration of Independence*. Cambridge, MA: Harvard University Press.

Ramirez, Mark D. 2009. "The Dynamics of Partisan Conflict on Congressional Approval." *American Journal of Political Science* 53: 681–694.

Rasinski, Kenneth A. 1989. "The Effect of Question Wording on Public Support for Government Spending." *Public Opinion Quarterly* 53 (3): 388–394.

Reeves, Andrew. 2011. "Political Disaster: Unilateral Powers, Electoral Incentives, and Presidential Disaster Declarations." *Journal of Politics* 73: 1142–1151.

Rehfeld, Andrew. 2006. "Towards a General Theory of Political Representation." *Journal of Politics* 68: 1–21.

Reich, Gary. 2002. "Executive Decree Authority in Brazil: How Reactive Legislators Influence Policy." *Legislative Studies Quarterly* 27 (1): 5–31.

Reinhart, RJ. 2018. "Republicans More Positive on U.S. Relations with Russia." *Gallup* July 13. https://news.gallup.com/poll/237137/republicans-positive-relations-russia.aspx.

Risen, James, and Eric Lichtblau. 2005. "Bush Lets U.S. Spy on Callers without Courts." *New York Times* December 16. www.nytimes.com/2005/12/16/politics/bush-lets-us-spy-on-callers-without-courts.html.

Roff, Peter. 2015. "Obama's Rule of Lawlessness." *U.S. News* June 23. www.usnews.com/opinion/blogs/peter-roff/2015/06/23/800-years-after-magna-carta-obama-needs-refresher-course-on-rule-of-law.

Rogowski, Jon C. 2016. "Presidential Influence in an Era of Congressional Dominance." *American Political Science Review* 110 (2): 325–341.

2020. "The Administrative Presidency and Public Trust in Bureaucracy." *Journal of Political Institutions and Political Economy* 1 (1): 27–51.

2019. *Unilateral Action, Public Opinion, and Presidential Responsiveness.* Working paper. https://scholar.harvard.edu/files/rogowski/files/unilateral_public.pdf.

Rogowski, Jon C., and Andrew R. Stone. 2021. "How Political Contestation Over Judicial Nominations Polarizes Americans' Attitudes toward the Supreme Court." *British Journal of Political Science* 51 (3): 1251–1269.

Rohac, Dalibor. 2018. "Hungary and Poland Aren't Democratic. They're Authoritarian." *Foreign Policy* February 5. https://foreignpolicy.com/2018/02/05/hungary-and-poland-arent-democratic-theyre-authoritarian/.

Roosevelt, Theodore. 1913. *Theodore Roosevelt: An Autobiography.* New York: Charles Scribner's Sons.

Rosen, Jeffrey. 2018. *William Howard Taft.* New York: Times Books.

Rossiter, Clinton. 2005 [1948]. *Constitutional Dictatorship: Crisis Government in the Modern Democracies.* New York: Transaction Publishers.

1956. *The American Presidency: The Powers and Practices, the Personalities and Problems of the Most Important Office on Earth.* Princeton, NJ: Princeton University Press.

Rubin, Jennifer. 2012. "Obama vs. the Rule of Law." *Washington Post* June 17. www.washingtonpost.com/blogs/right-turn/post/obama-vs-the-rule-of-law/2012/06/16/gJQAKm8dhV_blog.html.

Rudalevige, Andrew. 2021. *By Executive Order: Bureaucratic Management and the Limits of Presidential Power.* Princeton, NJ: Princeton University Press.

2012. "Executive Orders and Presidential Unilateralism." *Presidential Studies Quarterly* 42: 138–160.

2002. *Managing the President's Program: Presidential Leadership and Legislative Policy Formation.* Princeton, NJ: Princeton University Press.

Saffon, Maria Paula, and Nadia Urbinati. 2013. "Procedural Democracy, the Bulwark of Equal Liberty." *Political Theory* 41 (3): 441–481.

Sances, Michael W. 2017. "Attribution Errors in Federalist Systems: When Voters Punish the President for Local Tax Increases." *Journal of Politics* 79 (4): 1286–1301.

Savage, Charlie. 2007. "Barack Obama's Q&A." *Boston Globe* December 20. http://archive.boston.com/news/politics/2008/specials/CandidateQA/ObamaQA/.

"2016 Executive Power Survey Responses." 2016. *New York Times* January 25. www.nytimes.com/interactive/2016/01/25/opinion/sunday/document-savage-nyt-2016-executive-power-survey-aggregated.html.

Schenkkan, Nate. 2015. "Central Asia's Island of Democracy is Sinking." *Foreign Policy* September 30. https://foreignpolicy.com/2015/09/30/central-asias-island-of-democracy-is-sinking-kyrgyzstan/.

Schlesinger, Arthur M. 1965. *A Thousand Days: John F. Kennedy in the White House*. Boston: Houghton Mifflin Company.

1973. *The Imperial Presidency*. New York: Houghton Mifflin.

2004. *War and the American Presidency*. New York: W. W. Norton.

Sears, David O., and Richard R. Lau. 1983. "Inducing Apparently Self-Interested Political Preferences." *American Journal of Political Science* 27: 223–252.

Semple, Robert B. 1970. "Nixon Asks for Restraint on Wage-Price Demands." *New York Times* June 18. www.nytimes.com/1970/06/18/archives/nixon-asks-for-restraint-on-wageprice-demands-bars-mandatory.html.

Shane, Peter M. 2009. *Madison's Nightmare: How Executive Power Threatens American Democracy*. Chicago, IL: University of Chicago Press.

2018. "Testimony of Peter M. Shane Concerning the Nomination of Brett M. Kavanaugh to Serve as an Associate Justice on the Supreme Court of the United States." *Committee on the Judiciary of the U.S. Senate* September 7. www.judiciary.senate.gov/imo/media/doc/Shane%20Testimony.pdf.

Shapiro, Ilya. 2017. "Top 10 Ways Obama Violated the Constitution during His Presidency." *Cato Institute: Commentary* January 17. www.cato.org/publications/commentary/top-10-ways-obama-violated-constitution-during-presidency.

Shapiro, Sarah, and Catherine Brown. 2018. "The State of Civics Education." Center for American Progress. February 18. www.americanprogress.org/issues/education-k-12/reports/2018/02/21/446857/state-civics-education/.

Shear, Michael D. 2014a. "After Push by Obama, Minimum-Wage Action Is Moving to the States." *New York Times* April 2. www.nytimes.com/2014/04/03/us/politics/president-heads-to-michigan-to-press-minimum-wage-increase.html.

2014b. "Obama Delays Immigration Action, Yielding to Democratic Concerns." *New York Times* September 6. www.nytimes.com/2014/09/07/us/politics/obama-said-to-delay-executive-action-on-immigration.html.

2014c. "Obama, Daring Congress, Acts to Overhaul Immigration." *New York Times* November 20. http://www.nytimes.com/2014/11/21/us/obama-immigration-speech.html.

Shor, Boris, and Jon C. Rogowski. 2018. "Ideology and the US Congressional Vote." *Political Science Research and Methods* 6 (2): 323–341.

Shugart, Matthew Soberg, and John M. Carey. 1992. *Presidents and Assemblies*. New York: Cambridge University Press.

Shultz, George P., and Kenneth W. Dam. 1978. "Reflections on Wage and Price Controls." *Industrial and Labor Relations Review* 30 (2): 139–151.

Siegel, Rachel, and Andrew Van Dam. 2020. "U.S. Economy Contracted at Fastest Quarterly Rate on Record from April to June as Coronavirus Walloped Workers, Businesses." *Washington Post* July 30.

Siegel, Rachel, Andrew Van Dam, and Erica Werner. 2021. "2020 Was the Worst Year for Economic Growth since World War II." *Washington Post* January 28.

Sievert, Joel, and Ryan D. Williamson. 2018. "Public Attitudes toward Presidential Veto Powers." *Research & Politics* 5 (1): 1–6.

Skowronek, Stephen. 1993. *The Politics Presidents Make: Leadership from John Adams to Bill Clinton.* Cambridge, MA: Harvard College/Belknap Press.

Smith, Steven S., and Hong Min Park. 2013. "Americans' Attitudes about the Senate Filibuster." *American Politics Research* 41: 735–760.

Sniderman, Paul M., and Sean M. Theriault. 2004. "The Structure of Political Argument and the Logic of Issue Framing." In *Studies in Public Opinion: Attitudes, Nonattitudes, Measurement Error, and Change*, ed. by Willem E. Saris and Paul M. Sniderman, 133–165. Princeton, NJ: Princeton University Press.

Sorenson, Theodore C. 1975. *Watchmen in the Night: Presidential Accountability after Watergate.* Cambridge, MA: MIT Press.

Sorkin, Amy Davidson. 2020. "Trump's Impeachment and the Degrading of the Presidential Accountability." *New Yorker* February 10. www.newyorker.com/magazine/2020/02/10/trumps-impeachment-and-the-degrading-of-presidential-accountability.

Stebbins, Phillip E. 1971. "Truman and the Seizure of Steel: A Failure in Communication." *The Historian* 34 (1): 1–21.

Stein, Herbert. 1988. *Presidential Economics: The Making of Economic Policy from Roosevelt to Reagan and Beyond.* Washington, DC: American Enterprise Institute for Public Policy Research.

Stein, Jeff. 2016. "Americans Want Limits on Their Presidents – Even the Ones They Voted For." *Vox* February 3. www.vox.com/2016/2/3/10899242/americans-limit-presidents.

Stepan, Alfred, and Cindy Skach. 1994. "Presidentialism and Parliamentarianism in Comparative Perspective." In *The Failure of Presidential Democracy*, ed. by Juan J. Linz and Arturo Valenzuela, 119–136. Baltimore, MD: Johns Hopkins University Press.

Stephanopoulos, Nicholas O., and Mila Versteeg. 2016. "The Contours of Constitutional Approval." *Washington University Law Review* 94 (1): 113–190.

Stimson, James A., Michael B. MacKuen, and Robert S. Erikson. 1995. "Dynamic Representation." *American Political Science Review* 89: 543–565.

Sturm, Albert L. 1949. "Emergencies and the Presidency." *Journal of Politics* 11 (1): 121–144.

Sullivan, Sean, and Peyton M. Craighill. 2014. "Executive Order = Political Nothing Burger." *Washington Post: The Fix* January 29. www.washingtonpost.com/news/the-fix/wp/2014/01/29/executive-order-political-nothing-burger/.

Sundquist, James L. 2002. *The Decline and Resurgence of Congress.* Washington, DC: Brookings Institution Press.

Suri, Jeremi. 2017. *The Impossible Presidency.* New York: Basic Books.

Svolik, Milan. 2020. "When Polarization Trumps Civic Virtue: Partisan Conflict and the Subversion of Democracy by Incumbents." *Quarterly Journal of Political Science* 15 (1): 3–31.

Taft, William Howard. 1916. *Our Chief Magistrate and His Powers.* New York: Columbia University Press.

Temin, Jon. 2017. "The Alarming Decline of Democracy in East Africa: How Washington Can Help Reverse the Trend." *Foreign Affairs* November 27. www.foreignaffairs.com/articles/east-africa/2017-11-27/alarming-decline-democracy-east-africa.

Tesler, Michael. 2012. "The Spillover of Racialization into Health Care: How President Obama Polarized Public Opinion by Racial Attitudes and Race." *American Journal of Political Science* 56: 690–704.

The AP-National Constitution Center Poll. 2012. Vol. August. GfK Roper Public Affairs & Corporate Communications. https://constitutioncenter.org/media/files/data_GfK_AP-NCC_Poll_August_GfK_2012_Topline_FINAL_1st_release.pdf.

The Editorial Board. 2018. "President Trump, or King Donald I?" *USA Today* June 7. www.usatoday.com/story/opinion/2018/06/05/president-trump-king-donald-editorials-debates/670801002/.

"The Ills of Latin American Democracy." 2018. *The Economist* February 8. www.economist.com/the-americas/2018/02/08/the-ills-of-latin-american-democracy.

Theriault, Sean M., and Mickey Edwards. 2019. *Congress: The First Branch*. New York: Oxford University Press.

Thomas, Ginni. 2015. "Legal Expert: Obama is 'Undermining the Rule of Law.'" *Daily Caller* June 6. https://dailycaller.com/2015/06/06/legal-expert-obama-is-undermining-the-rule-of-law-video/.

Thompson, Cheryl W., and William Booth. 2009. "Obama Says Immigration Reform is a Priority, but Won't Happen Soon." *Washington Post* August 11. www.washingtonpost.com/wp-dyn/content/article/2009/08/10/AR2009081001797.html.

Thompson, Ginger. 2009. "Immigration Agents to Turn Focus to Employers." *New York Times* April 30. www.nytimes.com/2009/04/30/us/politics/30immig.html.

Thrower, Sharece. 2017a. "The President, the Court, and Policy Implementation." *Presidential Studies Quarterly* 47 (1): 122–145.

———. 2017b. "To Revoke or Not Revoke? The Political Determinants of Executive Order Longevity." *American Journal of Political Science* 61 (3): 642–656.

TIME. 1962. "The Administration: A Stroke of the Pen." November 30.

Time Staff. 2015. "Here's Donald Trump's Presidential Announcement Speech." *Time* June 16. https://time.com/3923128/donald-trump-announcement-speech/.

Tocqueville, Alexis de. 1963 [1840]. *Democracy in America*. Translated by H. Reeve. New York: Alfred A. Knopf.

Tomz, Michael. 2007. "Domestic Audience Costs in International Relations: An Experimental Approach." *International Organization* 61 (4): 821–840.

Tomz, Michael, Jessica L. P. Weeks, and Keren Yarhi-Milo. 2020. "Public Opinion and Decisions about Military Force in Democracies." *International Organization* 74(1): 119–143.

Toobin, Jeffrey. 2018. "Donald Trump and the Rule of Law." *New Yorker* January 6. www.newyorker.com/news/daily-comment/donald-trump-and-the-rule-of-law.

"Transcript of the Vice Presidential Debate." 2008. *New York Times* October 2. www.nytimes.com/elections/2008/president/debates/transcripts/vice-presidential-debate.html.

Trump, Donald (@realDonaldTrump). 2012. "Why is @BarackObama constantly issuing executive orders that are major power grabs of authority? This is the latest http://1.usa.gov/Lxe4xg." *Twitter* July 10. https://twitter.com/realdonaldtrump/status/222739756105207808.

Trump, Donald. 2016a. "Donald Trump Town Hall Meeting in Janesville, Wisconsin." *C-SPAN* March 29. www.c-span.org/video/?407408-1/donald-trump-town-hall-meeting-janesville-wisconsin.

———. 2016b. "Memo Explains how Donald Trump Plans to Pay for Border Wall." *Washington Post* March 31. www.washingtonpost.com/apps/g/page/politics/memo-explains-how-donald-trump-plans-to-pay-for-border-wall/2007/?tid=a_inl_manual.

———. 2017. "Remarks by President Trump in Joint Address to Congress." *White House: Office of the Press Secretary* February 28. www.whitehouse.gov/briefings-statements/remarks-president-trump-joint-address-congress/.

———. 2018. "President Donald J. Trump's State of the Union Address." *White House: Office of the Press Secretary* January 30. www.whitehouse.gov/briefings-statements/president-donald-j-trumps-state-union-address/.

Tucker, Patrick D., Jacob M. Montgomery, and Steven S. Smith. 2018. "Party Identification in the Age of Obama: Evidence on the Sources of Stability and Systematic Change in Party Identification from a Long-Term Panel Survey." *Political Research Quarterly* 72 (2): 309–328.

Tulis, Jeffrey. 1988. *The Rhetorical Presidency*. Princeton, NJ: Princeton University Press.

Turner, Ian R. 2020. "Policy Durability, Agency Capacity, and Executive Unilateralism." *Presidential Studies Quarterly* 50 (1): 40–62.

Tyler, Tom R. 2006. "Psychological Perspectives on Legitimacy and Legitimation." *Annual Review of Psychology* 57: 375–400.

Tyler, Tom R., Kenneth A. Rasinski, and Kathleen M. McGraw. 1985. "The Influence of Perceived Injustice on the Endorsement of Political Leaders." *Journal of Applied Social Psychology* 15: 700–725.

Tyler, Tom R., and Rick Trinkner. 2018. *Why Children Follow Rules: Legal Socialization and the Development of Legitimacy*. New York: Oxford University Press.

US Congress. House of Representatives. 1974. *Debate on Articles of Impeachment: Hearings of the Committee of the Judiciary*. 93rd Cong., 2nd sess., July 24, 25, 26, 27, 29, and 30.

US Congress. House. Committee on Rules. Subcommittee on Legislative and Budget Process. 1999. *The Impact of Executive Orders on the Legislative Process: Executive Lawmaking?* 106th Cong., 1st sess., October 27, 1999. www.govinfo.gov/content/pkg/CHRG-106hhrg62209/pdf/CHRG-106hhrg62209.pdf.

Urofsky, Melvin. 2020. *The Affirmative Action Puzzle*. New York: Pantheon Books.

Walsh, Lawrence E. 1997. *Firewall: The Iran-Contra Conspiracy and Cover-Up.* New York: W. W. Norton.

Washington Post. 2007. "Washington Post-ABC News Poll." June 4.

"Without the Benefit of Law." 1952. *Washington Post* April 10: 16.

Weber, Jennifer L. 2006. *Copperheads: The Rise and Fall of Lincoln's Opponents in the North.* New York: Oxford University Press.

Wildavsky, Aaron. 1966. "The Two Presidencies." *Trans-Action* 4: 7–14.

Will, George F. 2018. "Clawing Back Power from the President." *The San Diego Union-Tribune* December 16. www.sandiegouniontribune.com/opinion/commentary/sd-oe-george-will-presidential-power-trump-utcol-utak-20181216-story.html.

1997. "Line-item Veto Has Constitutional Flaw." *St. Louis Dispatch* January 13.

2014. "Stopping a Lawless President." *Washington Post* June 20. www.washingtonpost.com/opinions/george-f-will-stopping-a-lawless-president/2014/06/20/377c4d6e-f7e5-11e3-a3a5-42be35962a52_story.html.

2005a. "Why Didn't Bush Ask Congress." *RealClearPolitics* December 20. www.realclearpolitics.com/Commentary/com-12_20_05_GW.html.

2005b. "Why for GOP to Halt Filibusters Is to Hike Its Senate Numbers." *Desert Morning News* March 20.

Wilson, Woodrow. 1908. *Constitutional Government in the United States.* New York: Columbia University Press.

Wirt, William. 1817. *The Life and Character of Patrick Henry.* Philadelphia, PA: James Webster.

Woodward, Bob, and Robert Costa. 2016. "Trump Reveals How He Would Force Mexico to Pay for Border Wall." *Washington Post* April 5. www.washingtonpost.com/politics/trump-takes-to-the-campaign-trail-in-michigan-and-iowa/2015/08/13/9124f9bc-4206-11e5-8ab4-c73967a143d3_gallery.html.

World Values Survey 1981-2014, Longitudinal Aggregate v.20150418. 2015. World Values Survey Association (www.worldvaluessurvey.org). Aggregate File Producer: JDSystems, Madrid, Spain.

Yackee, Susan Webb, and David Lowery. 2005. "Understanding Public Support for the U.S. Federal Bureaucracy." *Public Management Review* 7 (4): 515–536.

Zaller, John R. 1992. *The Nature and Origins of Mass Opinion.* New York: Cambridge University Press.

Zechmeister, Elizabeth J., and Noam Lupu, eds. 2019a. *Pulse of Democracy.* Nashville, TN: LAPOP.

2019b. *Topical Brief #036: The 2018/19 AmericasBarometer.* Nashville, TN: LAPOP.

Zink, James R., and Christopher T. Dawes. 2016. "The Dead Hand of the Past? Toward an Understanding of 'Constitutional Veneration.'" *Political Behavior* 38: 535–560.

Index